MW01194119

Praise for

THE LAST DAYS OF BUDAPEST

"*The Last Days of Budapest* is a masterpiece. Immaculately researched, it is packed with larger-than-life characters and revelations about the unknown espionage history of the Second World War. Adam LeBor's vivid, taut prose brings the story of the 'Casablanca of central Europe' alive in glorious technicolor. From the naïve optimism of the late 1930s to the depths of depravity and bloodshed during the siege in winter 1944, LeBor takes the reader on an emotional rollercoaster. This is history as it should be written: utterly engrossing."

—Malcolm Brabant, coauthor of the *New York Times*–bestselling *The Daughter of Auschwitz*

"*The Last Days of Budapest* is not only an enthralling tale of wartime espionage and spycraft. It is a beautifully rendered portrait of heroism, tragedy, betrayal, and violence in the final hours of a grand city stuck between Hitler and Stalin. This superb account is not to be missed—and will haunt you."

—David McCloskey, former CIA analyst and author of *The Seventh Floor*

"A staggering achievement. *The Last Days of Budapest* is a must-read for anyone interested in the history of European espionage, offering readers a riveting journey through Budapest's turbulent past. This meticulously researched book delves into a complex web of astonishing intelligence operations, revealing how Budapest served as a crossroads for spies from East and West."

—Charles Cumming, author of the Box 88 spy fiction series

"This is an extraordinary book—an enthralling narrative that is full of extraordinary characters, both heroes and villains, and packed with the insights and subtle judgements that only someone with the author's knowledge of, and love for, the city can provide. What happened in wartime Budapest is virtually unknown outside Hungary. Now, thanks to LeBor, we have the story laid out in grim and absorbing detail, told with all the power and passion that a writer of his class can muster."

—Patrick Bishop, author of *Paris '44*

"A terrific account of Budapest in the middle of the twentieth century, culminating in the collapse of all civilized values as the Nazis retreat in 1944, and the Russian army advances. Part thriller, part astonishing personal history, this is a must-read for anyone wanting to know more about Hungary's grim role in the Holocaust. The stories LeBor tells will remain with you."

—Nicholas Best, author of *Five Days That Shocked the World*

"From the first to the final page, *The Last Days of Budapest* is difficult to put down. Using sources which offer chilling firsthand accounts and personal insight, LeBor expertly narrates one of the darkest periods in Hungary's history. This is an important and overdue book, and a must-read in the field of Second World War history."

—Sarah-Louise Miller, author of *Women in Allied Naval Intelligence in the Second World War*

"*The Last Days of Budapest* is both beautifully written and revelatory, with the kind of quirky detail that confirms LeBor's love and fascination for his subject country. Prewar Budapest comes alive as a nest of mischief and self-delusion, home for a beguiling cast of spies, adventurers, aristocratic lovelies, journalists, smugglers, thieves, and fellow travelers. ... LeBor offers an unblinking account of the last spasms of a ruined city. Deeply shocking. And long overdue." —Graham Hurley, author of *Dead Ground*

"A fascinating story of aristocratic spies, diplomats, and clandestine operations—and one of the finest histories of Budapest in the twentieth century." —Helen Fry, author of *Women in Intelligence*

THE LAST
DAYS OF
BUDAPEST

THE DESTRUCTION OF EUROPE'S MOST
COSMOPOLITAN CAPITAL IN WORLD WAR II

ADAM LEBOR

PUBLICAFFAIRS

New York

PublicAffairs
Hachette Book Group
1290 Avenue of the Americas, New York, NY 10104
www.publicaffairsbooks.com
@Public_Affairs

Printed in the United States of America

Originally published in hardcover and ebook by Head of Zeus Ltd, part of
Bloomsbury Publishing Plc in the UK in January 2025.
First US Edition: April 2025

Published by PublicAffairs, an imprint of Hachette Book Group, Inc.
The PublicAffairs name and logo is a registered trademark of the
Hachette Book Group.

The Hachette Speakers Bureau provides a wide range of authors for speaking
events. To find out more, go to hachettespeakersbureau.com or email
HachetteSpeakers@hbgusa.com.

PublicAffairs books may be purchased in bulk for business, educational,
or promotional use. For more information, please contact your local bookseller
or the Hachette Book Group Special Markets Department
at special.markets@hbgusa.com.

The publisher is not responsible for websites (or their content) that are not
owned by the publisher.

Library of Congress Control Number: 2024950288

ISBNs: 9781541700581 (hardcover), 9781541700604 (ebook)

LSC-C

Printing 1, 2025

In loving memory of Róbert Ligeti, 1930–2024
Maurice and Brenda LeBor

And for Zsuzsa Ligeti

Autumn and Buda were born of the same mother.

Gyula Krúdy

Contents

Prologue

Night was falling over the sports arena in Újpest, the air turning cold with the sharp bite of the winter to come, but the violence did not abate. The Arrow Cross militiamen tortured, abused and beat their captives, delighting in their sadism.

Róbert Lichtenstein flinched as another fusillade of shots rang out. Hundreds of Jewish men had been rounded up that day. They were gathered outside with no food, water, toilets or medical supplies. The arena was now an open-air concentration camp.

The men were supposed to form labour companies to dig trenches around Budapest as the Russians advanced. But the life expectancy of any Jew who fell into the hands of the Arrow Cross was usually short. Many would not even make it through the night.

Róbert – Robi to his relatives and friends – should not have been there at all. He was only fourteen years old. But he had been taken together with his neighbour, Artúr Schwarz. Artúr was elderly and had a bad leg. Neither of them were made for hard physical labour.

Artúr told Robi that he had to escape.

The shooting was getting more frequent now, the sound of the beatings and abuse ever louder. The war was lost, everyone knew, but the closer the Russians advanced on the city, the more frenzied the Arrow Cross became.

Robi waited, his heart thumping. For a moment, the guards' backs were turned.

He started running, faster than he had ever run before.

PART ONE

The Balancing Act

When Hungary is mentioned, then most people think of red pepper called paprika, of Gypsy bands, of picturesqueness, of big plains with herds of cattle upon it and semi-barbarous people to watch all over this. Now, as a matter of fact, we are quite on the same level of civilisation as any Western country in Europe is. We may say that we are the farthest outpost of Western civilisation towards the east.

Count Albert Apponyi, Hungarian diplomat and politician, speaking in the United States, 1929.

I was excited by the famous delights of the place.

British travel writer Patrick Leigh Fermor on his visit to Budapest in 1934.

I

The End of Empire

The Coronation of Charles IV unrolled the most superb film
I had seen to date.

Cyril Brown, writing in *The New York Times*.[1]

The great trek across the Danube began before dawn. Behind the
Buda Hills, the sun nudged higher, sending a faint tint of pink
across the horizon. The icy black waters shimmered in the misty
light and the damp air was still freezing. The city had never seen
such a procession, moving with such slow, steady determination,
some walking, some in horse-drawn carriages, all making their
way across the Chain Bridge, towards the Mátyás Church high
in the Buda Castle. It was 30 December 1916. Charles I, the newly
appointed Emperor of Austria, was to be crowned again, as King
Charles IV of Hungary. Budapest was alive with anticipation. For
once, in the midst of war, there would be a celebration. Cyril Brown,
the correspondent for *The New York Times*, planned to report on the
lavish ceremony – if he could ever get across the river and up into
the castle.

In normal times the journey from his room at the Astoria Hotel
in downtown Pest would take around half-an-hour. That day it took
three hours. But the spectacle, when Brown eventually arrived, was
extraordinary. 'Now followed reel on reel and tableau on tableau,
each one worth the price of admission of first night show', he
rhapsodised. The Hussars, the famed Hungarian cavalry, came
first, their perfectly groomed horses trotting along the cobbles,
followed by the mayor and magistrates of Budapest, and heralds

in red costumes 'blaring fanfares on trumpets from which hung bright banners'. The royal bodyguards wore cream-coloured capes and silver helmets with white kingfisher feathers, each carrying a pike with a blade like a scythe. Then came a trio of gilded Rococo carriages, bringing the highest-ranked ladies of the court, escorted by outriders in long, black cloaks. Last of all was the royal carriage, containing Charles, Queen Zita and their young son, Crown Prince Otto.

The spectators were bedecked in 'gold and jewels, velvet and costly furs', while the pillars of the cathedral were draped with purple velvet, bordered with gold. The cannons sounded at 9.00 am, followed by the crash of organ chords and the 'fanfares of trumpets and the exotic beatings of kettledrums'. The dramatic climax of the ceremony unfolded on nearby Szent György Square. The newly crowned king rode up a ramp on his horse and cut the air in four directions with his sword, to show that he would defend Hungary from attacks from anywhere. 'This was the signal to the waiting multitudes without the church. Batteries were fired, rifle salvoes from waiting Honveds echoed and the waiting crowds cheered', wrote Brown. The King stood while the Archbishop and Count István Tisza, the prime minister, set the sacred crown on his head. The crowd erupted, shouting '*Éljen, Éljen*, long live,' cheer after cheer resounding for long minutes.[2]

King Charles IV of Hungary now ruled over a nation whose lands reached east into present-day Ukraine and Romania, north into Slovakia, south into Serbia and Croatia and west to the Adriatic. Brown was an outsider, swept up in the pageantry of the moment. Katinka Károlyi, a young Hungarian aristocrat with a ringside seat, had a sharper eye. The crown was too large for Charles and slipped around his ears, she later wrote. The sceptre was heavy, his horse nervous. 'Charles seemed to shrink under the weight of them. His task was too heavy for his shoulders – to carry the load of a disintegrating empire and a war of which he disapproved.' The cheers were only those of the 1,500 or so nobles and aristocrats who had been admitted to the ceremonies. No crowds were allowed for fear of demonstrations. This was the last hurrah of a dying empire.

Among the cheering crowds was Katinka's sister Klára – Caja to her family and friends. Countess Klára Andrássy de Csíkszentkirály et Krasznahorka was born on 18 January 1898. The Andrássys had shaped Hungary's destiny. Caja's grandfather, Count Gyula Andrássy, had served as Hungarian prime minister and foreign minister of Austria-Hungary. His youngest son, also called Gyula, served as Hungary's interior and foreign minister. His oldest son, Tivadar, Caja's father, also a politician, had married a fellow aristocrat, Eleonóra Zichy. Caja was the youngest of four daughters, after Ilona, Borbála and Katalin (Katinka). The family divided its time between the ancestral home, a country manor house in Tiszadob, eastern Hungary, and their palace on the Buda side of the Danube embankment. The manor house was surrounded by a park filled with copies of Greek and Roman statues and a lake where the girls ice-skated in the winter. When the family went on a picnic, dozens of servants formed an advance party and went ahead with food and drinks. The Andrássy Palace was decorated in the typical style of the high bourgeoisie and aristocracy: stuffy, gloomy and over-furnished, with dark, heavy curtains that kept the light out and the dust in. The walls were covered in heavy oil paintings. Inside the rooms almost every inch of space was taken up with sofas, chairs, artworks and ornaments.

Eleonóra's marriage to Tivadar was troubled. A great society beauty, she had been engaged at the age of seventeen, in complete ignorance of men. The reality of marital relations, and her duties, appalled her. For her first few years of married life she would not leave the house unless veiled, and then only to see her family.

Eleonóra rigidly controlled her children's existence. They were not allowed to wear stockings or gloves, and wore summer dresses even in November. Their routine was set out in writing: three minutes for brushing teeth, three times a day. Four for washing hands. Seven for dressing. Six for brushing hair. There was a cold bath each morning and a hot one in the evening, each for five minutes and no more. Maids helped the girls dress and put on their shoes. Compared to most of their peers, the Andrássy girls led a life of great privilege; they never lacked for clothes, food or shelter and did not ever need to worry about material things. But the girls' relationship with their mother was cold and distant. In 1905, when Caja was seven years old, her father died of leukaemia. Four years later her mother married Count Gyula Andrássy the Younger, her late husband's brother. Caja's youth was spent in the usual routine of a young female Hungarian aristocrat: attending balls, dinners and charity events, and riding whenever she could – she was a skilled horsewoman. Beautiful, intelligent and high-spirited, a daughter of one of the country's best-known families, she attracted attention wherever she went.

The nineteenth-century Austrian statesman Klemens von Metternich once observed, with more than a hint of a sneer, that the Balkans 'begin at the Rennweg', a street in central Vienna. Budapest lay 150 miles east of Vienna. By Metternich's standards Hungary was deep inside the Balkans, but its citizens – especially those living in Budapest – mocked such Viennese snobbery. Hungarians can be prone to boasting, perhaps as a means of overcompensating for their position as a small, isolated people in the heart of Europe, with no natural allies or linguistic relatives. But there was plenty to boast about. Budapest was a thriving, modern, cosmopolitan city, home not only to Hungarians, but ethnic Germans, Greeks, Serbs, Gypsies, Armenians, Romanians, Russians and more. It was renowned for its art, literature and music, its restaurants and glamorous – sometimes even debauched – nightlife. The city boasted one of the largest and most prosperous Jewish communities in Europe – about one in four of the population. Its Jews were so entwined in its cultural and commercial life that the city was dubbed 'Judapest' by anti-Semites such as Karl Lueger, the mayor of Vienna. Budapest was a city of superlatives, certainly more beautiful than its Austrian rival. There the Danube was relegated to a distant quarter. In Budapest the majestic flow of the river defined its urban sweep, the rushing, whirling waters crossed with grandiose, ornate bridges. 'If only you were here for a moment to see with me the dead silver of the Danube, the dark mountains against the pale-red background and the lights of Pest glittering up to me; Vienna would go down in your appreciation compared to Buda-Pest', wrote Otto von Bismarck to his wife in 1852.[3]

That view was just as entrancing in 1916 and even today would be recognisable. The Chain Bridge, designed and built by British engineers, opened in 1849. Its graceful 200-metre span was adorned with giant lions at either end. Fifty years on, Hungary's engineers surpassed themselves with another suspension bridge – named for Erzsébet, the beloved empress and wife of Franz Joseph – with a span of 290 metres, then the longest in the world. Emperor Franz Joseph himself had inaugurated the Budapest Metro in 1896, the thousand-year anniversary of the arrival of the Magyar tribes from Asia. The Budapest Metro was the first electrified fully underground line on mainland Europe. New transport links bound the city to Western Europe – fast, modern trains and ferries ran from Budapest to Vienna. The Great Synagogue, a neo-Moorish extravaganza with space for 3,000 worshippers, stood on Dohány Street in the heart of downtown Pest. The largest Jewish house of worship in Europe, the Great Synagogue was the lavish, gilded embodiment of an increasingly prosperous community.

The view from the Buda Hills of the Erzsébet Bridge and the Chain Bridge spanning the Danube.

Overlooking the river by the Chain Bridge stood the pride of Budapest's artisans: the Gresham Palace. The art-nouveau building embodied all the flair and confidence of the resurgent city; its wrought-iron electric gates were shaped like peacocks, its staircases boasted delicate mosaics, stained-glass windows and Zsolnay glazed tiles, while the inner courtyard was topped with a glass dome. Budapest deserved such landmarks. It had taken just a century to transform three dusty provincial towns – Buda, Pest and Óbuda – into a single thriving, cosmopolitan capital. In 1799 around 54,000 people lived in Buda and Pest. By 1900 the city's population was nudging 1 million. The Hungarian capital was the eighth-largest city in Europe, bigger than Rome, Madrid, Liverpool and Brussels.[4]

But all the glories of the capital were not enough to save the empire. By late October 1918, as the war drew to an end, crowds gathered demanding independence, democracy, the release of political prisoners, the end of the war and for Mihály Károlyi, Katinka's husband, to be appointed prime minister. Many of the revolutionaries pinned an aster, a flower, on their lapels. Hungarians are a passionate, tempestuous people. Through the centuries they have launched numerous uprising and revolts. The Aster Revolution, as it came to be known, was the only successful revolution in Hungarian history.[5] On 31 October 1918 Mihály Károlyi was appointed prime minister. The Budapest-born writer Arthur Koestler had a ringside view. Koestler's father, Henrik, had his office on Kossuth Lajos Street, near the Astoria Hotel. Count Károlyi, 'a tall, dark, stooping man, with awkward gestures', stood on a balcony nearby bedecked in flags, while a 'huge, milling, cheering crowd blocks the street for half a mile'. Károlyi proclaimed Hungary's secession from the Habsburg Empire and 'its rebirth as a free, independent, democratic republic'. The crowd cheered and sang the national anthem. The Koestlers were elated, swept up in the patriotic fervour.[6]

The neighbouring states promptly invaded Hungary, capturing vast swathes of land. The victorious Allies demanded that Budapest cede more and more of what it saw as historic Hungarian territory to its neighbours. For a while in late 1918 the Astoria was the epicentre of the political upheavals. Mihály and Katinka lived in suite 414. The National Council, the new ruling executive that Károlyi chaired, met on the first floor, in rooms 105–109. More than twenty-five years later, when the Nazis invaded in March 1944, the Astoria's central location and proximity to the Great Synagogue and Jewish quarter meant it would once again take centre stage. But the noises echoing through the hotel, especially in its basement, would not be those of revelry or passionate debate.

Assailed by enemies inside and out, Mihály Károlyi's government did not last five months. On 21 March Hungary became the world's second Communist regime after Soviet Russia. The de-facto leader of the country was a Hungarian Communist called Béla Kun, born Béla Kohn. Captured by the Russians in the First World War, Kun became an ardent Communist, fighting with the Red Army during the Russian Civil War. Kun became close to Lenin, who later recalled, 'I knew Comrade Béla Kun very well when he was still a prisoner of war in Russia; and he visited me many times to discuss communism and the communist revolution.'[7]

Many, especially among the young, found the new creed exhilarating. The old world of dead empires, hierarchy and titles was ushered out – although not for long – and the new one, of freedom, equality and messianic promise, was welcomed in its place. Budapest's most talented artists and designers embraced the new creed of agitprop – Soviet-style artistic propaganda – with enthusiasm. The city was bedecked in red cloth and modern, futuristic posters extolling the virtues of the Red Army and the workers. For a brief interregnum, every day seemed full of promise. The factories were taken into public ownership; aristocratic titles and privileges were abolished; freedom of speech and assembly, free education and new rights for national minorities were all promised. The Hungarian Red Army (the old army with new badges) was performing creditably against the Czechoslovaks.

Unfortunately, the peasants, who produced the food that fed the capital, were not convinced. They refused to sell their produce. The new regime's banknotes, known as 'White money', were only printed on one side, which did not inspire confidence. There was almost nothing in the shops, except cabbages, turnips and, for some reason, ice cream. Communist Hungary reverted to an older economic system, recalled Arthur Koestler. 'The whole country lived on a barter system; the peasants came to town with their chickens, eggs, milk and butter, and went home laden with grandfather clocks, bronze statuettes, antimacassars, second hand shirts and suits.' Middle-class families were soon handing over their valuables for sacks of potatoes and a couple of ducks or chickens – scenes that would once again unfold in the later stages of the Second World War.

Koestler was born in Budapest in 1905 into a middle-class Jewish family, typical of the increasingly prosperous bourgeoisie. Thanks to the late Emperor Franz Joseph, Hungarian Jews enjoyed full civil rights. There were 'relatively large numbers of Jews in the highest judicial positions, among the great landowners, university professors, reserve officers and civil servants', notes the historian István Deák.[8] Hungarian Jews were also doctors, dentists, artists, poets, musicians, shopkeepers, carpenters, tailors and decorators. Budapest was home to numerous synagogues, Jewish schools, religious, community and welfare organisations, orphanages and old-age homes. On the Jewish High Holidays of Rosh Hashanah, the New Year and Yom Kippur, the Day of Atonement, the city centre fell notably quiet.

Jewish industrialists and businessmen owned many of the Hungarian mines and heavy industrial concerns, such as the Manfréd Weiss complex of factories on Csepel Island and a good part of the banking, wholesale and retail trades. Members of some families, such as the Weiss dynasty, were ennobled and sat in the Upper House of the Parliament. Many Budapest newspapers had Jewish proprietors, while more than two-thirds of their journalists were Jewish, as were about half of the city's university students. The Koestlers lived in an apartment on Szondi Street in District VI, near Andrássy Way. A short walk away were the crowded tenements and narrow back streets of Districts VII, VIII and IX, the rapidly expanding quarters between the two boulevards that encircled central Pest, home to many poor Jewish families, working as artisans or scraping a living as traders. Szondi Street was neither poor nor especially rich, its stolidly middle-class apartment blocks typical of the later-nineteenth-century explosion of building that turned Pest into a thriving urban centre.

Many of the revolutionaries were idealists, keen to educate the young and turn them into active citizens of the new state. New teachers arrived at Koestler's school, 'young members of the intelligentsia who had never taught in a school before', giving lessons in economics and politics, which 'opened new vistas and offered a new contact with reality'. On May Day a talented young student, a published poet, gave a speech extolling the French revolutionary leaders Georges Danton and Louis de Saint-Just, while the teachers listened in 'acid silence'. One day Koestler accompanied his cousin Margit to a factory on the outskirts of the city, where she was giving a course in political economy. Margit explained the history of money and the principle of barter. A few of the men fell asleep, but many 'drank her words in avidly, with a puzzled and rapt expression'.

Yet just as in Russia, the Communists were unable to govern. The nationalisations and appropriations triggered economic collapse. The aristocrats' estates were not divided up for the near-serfs who worked them, but instead were turned into collective farms, often under the same corrupt and brutal managers, causing fury among the peasants. The Kun regime deployed brutal, anarchic paramilitaries known as the 'Lenin Boys' who randomly arrested, imprisoned, tortured and shot their captives. Hundreds died in their custody. A good number of the regime's leaders and high-ranking officials, including Kun himself, were Jewish. For some young Hungarian Jewish intellectuals, like their co-religionists in Russia and elsewhere, Communism proved attractive. It offered the promise of messianic deliverance, with its own dense works of theology to pore over and discuss late into the night and the chance to rebel against patriotic, assimilated parents and their stultifying bourgeois lifestyles. The Jewish Communists did not spare their co-religionists. Jewish institutions, societies and publications were closed down. Jewish businessmen and traders lost their source of income. Jewish artisans' workshops were confiscated.

Meanwhile, in Szeged in the south of Hungary, Admiral Miklós Horthy, the former commander of the Austro-Hungarian Navy, was plotting, preparing to deploy his 'National Army' to bring down the revolutionary regime. Under attack from the Romanians and the Czechoslovaks, with Horthy mustering his forces for a coup, the Hungarian Army collapsed, the Communist regime itself following swiftly. The Romanian Army entered Budapest on 1 August 1919. The Communist republic had last lasted 133 days. The Romanians stayed until 14 November 1919, their presence a national humiliation. Two days later Admiral Horthy entered the capital on a white horse, trotting up Fehérvari Way on the Buda side of the Danube to establish his headquarters at the Hotel Gellért, a famed landmark overlooking the Danube. Horthy's first speech decried the city as treacherous, depraved and corrupt.

> We loved and respected this city, which over the past year became the depraver of the nation. Here on the banks of the Danube I arraign the Hungarian capital: this city denied its one-thousand-year history and trampled the crown and national colours into the mud and clothed itself in red rags. This city threw into jail and drove into exile the finest people of the homeland and in one year squandered all our wealth.[9]

In fact it would be Horthy's authoritarian regime and series of anti-Jewish laws that would, through the 1920s and 1930s, drive many of Hungary's 'finest people into exile', among them numerous scientists, writers and thinkers, just the kind of people the country needed to navigate the complicated, turbulent currents of modernity and the twentieth century. Meanwhile, the city's writers came to Budapest's defence. Gyula Krúdy, one of Hungary's best-loved and most lyrical novelists, hit back at Horthy's sour condemnation.

Well, Pest has never been an agreeable town. But desirable, yes: like a racy, full-blooded young married woman about whose flirtations everyone knows and yet gentlemen are glad to bend down and kiss her hand ... Here the dancing in the theatres is the best, here everyone in a crowd may think that he is a gentleman even if he had left prison the day before; the physicians' cures are wonderful, the lawyers are world famous, even the renter of the smallest rooms has his bath, the shopkeepers are inventive, the gentlefolk are agreeable, the streetlights burn until the morning.[10]

And so Krúdy's lyrical defence of the capital continued at some length.

The Kun interregnum, the time of 'red rags', was short-lived but profoundly significant. For many Hungarians, especially the nationalist-minded, Jews and Bolshevism were now entwined. Horthy's detestation of the capital, most of whose population, including its Jewish citizens, had not supported the brief Magyar–Soviet interlude, would shape his policies during the decades to come.

In September 1920, his government drafted modern Europe's first anti-Jewish law, known as the 'Numerus Clausus'. It set a quota of 6 per cent for Jewish students at Hungarian universities. The law caused outrage, but was still passed.[11] Hungary's Jewish leadership was shocked and dismayed, but remained proudly – even fiercely – patriotic. Vilmos Vázsonyi, a former minister of justice, told the 1925 Hungarian National Jewish Congress that 'We are not Hungarian Jews but Jewish Hungarians ... We adhere to our ancestral religion but this fatherland is also ours.' But not everyone agreed. The precedent was now set; legally, politically and, perhaps most important of all, in many Hungarians' minds Jews were not really Hungarian, and were therefore unable to enjoy the same legal rights as their compatriots. Instead they were a distinct and separate minority. Their lives and their activities could be controlled and restricted by laws that did not apply to Christians. Soon after delivering his rousing speech Vázsonyi was severely beaten up. He died the following year.[12]

2

A Nation Traumatised

Nem, nem, soha! (No, no, never!)

Hungary's response to the 1920 Treaty of Trianon, imposed
by the Allies, that excised two-thirds of its territory.

Claud Cockburn was sixteen when he arrived in Budapest with his
father, Henry, a British diplomat in charge of an Allied mission to
manage Hungary's finances. He had served in China for twenty-
five years. Henry was an Asia specialist and knew nothing about
Hungary or finance. His predecessor had a solid knowledge of
both, but he had committed a terrible faux-pas, so he had to go. 'He
had been seen picking his teeth with a tram-ticket in the lounge
of the Hungaria Hotel', explained Claud many years later in his
autobiography. Such behaviour 'was regarded as socially impossible'.[1]

Much worse than poor dental hygiene was unfolding. The
Cockburns arrived in 1920 to a city traumatised by war and the
collapse of empire, government and the rule of law. Budapest 'was
a battlefield where everyone has come to a bad end, where all the
heroes are dead and all the great causes betrayed', wrote Claud.[2]
After the Red Terror came the White Terror, the campaign of
violence, torture and murder waged by right-wing military officers
and their followers. The Prónay Battalion, led by Pál Prónay, the
head of Horthy's bodyguard, spearheaded the White Terror.
Prónay set up shop in the Hotel Britannia, close to the Nyugati
('Western') Station. By the end of 1919 he had 800 men under his
command, looting and killing at will. 'It was a city where everyone
was frightened – frightened of being arrested, frightened of being

murdered, frightened of just being ruined', wrote Cockburn, who later became one of Britain's best-known journalists. Among the victims, Arthur Koestler believed, was his schoolmate, who had praised the French revolutionary leaders. Once the Kun regime had collapsed, he had been expelled from school and, according to rumour, murdered.

The savagery of the White Terror, and its revenge on supporters of the Kun regime, whether real or imagined, was not state-organised. But it was state-tolerated, at the highest level. Jews were disproportionately targeted. The historian Béla Bodó estimates that between August 1919 and the end of 1921, 'officers' detachments, supported by the civilian militias and patriotic organisations, killed at least 3,000 individuals, mainly in the western and central parts of the country and in Budapest'. At least a third of the victims were Jewish – in 1919 and 1920 more than sixty pogroms took place in the Hungarian countryside. Around 70,000 innocent people were incarcerated in prisons or ramshackle internment camps, many on the basis of denunciations from jealous neighbours or work colleagues. Thousands of Jews were classified as 'illegal aliens' and deported, even though many had lived in Hungary for generations. Tens of thousands of everyday people were sacked from their jobs for supposedly supporting the Soviet regime. At least 100,000 people left Hungary for good.[3]

The Prónay Battalion moved across the country in an armoured train, rampaging through villages and hamlets and setting up kangaroo courts. In Fonyód, on the southern shore of Lake Balaton, Prónay militiamen organised a lynching of three Jewish men: Albert Tószegi, Albert Graner and Ede Hamburger. Their supposed crime was supporting the Kun regime, which was absurd. Tószegi owned substantial holdings and was a high-ranking municipal official in Budapest's inner-city District VI. Graner was his estate manager and Hamburger a local businessman. Their real 'crime' was being Jews. All three were hanged from trees while a large crowd of locals cheered and jeered. The rope around Tószegi's neck broke twice. His wife watched, screaming and pleading. She had even managed to obtain an order from Admiral Horthy that the men should not be executed, but to no avail. On the third attempt Tószegi's neck finally snapped. His wife later had a nervous breakdown and died a year later.[4]

Another militia, led by Count Anton Lehár, brother of the composer Franz Lehár, was involved in one of the most infamous political murders, that of Béla Somogyi, the Jewish editor of the social democrat newspaper *Népszava* (*People's Voice*), and his colleague Béla Bacsó. *Népszava* had extensively reported on the White Terror. Somogyi had been warned off but continued to run the stories. One evening in February 1920 he and Bacsó stepped outside the newspaper's office and were kidnapped by militiamen led by Emil Kovarcz, an extreme-right military veteran. The journalists were forced into a car, driven out of Budapest and then shot. The killings caused uproar in Hungary and around the world. The crime was investigated and the perpetrators identified, but Horthy pardoned them all, as well as many others who had carried out atrocities during the White Terror, including the Fonyód killers and their numerous local accomplices.[5]

Despite the Prónay Battalion's avowed anti-Communism, there was some overlap with the Lenin Boys. They used the same slang; 'half-English' (*fél-angol*) meant a roughing-up but not murder, whereas 'English' (*angol*) meant murder. But what distinguished the White Terror from the Red was the degree of sadism and torture. In his diary Prónay himself praised the enthusiasm of his 'new, overly ambitious and highly motivated recruits' to beat up Jews outside the barracks, or 'bring them in where they can give them a real thrashing'.[6] One Jewish victim, beaten almost senseless, had sugar sprinkled on his wounds so that flies gathered and feasted on his bloodied flesh. Bodó notes:

He [Prónay] and his men organised pogroms, raided prisons and murdered their inmates, kidnapped and blackmailed rich Jewish merchants, cut peasant and Jewish women's breasts off, collected ears as 'talismans', hung estate servants by either their necks or legs and fed the boiler of their armoured train with the bodies of their victims, many of them still alive.[7]

Post-war Hungary, dismembered, traumatised and impoverished, was not alone in bringing forth violent, often murderous nationalist paramilitary formations. In Germany the Freikorps fought pitched battles with the Communists in the street. Freikorps troops summarily executed Rosa Luxemburg and Karl Liebknecht, two Communist leaders. Italy had Mussolini and his black-shirted Fascist Squadre d'Azione (Action Squads). But only in Hungary was the connection between the death squads and the head of state, Admiral Horthy, so direct. Count Pál Teleki – soon to be prime minister – also employed Prónay's thugs as bodyguards, as did his successor, Count István Bethlen. As Bodó notes:

> Without the support of the political and military elite, the two most important paramilitary units could not have survived for more than two years. The countless murders, robberies and petty thefts that they had committed would not have been possible without either the active cooperation or the connivance of the authorities, which received their cues from the political and military elites.[8]

But even Horthy eventually realised that the White Terror was bad for business, the economy, Hungary's international image and life in general. Leading businessmen and industrialists had been pressurising him for months to stop the rampage. The atrocities were gaining increasing publicity in the foreign press at a time when Hungary needed all the allies it could find. In November 1920 government forces finally raided both the Hotel Britannia and the Prónay Battalion's barracks. By the end of 1921 the White Terror had faded away. The paramilitary formations dissolved themselves. Their members and officers either returned to their old lives or became active in Hungary's now-thriving far right. But the legacy of the short-lived Kun regime shaped and poisoned Hungarian politics for decades to come. The radical right had tasted power: physical, on the streets and in its torture chambers, and political, in the corridors of power. Such savagery would erupt again in the winter of 1944–1945, but on a much larger scale.

Caja Andrássy grew into an attractive young woman, warm, intelligent and highly sought-after. By the time the war was over she was almost twenty. There was no shortage of suitors among the aristocracy. But Caja wanted more than the traditional arranged – or semi-arranged – dynastic union. She wanted a soulmate, with the same sensibilities and passionate interest in politics. Unlike many Hungarian aristocrats, Caja had a social conscience and strong sense of *noblesse oblige* that privilege and riches brought duty. Politics was in her blood. In 1919 Caja travelled to Switzerland for the Socialist Congress in Lucerne. Caja also fell in love with Archduke Albrecht Habsburg. But Albrecht's mother Isabella refused her consent. The Andrássys were a venerable Hungarian family, but of lower rank than the Habsburgs. In addition, there was the problem of Katinka and her husband. Albrecht broke off the relationship. Caja, heartbroken, returned to Budapest, where she completed a nursing course and worked in children's nurseries. Meanwhile she and Katinka angrily parted ways. Caja was still an ardent monarchist and could not forgive the Károlyis for turning Hungary into a republic. The two sisters would not communicate for years.

By May 1921 Caja was finally betrothed – to Prince Károly Odescalchi, a friend of Archduke Albrecht. The Odescalchis were originally of Italian origin but had deep roots in central Europe.[9] Count Gyula, Caja's stepfather, was opposed to her marrying Károly. He had a fine title, but he had no proper job and few assets. The Odescalchi estate remained in the family's posession, but was now in Czechoslovakia, part of the lands lost at the 1920 Treaty of Trianon, which redrew Europe's post-war borders. The Hungarian delegation was humiliated during the negotiations and not allowed to participate in the discussions. Count Apponyi was finally permitted to address the conference for a few minutes to plead Hungary's case. His eloquence was to no avail. The decision had already been made: Hungary was to be dismembered. Trianon was a savage punishment. Hungary lost two-thirds of its territories – 125,000 square miles – and 3.3 million people. In comparison, Germany lost just 15 per cent of its lands. Before the war Greater Hungary stretched from the forests of Transylvania, in present-day

Romania, to Istria and the port of Fiume – now Rijeka – on the Adriatic, a journey of around 800 miles. Hungary then was a cosmopolitan, multi-ethnic nation. The Croat, Romanian, German, Slovak, Serb, Ukrainian and Ruthenian minorities made up about half the population. There was a substantial Roma community and smaller Greek, Armenian and Polish minorities, while the Jewish community numbered over 900,000. Recognised national minorities could use their own languages and had their own autonomous churches. Banknotes issued by the Austro-Hungarian central bank showed their value in Hungarian, German and eight minority languages.

But the minorities did not want to be subject people. They wanted independence. Trianon forced Hungary to cede vast areas of present-day Slovakia, northern Serbia, Croatia and Romania, as well as lands now in Ukraine, Poland, Slovenia and Austria. Some of these, such as the Istrian ports, were peripheral. But large swathes were historically Hungarian. Millions of Hungarian citizens – many of them ethnic Magyars – were cut off from their motherland and marooned in new states to which they had no allegiance, whose bureaucracies they had to navigate in a foreign language. As Géza Jeszenszky, a former Hungarian foreign minister, notes, Central and Eastern Europe, once a single space with a shared currency, suddenly sprouted visa regimes and arbitrary border crossings – which often made no sense to the locals.[10] The pain, anger and resentment did not fade. Rejection of Trianon became the central tenet of Hungarian politics, under the phrase *Nem, nem, soha!* 'No, no, never'. Across the political spectrum there was a widespread determination to reverse the terms of the treaty.

Much of Admiral Horthy's rule overlapped with those of Hitler and Mussolini. But Horthy was neither a Nazi nor a Fascist. His ideology was a synthesis of authoritarian national conservatism, while Hungary was a managed quasi-democracy. The Communist Party was banned – and, later on, the far-right Arrow Cross – but other opposition parties organised more or less freely and won seats in Parliament. Trade unions operated, there was a lively press, with hundreds of newspapers and magazines. Journalists wrote critical articles, although censorship became more intrusive over the years. But the political system was gerrymandered. Strict educational and residential requirements and the widespread abolition of the secret ballot ensured that Horthy and his allies maintained an iron grip on power.

Like many Hungarian nationalists, Horthy idealised the countryside, seeing it as free from cosmopolitan, liberal and Jewish influences (even though many Jews lived in small towns and villages). That pastoral idyll was wholly imaginary. György Pálóczi-Horvath, a Hungarian writer who later worked for Britain's Special Operations Executive in Budapest, recalled in his memoir a visit to his uncle's estate. Living conditions were medieval. The peasants were treated as less than human, often forced to work without pay, subsisting off the wheat and barley they were given and the chickens they kept in the yard. Children were malnourished and barely educated. Disease was rampant. The lord of the manor was a god-like figure, whose wishes and instructions had to be obeyed, for fear of brutal punishment.

Perhaps twelve people shared a filthy space, often with their animals. There was very little to eat, and there were no proper washing facilities, no means of keeping the rooms clean and no privacy. Four women, two middle-aged and two elderly, stood to attention as they greeted Pálóczi-Horváth and his companion, an estate manager called Labay. There was no question of the women asking for help or highlighting their dreadful living conditions. They proclaimed 'God's welcome to your honours', the phrase indicating their respectful subservience. Such conditions were the norm. Many agricultural day-labourers only had work half the year and for the rest were on the brink of starvation. There was no welfare system. Not for nothing was Horthy's Hungary known as the 'land of three million beggars'.[11]

Pálóczi-Horváth and Labay left quickly, the foul air lingering in their noses. Labay asked Pálóczi-Horváth if he wanted female company later. The peasant girls were expected to make themselves available at any time, for which they received a few crowns. 'It's the custom, or tradition if you like, that we landowners, estate managers, overseers, "use" the girls ... We use the girls if we feel like it and they are in no position to refuse.' This utter disdain for everyday people was considered quite normal among much of Hungary's ruling elite, even among enlightened families. Katinka Andrássy, Caja's sister, recalled in her memoir how their uncle Géza 'would make love to ladies and beget children by the peasant girls in the village'. The lands around the Andrássy country home were inhabited by Romanian peasants, whom the Hungarians called 'Oláhs', a derogatory term derived from the word 'Vlach'. The Oláhs, recalled Katinka, 'looked less human than their beasts. We indeed considered them so.'

The upheaval of the post-war years had barely affected a deeply engrained deference. Hungary remained a traditional, hierarchical and conservative society, especially outside the capital. Each rank or social stratum had a different form of address, each jealously guarded. Ministers, bishops and high-ranking counsellors of state were addressed as *Nagyméltóságú*, 'your great Eminence' or *Kegyelmes*, Gracious. MPs, Mayors, high-ranking civil servants, counts and barons were *Méltóságos*, 'Eminence'. Further down, military officers, business people and intellectuals were Nagyságos, 'Greatness'. Artisans and manual workers were addressed as Tekintetes, 'Respected'.[12] Women were called by the female equivalent of their rank, so the wife of a baroness would be addressed as *Méltóságos baroné*.* Along with this came anti-Semitism. But there were gradations of the oldest hatred. Horthy's anti-Semitism was not the same as Hitler's. Horthy regarded Jews not with hatred but fluctuating degrees of distaste. He believed Hungary's Jews should be controlled, their political, cultural and economic influence minimised. But he also saw the value they

---

* These terms have now mostly vanished, but Hungarians still place great importance on correct greetings and politesse when encountering strangers. It would be considered rude to enter and leave a lift, for example, without greeting the other passengers and saying goodbye to them. Children still greet older women with *Kezét csókolom*, 'I kiss your hand', often shortened to *Csókolom*, which literally means 'I kiss it'.

brought to the economy. Emperor Franz Joseph had ennobled over 120 Hungarian Jews. Some sat in the Upper House of the Hungarian Parliament. Horthy enjoyed their company, regarding them as 'honorary Magyar gentry', when they socialised together or played bridge.[13]

The Horthys were modest gentry and landowners in the village of Kenderes, ninety miles east of Budapest. Born in 1868, Miklós Horthy joined the Imperial and Royal Navy as a cadet and served with distinction, rising to be aide-de-camp to Emperor Franz Joseph. In May 1917 he commanded a flotilla at the Battle of Otranto. Horthy fought with valour until he was seriously wounded and fell unconscious. A year later he was promoted, at the young age of fifty, to commander of the Imperial Navy. Horthy was a physically imposing leader, charming when needed, with an athlete's build – he was an excellent fencer, tennis player and horseman. He spoke seven languages and was fluent in German, French, Spanish, Italian, Croatian and English. Horthy was an Anglophile, was not corrupt and was devoted to his family. He took power in a country thoroughly traumatised by its defeat in the war and the losses of Trianon. At a time of widespread international political turbulence, he held Hungary together as a unitary state – a remarkable achievement. In comparison to Germany and Italy, even France, Hungary was an island of stability.

But Horthy was also a man out of time: blinkered, block-headed and lacking enough self-knowledge to acknowledge his very limited vision. Central Europe during the 1930s and especially in the early 1940s was a whirlpool of deadly, swirling currents. Navigating a path through such dangerous waters would have tested the most astute and perceptive political leader. Horthy was neither. Instead of policies that evolved and were adjusted according to sometimes rapidly changing circumstances, he had a set of pre-ordained responses, shaped by the demands of his fervent Magyar nationalism – most of all the determination to reverse Trianon and regain the lost lands. Hungary was firmly under his control. The wider world was not. Horthy's poor strategic choices would, within a few years, cost the lives of hundreds of thousands of his citizens, both Jews and Christians.

Caja and Károly Odescalchi were married in October 1921 at the Batthyány Castle in Polgárdi, a village southwest of Budapest. They set up home in the Andrássy Palace where they lived comfortably. But while Károly was the scion of a grand and respected dynasty, he lacked a substantial income. He worked as a banker. Soon after her marriage Caja took half-ownership of a hairdressing salon on Haris Alley, just off Váci Street, the city's most glamorous shopping street. The news caused a sensation. But the young couple needed the money that the business brought in. Money, and Caja's difficulties carrying a child to full term, were also putting their marriage under stress. Caja gave birth to twins who died prematurely, but then finally in September 1923 gave birth to a son, the couple's only child: Pál Ottó Odescalchi. It was not enough to keep Caja and her husband together. In 1926 she announced that they were to divorce. Their paths, their interests, diverged too far, but they stayed friends as they raised their son.[14]

Caja was just one of Budapest's legion of attractive women. Waves of invaders from the Tatars to the Turks and Austrians had combined with the indigenous Slavic tribes and Hungarian gene pool to produce a female population of rare beauty. It was something beyond physical appeal, a vivacity and flirtatious, proudly feminine confidence that frequently entranced male visitors, especially those from colder, more reserved lands. 'The city was blessed with its cult of women', proclaimed Gyula Krúdy. 'The eyes of men trembled, the women were so beautiful: black-haired ones, as if they had come from Seville, and in the tresses of the blonde ones tales from an Eastern sun were playing hide and seek, like fireflies in the summer meadows.'[15] Francesca Wilson, an American aid worker who became friends with Caja in the late 1930s, was also full of praise. Wilson's memoir, *In the Margins of Chaos*, includes a sharply observed and informed account of Hungary in 1939 and 1940, studded with perceptive pen-portraits.

'At the best Hungarians – especially the women – are admirable: lively, warm-hearted gracious with the charm of Austrians but more dynamic and vivacious; in the simplicity of their manners not unlike the English, but with the spontaneity of which the Puritan movement deprived us and which we have not yet regained.'[16]

Poverty and the lack of opportunities in a highly class-based society drove some women into prostitution. Budapest was home to a busy sex industry. A range of brothels from the cheap to the luxurious catered for both local men and visitors. Many were officially licensed and regularly inspected; in 1906 Budapest had twenty-one. The most upmarket, Madame Roza's, was on Magyar Street, in District V. The entrance fee was 200 crowns, a substantial sum of money, equivalent to a teacher's salary. The madame, Roza Pilisy, offered poetry dinners and live music while the working girls wandered among the clients. Gyula Krúdy was a regular and Madame Roza fell in love with him.[17] The government clamped down on the sex trade in the 1920s, but with no great enthusiasm. Madame Roza's closed, but across the road Madame Frida's stayed open. Its calling card showed a luxuriously furnished bedroom, with a four-poster bed and mirrored dressing table.[18]

Viscount Rothermere, the British newspaper proprietor, was a rare ally. In June 1927, beguiled by Princess Stephanie von Hohenlohe, a socialite on the Hungarian government payroll, he wrote two articles in the *Daily Mail* decrying the injustice of Trianon. The lands ceded to Czechoslovakia, Romania and Yugoslavia were the 'greatest frauds that have ever taken place in the public life of Europe' and should be reversed as soon as possible. Hungary erupted in joy and gratitude. Rothermere became a national hero. An address of gratitude was prepared. Within a few days 1.2 million people had signed it, their names bound in twenty-six volumes.[19] Streets were named after him. Some even called for Rothermere to be crowned King of Hungary. Even now a statue of him stands in downtown Budapest. Rothermere's articles had no effect whatsoever. Hungary's borders remained the same. The British government regarded his meddling with irritation. But Rothemere's clarion call, and the reaction to it, highlighted how

Trianon – and the attempts to reverse its losses – were the most important factors in Hungarian politics and diplomacy. Almost every decision that Horthy took, including Hungary's disastrous alliance with Nazi Germany, was driven by the attempt to reverse Trianon. Some of the lost lands would eventually be returned, but only temporarily, and at a very high price.

3

The Most Seductive City

One cannot breathe hot and cold air from the same mouth. The country cannot stay within the German-Italian line in foreign policy and successfully defend itself from Hitlerism from within.[1]

Caja Odescalchi to Klotild Apponyi, April 1937.

Patrick Leigh Fermor was sitting in the Ruszwurm Café in Budapest's historic Castle District, trying to learn some Hungarian. The nineteen-year-old Englishman had arrived on 1 April 1934, stopping off on his journey on foot and horseback to Turkey. Like most foreigners, especially those whose native tongues are Indo-European languages, Leigh Fermor was struggling. 'On a printed page the fierce-looking sentences let slip no hint of their drift. Those tangles of S's and Z's', he wrote in *Between the Woods and the Water*, his classic work of travel writing.[2] Hungarian is not Indo-European but Finno-Ugric, distantly related to Finnish and Estonian. Its grammar, syntax and structure are complex. Hungarian has three modes of formality, with verb forms distinguishing between the definite and indefinite, and is agglutinative. Syllables and suffixes that indicate position, possession, direction and more are piled one after another onto the base word, like the layers in Hungary's justly famed *Dobos torta*, a cake with a crunchy topping. Hungarian's crunchy topping is that it requires rhyming vowel harmony. It is a language of great beauty with some words of visceral simplicity. 'Sibling' is *testvér*, literally 'body-blood'. 'Sister' is *nővér*, 'woman-blood'.

Until Ferenc Kazinczy modernised and codified Hungarian in the early nineteenth century, the educated middle classes spoke German. Buda – Budan to the Ottomans – was known by its German name of Ofen. Many streets had German names. Hungarian was archaic, almost impossible to use for everyday commerce and conversation. Across the Austro-Hungarian and Ottoman Empires, subject peoples were modernising their languages as a means of asserting their national identities. The new word for 'revolution', a frequently used term in Hungarian history, was *forradalom*, 'on the boil'. 'Secretary', *titkár*, comes from the ancient word for 'secret', *titok*. Language was the twine that bound together the Hungarian nation, especially after Trianon, when one third was scattered beyond the new borders. Hungary's growing Jewish community was one of the most enthusiastic early advocates of the modernised tongue. Speaking Hungarian was both functionally useful and also a means of showing their loyalty to their new homeland.[3]

Leigh Fermor was staying not far from the Ruszwurm Café, at 15 Úri Street, hosted by Tibor and Berta von Berg. Úri Street ran through the heart of the Castle District. It was a pretty thoroughfare of Gothic, Baroque and later houses, many inhabited by noble or aristocratic families. The von Bergs were proud Anglophiles. Tibor's mother was American and he had been educated in England. On his father's side he was related to the Swedish aristocracy. Berta was a countess. The von Bergs' house was called a *palota*, meaning a small palace. It was a double-fronted, two-storey house, spacious and comfortable but less grand than its description. As Berta noted in her brisk, idiomatic English, 'All rot, of course. We seem to have a passion for grand styles in Hungary. It's a perfectly ordinary townhouse.' But 15 Úri Street would not have a perfectly ordinary fate. Ten years later, in the winter of 1944, the house and its cellars would serve as a secret base for Raoul Wallenberg, the Swedish diplomat, and his rescue operation.

Leigh Fermor experienced nothing but warmth and lavish hospitality on his visit. 'Life seemed perfect: kind, uncensorious hosts; dashing, resplendent and beautiful new friends against the background of a captivating town; a stimulating new language, strong and startling drinks, food like a delicious bonfire and a prevailing atmosphere of sophistication and high spirit that would have been impossible to resist even if I had wanted.'[4] After attending a ball in Buda where a young couple danced a *csárdás*, a traditional Hungarian folk-dance, 'throwing themselves into it with a marvellously fierce and stamping brio, their hair flinging about like the manes of ponies', Leigh Fermor squeezed into a car and 'whirled downhill and across the Chain Bridge' to Budapest's most famous and glamorous nightspot: the Arizona on Nagymező Street, known as Hungary's Broadway. Leigh Fermor was entranced. So was Cecil Beaton, the British society photographer, who visited the following year: 'There were revolving dance floors and a cabaret that went on from ten o'clock until three in the morning. The walls had breathing shells; balconies suddenly shot ceilingwards on the trunk of a palm tree; stars flashed and chorus girls, suspended by their teeth, twirled at the end of ropes.'[5]

One of Leigh Fermor's former hosts had written to the former prime minister Pál Teleki, introducing him. Teleki was a renowned geographer and cartographer. His 'alert, pointed face, behind horn-rimmed spectacles, lit by a quick, witty and enthusiastic manner, had an almost Chinese look', wrote Leigh Fermor. Teleki was Hungary's Chief Scout and the two men spent much time poring over maps and planning Leigh Fermor's journey to Transylvania. 'It is hard to think of anyone kinder', he wrote, but Hungary's Jews might not have agreed. One of Teleki's first acts in power was to draft and push through Parliament the 1920 Numerus Clausus Law restricting the number of Jewish students at Hungary's universities.

There was a dark side to the world of the Hungarian aristocracy. Not all were modern-minded Anglophiles like the von Bergs or the Andrássys. As previously noted, a good number had been supportive of the White Terror. Some, in common with their British equivalents, were anti-Semitic and openly admiring of Hitler. The British socialite and ardent Nazi supporter Unity Mitford was a frequent visitor to Hungary and Budapest in the 1930s, finding plenty of kindred spirits. Unity was entangled in a

The Club Kávéház in downtown Budapest. The city was renowned across Europe for its glamorous café society where artists, writers, aristocrats, politicians and everyday people gathered.

dark, obsessive sexual relationship with János Almásy, the brother of the Hungarian explorer László Almásy, a version of whose life was fictionalised in the film *The English Patient*. Almásy was the lover of Unity's brother, Tom, and quickly seduced her. When their violent, frenzied sex life palled, Almásy took Unity and his other guests to stay at the family apartment, not far from the Gellért Hotel. There, she threw herself into Budapest's social whirl, meeting friends for drinks on the terrace of the Dunapalota Hotel, shopping on Váci Street and attending endless parties.

The morning of Leigh Fermor's visit to the Ruzswurm Café there was one other customer: a white-haired, elderly man reading the newspaper *Pesti Hírlap*. The headline announced 'Ó Boldog Angolország!', meaning, 'Oh, Happy England!' – happy because it had a prince as promising as Edward, Prince of Wales. He arrived the following February by train from Vienna. A crowd of journalists boarded the train, records the police report, 'but absolutely nobody was permitted' to get near him. The prince's party had reserved the first carriage behind the locomotive, and behind that was the dining car, so they were sealed off from curious fellow passengers. There they had eaten numerous dishes of rich and spicy Hungarian food, washed down with copious quantities of the famed Tokaj wine and pálinka (fruit brandy), while smoking plenty of cigarettes and cigars. Peter Hain, Horthy's security chief, was travelling with the royal party, in charge of their safekeeping.[6]

Together with their fifty-one yellow pigskin suitcases they travelled by car straight to the Dunapalota Hotel, by the Chain Bridge. The Dunapalota, opened in 1913 as the Grand Hotel Ritz, was the most sought-after of the cluster of hotels along the Danube promenade known as the Corso. Its roof garden, grand café and restaurant were frequented by aristocrats, businessmen, writers and artists as well as everyday people seeking a slice of the city's glamorous social life. After freshening up, the prince and his entourage headed out into the night. Their first stop was the Arizona nightclub. In later years, one of the Arizona's most popular cocktails was 'The Prince of Wales', a mix of Canadian rye whisky, apricot pálinka, bitters, water, sugar and garnish of orange peel. Over the next few days Edward and Wallis Simpson also went shopping for jewellery and antiques, took long walks on Margit Island and bathed in the mineral waters of the Gellért Hotel. They dined at the famous Kakukk restaurant, where they were serenaded by Gypsy violinists. There were some official duties as well, such as drinks with the British ambassador and a visit to Admiral Horthy.

Színházi Élet (*Theatre Life*) published an extraordinarily detailed account of the royal visit by Attila Petschauer. A Jewish sabre fencer famous for the speed and accuracy of his attacks, Petschauer won several medals at the Olympics. Fencing is one of Hungary's national sports and Petschauer was a well-known and popular figure in Budapest high society. He wrote: 'The journalists and the photographers chased the Prince of Wales for four days. Where is he going? What is he doing? Until when did he party? Where is he having dinner tonight?'[7] The list of names is a roll-call of the city's best-known and most influential historical dynasties, gathering at Budapest's most glamorous nightspots. At the Parisien Grill,

Dancers at the Arizona, the best-known and most glamorous
of the city's nightclubs.

where dancers cavorted down a catwalk between the diners, the
party included Caja Odescalchi, György Pallavicini and Admiral
Horthy's two sons, Miklós and István.

Edward enjoyed his time in Budapest, so much so that he
returned in September for several days. This time he checked in at
the Dunapalota as the Earl of Chester, in a vain attempt to avoid
publicity. An enterprising photographer from *Színházi Élet* perched
on the glass roof of the Operetta Theatre to take paparazzi shots of
the prince. The accompanying police saw the flash and confiscated
the photographer's camera – but he had already removed the film
and hidden it behind one of the statues. He returned the next day
and his shot made the magazine's cover. Edward finally and briefly
passed through Budapest in September 1936 as King Edward VIII.
The royal train stopped at Keleti (Eastern) Station, where he met
with the staff of the British Embassy for an hour. Three months
later he abdicated, to be with Wallis Simpson. His departure was

viewed with regret in Budapest as the loss of a potentially useful ally and sympathiser.

The rift between Caja and Katinka steadily healed over the years. After Hitler took power in 1933 their once-passionate arguments seemed irrelevant. Fascism, and its growing number of supporters in Hungary, had to be stopped. For Katinka and Mihály Károlyi, like many left-wingers at that time, the Soviet Union would help achieve that. The Károlyis travelled to the Soviet Union in 1931, where they were feted as honoured guests. They took part in propaganda tours, turning a blind eye to the state terror, the shortage of food and the feral children living on the streets. In Moscow they met Béla Kun. He was not very friendly, perhaps from jealousy at the attention the Károlyis were receiving. In a few years he would be dead, one of many foreign Communists to perish in Stalin's purges.

In the early 1930s the Károlyis moved to Paris. They became close to Willi Munzenberg, the charismatic German Comintern operative and propaganda genius. Katinka showed extraordinary bravery in a mission for Munzenberg. Across Germany Communist operatives and sympathisers gathered evidence of the brutality of the Nazis. It detailed their violence and torture, the concentration camps and persecution of Jews and everyday people. The material needed to be smuggled out. Katinka volunteered to travel to the Third Reich, confident that her name and social standing would protect her from the Gestapo. It worked. The material she brought back was published in *The Brown Book of the Reichstag Fire and Hitler Terror*. Co-authored by Willi Munzenberg and published in Paris in August 1933, it was an instant bestseller and enraged the Nazis.

The following year Katinka and Caja spent some time together in a Czech spa town and met again in Switzerland in 1936. That summer war broke out in Spain. Spain was a testing ground for the great powers. The Nazi pilots of the Condor Legion honed the tactics of dive-bombing and strafing columns of civilian refugees. Hitler and Mussolini supplied Franco's fascists with arms, advisers and funds, while the Soviet Union sporadically aided the beleaguered Republican government. Spain galvanised a generation. Caja travelled to Spain to report on the war, writing for the French newspaper *L'Ordre* and the Danish *Politiken* while her articles were also reprinted in *Újság* (*News*), a Hungarian newspaper. She travelled across the country and in Madrid met Ernest Hemingway at the Hotel Florida. The facade was peppered with bullet holes and gouged by shrapnel. 'I would not leave here even if I was forced to, This is a great city, how could one live anywhere else', he told her, 'with a robust joie de vivre'.[8]

Caja reported from the Madrid front at the university – where Nationalist forces were just a few metres away – with a fine eye for detail: 'The underground corridors are a reminder of Dante's vision of hell ... damp cellars lit by the red flames of open fires. Thick smoke everywhere. People with weathered faces sit by the flames, their eyes gleaming white in the light of the fire. The plumbing has been shattered by a shell and damp leaks onto the floor. A few metres away, facing us, the building is held by Franco's troops.'[9]

Countess Klara Andrássy, later Princess Caja Odescalchi, turned the Andrássy Palace into a centre of anti-Nazi resistance.

According to Katinka, Caja had another, secret mission in Spain: 'None of us knew until after her death what dangerous tasks she had undertaken, as, for instance, carrying large sums of money to the Republican fighters. No one would have suspected her, Princess Odescalchi, of such subversive activities', wrote Katinka in her memoir.[10] Whatever the truth of Caja's activities in Spain, the time she spent there gave her experiences of dangerous missions that would prove very useful after the outbreak of the Second World War. For Caja, Spain was a dark portent of Europe's future. She left, with a 'heavy heart', she wrote, a country that was a 'wilderness of thousands of cries and tears'.

But if the war for Spain was lost, the battle for Hungary's hearts and minds continued. Caja opened a literary salon in the Andrássy Palace where liberal-minded and anti-Fascist writers and intellectuals gathered over fine English tea and cake. There were French, English and Swiss newspapers, as well as copies of *The Economist* and musical interludes, with performances of works by Béla Bartók and Zoltán Kodály, Hungary's best-known modern composers. 'We talked and discussed, what we had read, what we were writing, what we would like to do, how we imagined the country after the war', recalled Iván Boldizsár. For war, he was certain, was coming. Boldizsár had started his literary career writing poems for the journal *Nyugat* (*The West*), one of the centrepieces of Hungary's thriving literary culture. Those Hungarians who were not writers were readers; one positive result of the Horthy era was the reform and modernisation of the school system. By 1938 only 7 per cent of the school-age population was still illiterate, much less than in Hungary's neighbouring countries.

The Andrássy Palace stood on the Buda side of the river, by the Chain Bridge. With its long, dark corridors and heavy, old-fashioned furniture and paintings, it seemed an unlikely gathering-place for maverick liberal and dissident writers. Francesca Wilson, the British aid worker who became close to Caja, noted that stepping inside the building was like 'going into a museum', entering through the large, iron-barred doors, up a wide staircase through 'vast rooms decorated with ancient tapestries and Old Masters that had lamps burning under them'. Yet in the midst of this gloomy, feudal setting was Caja, with her 'electric vivacity and modern outlook'. Caja read her guests' writings and listened attentively to what they had to say. As Boldizsár recalled, 'they had no more diligent reader than her', and of course her attractiveness was an added bonus. Wilson noted her 'fair hair piled up high, expressive blue eyes, a mouth that was rather large – a face that was not beautiful but was a real face, that one couldn't forget'.[11] Iván Boldiszár was more direct: 'She had the loveliest legs I had ever seen.' But the salon was more than a literary affair. Caja was engaged in high politics, trying to steer the Hungarian government away from Berlin and towards London. Many of the guests were known for being anti-German and pro-Allied. They lobbied the British diplomats who also attended, gathering snippets of useful intelligence. Caja's connection with London, and the British Legation in Budapest, would grow much stronger as the Andrássy Palace became an open centre of anti-Nazi opposition.

Despite the country's lurch rightwards and the dark news from Germany, Budapest's irrepressible spirit still fizzed like a glass of *pezsgő*, Hungary's version of champagne. György Pálóczi-Horváth was a reporter on *Pesti Napló*, an open-minded liberal newspaper. Each night, after the journalists put the newspaper to bed, he met his colleagues at the Parisien, where they stayed until five in the morning. Every night club had a special table for journalists, where they could buy food and drink at a discount, in exchange for the latest news and gossip. When the Parisien closed, the journalists went on with the hostesses to a café to have an enormous breakfast, and then went back home to sleep, before returning to work and the social whirl afterwards. 'Naturally it was nearly four in the afternoon before we got up, so our life was spent entirely in the office and in nightclubs.'[12]

Pálóczi-Horváth's description of an evening at the terrace of the Café Japán, on Andrássy Avenue, is a lyrical evocation of a pre-war world of literary glamour and sophistication.

It's just past eleven; the city is very much alive. People dine on the terrace, shielded from the other half of the busy pavement by a stone balustrade with flower pots. The bright electric bulbs throw their light up to the heavy green foliage of the pavement trees. Cars swish by on the smooth wooden blocks of the avenue, bright blue buses sail along, streetwalkers flutter past ... Everybody dashes from table to table always in the way of perspiring waiters sailing by with big trays and flopping frock-coat wings.[13]

Yet there was also a darker, melancholy edge to the city's endless partying, one embodied in perhaps the city's best-known song. Rezső Seress, a well-known lyricist and composer, had co-written and composed a song which became 'Szomorú Vasárnap' ('Gloomy Sunday'). Hungarians, already prone to melancholy, quickly adopted the sad ballad. Some were supposedly so captured by its lyrics that they committed suicide. Myths soon sprung up about the song – heartbroken lovers supposedly left copies of the lyrics by their bodies, or simply jumped off the Chain Bridge into the Danube. Seress was horrified. 'I've become the suicides' singer? I'm devastated that this has become the song's fate', he said. Yet when Europe, perhaps even Hungary itself, was sliding towards a kind of suicide, 'Gloomy Sunday' seemed more and more apt.[14]

For a while, Hungary had taken another path. István Bethlen, who served as prime minister between 1921 and 1931, was also a Transylvanian aristocrat. A moderate conservative, he built bridges between the aristocracy and the labour unions. He kept good relations with Jewish business leaders and opposed the anti-Jewish laws. Hungary remained politically stable, especially in comparison to Germany and Italy. But while the far-right were far from power, they were still organising, gathering their forces, especially at the universities. When Bethlen passed an amendment to the Numerus Clausus in 1927 that allowed more Jewish students to study at university, nationalist students launched violent attacks on their Jewish peers.[15]

Bethlen was succeeded in 1932 by Gyula Gömbös, a former militia leader. Horthy regarded Gömbös with sympathy, seeing him as an old comrade from their days in Szeged after the end of the war, fighting the Reds. Gömbös was an extreme Hungarian nationalist and openly anti-Semitic. It was his thugs who had beaten up Jewish students. As minister of defence in the 1920s Gömbös had had rebuilt Hungary's shattered and traumatised armed forces. Gömbös was the first foreign leader to visit Hitler. Yet at home he moderated his tone and proved surprisingly pragmatic. He pledged to prevent any further anti-Jewish legislation, and kept his word. But if the Jewish question had been at least put aside for a while, Gömbös ensured that the centralisation of power and the erosion of democratic freedoms continued. The ruling Unity Party was renamed the Party of National Unity. It took control of the state machinery and local administrations. Press censorship was increased, telephones were tapped, mail was opened and a legion of paid informers was recruited. Elections became even more corrupt and marked by intimidation. By 1936 Hungary seemed to be sliding from a managed quasi-democracy into actual fascism. Gömbös placed his allies across the civil service and ministries, in preparation for an internal coup. It was too much, even for Horthy. But he did not have to depose his old comrade. Gömbös had long been sick and died in October 1936 of kidney failure.[16] But his long-term plan to make Hungary's machinery of state a servant of Berlin continued without him – and would bear fruit in 1944.

4

Diplomatic Dances

All doors are open. The best of entertainment is offered and anything anywhere he wishes to do or see will be arranged with all the goodwill in the world.

Owen O'Malley, British minister to Hungary.

Owen O'Malley arrived in Budapest in May 1938 to witness the passing of the country's first anti-Jewish law. Born into an Anglo-Irish family, O'Malley had previously served in China and Spain. Like much of Britain's ruling elite, O'Malley was sympathetic to Franco, believing that he ensured stability. O'Malley was a minister, one rank down from ambassador, and the British premises was a legation rather than an embassy, but a legion of servants met the family's needs. The legation was housed in a four-sided Ottoman-era and Baroque mansion with an inner courtyard at 1 Werbőczy Street, in the Castle District (now Táncsics Mihály Way). The prime location gave him easy access to ministries and government leaders. The flow of invitations to drinks, lunches, dinner and weekends away was never-ending. The Anglophile aristocrats O'Malley met were especially welcoming, their lifestyle comfortable and familiar. Weekends in the Hungarian countryside followed a familiar British pattern of a hearty breakfast and long tramps through while shooting hundreds of pheasants.

Francesca Wilson took a sharper view. 'The English especially, invited to exquisite meals in the feudal homes that overlook the Danube, or for a weekend's wild goose shooting at a country castle, used to come back denouncing Trianon and sighing for a restoration of the Habsburgs', she noted. O'Malley's wife, Mary Dolling Sanders, was another sceptical observer. Perhaps because of her American mother, she was more of an outsider. Her fine eye for detail, and subtle understanding of human relations – especially between men and women – are evident in the series of best-selling novels she wrote under the pseudonym of Anne Bridge. Dolling Sanders published two novels set in Hungary in 1940 and 1941, unfolding in those strange months when Hungary was allied to Berlin and Rome but was still neutral and keen to keep channels open to London and the West. *The Tightening Spring*, an almost undisguised account of her life in Budapest, tells the story of a group of English diplomats in the Hungarian capital and their efforts to send food and clothing to the tens of thousands of British POWs in Germany. It includes an evocative description of the legation and its courtyard. 'It was really an old palace dating from the Turkish occupation in the seventeenth century ... and the garden itself had once constituted the *harem-lik*, or women's quarters.' Meanwhile, across the street, sitting in the first-floor window of a small greengrocer's shop, sat a small man with binoculars, and another with an open notebook on the window sill, noting whoever entered the legation.

The book also has a lively account of the daily information service that O'Malley, Sir Hugh in the novel, had set up. 'To accommodate it Sir Hugh had sacrificed most of his spare rooms, over in the old harem quarters on the ground floor on the far side of the courtyard ... the huge and enormously powerful radio receiver lived in the bathroom – where whoever was doing the monitoring perched uncomfortably on a cork-topped stool.' O'Malley's teenage daughter, Kate – renamed Lucilla – monitored the broadcasts and took shorthand notes, then compiled the newssheet with a colleague. Subscribers had to collect their copies, either from the legation or the consulate in Pest, but it had a daily circulation of over 1,200 copies, printed on a Roneo machine. *A Place to Stand*, set in Budapest in Spring 1941, features a classic Bridge heroine: a young American woman called Hope Kirkland who falls in love with a Polish refugee. Hope smuggles blank

Yugoslav passports into Hungary, hidden in a box of chocolates, and is soon drawn into a web of danger and international intrigue, based on the actual Polish underground rescue operation. Many characters are barely disguised versions of real-life people. The Dendrassys are the Andrássys. The Weissbergers, a noble dynasty of Jewish origin which had converted to Christianity, are the Weiss family of industrialists, some of whom had converted to Christianity from Judaism.

The American ambassador, John Flournoy Montgomery, arrived in June 1933 and stayed until March 1941. Flournoy was not a career Foreign Service officer, but a political appointee who had made his fortune in the dairy industry. A close ally of President Roosevelt, Flournoy donated substantial sums to the Democratic Party. Montgomery was a keen bridge player and golfer. He soon became close to Admiral Horthy and played bridge with Horthy and Gyula Gömbös. Like O'Malley, Montgomery was an admirer of Hungary's leader. His memoir, *Hungary: The Unwilling Satellite*, published in 1947, is studded with illuminating anecdotes such as his account of a gala performance at the Royal Opera House in Budapest on 15 March 1939, celebrating Hungary's day of national independence – the same day that Nazi tanks rolled into Prague. The performance was in aid of the Boy Scouts. It opened with a young Boy Scout giving a speech, which was quickly interrupted by demonstrators chanting 'Justice for Szálasi' – meaning the imprisoned Ferenc Szálasi, the leader of the extreme-right Arrow Cross party.

Montgomery and his son-in-law quickly left their seats to find out what was happening. Horthy himself had rushed out of his box, past his bodyguards, down to the demonstrators. Two had been knocked down and Horthy had a third by the throat, slapping his face while he shouted, 'So you would betray your country, would you?'. Horthy threw him to the floor and walked away, mumbling to himself while passing Montgomery. A few days later Horthy asked Montgomery to call on him. He presented him with his picture. 'The whole incident was typical not only of the Regent's deep hatred of alien doctrine, but of the kind of man he is', wrote

Montgomery. 'Although he was around seventy-two years of age, it did not occur to him to ask for help; he went right ahead like a skipper with a mutiny on his hands.'[1] His attempts to connect Horthy and Roosevelt through their shared love of sailing, however, failed. Roosevelt did not share his ambassador's enthusiasm for the qualities of Hungary's leader.[2]

Montgomery spent much time entertaining and mixing with Hungary's political and social elite. He and his family lived on Lovas Way, in Buda, but the American Legation was located downtown on Szabadság Square, near Parliament and the government ministries. Montgomery led a busy, highly organised social life. He and his staff kept a detailed list of the hundreds of people invited to lunches, dinners, teas and the Wednesday concerts. An invitation was highly prized by pre-war Hungarian society – in part because it was a merry-go-round of familiar faces. 'Socially everything is very lively here, and I am kept very busy with luncheons, dinners, teas and goodness knows what. It gets very tiresome but it is necessary and in this business you have to keep in touch with your contacts all the time', Montgomery wrote to a friend in 1935.[3]

Despite his years in Hungary, Montgomery did not speak Hungarian and rarely mixed with everyday people. His contacts, notes the historian Tibor Frank, were 'an extensive but closed world' that mirrored the 'odd, semi-feudal establishment of Hungary between the two world wars'. Montgomery loathed Hitler and was an outspoken critic of the Nazi leader. But like much of the American political establishment, he shared some of what Frank describes as 'snide drawing room anti-Semitism', dismissing the fears of the upper-class Budapest Jews he knew. On 12 May 1938 he wrote to the US minister in Copenhagen, 'the Jews are so scared and they have such wonderful imagination they turn out the most beautiful assortment of stories you ever heard and one keeps thinking some of them must be true'.[4] Had Montgomery enjoyed a wider circle of contacts, and a more sceptical view of his friends in the ruling elite, he would have realised that his Jewish acquaintances had good reason to be scared – and proof was coming in just a couple of weeks.

O'Malley also enjoyed cordial relations with Admiral Horthy, and often spoke frankly with the Hungarian leader. But his closest contact was Pál Teleki, then the minister of religion and education. O'Malley was an admirer. 'He lived a dedicated life, untortured by conflicts originating in his own character and beliefs. All the conflicts came from outside; from the ineluctable pressure of political circumstance on his judgement and conscience.'[5] Teleki modernised the Hungarian state, and while he ushered Hungary deeper into the Axis, he recognised that Germany and Hungary had different national interests, attempting a geopolitical balancing act between London and Berlin. Teleki strongly believed that Hungary also needed to keep healthy relations with the Western powers – one reason why he always had time for O'Malley. But he was a driving force behind the first anti-Jewish law. Teleki's anti-Semitism was different to that of the Arrow Cross. His 'civilised' version sought to first restrict, then eliminate Hungarian Jews' social and economic influence. Hitler's demands would be refused. Hungary's Jews would not be rounded up or placed in camps or deported. They could stay, and stay alive, but as weak, dependent second-class citizens. Ultimately, of course, such fine distinctions proved irrelevant.

The First Anti-Jewish Law was drafted by early 1938. Many among the country's cultural and political leaders were horrified. István Bethlen, the moderate conservative who served as prime minister through the 1920s, wrote to Horthy expressing his dismay, warning that the million Jews living in Hungary would be transformed into 'desperate internal enemies of the Hungarian nation'. The journalist György Pálóczi-Horvath helped organise a large-scale protest. Hungary's greatest living composers, Béla Bartók and Zoltán Kodály, signed. So did numerous other liberal politicians, painters, artists, writers and scientists. It was to no avail. The law passed in May with an overwhelming majority in both houses of Parliament. It limited the proportion of Jews in the professions such as law and medicine, and in firms employing more than ten people, to twenty per cent, with some exceptions. This was enormously significant and a radical constitutional step.

The law essentially amended the 1868 law, passed under Emperor Franz Joseph, emancipating Hungarian Jewry. If there was a moment when Teleki's bill might have failed, it was lost when the churches came out in its support. One after another, high-ranking churchmen of all the main denominations, Lutheran, Calvinist and Catholic, called for the bill to be made law. All this contributed to the legitimisation of anti-Semitism and boosted the far right. As Randolph Braham – the foremost historian of the Hungarian Holocaust – notes, the churchmen's failure to defend their Jewish compatriots would have catastrophic consequences.

> Their position on this and several other anti-Jewish laws prepared the ground for the effective implementation of the ghettoisation and deportation programme in 1944. Their public declarations in support of discriminatory laws contributed to the psychological conditioning of the Hungarian people. This explains in part the passivity with which the Hungarian masses witnessed the suffering of their fellow citizens of the Jewish faith and the lack of any meaningful organised resistance in the country following the German occupation in March 1944.[6]

Some of the law's supporters argued that it was necessary to reduce the pressure from the far right. Arguably the anti-Jewish legislation did ease some of the pressure from Berlin, but it seems highly unlikely that without such laws Nazi Germany would have then invaded Hungary. Hitler needed Horthy as an ally and easy access to Hungary's resources, military and the Danube. Some Hungarian Jewish leaders even argued that compared to what was happening in Nazi Germany, and neighbouring Romania, where an anti-Semitic government was stripping Jews of their citizenship, these comparatively moderate measures would defuse the demands for stronger action.[7] Predictably, the opposite occurred. Buoyed by its legislative success – and the support of the churches for the anti-Jewish law – Hungary's far right demanded further, more oppressive measures.

Adolf Hitler welcomed Admiral Horthy to Berlin in 1938, the same
year that Hungary passed its First Anti-Jewish Law.

Not only Hungary's Jews were legislated against. Hungary
had an ambivalent relationship with its Roma community. Its
music was celebrated as an authentic part of Magyar culture, its
energy and *joie de vivre* an essential part of any serious celebration.
But the people who played the instruments were usually not
celebrated. They were stigmatised, marginalised and discriminated
against, especially those living a nomadic lifestyle. The anti-Roma
discrimination had deep roots in the Austro-Hungarian Empire.
Many still travelled across the country in caravans with their
families, trading and working as horse-traders, artisans, musicians
or handymen. During the First World War a decree had been
passed to tie travelling Roma to a specific place and forbid them
to leave. Their possessions were confiscated and those who defied
the rules were to be interned in labour camps. Many settled Roma
lived in conditions of extreme poverty and deprivation. Towns and
villages had their own 'Gypsy quarter', where a kind of de facto
apartheid operated. The area was ignored by the municipality and

usually lacked running water, electricity or heating. Families often lived in shacks made of mud and wood or even tents, cooking outside on an open fire. Few Roma children went to school and most were barefoot. Conditions were somewhat better in Budapest, where the Roma at least inhabited proper buildings.

In 1928 the Interior Ministry passed a decree authorising the authorities to carry out bi-annual raids on Gypsy settlements. These were essentially a licence for the gendarmes to beat up anyone they cared to. A flurry of other arbitrary laws and decrees allowed local authorities to deport Roma from their lands, banned them from appearing as witnesses in certain court cases and from owning horses, building on village greens and more.[8] Unlike the Jewish community, the Roma had no communal organisations, political leaders or connections to the ruling elite. Weak and powerless, with no protectors, they were easy prey for the gendarmes in the countryside and the Horthy regime. Eventually the government outlawed almost all of the travelling professions. From then on a work permit was only valid where the Roma lived – and needed the consent of the local council. A powerful extreme-right-wing Hungarian politician called László Endre had both the Roma and Hungary's Jews in his sights. In 1944, after the Nazi invasion of Hungary, Endre would be a driving force in the Hungarian Holocaust. A decade earlier he demanded that travelling Gypsies be incarcerated in camps and males sterilised. In 1938, the same year that Hungary's First Anti-Jewish Law was passed, another decree was issued. From then on, every Roma person was to be regarded as potentially 'suspect'. Just as it was doing with the Jews, the Hungarian state was preparing the ground for the separation of the Roma.[9]

'Autumn and Buda were born of the same mother', Gyula Krúdy once wrote, in happier times. The trees along the Danube still slowly turned brown and golden that autumn. A cool breeze blew across the water in the evenings, through the crowded terrace cafés. Imre Magyari's Gypsy band played on the terrace of the Grand Hotel Hungaria, and those who could not afford a meal or drink there could rent a chair nearby, and listen for a few pennies.

But it was clear that Europe was sliding to war. German agents masquerading as 'tourists' were everywhere, it seemed, sitting in cafés, eavesdropping, watching and sometimes noting movements of people, traffic and the river cargo along the Danube. The police were ever more intrusive, the far right more confident. Left-wingers and those considered subversive were kept under intrusive surveillance. József Attila, one of Hungary's most talented poets and an independent-minded Communist, wrote:

> They can tap all my telephone calls
> (when, why, to whom)
> They have a file on my dreams and plans
> And on those who read them.
> And who knows when they'll find
> Sufficient reason to dig up the files
> That violate my rights.[10]

Czechoslovakia was soon dismembered, its passing little mourned in Budapest. The Sudetenland, the border area inhabited by ethnic Germans, was ceded to Germany at Munich in October 1938. In November the First Vienna Award gave swathes of southern Slovakia, known in Hungarian as the *Felvidék*, or 'Upper Lands', to Hungary. Finally, the injustice of Trianon was being reversed and some of historic Hungary had been returned. But for the far right this was a cause for concern as well as celebration. Unfortunately some of those living there were Jews. As Béla Imrédy, the prime minister, noted: 'With the reacquisition of the territories of the Upper Lands, the proportion of the Jews, which was already unfavourable, became even more so and the infiltration became much wider.'[11]

In Budapest Teleki was busily working on the Second Anti-Jewish Law, with further restrictions. This time the Jewish leadership took a stronger line. Jewish organisations submitted petitions and appeals. The bill, they argued, violated the constitution, breached the principle of equality before the law, was in conflict with justice and harmed Hungary's interests. Jewish leaders published pamphlets, postcards and leaflets emphasising their loyalty and patriotism through the ages. István Bethlen was again a powerful critic. A key moment, as with the First Anti-Jewish Law, was the attitude of the churches, which had not changed. Newly emboldened, the far right moved to bloodshed. On 3 February 1939 members of the Arrow Cross threw hand grenades at Jewish worshippers as they left the Sabbath service at the Great Synagogue on Dohány Street. Twenty-two were wounded and several died. Budapest had not seen such anti-Semitic violence since the early 1920s. The attack sent shock waves through the Jewish community and caused outrage in wider society – and was indeed rooted in the White Terror. Emil Kovarcz, who had helped organise the kidnapping and murder of two left-wing journalists in 1920, was a key figure in the synagogue attack. Kovarcz was arrested and tried but somehow escaped to Germany.

Soon after the grenade attack Teleki returned to power as prime minister. He was one of the Second Anti-Jewish Law's most outspoken advocates, steering it through Parliament. The bill became law on 4 May 1939. The law, like the Nuremberg legislation, gave a detailed definition of who was a Jew: anyone who belonged to the Jewish community, or had one parent or two grandparents who belonged to the community. The list of restrictions was long and thoroughly drafted. The law also re-established the 1920 Numerus Clausus 6-per-cent quota for Jewish students and set the same limit for Jewish membership of professional chambers, cutting back from the 20 per cent of the First Anti-Jewish Law.

The legislation accelerated Hungary's slide into darkness. At the end of the month parliamentary elections were held. Teleki and Horthy's party swept to victory with 181 seats, but the real winner was Hungary's ever-growing extreme right. The Arrow Cross, standing for the first time, won 530,000 votes and 29 seats. Other far-right groupings won around 20 seats, making the bloc the second-largest in Parliament. The Social Democrats and their liberal allies won just 8 seats in the May 1939 elections. The Arrow Cross drew support from aggrieved workers, impoverished city dwellers, the unemployed, the poorly educated and convicted criminals. Its ideology was a mishmash of Nazism, Fascism and its leader Ferenc Szálasi's creed of Turanism, itself a mix of sentimental pastoralism, anti-Capitalism, anti-Communism and, most of all, virulent anti-Semitism. Yet Szálasi differed from the pro-Nazi faction on the extreme right. He was not a Hitlerite who wanted Hungary to be absorbed or ruled by the Nazis. In his own dark worldview, he was a Magyar patriot, who put Hungary first. Ironically, despite Szálasi's own obsession with Magyar purity, he himself was a true child of the multi-national Austro-Hungarian Empire, being of mixed Hungarian, German, Armenian, Slovak and Ruthenian ancestry.

Gyula Gömbös had used his four years as prime minister during the early 1930s effectively. His deployment of far-right and pro-German sympathisers throughout the bureaucracies now bore fruit. The new laws needed to be interpreted. Many officials inclined to the most rigorous implementation, as Alexander Szanto discovered. Szanto, a Hungarian Jewish man who had lived in Germany for thirty years, returned to Budapest in December 1939. He survived the war and later wrote a detailed memoir. At first he was struck by the apparent normality of life in the Hungarian capital. In Germany food was strictly rationed and there were many shortages. In Budapest the shops were full. Upmarket restaurants such as Gundel even offered delivery. Károly Kresz, an adviser to the Treasury, put in his order in April 1940. Kresz ordered cold catfish with a remoulade sauce, two servings of goose liver mousse and a poultry galantine in aspic, a kind of terrine, with Cumberland sauce. The total cost was 84.40 *pengős*, plus another 26 *pengős* for delivery, a substantial sum. Károly Gundel himself, the owner, signed a note on the receipt: 'Thank you for your order and I am always gladly ready to serve you, with exceptional respect'.

Yet the appearance of plenty did not mean that all the goods were easy to afford, especially for Jews. Inflation was soaring, wages were sliding, much of the economy was in decline and there was no unemployment benefit. The Jews were hardest hit. The First and Second Anti-Jewish Laws were biting hard now, triggering waves of job dismissals. Szanto witnessed thousands losing their livelihoods.

Most women did not work so the loss of the male bread-winner's income had catastrophic consequences. No public contracts could be awarded to Jewish firms, a serious blow in a bloated bureaucratic state like Hungary. The professions were steadily 'de-Jewified'. No Jews could work in state monopolies like the tobacco trade. The Jewish community, solidly established and well organised, rallied to help their impoverished co-religionists, setting up a new agency to find work for those who had lost their jobs. Samu Stern, the president of the Pest Jewish community, asked Szanto if he could help, as he already had experience of this kind of work in Berlin. Stern embodied the Jewish establishment – a prosperous and successful businessman who was close to Horthy and Hungary's ruling elite. Some of those who lost their jobs were found positions at Jewish businesses which had not exceeded their quota of Jewish employees; others were allocated training for manual occupations.

The problem was the Hungarian authorities. The Jewish laws set out the general framework but their implementation was mercurial and arbitrary, depending on the whims and prejudices of the bureaucrats. But for all the difficulties many Hungarian Jews still had a *laissez-faire* attitude, noted Szanto. When a retraining course did finally take place, the numbers attending soon fell away. Budapest's Jews believed they had no need to learn new skills. If something hit the Hungarian Jews hard then they could easily panic, but that was usually temporary and 'gave way to the general nonchalance which is a fundamental trait not only of the Hungarian Jews but of Hungarian people as a whole, above all in Budapest'.[12]

Meanwhile, the exodus of Hungary's scientific and cultural elite continued. For a small country, Hungary produced an unusually high number of world-class scientists, writers, artists and musicians. Part of that was due to Budapest's modern education system. Two schools in particular, the Minta Gymnázium and Fasori Gymnázium in Budapest, produced a steady stream of scientific geniuses and Nobel laureates. Their alumni included Eduard Teller, János Neumann and Leó Szilárd, key contributors to the Manhattan Project that developed America's atomic weapons. All

Király Street, the main shopping avenue of the Jewish quarter,
was one of Budapest's liveliest thoroughfares.

were Jewish and all left Hungary. So did the conductor György Solti and the film directors Sándor Korda, Emeric Pressberger and Mihály Kertész, who had filmed the coronation of King Charles in 1916 and later directed *Casablanca*. Not only Jewish Hungarians found life in the country unbearable. The composer Béla Bartók, a staunch anti-Nazi who had loudly and publicly opposed the Anti-Jewish Laws, started sending his manuscripts abroad. In October 1940 he emigrated to the United States with his wife and youngest son, to work as a research fellow at Columbia University.

5

Brothers in Sword and Glass

Beware of spies – rumour and gossip are treason.

Government posters on the streets of Budapest after the
Nazi invasion of Poland on 1 September 1939.

The posters' warnings were apt. By the time the Second World War
finally broke out the Hungarian capital was thick with secret agents
working for the Nazis, the Allies, the Soviets and the Hungarians
themselves. Neutral Budapest, a crossroads that valued its good
relations with both Berlin and London, was about to take centre
stage as the Casablanca of the Carpathian Basin – an epicentre of
espionage, smuggling, intrigue and escape. The war, or news of the
war, was everywhere. Between dance music and Gypsy bands, the
radio broadcast a lecture about air-raid shelters. Yet normal life
continued; there was no sense of panic and there were no shortages
of food or drink. The trams still trundled along the Danube Corso,
lovers strolled on Margit Island and the Danube glittered silver in
the warm seasonal sunshine.

The city's legendary nightlife was as lively as ever. 'Nowhere else
could have seen so many well-dressed people as at a cocktail party
in Buda or at the Regent's ball', wrote Francesca Wilson. 'In the
middle of the black-out of Europe this city glittered like a Christmas
tree.' At the Arizona Nightclub, a new revue, *Madame Folies*, had
its premiere. Cinemas showed the latest Western films. *Huckleberry
Finn*, starring Mickey Rooney, was playing together with the new
releases from Joan Crawford and Betty Davis. A new star was born
– from an unlikely background. Katalin Karády grew up in poverty

on the outskirts of Budapest, one of seven siblings. A charity sent her to Switzerland for her education. On her return she took acting classes and worked as a nightclub hostess. Her first film role, in *Halálos tavasz* (*Deadly Spring*), catapulted her into instant fame as a *femme fatale*. Her classic beauty and smouldering sex appeal brought rapturous reviews. 'The big surprise of the film: Katalin Karády', wrote the reviewer in *Újság* (*News*). 'This panther-like, acerbic, often lazily moving, strangely mysterious actress can boldly compete with the biggest stars. One look, one twinkle of her eye, a barely noticeable move are full of sex appeal. She knows everything and she does it by instinct. Excellent.' Wilhelm Höttl, later the Nazi regional intelligence chief, was not a fan. He described her in his memoir as 'A brunette of striking physique, full-lipped and of passionate temperament, this woman wanted to be great film star, although her talent for the drama was slight.'[1] Karády, a staunch anti-Nazi, would soon be drawn into a much more dangerous masquerade, involving espionage, intrigue and betrayal at the highest levels of state.

Katalin Karády, Hungary's best-known actress,
was a staunch anti-Nazi.

Across the Danube on the other side of the city, the Hotel Majestic was advertising for tenants. The Majestic, perched on the top of Sváb Hill in Buda, was a luxurious five-storey serviced apartment building. Tenants enjoyed a meal service delivered to their rooms – special diets were available on request – an in-house doctor, laundry, central heating, hot and cold running water, 'prime service' and magnificent views over the city. There was cellar space as well in the basement – which would prove useful when Adolf Eichmann set up his headquarters there in 1944. Meanwhile, guidance was available for those unsure how to implement the latest anti-Jewish legislation. Parliament could pass laws limiting the number of Jewish members of professional associations, but what did companies and professional associations actually need to do? The newspaper *Az Est* (*Evening*) was there to help. A detailed guide on the new anti-Jewish law, complete with examples and specimen documents, explained in detail how to implement the new regulations. It cost two *pengős* at the newspaper's book department.

Meanwhile Teleki instructed the Foreign Ministry to set up the new Foreign Press Control Department, which would manage censorship of foreign newspapers which were still available in Hungary. His new press secretary and deputy censor was a multi-lingual Transylvanian Hungarian called László Veress. Born in 1908, he and his sister had been brought up in the aristocratic manner, by governesses. After Trianon, their hometown of Sepsiszentgyörgy reverted to Romania. Veress's father refused to take an oath of allegiance to the new state and the family moved to Budapest. Fluent in French, German and English, Veress studied law in Paris for several years and then lived in London, where he worked for a lawyer. Veress was highly intelligent and politically sophisticated. His father wanted him to go into business. But ever since his childhood, he wanted nothing more than to be a diplomat, at the centre of international intrigue and geopolitical dramas. An ardent Anglophile, he eventually took a job at the Revisionist League, which campaigned against the Trianon settlement.[2] Veress's main role was to read foreign periodicals, including newspapers, books and pamphlets, and censor any material which could be harmful to Hungary and to black out any unfavourable coverage of Germany. Here he usually only blacked out part of the offending sentences, leaving enough that the meaning would be clear. Veress reported directly to Teleki, who wanted to see all the foreign press coverage of Hungary. Veress had another, highly confidential assignment: to maintain contact with the Hungarian anti-Nazi resistance and Western Allies. That role would soon place him at the heart of Hungary's first, stuttering attempts to change sides.

Teleki also set a clandestine propaganda anti-Nazi operation to help counter German influence and ensure Hungary's independence. A special unit in the Prime Minister's Office, staffed by high-ranking officials of proven loyalty, oversaw a covert printing and publishing campaign. Teleki provided the editorial guidelines and oversaw the publication of a range of anti-German pamphlets and a news magazine. The covert unit's material was carefully customised for the intellectual level and interests of its intended recipients. It contained analyses of domestic and international politics, *exposés* of German activity and propaganda catchphrases. The leaflets and magazines were posted to a select audience with paid-for stamps as government facilities could not be used. High-ranking Church figures used their local networks to disseminate the material. In addition these local agents, many of them clergy, reported on Arrow Cross and German activity.[3]

With the Jewish question solved, or so they hoped, Teleki and Horthy continued their balancing act between Berlin and London – annoying both, satisfying neither, while planning how to regain Transylvania from a weakened Romania. Before the outbreak of war Teleki had assured Mussolini and Hitler that Hungary would confirm to Axis policy but would also not take part in armed action against Poland on 'moral grounds'. Predictably, Hitler reacted with fury, pointing out, correctly, that Hungary would never have regained much of Slovakia without Germany's support. Meanwhile, Teleki also wrote to Lord Halifax, the British foreign secretary, informing him that Hungary would not take part in any attack on Poland and would remain neutral – although the geographical situation meant that Hungary could not actually declare itself as neutral. It was a very Hungarian compromise, and deeply unconvincing. As the historian Bryan Cartledge, a former British ambassador to Hungary, notes succinctly, 'The Hungarian government now pursued the hopelessly contradictory objectives of fending off insistent requests from Berlin for logistical support for the German invasion of Poland; securing German acquiescence in the recovery of Transylvania from Romania by force; and at the same time persuading the Western powers of Hungary's essential virtuousness.'[4] Hungarians have long been known for their inventiveness and ingenuity. But even the most *ügyes*, 'capable', Magyar could not square such a circle.

Eventually, Teleki and his ministers took a moral stand. Hitler demanded that German troops be allowed to attack Poland from the south, from Hungarian territory, through Slovakia. Teleki's government refused – although it did allow German military supplies to transit by rail. Hungary's defiance was rooted in a centuries-old alliance, one immortalised in verses that celebrated the Magyars' and Poles' brotherhood. Both had been caught between great empires – the Hungarians between the Ottomans and the Habsburgs, the Poles between Russia and Germany – and both saw themselves as fiery freedom fighters, with a strong tradition of chivalry. Poles, too, kissed a lady's hand upon greeting and departing. During the nineteenth century Hungarians had supported the Poles against the Russians and the Poles had returned the favour in 1848 when the Hungarians had risen up against the Austrians. Thousands of Poles joined the revolutionary army, including two generals – Jozef Bem and Henryk Dembinski – whom Lajos Kossuth, the Hungarian leader, appointed commander-in-chief. The rebellious Poles suffered a worse fate than the Hungarians – by the mid-nineteenth century the country no longer existed and was partitioned between Austria, Prussia and Russia. Poland regained its independence after the First World War and was quickly invaded by the Bolsheviks. Partly in gratitude for 1848, Hungary supplied the new Polish government with a massive arms shipment to use against the Russians. This historical alliance would lead to one of the least-known but largest rescue operations of the Second World War.

In March 1939 Hungary annexed a part of Czechoslovakia in the far east of the country, known as Carpatho-Ukraine. Once again, Hungary and Poland shared a border. On 18 September 1939, just over two weeks into the war, Teleki ordered that the frontier, around 150 miles long, be opened to the fleeing Polish forces. Whole units, brigades and regiments of the Polish Army crossed: mountaineering sharp-shooters, sappers, the famed Uhlan light cavalry, signal specialists, police officers, border guards, motorised infantry and artillery over the next few weeks, around 100,000 soldiers in total. One general arrived in front of the Polish Legation in his army car, flags fluttering, wearing his uniform, together with his aide-de-camp. The Polish minister quickly ushered him inside – the German Legation was just a block away and their watchers were everywhere. The general changed into civilian clothes and was quickly moved on to France.

Tens of thousands of civilian refugees also crossed, like the soldiers, to a warm welcome. Together with the Defence and Interior Ministries and the Red Cross, a network of organisations quickly sprang up to feed, clothe and house the refugees. There were soon almost 200 camps, fairly evenly divided between those for the military and civilians. The Polish relief operation was public knowledge – and would have been impossible to keep secret. Across the country the Hungarians were so welcoming, even wearing Polish military insignia, that the authorities became concerned it would provoke Germany. One group of Polish soldiers was greeted by a military band. In Budapest the Poles were brought to the city centre, where locals gave them water, bread and fruit. Hungarian aid workers set up a ticket system for restaurants giving free meals.

The man in charge of the relief effort was a high-ranking official in the Ministry of the Interior called József Antall. The Antalls were an old Hungarian noble family. Born in 1896, Antall had fought on the Russian front. Like Béla Kun he had been taken prisoner. Antall did not become a Communist, but the time he spent with his fellow Hungarian POWs, many of whom were from deprived backgrounds, fuelled his burgeoning social conscience. After finishing his legal studies he joined the civil service, working on welfare and poverty relief programmes. Antall recalled in his memoir that he never received any orders from either the prime minister or the interior minister. Instead, they let him act as he saw fit. Some of the Poles were Jewish, including unaccompanied children. Antall gave verbal orders that all the Jewish refugees, whether military or civilian, were to be given Christian identity papers – unless they insisted on being registered as Jews. The Office of the Polish Apostolate then certified that the religious registration was correct and valid. The refugees were then handed copies of Catholic prayers to learn. The Jewish children, masquerading as Hungarian Catholic orphans, were later sent to children's homes, where they were taught Hungarian.

Other refugees, who may have been on the Nazis' watchlists, or whom the Germans wanted to be extradited, were also given false identity papers. This was dangerous work. Antall may have had the support of the government, but he was surrounded by enemies. Much of the army, especially among the Hungarian General Staff, was sympathetic to the Nazis. The far right was growing in power and influence, as was the Volksbund, the organisation of Hungary's ethnic German minority. The Gestapo and the Nazi intelligence services had thoroughly penetrated Hungary's ruling elite – many of whom were anyway sympathetic to Berlin. Yet Antall and his colleagues persevered. With Teleki's full support, Antall and his colleagues ran a courageous and well-organised rescue organisation – one that showed how many lives could be saved with sufficient will and political support.[5]

With the Polish government-in-exile relocated to France, Budapest became a centre of the resistance against the Nazis. The Andrássy Palace quickly became a central hub for the Polish refugee and aid organisations. The mezzanine floor was given over to a clinic while another part of the building housed the Hungarian branch of the Polish Red Cross. Both Caja and her cousin, Erzsébet Szapáry, joined the new Hungarian–Polish Committee for Refugee Care, together with another of her sisters, Ilona, and a young student and soldier called Tamás Salamon-Rácz, who served as secretary, and Erzsébet's brother, Antall. The Szaparys' mother was Polish. The group quickly set to work; the Poles needed to be fed, clothed, housed and ferried to the border. The Andrássy Palace also became a centre of liaison with Polish intelligence and the British Embassy. Caja's clear-eyed assessment of her homeland – and the need for decisive action – was unusual among her peers, recalled Francesca Wilson. 'She was able to look at her country from the outside – a power rare in the Hungarian upper class who are as complacent as though they lived in an island; she understood and sympathised with the needs of the people who are still treated almost like serfs by their masters in Hungary.'[6]

Three weeks into the war, some of the Polish General Staff arrived in Budapest, where they set up Ekspozitura-W, the Polish Military Agency. Its two main tasks, noted Károly Kapronczay, author of a study of Polish wartime refugees in Hungary, were to set up courier services and to get the soldiers out of Hungary to Yugoslavia, then on to France, which was then still at peace. The evacuation effort was run out of the Polish Consulate at 36 Váci Street. The Poles also set up their own committee to deal with the myriad of new tasks: organising education and cultural events, publishing books and newspapers and providing religious services. József Antall's interpreter was an ebullient Polish reporter and Socialist named Henryk Slawik. Slawik told Antall at their first meeting, 'This will be a long war. We, the Poles, will win this war. But because of this, the Poles will have to work, and they will need schools, so they can play an active role in the future Poland.' Slawik was soon running the Polish organisation.

Meanwhile, József Antall helped ensure that the clandestine courier services kept running, supplying false papers, safe houses and places to safely rest and recuperate. The Hungarian diplomatic service sent Polish documents in the diplomatic bag to Rome or Lisbon, where they were picked up by Polish couriers. The Polish Military Agency worked closely with Antall and his staff in the Hungarian Interior Ministry. Many of the soldiers heading west changed their identities and pretended to be civilians. Caja and her fellow committee members bought civilian clothes, hired cars and trucks for the exodus and sometimes drove the Poles to the frontier themselves. Some of the Poles crossed at the 'green border', the woods and open countryside that led to Yugoslavia, where they were helped across by locals who knew the terrain. Others left by train, crowded into sealed compartments, aided by railway workers. Border crossings were easier in the winter of 1939–1940, when the Drava River froze over. Slawik and Erzsébet Szapáry also set up an orphanage in the small town of Vác, just north of Budapest, for dozens of Jewish Polish children. The children were disguised as Catholics, instructed in the Catholic faith and publicly attended church on Sundays. Erzsébet even arranged for Angelo Rotta, the papal nuncio, to visit and so give the home the Vatican's imprimatur. Meanwhile the children were secretly taught Hebrew and Jewish studies.

In his memoir Salamon-Rácz recalls how the division between sympathy for the Allies and the Nazis was mirrored in the government ministries. One part of the Interior Ministry tended to side with the Germans. After Trianon many thousands of ethnic Magyars moved from neighbouring countries to the motherland. They found jobs in Hungary's bloated civil service. 'Hungary's bureaucracy was the most overstocked and underpaid in the world', noted Francesca Wilson, 'and as in Vienna became a good seed bed for Nazi doctrines'. Yet other civil servants were keen to help the Poles. Border guards were told to turn a blind eye when the Poles 'escaped' across the green border, although police officers still sometimes opened fire.[7]

The Polish Military Agency soon expanded its clandestine courier network through Budapest. One line ran from Warsaw to Krakow in the south of the country, down to Budapest then to London or across the Mediterranean to the Vatican. Others connected the Hungarian capital to Stockholm and Istanbul. The courier service was run under condition of the highest secrecy – a system of five or six relays where each courier only knew from whom they received the information and to whom they passed it on.[8] This was extremely dangerous work, especially when crossing

Nazi territory or Poland itself. The couriers smuggled documents and money. If they were caught, they would be arrested and handed over to the Gestapo and tortured before being executed or sent to a concentration camp.

The contrast between the treatment of the Czech and Polish refugees was stark. The Czechs arrived in far smaller numbers and could easily have been absorbed into the wider relief effort. Instead they were arrested and imprisoned in miserable, filthy conditions. In early 1940 a contact at the British Legation told Francesca Wilson that 120 Czech prisoners were imprisoned in the Citadel, an ancient building in Buda. They were living in damp cells on filthy straw with no proper sanitation and just two litres of water a day for drinking and washing. The Czechs had been arrested in autumn 1939 and still wore the clothes in which they had fled. All the conditions were in place for an epidemic of typhus. Some were even charged with espionage. Others were imprisoned for a while, then handed over to the Germans.

Wilson visited one of the prisons where the Czechs were held with a Jewish lady, probably Edith Weiss. The Weiss family was engaged in extensive philanthropic work. Incarcerated in a long room with concrete walls and floor and no furniture were 200 men. 'They were standing up when we came in and had a look of drooping dejection, impossible to describe. They were filthy, ragged and underfed. Some of them had been there for months. They had no change of linen, no soap or water to wash in. There was no positive cruelty shown to them – they were just forgotten,' wrote Wilson.[9] The Czechs, like the Poles, had an extensive underground organisation operating in Budapest. The question was how to get the men out of prison and into the city where they could go into hiding. It is clear from her account that wartime Budapest was also home to a highly organised Czech resistance group, moving refugees and exiles through networks of safe houses and spiriting them across the border to Yugoslavia. 'Because of my innocent enquiries as to how to send shirts to the Citadel, I became more and more involved in this organisation ... The leaders were – most of them – single-minded, courageous men and women. Although they all had foreign passports, real or false, they were in great danger.'

Wilson was puzzled why Poles were treated so well and Czechs so badly. One reason, it seemed, was Trianon. The Czechs were traitors, Wilson's Hungarian contacts told her. They had brought down the monarchy and as a reward had received Slovakia, which was really historical Hungarian territory. Any Czechs who could move freely were closely watched by the Hungarian police and German agents. The Czechs often met in cafés, but Wilson was careful to meet them in public as rarely as possible. Wilson came to admire how, in their unassuming way, the Czech exiles ran an efficient resistance network. 'These men in danger of their lives were most of them quiet, self-composed, unostentatiously brave.' About half of the prisoners in the Citadel eventually escaped, and hundreds more from other prisons. Some made it to London. There, later in the war, Wilson met several whom she had last seen in hiding in Budapest living as 'hunted hares'.

The Germans were pleased with Hungary's cooperation over the Czechs but increasingly angry over Hungary's open support for the Poles. Berlin's ambassador to Hungary, the German foreign minister and the Nazi press all protested furiously. There was particular fury that the Polish Legation, a defiant symbol of Polish freedom and independence, was still functioning freely in Budapest. 'The Germans were continually putting pressure on the Hungarian authorities to hand back Poles to them', wrote Francesca Wilson, 'or at least make the supervision of their internment camps tighter'. Teleki resisted and ensured the Polish ambassador, consul and military attaches retained their diplomatic status.

A German diplomat informed the Hungarians about the Polish Military Agency on Váci Street, the name and location of every camp where the Polish soldiers were staying and the names of the leaders guiding the evacuations across the borders. The message was clear: we know everything and this has to stop. As autumn moved to winter and the onslaught on Poland intensified, the lights burned almost non-stop at the Andrássy Palace. By the end of the year it was clear that this would not be a quick war. There were days when Caja despaired. 'I myself am so terribly unhappy – but why talk about it', she wrote to her brother-in-law Mihály Károlyi at the end of December 1939. 'I believe that the war is spreading to the whole of Europe and we have to play our part in it. When will that be? I would like to know. One scenario is as impossible as all the others. And what will this destruction bring? I have lost all hope of a "new world" because I am in the depths of despair at the moment.'[10]

But her determination to do whatever she could to stop or impede the Nazis did not waver. All this was well known and placed Caja in growing danger. Somewhere in the German Embassy, doubtless in Berlin as well, her name was on a list. She was an avowed and very public anti-Fascist who had reported from Spain. She had never hidden or camouflaged her involvement with the Poles. Her secret work for Britain with the Polish rescue operation was also known to the Hungarians and the Germans. Her home, the Andrássy Palace, was a landmark building in the centre of the city and now a base for the anti-Nazi resistance. In the first year of the war Caja's family name and her network of connections gave her a degree of protection, but the day was coming when they would no longer be a shield.

6

A Sackful of Trouble

There is important work to be done by this section in Hungary.

SOE report on the Section D sabotage and propaganda operation, August 1940.[1]

Basil Davidson's wartime career as a British agent in Budapest began in October 1939 with a simple instruction: go to Simpson's in the Strand, a smart restaurant in Central London, at 12.45 pm and find a man reading the *Evening Standard*. This was easier said than done. Simpson's was a very popular meeting place, near to several ministries and government offices. It was always crowded with government officials, many of them reading the *Evening Standard* while they waited for the restaurant's famed roast beef. Eventually Davidson found his recruiter, a man of 'saturnine allure', who had seemingly stepped out of the pages of an Eric Ambler novel. Davidson was a journalist, with a fine eye for detail. Born in Bristol in 1914, his first writing job was as editor (and sole employee) of *Quarry and Roadmaking*. After a spell travelling across Central Europe and the Balkans, he joined the staff of *The Economist*, reporting from Vienna after the Anschluss in March 1938. When war broke out Davidson was diplomatic correspondent for *The Star*, the rival to the *Evening Standard*. He had been talent-spotted by Section D of the Secret Intelligence Service.

'D' stood for demolition, meaning blowing things up. Davidson's lunch companion was George Taylor, an Australian who ran Section D's Balkan department, which included Hungary. He asked Davidson if he knew anything about explosives. Davidson nodded – of course, he replied, he had been editor of *Quarries and Roadmaking*, dealing with explosives 'all the time'. This was complete nonsense – Davidson had no experience of explosives at all – but was well received. Taylor asked Davidson what he knew of the Balkans. Here Davidson was on firmer ground, as a year earlier he had reported from the region. Davidson chatted about his adventures, making sure to drop the names of the best hotels in the Balkans, the Majestic in Belgrade, the Athénée Palace in Bucharest and so on.

By mid-December 1939 Davidson was recruited to Section D. Davidson was jubilant, hoping, if not expecting, to be despatched to the Balkans. After ten days of training Davidson was told he would be leaving on 1 January 1940 – for Hungary. He protested that Hungary was not actually in the Balkans and that he did not know a thing about the country. His protests were ignored. Budapest bordered the Balkans. It was a crucial listening post, home to numerous Nazi spies, the capital of a country bordering both the Third Reich and the Soviet Union, one aligned with the Axis but which still wanted good relations with the Allies. Hungary was of immense strategic importance: the gateway to the Balkans and the Black Sea, and now a transit route for thousands of fleeing Poles. It was bisected by the Danube, a crucial shipping route along which flowed oil and grain from the Balkans to Germany. There was no more discussion.

As Davidson prepared for his departure, one of Section D's most intrepid operatives also arrived in the Hungarian capital. Her courage, determination, vivacity and good looks captivated almost everyone she encountered. Krystyna Skarbek was born in Warsaw in 1908, to Count Jerzy Skarbek and Stefania Goldfeder. Count Skarbek was a typical Polish aristocrat, a charming, handsome womaniser. He inherited a substantial estate, much of which was frittered away. Stefania, the daughter of a Jewish banking dynasty, was a highly cultured, intelligent woman. Their marriage was unhappy – Count Jerzy did not change his ways. But he doted on his daughter and Krystyna enjoyed a privileged childhood. She learned to ride at an early age, to shoot, traverse open countryside and manage dogs and horses – all skills that would prove useful in her later life as a British intelligence operative.

Krystyna had her mother's intelligence and subtle understanding of human nature. But it was perhaps her father's lust for life and hunger for new experiences that most shaped her character, bringing a wild streak that was never truly tamed. As a young woman of aristocratic background she was invited to Warsaw's high-society parties. But she preferred the city's demi-monde. Warsaw, like Budapest, was a city relishing its turn to modernity, filled with cafés, restaurants, cinemas and theatres. And few in that bohemian crowd cared that Krystyna was half-Jewish and her family now impoverished. She took a job at Warsaw's Fiat dealership. Unbeknown to Krystyna, her lungs were being steadily damaged by exhaust fumes from the garage below – leaving scarring that would, years later in wartime Budapest, help save her life.

A short-lived marriage to a curtain manufacturer failed, but left her with a settlement enough to pay for a small apartment downtown. Krystyna spent much time in Zakopane, a ski centre and resort town in the Tatra Mountains, in the far south of Poland. There she met Jerzy Gizycki, a Polish man almost twenty years her senior. Gizycki was an adventurer and had spent time in the United States working as a cowboy, trapper and chauffeur for J. D. Rockefeller. Gizycki had also worked for the Polish Diplomatic Service in Ethiopia and Rome. The two were quickly inseparable. She was, he later wrote, an 'excellent horse-woman, fair skier and the most intrepid human being I have ever met – man or woman'.

They married in Warsaw in November 1938, travelled to Paris and Switzerland and then moved to Kenya, where Jerzy opened a Polish consulate covering much of Africa. When war broke out they managed to buy passage on the *Cape Town Castle*, a mail steamship heading for Southampton. The journey took several long and frustrating weeks, eventually arriving on 6 October. Jerzy quickly travelled to Paris to offer his services to the Polish government-in-exile. Age and several ski injuries meant he was rejected for military service. Meanwhile, in London, Krystyna quickly found her way to George Taylor, possibly through Jozef Radziminski, a journalist and intelligence operative whom she had met some years earlier in Poland. Radziminski was already besotted with her – an unrequited love that would later lead to behaviour by him in Budapest so reckless that it threatened the security of the whole Section D network.

George Taylor was also taken with Krystyna, although in a professional sense. 'She is a very smart looking girl, simply dressed and aristocratic. She is a flaming Polish patriot. She made an excellent impression. Her husband has or had here a post at the Polish consulate. Her idea is to bring out a propaganda leaflet in Buda and smuggle it over the frontier herself.' Krystyna had already planned how the smuggling operation would work. She already had an extensive network of contacts in Zakopane. The smugglers, she was certain, would still help now. 'She is absolutely fearless and certainly makes that impression. She says the matter is urgent and they should leave at once', wrote Taylor. The mission was authorised, funding was approved and Krystyna was given a number, 4827, and a code-name: Madame Marchand.[2]

A couple of weeks later, on 21 December, she flew to Paris and took the train to Budapest's Keleti Station. She had £250, a cover story as a French journalist, some contacts and basic instruction in the use of explosives. Arriving in the city, she made her way to her new home, a small serviced flat on Derék Street, in an unremarkable area of Buda. There was a kitchenette, a small bathroom and a large room with a sofa-bed. A maid arrived each morning with her breakfast; otherwise she would eat in one of the city's numerous cafés or restaurants. She quickly made contact with the Polish Consul, whom she already knew, and often called there in the afternoons. Another point of contact was Hubert Harrison, the British correspondent for *The News Chronicle* who was also working for Section D. Harrison was not captivated by her. 'He had been told to help me technically with all I needed and he in turn asked me to be an intermediary between himself and the Poles', Krystyna later recalled in a lengthy report to SOE. 'As a result my flat in Budapest became a dump for everything being sent to Poland including high explosives.'[3]

Jozef Radziminski was far more enthusiastic, introducing her to the rolling circus of journalists and diplomats that moved between embassy and legation parties and receptions, and the smoky bars, cafés and nightclubs of Budapest's busy nightlife.[4] Soon after her arrival Krystyna was invited to Café Floris on Vörösmarty Square in the heart of downtown. Floris was famed for its cakes and patisserie, but had a bohemian edge. The city's demi-monde – including the growing cohort of exiles, refugees, foreign spies and journalists – gathered there in the evenings for gossip, intrigue and love affairs, a real-life version of Rick's Café in the film *Casablanca*. Krystyna walked into a back room, thick with smoke, to see a handsome – and familiar-looking – Polish officer telling his war stories to a growing crowd of admirers. Andrzej Kowerski, an old friend from her childhood, was the very embodiment of a dashing Polish officer – charismatic and flirtatious. Despite only having one leg – he lost a limb after a friend accidentally shot him in the foot on a hunting trip – he joined the Black Brigade, the only motorised unit of the Polish armed forces, named for their black leather jackets.

After the Nazi invasion, when his unit could fight no more, Kowerski stole an Opel and drove to Hungary, where he was promptly interned. He escaped and drove the Opel to Budapest, dumped his uniform and found some civilian clothes and made contact with his fellow Poles. Like most of the Polish soldiers, he planned to get to France and rejoin the Free French forces. But General Maczek, the commander of the Black Brigade, ordered him to stay in Budapest and set up escape lines out of Poland. Andrzej and his comrades were soon running a complex and highly efficient escape network, running from southern Poland, through Slovakia, into Hungary and on to Yugoslavia. He often drove the escaping soldiers himself, in an unheated Chevrolet, sometimes asking local villagers to drag the car out of thick snow.

Kowerski and Krystyna caught each other's eye. The mutual attraction was instant. 'Ten minutes after I had began talking, the door opened and a girl walked in. I stopped and stared at her', he later recalled. 'She was slim, sunburnt, with brown hair and eyes. A kind of cracking vitality seemed to emanate from her … After a moment I realised that we had met before.'[5] Krystyna reminded him that they had met at Zakopane. Later that evening she asked him to dinner. Eventually they managed to snatch an evening together. They met by the Chain Bridge, Andrzej watching admiringly as she walked with her graceful poise. They dined at the Café Hangli, an elegant art-deco downtown restaurant, near the Corso. Its panoramic windows looked out over a small park and the river. After dinner they went back to her flat for coffee. 'I sat and watched her, marvelling at her extraordinary grace', he later recalled. 'Then she gave me a cup of coffee and suddenly we were in each other's arms.' The following morning, when Krystyna's maid arrived with breakfast, Andrzej hid in the cupboard – their affair, they decided, should be kept secret.

Secrecy was key to the Polish rescue operation. The Hungarian authorities gave the Poles a nod and a wink but if Andrzej was caught actually helping escape interned POWs there would have to be consequences. Sometimes there were ten men sleeping on the floor of his room. He was staying at the Metropole on Rákóczi Way, not far from the Astoria. One night he returned to his room to find two Hungarian policemen waiting for him. They had been tipped off, he was certain by the hotel porter, that he was up to something suspicious. Wartime Budapest was also a city of snitches, part of a long tradition of denunciation to the authorities. Porters, taxi drivers and apartment houses' concierges all often fed a steady stream of information to the police. Andrzej managed to talk his way out, in part by placing his wooden leg on the table. What kind of smuggler had one leg? Soon after he moved his operation to an apartment in the heart of the city's red-light district. There nobody worried about strange comings and goings at all hours, and mud-spattered cars parked nearby.

Krystyna was still married to Jerzy, who was stuck in France. Yet she managed to bury any guilt she might have felt about cheating on her husband. She and Andrzej spent every moment together that they could. Danger and adrenaline were potent fuel for their love affair. But her plans were running aground. By late February 1940 she had been in Budapest for two months and had still not crossed into Poland. She pushed to set up a radio station, broadcasting Allied propaganda into Poland. But that was a complicated venture and sooner or later would be noticed by the Hungarian authorities and the Gestapo. The Polish underground was wary of Krystyna. She was Polish, yes, but she was on London's payroll. Who really knew where her ultimate loyalty lay? And what if she was recruited and then captured? She might, under torture, betray the resistance networks.

Basil Davidson finally set off in January 1940 to Budapest by train with a colleague from Section D. As well as their luggage, Davidson and his companion had several heavy blue sacks. The two men travelled via Milan to northern Yugoslavia and the frontier station at Subotica. It was imperative that the Hungarian Customs did not inspect the contents of the sacks, explained Davidson's companion as they approached the frontier. What if the officers insisted, asked Davidson. 'You'll make a diversion. Throw a fit, threaten to jump out of the window, almost anything may do.' This advice was even less reassuring when the other Section D man explained that there was no need to worry about him, as he had diplomatic immunity – which Davidson did not. Davidson's cover was journalistic: he was going to write for *The Economist*, *The Observer*, *The New York Times* and *The Star*.

In the end the oldest gambit in the book worked: a bribe to the Hungarian Customs officers ensured that the blue sacks remained untouched. As the train trundled through the flat plains of southern Hungary, towards the capital, Davidson asked what was inside. 'Plastic and such, a few toys', replied his companion. The plastic was plastic explosives, as well as limpet mines – to be used to blow up shipping in the Danube. Sabotage was just part of Section D's mission in Hungary. It was also to liaise with the Polish resistance and supply it with materials and weapons to be used in Poland, to circulate Allied propaganda into Austria and around Hungary and to develop contacts with anti-German elements in political and especially military circles. Davidson was not the only journalist to work for Section D in Budapest. As well as Hubert Harrison, there was Ted Howe, a reporter for *The London News*, who worked on sabotage and penetrating neighbouring countries.

Davidson and his companion arrived safely in Budapest. They took a taxi from the station across the river to the British Legation on Werbőczy Street and left the explosives there – without the knowledge or agreement of O'Malley, who, had he known, would have exploded with anger. Davidson checked into a hotel and considered his next move. His main function was propaganda and contact development. Others would focus on sabotage and using the blue sacks of explosives. Davidson planned to legally and openly set up a bureau of the Britanova news agency to distribute British news to the Hungarian press and radio. His second, covert, mission was to arrange the printing and distribution of anti-Nazi leaflets. It took almost three months for the Hungarian Foreign Ministry to grant Britanova a licence to work in the country. For a while Davidson felt lost. He spent much time staring dolefully at a large neon sign which advertised the *Központi Takarékpénztár*. The incomprehensible words seemed somehow menacing. Their meaning, he eventually discovered, was 'Central Savings Bank'.

These early months of the war in Budapest were a strange interlude. Hungary was firmly aligned with Nazi Germany but was not engaged in the conflict. Teleki and Horthy's balancing act – and their vain hope that Britain and the West could somehow liberate Hungary from its geography and malevolent neighbours – meant that the British Legation was under continual surveillance but functioned freely. O'Malley was always welcome at Teleki's quarters or Horthy's apartment. O'Malley certainly did his best to ensure good relations. He wrote to London in late February 1940 that he planned to mark the anniversary of Horthy's accession as regent by presenting him with a signed photograph of the king and 'a personal message from his Majesty'. O'Malley also asked that the BBC and the press give more 'sympathetic reviews' of Horthy's term in office. Horthy, he said, was continuing the Hungarian tradition of standing firm against 'oriental barbarism' and stood for Christian and gentlemanly qualities.[6]

For the Hungarians, allowing a British news agency to operate freely was another gesture that would usefully annoy the Germans and show London and Washington that Hungary still retained some independence of spirit. Once Davidson's licence came through on 24 April the news agency, now called *Külföldi Hírek*, 'Foreign News', was soon up and running. The Hungarian Foreign Ministry proposed Viktor Stankovitz, a local man, as editor. Davidson agreed. He rented a spacious office on Petőfi Square, overlooking the Danube by the Erzsébet Bridge. Davidson took on half-a-dozen employees, including the journalist György Pálóczi-Horvath. The agency soon had plenty of customers. *Külföldi Hírek*'s material was used in every Budapest newspaper except *Új Magyarság* (*New Hungarianness*), which supported the extreme right, and over 100 provincial newspapers. The Ministry of Information in London sent the daily newswires from which Davidson wrote his news briefing for the agency's customers.

Section D's sabotage and resistance networks, however, were not going so well. The section was fighting a turf war on two fronts inside the legation. O'Malley was completely opposed to any sabotage activity, perhaps fearing that it would draw unwelcome attention and disrupt the Polish rescue operation. He was certainly proving a major obstacle to Section D's plans and work. At the same time the Secret Intelligence Service station and Military Attache's Office were on manoeuvres, trying to take over Section D's supply lines to the Poles. The SIS Budapest station was the largest in the region. William Hindle, the head of station, had six secretarial staff, a wireless operator, twenty-one agents on a retainer and another cohort paid on an ad-hoc basis, depending on what they supplied.[7] Another problem for Section D was that the Hungarians had handed over control of the Danube to the Germans so the policing and surveillance of the river was far more intense. Key Czech personnel had been arrested, noted a Section D report, and 'it has been quite impossible to organise a smuggling system by which material required could be got into Hungary and distributed to the Poles'. The Hungarian government had also started putting the Poles under pressure. By August 1940, 'the whole of our organisation in Hungary for the delivery of supplies to the Poles and for sabotage collapsed and had to be temporarily abandoned'. But the Poles had appealed for help. The Section D report concluded that O'Malley needed to get on board.

> There is important work to be done by this section in Hungary. It cannot be done unless the non-cooperative attitude adopted by the Minister in Budapest is reversed. We would be glad, therefore, if the necessary approach could be made to the Foreign Office so that pressure can be put on Mr O'Malley to revise his attitude.

But there was one bright spot on this gloomy horizon. Davidson's propaganda operation was 'flourishing at the moment to an unexpected degree'.[8]

Davidson's network of contacts was expanding rapidly across Hungarian society, albeit within limited circles. One of his most high-profile – and best-connected – recruits was László Békeffi, a famous actor, comedian and cabaret performer. During the late 1930s Békeffi had had his own cabaret show at the Gresham Palace Café. As the world grew darker through that decade, Békeffi's satire became ever more biting and courageous. The tiny, smoke-filled theatre became one of the centres of the city's nightlife and high-level diplomatic intrigue, a haven for likeminded spies and Anglophiles, journalists, artists, free-thinkers, anti-Nazis and diplomats. After the passing of the Second Anti-Jewish Law in May 1939, Békeffi included the new rules in his satirical performance 'Forward with the Documents!'.[9] The SOE operation was closely watched by Hungarian intelligence, as István Ujszászy, Hungary's intelligence chief, testified after the war.

> British intelligence in Hungary worked mainly through social, political and commercial channels, but it also had properly paid agents as well. Socially, it looked for contacts

with the aristocracy, the Anglophile elements and Jewish industrialists and bankers known for their snobbery. It also kept in touch with politicians of the moderate and centre-left, and businessmen and sportsmen who had connections with England ... British tourists staying in Hungary and their connections in society also supported British intelligence.[10]

Davidson was also distributing a confidential, insider's news service covering stories that were suppressed by the censor to high-ranking officials, businesspeople and senior journalists.[11] London decided that as Horthy might still help the Allies, his regime would not be undermined. Instead, Section D would also focus on shaping public opinion against the Nazis through illegal leaflets. Over a million were eventually distributed. László Békeffi worked with György Pálóczi-Horvath drafting the leaflets. There were three versions: one for the largely Catholic bourgeoisie, another for the aristocrats and a third for the working class.[12] They all infuriated the Arrow Cross and angered the government. 'Evidence of the effectiveness of this work could be seen from time to time in the bitter attacks of the Government Press on "underground trouble-makers" and by the care to which the Police went to trace the origin of the leaflets', notes the SOE's history of its Hungarian operation.[13]

Davidson also supported the Peasants' Party and its newspaper, *Szabad Szó* (*Free Word*). Imre Kovács, the party leader, received SOE funds through Caja Odescalchi and became an agency asset. By summer 1940, Davidson was feeling productive and useful. 'It was like winning the Irish sweepstake and the war into the bargain', he wrote. 'I acquired an executive desk, and I sat down by the waters of the Danube and rejoiced'.

7

A Surfeit of Spies

I shall denounce you to the Hungarian police.

Owen O'Malley's threat to Basil Davidson if he brought
in any more plastic explosives.

Jozef Radziminski, the Polish spy who introduced Krystyna to Budapest's nightlife, became so infatuated with her that she referred to him as her 'lapdog'. When she rejected his advances he threatened to shoot himself in the groin. He shot himself, but in the foot. Once Radziminski could walk again, he threw himself off the Erzsébet Bridge. The river was half-frozen, so he did not drown, but he broke his other leg. Radziminski was dismissed from Section D. Krystyna recommended her lover, Andrzej, as the new liaison with the Polish resistance. Her superiors agreed, and then finally, in February 1940, she was on the move to Poland.

Krystyna spent five weeks there, gathering information about troop and armaments movements and industrial production. She made contact with resistance groups and drew up plans for spreading news by radio and by illegal news-sheets. In Warsaw she tried in vain to persuade her mother to leave. Meanwhile, her love life had become even more entangled. In Poland she had started an affair with Count Wladimir Ledóchowski, who had escorted her back across the mountains to Hungary. When Andrzej was in Budapest she spent time with him, but when he was away on a mission she met Wladimir. As if that were not complicated enough, Kate O'Malley, the British minister's pretty daughter, had a crush on Andrzej. Krystyna's next mission ended in disaster when she and Wladimir were caught in Slovakia. They made a run for it, dodging bullets as the Slovak police shot at them. Two days later they were back in Budapest. It was now too dangerous for her to return; her photo was posted on every railway station with a reward for her, 'dead or alive'.

That winter was one of the harshest in memory. The city was battered by snowstorms, temperatures plunging far down to minus thirty, while great shards of ice floated down the Danube. Yet despite the weather, and the war – or perhaps because of it – the social season was in full swing. The most anticipated event was the *Living-Art* exhibition and charity ball at the Opera House on Andrássy Way. The exhibition had been organised by Admiral Horthy's wife Magdolna and showcased some of the city's best-known and most attractive society women, portraying fifty famous works of art by renowned painters. Among those in attendance was Countess Ilona Edelsheim Gyulai, a young society beauty. Ilona had no idea she was being watched by a secret admirer: the Horthys' older son, István.

The Horthys had four children: Magdolna, Paulette, István and Miklós junior, known as Niki. Magdolna had died tragically young at the age of sixteen and Paulette was terminally ill with tuberculosis. Niki had suffered two accidents, one on his motorcycle and another at a polo match when his horse fell on him and stood on his head as it got up. Ilona had never spoken to István, nicknamed Pista. Pista was an attractive figure, intellectually curious, open-minded and adventurous. A keen flyer, he joined the Hungarian Air Force in 1929. He trained as an engineer and worked on the assembly line at the massive engine factory on Csepel Island, then went to the United States. There, he spent eighteen months at the Ford Works in Dearborn, Detroit, learning as much as he could about modern industrial production and workforce organisation. On his return István joined MAVAG, the state-subsidised engineering works. At a time when the far right was growing in strength and confidence, and many Hungarians turned inward, nurturing their bitter resentment about Trianon, István Horthy embodied another Hungary – modern, forward-looking and open-minded – and very hard-working. István and Ilona spent a very enjoyable evening together at the ball. Those few hours would decide the course of her life.[1]

Budapest's aristocratic families had also laid on a lavish buffet, enjoyed by the diplomatic corps, including J. S. Somers-Cocks of the British Legation. He sent a wry account of the event to London. Each dish bore the name of the family who had donated the food. 'One found oneself eating exquisitely underdone roast beef, marked, say "Countess Apponyi", or a slice of luscious Sachertorte marked "Countess Szechenyi".' The sharpest touch was that the buffet's principal dish was named 'Miss O'Malley'.[2] Yet beyond the social barbs a serious struggle for power and influence was playing out, which Germany seemed to be winning.

After their evening together, Ilona Edelsheim Gyulai and István Horthy went skiing several times. They spoke regularly on the telephone. Then, after a couple weeks, out of the blue, István proposed. Ilona, once she had got over her surprise, accepted. The betrothal was huge news. *Képes Vasárnap* (*Sunday Pictorial*) ran a large spread of photographs, captioned 'Countess Ily Edelsheim Gyulai, the country's happiest bride-to-be'. In the meantime, she learned to fly. Their civil wedding took place on 26 April, with a religious ceremony the following day at the Calvinist church, a short walk along the riverbank from the Andrássy Palace. The red-brick neo-Gothic church, with its sixty-two-metre-high tower, was a landmark building. About two-thirds of Hungary's Christian population were Catholics and the remainder were mostly Protestant, with a few smaller denominations such as Greek and Serbian Orthodox. Hungary's Christians were unusually tolerant of each other. Many families, like the Horthys and Ilona's own, were a mix of both faiths. Ilona was a Catholic, like her mother and sisters, while her father was a Lutheran. The Horthys were similar. The regent and his sons were Calvinists, but his wife, mother and two daughters were Catholics.

It was a perfect spring day, white clouds scudding across a blue sky, the river glittering silver in the sunshine – a time of great joy but also tinged with sadness. Before they arrived at the church Ilona and István went to visit his sister, Paulette. She was now bed-ridden, breathing with the help of an oxygen cylinder. When the ceremony ended the newlyweds came out of the church, where two young pilots stood on both sides of the steps, holding up a triumphal arch of propellers. After the reception at the Royal Castle Ilona and István went to the airport. There his Arado 79 sports aeroplane was waiting for the start of their 8,000-kilometre honeymoon journey. As the small red aeroplane roared down the runway and soared into the sky, it was escorted by two Hungarian fighter planes, one on either side. The fighters overtook István's aeroplane, then looped back again, before peeling off into the distance. That evening István landed at Venice. 'It seemed to me', wrote Ilona, 'that nobody could imagine how happy I was'.

Around a mile and a half upriver from Basil Davidson's office near the Erzsébet Bridge, the Abwehr, the German military foreign intelligence service, was running a busy operation at its offices on Pozsonyi Way in District XIII. The wide, tree-lined street was one of Pest's most pleasant thoroughfares, lined with art-deco apartment houses, cafés and restaurants. This upmarket part of District XIII was the city's middle-class Jewish area, to which families moved from the cramped tenements of District VII and VIII as they became more prosperous.

Nazi Germany had two intelligence agencies, the Abwehr and the Sicherheitdienst (SD), which was run by the SS. Both operated freely in Budapest, using a wide network of agents and collaborators. They included army officers, intelligence operatives, civil servants, impoverished chancers, thieves, art dealers and black marketeers. A network of currency smugglers linked to the Abwehr moved back and forth between Budapest and Istanbul, bringing funds and intelligence for Jewish organisations. The Abwehr was run by Admiral Wilhelm Canaris. His and the service's loyalties were to Germany and the German state, rather than Hitler, which is why Heinrich Himmler had created the SD. This was a new, ideologically pure party organisation, staffed by fervent Nazis. The SD was commanded by Reinhard Heydrich, Himmler's deputy. In September 1939 Heinrich Himmler set up the Reichssicherheitshauptamt (RSHA) which combined the Kripo (criminal police) and Gestapo (political police) with the SD, all under the command of Reinhard Heydrich.

The Abwehr had worked together with the Hungarian intelligence service since the early 1920s, and the two had signed a cooperation agreement. As Hungary remained neutral, its diplomats and spies could still operate in countries at war with Germany. They would then feed intelligence back to the Abwehr. Colonel István Ujszászy, the Hungarian military and counter-intelligence chief, was sceptical about the new arrangement. He was a Hungarian patriot and not part of the pro-Nazi faction in the military leadership. Ujszászy's sharp instincts and ability to process and evaluate Hungary's ever-changing situation were combined with an extraordinary capacity for conspiracy. Born in 1894 in the town of Nagykőrös, southeast of Budapest, Ujszászy was slim, dapper and a notorious ladies' man. Fluent in German, French, English and Serbian, during the 1930s Ujszászy served in Paris, Warsaw and Prague as a military attache. Ujszászy reported directly to Horthy, rather than the defence minister, according to his biographer Lászlo Pusztaszeri, and was also in contact with the British and American military attaches in Budapest.[3] A central figure in the Polish rescue operation, Ujszászy for years carried on a passionate love affair with the actress Katalin Karády. That relationship would eventually exact a high price for both.

One of the most senior Abwehr officers in Budapest, Rudolf Konitz (or Kanitz), known as Korda, was Jewish – as were his chauffeur and a good number of his agents. Working for the Abwehr provided protection, although some Jewish Abwehr agents were coerced, or claimed to be. Others were connected to the smuggling networks bringing funds and valuables from the Zionist organisations in Istanbul. These were days of fluid loyalties, where choices were decided by the need to survive. Perhaps not surprisingly, life as a Jew working for the Abwehr was extremely stressful. Korda was a heavy smoker, who suffered from stomach trouble. Korda's girlfriend was an attractive blonde woman called Itza Szabó, who worked as a singer and hostess in the glamorous Prince of Wales bar by the Corso. Szabó was also an Abwehr agent, and reported back to Korda snippets of news and information about the bar's customers.

The Abwehr operation in Budapest sometimes lurched into farce, as evinced by the case of Wilhelm Götz. Götz had a comfortable job working for the Hungarian–German Chamber of Commerce, until March 1940, when he was summoned to the consulate in Budapest and ordered to return to Germany for military service. He managed to join Korda's operation instead. Götz survived the war and was eventually interrogated at length by British intelligence. 'Götz seems to have been the complete adventurer whose only detectible principle was to avoid military service. I should regard him as a perfect instrument for the passing of deception material', noted one British officer.

Korda asked Götz if he knew any Allied personalities in Budapest. Götz said he knew Colonel Barclay, the British military attache, through Teleki, the prime minister. Korda told Götz to go and see Colonel Barclay with Teleki. Teleki agreed. Götz asked the British officer if he was interested in plans for the new seventy-ton German tank. Colonel Barclay, rightly suspecting some kind of trap or provocation, was non-committal. The next time Götz visited Vienna he was arrested by the Gestapo. Teleki had reported him to the German authorities. Eventually Götz was released. After what the interrogation report describes as Götz's 'abortive attempt to work as an agent provocateur' he took a position in Korda's office, typing and collating reports from other Abwehr agents. Some time later Korda sent him to Bucharest to recruit agents. Götz spent six weeks there and 'achieved nothing whatsoever in the C.E [counter-espionage] line and made no useful contacts'. He went back to Korda's office, compiling and editing reports. But within a few months his comfortable life was about to be upended.[4]

By the summer of 1940, thanks in part to sustained German pressure, the Hungarian attitude to refugees – especially Jewish refugees

– had hardened. Christians were required to register with the police but lived more or less freely. Jewish refugees were interned in special camps, supervised by a new unit in the Ministry of the Interior, the Alien Control Office, known as KEOKH. Jewish communal leaders lobbied for the internees to be released on the same basis as the Polish Christians. This was refused, but KEOKH did allow the Jewish refugees to receive kosher food, clothing, medicines, pocket money and bed linen. Those who fell ill could be treated in the Budapest Jewish hospital. Visiting days were allowed and some internees were given permission to go into the city. Their situation was not ideal, but they were safe, fed and clothed.

That summer Alexander Szanto, the Jewish Hungarian who had returned to Budapest from Berlin, was called up for *Munkaszolgálat*, labour service. Jewish men were not allowed to serve in the army proper. Together with others considered politically unreliable, they were drafted into work companies, to build roads, work on construction and perform menial work such as cleaning army barracks. The work was physically demanding for often unfit middle-aged family men, and the living conditions were harsh, with often anti-Semitic officers and poor, inadequate food. But this first round of labour service was restricted to Hungarian territory. The labour servicemen were usually not subjected to violence, and they could correspond with their relatives and receive packages.

Ignatz Katz wrote to his wife, Ilona, on 21 August. A former sports journalist from Nyíregyháza in eastern Hungary, Katz had also been a well-known competitive wrestler in his younger days. Photos of Ignatz show a man in the prime of life, with a honed athlete's physique. Jewish athletes, especially fencers and swimmers, reached the highest levels of their sports, and several competed for Hungary in the Olympics. Their athletic prowess and patriotism would bring no protection against what was to come. Ignatz had received a letter from Ilona the previous day, a national holiday in honour of St István, the first king of Hungary. Ignatz and his fellow labour servicemen were given the day off and went to church. 'It was a nice service, the whole unit was there', he wrote. His postcards may not always arrive, he added, but that did not mean he was not thinking of Ilona. He also congratulated her on her name day, on 18 August.[5]

By late autumn 1940 the labour servicemen had returned and Ignatz was back home with Ilona at the family apartment on Kálvin Square in central Pest. The following year, after Hungary joined the invasion of the Soviet Union – indeed, for the rest of the war – the labour servicemens' conditions would be far harsher, most of all for those sent to the Ukrainian front. There tens of thousands would lose their lives, many at the hands of their own Hungarian officers. And a much tougher crackdown on the Jewish refugees was coming, one that would eventually result in the deportation and murder of many thousands. Before his labour service, Alexander Szanto had frequently inspected Budapest's Jewish internment camps for the Jewish communal leadership. He little suspected that, 'one year later I would be in one of them'.

Around this time Krystyna and Andrzej moved in together. Andrzej developed a sophisticated network of courier routes to smuggle money, arms and explosives into Poland and bring out intelligence and people. Andrzej's SOE file records that he, 'in the course of numerous operations transferred some 5,000 Poles and Czechs to appropriate destinations'. Even while under 'constant Gestapo surveillance' in Budapest, Andrzej 'distributed arms and explosives from Britain to Poles in Hungary and Poland'. He also organised escape routes for British POWs in Poland. He managed to obtain a pass from a Hungarian ministry and an official car that allowed him to drive to the border region – extremely useful as the borders were under continual surveillance by the Hungarian police and the Gestapo.[6]

But his prosthetic leg was giving him terrible trouble – especially as he often had to walk through the mountains on his rescue operations. Andrzej was repeatedly arrested by the Hungarians. O'Malley strongly advised him to leave Budapest. In November 1940 Krystyna returned to Warsaw. The reports she brought back included information about new gases the Nazis were developing, the location of munitions factories in Germany and Poland, plans of airfields, aeroplanes, aircraft factories, torpedoes and U-boats,

Krystyna Skarbek, later known as Christine Granville, was a key SOE agent, moving between Budapest and Nazi-occupied Poland.

as well as a detailed outline of an underground radio network. She immediately handed over the report to an official at the legation and 'daily badgered' him to read it. But the official, unnamed in the report, sat on it for two months, saying he had no time.[7]

Krystyna and Basil Davidson were now part of a new organisation. In July 1940 Section D was merged with Department EH, which ran propaganda operations, and MI/R, which researched guerrilla warfare, to form the Special Operations Executive. Hugh Dalton, the minister of economic warfare, was placed in charge. Churchill ordered him to 'set Europe ablaze' through sabotage, propaganda and local resistance movements. SOE operatives, often parachuted into enemy territory, were quickly dubbed the 'Baker Street Irregulars', after their wartime headquarters at 64 Baker Street. The SIS and much of the wartime establishment was much less enthusiastic. Many of its officers regarded the SOE as amateurish diletanttes, whose enthusiasm for blowing things up only brought retribution onto civilian populations and disrupted long-nurtured and delicate intelligence-gathering operations.

As did Owen O'Malley. In September 1940 O'Malley summoned Davidson to the legation. O'Malley was furious. The military attache had found the blue sacks of plastic explosives and limpet mines. O'Malley had ordered him to throw them all into the Danube. O'Malley threatened Davidson that if he brought any more explosives into Budapest he would denounce him to the Hungarian police.[8] Davidson immediately informed London. O'Malley's threat caused consternation at the Foreign Office. A flurry of telegrams flew back and forth between Budapest and London. On 9 October Sir Alexander Cadogan, one of Churchill's most important advisers, wrote to O'Malley, laying down the law. Davidson had been authorised to resume his 'subsidiary' activities.[9] O'Malley replied that Davidson was 'a clever journalist but a fledgling in other matters'. He was provoking attention by displaying large sums of money and had also become deeply involved with the 'wife of an agent' of the Hungarian government – 'Are you aware of these facts?'[10] O'Malley demanded that Davidson be replaced. But O'Malley lost and Davidson stayed.

O'Malley would have better spent his time checking on his own security procedures. The Abwehr had placed an agent inside the British Legation. A Hungarian employee, possibly named 'Peters', had been recruited by a Hungarian working for the Nazis. William Hindle, who ran the SIS station, and others, were not using a shredder or destroying all their confidential documents. Instead, they simply put them into the waste-paper baskets in their offices. These were gathered by 'Peters' and passed to the Hungarians and the Abwehr. A British intelligence report notes drily: 'The waste-paper basket of Mr HINDLE, regarded by the Hungarians as one of the leading British Secret Service officials in Budapest, was so productive in addresses etc that [Abwehr department] III F received a wealth of information of suspect personalities in BUDAPEST.'[11]

That winter Budapest's intelligence battle heated up. Hungary had joined the Tripartite Pact between Germany, Italy and Japan in November 1940, and so was a member of the Axis, but had not yet entered the war. This left O'Malley and the British Legation in a strange, anomalous position. Britain was at war with Germany and Italy, although not with Japan. The diplomatic dance continued. Embassy and ministry receptions were crowded with Allied and Nazi officials at the same event, circling, watching, listening and intriguing. In February 1941 the British military attache met his American counterpart at a gathering hosted by the Hungarian Army, a Foreign Office report reveals. The American military attache had heard that his Nazi counterpart had, 'while in an intoxicated condition severely criticised the D.O.M.I [director of military intelligence] for his friendliness to us and his lukewarm support of the Axis cause'. The British military attache also noted that the 'American embassy thinks that Germans might exert pressure to have D.O.M.I removed'.[12] But with Horthy's backing, István Ujszászy was secure.

One morning in February 1941 Krystyna and Andrzej were finally arrested. They were taken to the Hadik barracks on Horthy Miklós Road, which housed the headquarters of Hungarian military counter-intelligence and a small prison. There they were separated and then interrogated by Hungarian counter-intelligence and the Gestapo. Andrzej was questioned for nineteen hours by two Germans, knocked around, although not severely, and then held overnight. Krystyna was also harshly interrogated but gave nothing away. Her interrogators produced a copy of a fake identity card in the name of Zofia Andzrejewska that she had used. Krystyna shrugged – there was a resemblance, but the girl in the photo was prettier, she said.

The next day Andrzej and Krystyna were returned for more questioning. She looked very pale. She coughed and coughed until her body was shaking, then bit her tongue as hard as she could, again and again until her mouth was bleeding. Coughing up blood was a symptom of tuberculosis, which was highly infectious and, in the days before antibiotics, incurable. The Germans called a doctor, who sent her for an X-ray. There were indeed dark shadows on her lungs – not from tuberculosis, but from the exhaust fumes at the Fiat garage in Warsaw, where she had worked fifteen years earlier. The doctor recommended her release on humanitarian grounds. Her interrogators, fearful of catching tuberculosis, agreed. Krystyna and Andrzej were freed on the condition that they stayed in their flat and reported to the police.[13]

Once home Krystyna and Andrzej realised they had to leave Budapest – as soon as possible. Andrzej had two cars. His Chevrolet, which he used on his border missions, was known to the Germans. He also had the stolen Opel that he had first driven from Poland to Hungary. That evening a friend came round. He created a diversion with the Chevrolet to distract the watchers. Meanwhile Andrzej and Krystyna drove up the hill in the Opel into the Castle District. Andrzej telephoned Kate O'Malley, alerting her that he and Krystyna needed help. They parked the Opel and walked through the legation's main gate, past the policeman, into the courtyard. They were quickly ushered through to O'Malley's quarters. Here, at last, they were safe under British diplomatic protection. British passports were issued in new names: Andrew Kennedy and Christine Granville. The plan was that Krystyna would hide in the boot of a legation car and be driven into Yugoslavia. The vehicle had diplomatic status, so should be safe from inspection. Andrew would follow in the Opel, using his Polish passport. It worked. Once the embassy car was well inside Yugoslavia the driver pulled over and released Krystyna from the boot. All three toasted their freedom with some pálinka. A few hours later they arrived in Belgrade.

Some days later O'Malley was woken from a nap by his daughter, Kate. Two British POWs had escaped from Poland and were being hidden in Pest in a nursing home. O'Malley agreed that they should be brought to the legation. The POWs had to stay in conditions of utmost secrecy – the embassy's local staff could not know of their presence. The question for O'Malley was how to get them out. O'Malley had been planning to visit his counterpart in Belgrade. Now, it seemed, was the time to visit the Serbian capital. The two soldiers would be disguised as members of his staff, he decided. They needed false names that were not too obvious. The passport control officer decided to call them Hardy and Willis, after a popular chain of British shoe shops. Passports for both, stamped with fake Hungarian exit visas, were produced. O'Malley and the POWs took the night train from Budapest. The border guards were suspicious of the fake stamps. But when an indignant O'Malley threatened to call Admiral Horthy himself, they backed down and the party passed into Serbia.

Jerzy Gizycki was finally reunited with Krystyna in Istanbul in March 1941. He immediately understood that she and Andrzej were lovers, writing in his memoir that 'I told him not to take it hard, that it was not his fault but the war's and that I understood how it had all happened'. Jerzy agreed to assume Krystyna's old role as British liaison with the Polish underground in Budapest. He was issued a British passport and arrived on 1 April. O'Malley appointed him clerk to the legation's military attache. O'Malley had drawn extensive plans for the rescue network. To his amazement the Foreign Office said he could have as much funding as he needed. Everything seemed set for a properly organised and funded international escape route. But it was not to be.

8

The Die is Cast

The Gestapo is after us yet for the moment they cannot harm us. If you shouldn't hear from me for some time, don't worry. It would only mean that I have left for some time.

Caja Odescalchi to her sister, Katinka, and husband,
Mihály Károlyi, 16 March 1941.[1]

Jerzy Gizycki's new job at the British Legation did not last. It was clear that Germany would soon invade Yugoslavia – and through Hungary. But would Budapest aid or obstruct Berlin? The pro-Nazi faction in government was growing in confidence. The Gestapo and the Hungarian secret police had the Andrássy Palace under ever more intrusive surveillance. But Caja and her colleagues were defiant. They continued with the Polish rescue operation, getting the soldiers to the Yugoslav frontier, frequently driving them there themselves. For now, Caja still – just – had the protection of the government. 'If you hear or read a lot of Poles have been imprisoned, don't be anxious of [sic] me. I believe that as long as this government stays in power, nothing will happen to me. They are putting up quite a brave stand so far', she wrote to Katinka and her husband in English. One of the couriers took the letter to neutral Lisbon, from where it was sent on to London. O'Malley had promised to let Katinka know if Caja ended up in prison, but meanwhile she would stay. 'I long to see you yet I believe that I am more useful here just now. Life is very hectic, it might be more so! All my fondest love to you all, my thoughts are always with you, please find some means to write.'[2]

Korda's Abwehr operation was also in full operational mode. Wilhelm Götz was handling a stream of reports from the border region. The dwindling band of optimists in Budapest took comfort in the Treaty of Eternal Friendship between Hungary and Yugoslavia that the two countries signed on 14 March. Eleven days later Yugoslavia joined the Axis. Two days after that, on 27 March, the Yugoslav government was overthrown in a pro-Allied coup. The last shreds of optimism, that somehow Hungary could avoid the coming conflict, evaporated. Hitler immediately demanded that Hungary join in his planned invasion. In London, Anthony Eden, the British foreign secretary, sent a telegram informing Budapest that if Hungary did not resist the passage of German troops through its territory, London would break off diplomatic relations.

Teleki now faced a fateful dilemma. If he acceded to Eden's demands, Germany would likely invade Hungary. If he refused and let the Nazis through, London – and the Allies – would eventually declare war. In Budapest O'Malley tried to persuade Horthy to send moderate politicians such as István Bethlen abroad to form an émigré government. Then, when the Germans arrived, Horthy would muster his loyalist troops – those that had not been Nazified by the High Command – on the border with Yugoslavia and make a stand. It was a fantasy. Germany had the country in a stranglehold. Wartime Budapest had no secrets, wrote Wilhelm Höttl in his memoir. Höttl, a senior officer in the SD, was based in Vienna and spent much time in Budapest. He was extremely well informed about the inner workings of the Horthy regime. High-ranking Hungarian politicians on the extreme right fed a stream of information to the Nazi intelligence services. Horthy and Teleki's supposedly secret overtures to the Allies and subtle, covert manoeuvres were nothing of the sort. Hitler viewed Horthy with distrust, bordering on contempt, wrote Höttl, 'regarding him as a fossilised old Austrian admiral, completely in the hands of his Anglophile and Jewish entourage and imbued with a strong aversion of National Socialism and the person of its Fuhrer ... He was kept well informed by the

German secret service of the secret diplomatic activities of the Hungarians.'[3]

Faced with a choice that would decide the country's fate, Horthy could not decide. Hungary needed a leader with courage and strategic vision. It had an aged admiral, one far out of his depth, his government flailing. Teleki's anguish is evident in the letter that he wrote to György Barcza, the Hungarian minister in London, asking him to explain Hungary's position to the British government. The letter was intercepted by British intelligence and included in a report compiled for Stewart Menzies, the head of the SIS. Teleki had written to Barcza:

> I fully realise that you on the other side often watch with desperation our activities here, seeing the marvellous behaviour of the English and their chances of victory. Believe me, it is very difficult for us here and one cannot judge without seeing the whole situation. The Allied powers prevented any friendly understanding between us and our neighbours during the last twenty years. They did that until the last moment and now they expect us to resist Germany together … Hungary is financially balanced and can hold on for one – two years; not longer. England should understand the problems of the small countries. I trust you will have the chance to explain this to authentic quarters. We do worry a lot but keep on hoping for the best.

At the end of the letter Teleki urged Barcza to keep holding his ground, and advised him that even if Hungary and Britain were to break off diplomatic relations, Barcza should stay in London. The SIS report also notes the military attache brought with him 'a large quantity of papers and documents proving the number of German requests which the Hungarian government has refused'. But no matter how many heartfelt letters were written and detailed dossiers compiled, the key factor driving Hungarian policy could not be obscured: the overriding desire to reverse Trianon. Hungary had poor relations with its neighbours not because of the Allies, but because it had aligned with Nazi Germany so it could annex swathes of its former territories. And as German troops massed, northern Yugoslavia was surely next.

The following day Barcza sent a radio message to Teleki from the legation's radio transmitter. British intelligence allowed the Hungarians to operate the radio on condition that they kept it secret. There was a trade-off; the British Legation in Budapest also had a transmitter. If Hungary's London transmitter was shut down, the transmitter in the legation in Budapest would soon follow. Barcza's message, which was intercepted by British intelligence, warned Teleki that Britain had stayed friendly with Hungary because of his and Horthy's opposition to Germany using the country as a base. But if Germany attacked Yugoslavia from Hungary it would cause an immediate break in diplomatic relations and make it impossible for Hungary to have a seat at any future peace conference.[4]

Some time in the early hours of 3 April Teleki wrote a farewell note, placed his gun against his head and pulled the trigger. His valet found him the next morning. Teleki's note was addressed to Horthy.

Your Serene Highness: We broke our word, out of cowardice, with respect to the Treaty of Permanent Peace [with Yugoslavia] …The nation feels it, and we have thrown away its honour. We have allied ourselves to scoundrels … We will become grave robbers, the most rotten of nations. I did not hold you back. I am guilty.

The Transylvanian nobleman had embodied the contradictions of wartime Hungary: trying to steer a path between the Allies and the Axis, while passing repeated swathes of anti-Jewish laws and more than 100 decrees restricting the rights of Jewish Hungarians.[5] But Teleki's – and Hungary's – balancing act was over.

O'Malley, once he had got over his shock, moved quickly. Diplomatic relations would soon be broken. The legation needed to be packed up as quickly as possible, its personnel – and Caja

Odescalchi and Erzsébet Szapáry – evacuated at speed. But O'Malley first needed to say goodbye to Horthy and pass on his condolences about the death of Teleki. He found the regent in a strangely good mood, doubtless happy at the prospect of retaking the *Délvidék*, the 'Lower Lands', the part of northern Yugoslavia that had once been Hungarian. Horthy's 'optimism was ridiculous'; O'Malley recalled that he told the regent, 'You've got this all wrong. Things are a damn site worse than you suppose.' Horthy told him that Hitler had promised Hungary the return of Croatia, including the port of Fiume, in exchange for supporting the invasion of Yugoslavia.

O'Malley snapped back that if Hungary acted as a 'jackal' for the 'German lion', with regard to a state with which Hungary had just signed a Treaty of Eternal Friendship, Hungary could expect no indulgence, sympathy or mercy from a victorious Britain and United States. Moreover, Horthy personally would be 'covered in a well-deserved contempt and dishonour'.[6] O'Malley left and then informed the Hungarian government that Britain was breaking off diplomatic relations. His mission was over. Northern Yugoslavia was added to the lands returned under the two Vienna awards and the occupation of Carpath-Ruthenia. By the end of April Hungary had recovered 53 per cent of the territories lost at Trianon.

Pálóczi-Horváth was woken by a friend to hear the news of Teleki's suicide. He immediately called Basil Davidson. Davidson said he would be leaving Budapest that evening and urged Pálóczi-Horváth to do the same. Pálóczi-Horváth headed to the Foreign Ministry in the Castle District to meet his friends. 'Budapest was bewildered; people in the trams and buses wept; most of the city was in mourning. On the Buda side of the embankment huge German military lorries, tanks, Panzer cars, all kind of military vehicles were rolling southwards', he wrote in his memoir.[7] There was no free travel at that time and Pálóczi-Horváth asked one of his contacts if he could help him obtain an exit permit. 'Now that the old man shot himself? Out of the question', came the reply.

O'Malley, recognising the danger both Caja and Erzsébet Szapáry were in, moved quickly. On the afternoon of 4 April he sent a telegram to the Foreign Office.

On my insistent advice Princess Odescalchi and Countess Szapáry are leaving for England immediately to avoid internment in concentration camp. They have rendered signal services to our cause and I am defraying their expenses from public funds as far as Athens. They are highly accomplished linguists and efficient and devoted workers.[8]

From there, he asked that the British Legation arrange and pay for their onward journey, unless they could be found useful work in the region or Middle East.

Caja's request for an exit permit had also been turned down. She appealed to Horthy personally. The regent, always susceptible to attractive young women, especially of aristocratic background, succumbed. Caja got her papers. She and Pálóczi-Horváth met in a café to decide what to do next. Caja said he should leave with her – she was travelling in a British diplomatic vehicle into Yugoslavia the next day, driven by Captain Larkin, the naval attache. Erzsébet Szapáry had decided to stay in Budapest. Davidson took the train to Belgrade that night. He had also managed to organise the escape of Viktor Stankovitz, the nominal editor of *Külföldi Hírek*, and his wife, and another of his journalists. Pálóczi-Horváth waved off Davidson, promising him he would try and get to Belgrade as soon as possible. He spent the night at a friend's house, thinking it wise to avoid going home.

The next morning he obtained a forged identity document in the name of 'George Peter Howard', saying he was a Canadian from Quebec. But there was bad news when he called home and spoke to the maid. A telegram had arrived to inform him that he had been drafted into the army and needed to report for military service. If he was caught now he would be imprisoned. It really was time to leave. But first he needed to see his girlfriend, Flóra, and say goodbye. Pálóczi-Horváth's personal life was chaotic. Flóra was his wife Márta's best friend and married to István Örkeny, later one of Hungary's best known writers.

The two lovers met for lunch at Gundel, although fine food was the last thing on Pálóczi-Horváth's mind. A few hours later they said goodbye at the station. The train pulled out. Pálóczi-Horváth undressed, got into his new pyjamas and started reading Thomas Mann's *Magic Mountain*. The book and the rhythm of the wheels on the tracks soon sent him to sleep. The sleeping car attendant woke him hours later. 'The train will not go on. Monsieur has to get out.' Pálóczi-Horváth looked out of the window. The sign said Subotica. He was in Serbia. Nobody was interested in his papers. Pálóczi-Horváth teamed up with a British diplomat, the only other passenger in the sleeping car. They found a driver and headed to Belgrade.

The Serbian capital was a smouldering ruin. The Nazis had sent wave after wave of bombers, killing thousands of civilians, levelling the city centre. They headed south, to a summer resort called Vranika Bania, where the Yugoslav government had regrouped. There he met Basil Davidson and Caja Odescalchi. The next morning they all set off in a convoy of seven cars to Sarajevo. The journey was slow, arduous and very dangerous. From Sarajevo the party headed to the coast. Captain Larking went with Caja to Dubrovnik. Pálóczi-Horváth, Basil Davidson and another passenger, a British woman, headed west via Mostar in the Bosnian mountains. Larking and Caja eventually arrived in Dubrovnik, on the Adriatic coast, on 10 or 11 April. From there the plan was to take Caja and the others by submarine to Athens.

It took three days for O'Malley and his family to say their goodbyes, but by 11 April they were ready to go, possessions packed into eighty-five suitcases. Many tears were shed, O'Malley records, including by his butler, who kissed his hand again and again. The tears, everyone knew, were for more than the departure of the O'Malleys. By now Hungarian troops had invaded northern Yugoslavia, together with the Germans. Hungary was now an active participant in the war. Together with the British, the Belgians and Dutch also evacuated. The party of fifty or so diplomats and their families took a train eastwards to the Soviet border. Three days later, they were in Moscow.

By 16 April O'Malley was increasingly worried. There was no news of Caja. He sent a telegram from Moscow to the Foreign Office.

Only one lady finally went. She is a Princess Odescalchi who has done very special work for us in connexion with escape of Poles from Hungary and her liberty was definitely in danger after break of relations. I telegraphed direct to Hopkinson about her. I am most anxious to learn if she and the Naval Attache are safe.[9]

The reply from London came on 19 April.

Your Naval Attache was last heard of at Kotor. He should be with Mr. Campbell who is being asked for latest information, but communications are now very difficult.[10]

The same day the Foreign Office asked the British Legation in Athens if Caja had reached the Greek capital safely. Athens replied on 21 April – there was no news of Princess Odescalchi. There was news, terrible news, but it had not yet reached the Foreign Office and O'Malley. On Easter Saturday, 12 April, Caja was having breakfast in a restaurant when the Italian Air Force began bombing the city. She remained calm, and after she finished her breakfast she took out a book and began to read. She was so calm that those around her thought she must be British. Some time later, Caja was walking on the city's main street when several bombs landed, causing heavy casualties. She was taken to hospital with severe wounds to her left leg and to her head. She did not survive her injuries.

The news of Caja's death stunned Pálóczi-Horváth. He wandered the streets of Sarajevo that night, his head full of memories. Caja was just forty-three, steadfast, brave and honourable and with so much still do for the Allied cause. 'I went out and moved blindly about in the crowded streets till late at night. I remembered her speaking at political meetings, standing by her car when I saw her off in Budapest, waving her hand as she left for Dubrovnik. At home in Hungary she had left a fourteen-year-old son. Somewhere in London the Károlyis would mourn her.'[11]

In her memoir Katinka claims that Caja did much more than bring Polish soldiers in and out of Hungary. 'After her death, Caja's

THE LAST DAYS OF BUDAPEST

travelling companion [Captain Larkin] found in her bag letters of introduction from the British minister in Budapest to personalities in London. They referred to her important work for the Allies, organising the sabotage of trains and other transport in Poland. Scared, the naval attache burned them.' O'Malley's telegrams to the Foreign Office and their responses give some sense of Caja's vital role in wartime Budapest. In November 1941 O'Malley wrote, 'She had for long been active in Polish and British interests. She had in fact acted as an extremely useful agent in work both legal and illegal for me and for members of my staff. These facts were well known both to the Hungarian authorities and to the Gestapo.'[12]

Such illegal work may well have included sabotaging trains in Poland, planning such missions and organising the necessary supplies and munitions. Colonel Jan Emisarski, Polish military attache in Budapest from 1938 to 1940, wrote that Caja took Polish soldiers to the frontier herself: 'Many Hungarians took the Poles to the border in their own cars, thus assuring their travel and the border-crossing ... I would like to mention those Hungarians who gave decisive help to the evacuation: Countess Károlyi, Princess Klára Odescalchi, Countess Erzsébet Szapáry, Tamás Salamon-Rácz and his wife, Countess Edit Weiss as well as Ilona Sacellary and Countess Ilona Andrássy.'[13]

The full story of Caja's wartime work for Britain and the Poles is yet to be told. The details are likely to be held in SIS archives, which remain closed. At the end of the war, or soon afterwards, Basil Davidson listed SOE's surviving Hungarian agents and contacts, and outlined Britain's obligations to them. But Caja was not part of Section D or SOE. She was part of a Hungarian resistance network, working with O'Malley.[14] Any obligations to her family, Davidson wrote, were for the Foreign Office, not SOE.

It is not possible, or necessary, to regard the Princess as an agent. For her part in the scheme of things was to help the Poles to escape through Hungary into Jugoslavia and this she did independently of us and with the connivance of some sections of the Hungarian government.[15]

For Davidson here, 'us' means SOE, rather than Britain. Yet O'Malley clearly states that Caja was an 'extremely useful' British agent. Before Caja left she took a case of her most important papers to her former husband, Károlyi, and asked him to look after them. They remained on friendly terms – he readily agreed. The papers survived the war but tragically were later lost.[16]

What is clear is Caja's courage, determination and her legacy: turning the family home, the Andrássy Palace, a high-profile building in the centre of the city, into an open centre of anti-Nazi resistance; working with the Poles to organise the evacuation of tens of thousands of Polish soldiers, helping to run a relief operation for those who stayed behind and never wavering even as the Gestapo had her in its sights. Perhaps most of all, showing that there was another Hungary, one where the Nazis and their willing local allies were despised, a Hungary that stood in plain sight for courage, decency and simple humanity. In his memoir Mihály Károlyi recalls an especially heavy night of bombing in London soon after he and Katinka learnt of Caja's death. Her passing seemed to symbolise the start of an even darker era. 'All round the horizon flames were devouring the city ... It was a tragic night. It seemed as if the dark forces had all united to destroy the civilised world.'[17]

In Budapest it fell to Caja's former husband, Károlyi, to break the news to their son, Pál. Károlyi, known as Carlo to his relatives, had joined the board of Ganz, one of Hungary's largest machinery and engineering firms in 1935, and built a very successful career. Pál had come to live with his father in 1938. With Caja busy with her political activities and then away reporting on the Spanish Civil War, Károlyi wanted to take responsibility for Pál's education. Father and son divided their time between Károlyi's villa in Buda and the Odescalchi family estate at Szolcsány (now Solčany in Slovakia) where Károlyi had been born. Pál, now seventeen, now relished the outdoor life and liked nothing more than spending a few days deep in the woods with one of the gamekeepers. He became an excellent skier and a first-class shot. Pál was devastated to learn of his mother's death and was grief-stricken for a year. 'Caja's political opinions had become very left-wing during the years between the wars', recalled Károlyi in his private memoir, 'and in the last few years I had not shared many of her views; nor had the majority of her relations. Nevertheless we respected her for her sincerely held and openly expressed beliefs, so that I was one of many who mourned her tragic end.'[18]

Pál determined to excel in his studies, to honour her memory. Three years later, after the Nazis invaded, he would follow in Caja's footsteps, and join the anti-Nazi resistance.

9

City of Spies

Of all the posts in German dominated countries, Budapest is the most independent, and the one from which it is most likely that any serious ballon d'essaie [trial balloon] will be sent up.

> Herbert Pell, American minister in Budapest, May 1941,
> arguing that Hungary might yet break away from Germany.[1]

Imre Cserépfalvi was suspicious of the pretty young woman who had just walked into his shop on Váci Street. It was spring 1941 and Budapest's streets were full of attractive females in their finery, but even by the standards of the Hungarian capital Aranka Starosolszky was notably eye-catching – and, he thought, trying too hard. She was dropping names of his friends and contacts, praising the work of his publishing house, asking if he would consider publishing her manuscript. Cserépfalvi's shop, Librairie Française, was an anti-Nazi landmark, especially for the Budapest literati. Arthur Koestler had once been a regular customer. Cserépfalvi was an SOE asset, working with Basil Davidson. He was friends with György Pálóczi-Horváth and György Bálint, another pro-Allied journalist writing for *Pesti Napló*. He knew he was under surveillance.

Cserépfalvi politely declined her offer. His instincts were right. Cserépfalvi was later tipped off that Aranka Starosolszky was an agent provocateur working for Hungarian intelligence. Some time later she tried again at the publishers, this time with Imre Kovács, the politician who was also an SOE asset. Kovács worked for Cserépfalvi as a proofreader. He listened to her story about being an anti-Nazi and the political manuscript that she had supposedly written. He advised her to write a romance novel instead as the publishers had enough political books. Kovács too did not fall for her story, but was impressed with her performance. Her confidence and good looks, he was sure, would soon bring her results.

A few months later, Kovács met László Békeffi, the cabaret artist who was a well-known figure in the resistance and was also working for SOE, at the Hangli Café. Békeffi was in a state of high excitement. A new opportunity had arisen to make contact with British intelligence in Istanbul. His girlfriend, a highly educated, completely trustworthy person, well connected in diplomatic circles, would soon be leaving for Turkey. She would be able to bring back all the plans to start serious sabotage. Kovács asked Békeffi about this girlfriend – was she young, pretty, good-looking? Békeffi nodded – yes, she was all of these. Kovács then enquired if this 'completely reliable courier' was not Aranka Starosolszky? Békeffi nodded in astonishment – how did Kovács know her? Kovács did not give a straight answer, but did tell Békeffi that he should immediately break off his connection with her. Békeffi protested indignantly that it was unimaginable to be so distrusting. Unfortunately for Békeffi, Kovács would later be proved right.[2]

The SD was also recruiting across the city. In April 1941 Wilhelm Götz met a friend at the Hotel Gellért together with a Dr Meier. As an Abwehr agent – and someone with an eye for the main chance – Götz was always ready to make new contacts. The three men introduced themselves but this soon turned out to be a much sharper-edged encounter than Götz had expected. 'Dr Meier' knew all about Götz's background and personal life. He told Götz that he was friendly with a number of Jews, including his Jewish girlfriend, Tilde, with whom he was living. This kind of behaviour could have unpleasant consequences for Götz, but any 'unnecessary complications' could be avoided if Götz came to work for the SD. 'Dr Meier' was in fact Wilhelm Höttl, the high-ranking SD officer and Hungary expert. Götz protested that he did not know that Tilde was Jewish, which seems unlikely, and that in any case he was already working for the Abwehr. Höttl said that it did not matter, although he was strictly forbidden from telling anyone at the Abwehr that he was also now working for the SD.

Götz could only agree. Höttl was extremely dangerous. He reported to Walter Schellenberg, a rising star in the Nazi intelligence service, and ally and protégé of Heydrich. A call from Höttl and Götz – and Tilde – would be in the hands of the Gestapo. Götz listened as Höttl outlined his new duties: to report on 'suspicious activities of individual and movements of enemy agents'; to provide 'Intelligence on Polish underground movements in Hungary and their means of contact with Poland'; and finally to gather information about the Social Democrat, Communist and Arrow Cross parties. Götz, Höttl continued, would write fortnightly reports and hand them to a Dr Marek who would then forward them to Höttl's office in Vienna.[3]

Perhaps the threat of incarceration spurred Götz on. He compiled reports for the SD, albeit mostly using the Abwehr's information. One day Götz met a man called Andor Grosz at Korda's office. Grosz had been born Jewish but had converted to Catholicism. Grosz, nicknamed Bandi, was a ne'er-do-well: a well-known figure in café society and the more disreputable end of the city's nightlife. Grosz was a currency trader and smuggler who moved gold, diamonds, cash and even Persian carpets. He also went by the names of György, Grainer and Gregori. Despite his connections and colourful past, Grosz was often impoverished. 'In 1940 and 1941 Grosz never had very much money and sometimes had to borrow from his friends enough to buy a cup of coffee', noted a British intelligence report written later in the war. Grosz had been arrested and sentenced to eighteen months in prison for currency smuggling. He wanted Korda's help to get the sentence annulled.

Korda refused, so Grosz joined the Abwehr's station in Stuttgart instead. He somehow managed to avoid being sent to prison, but the sentence had not been cancelled. Grosz's tasks for the Germans included buying consumer goods such as chocolate, cocoa and rice; working out how to get the goods to Germany; and discovering which transport firms were moving similar commodities for the

British. Grosz obtained a German passport in the name of Grainer. In summer 1942 he also became an agent for Anton von Merkly, the new chief of Hungarian military intelligence. If being a double agent was not enough, Grosz, now known as the 'smuggler king' of Budapest, was also working as a courier for the Hungarian Zionists. Grosz moved between Budapest and Istanbul bringing money and valuables for the Zionists, while also feeding information to the Abwehr and Hungarian military intelligence. It was a perilous juggling act but the stakes would later become much higher.

In the summer of 1941 the Abwehr operation in Budapest came crashing down. There had long been suspicions about Korda's business activities and rumours of smuggling, but it seems one of his own agents helped deliver the coup de grace. An investigation was opened which found that Korda and a colleague had been 'involved in large-scale illegal currency smuggling and had failed to pay their agents regularly or sufficiently'. By September 1941 Korda's operation was closed and all his agents dismissed. Götz resigned from the Abwehr. He started a new career as a journalist, essentially rewriting Hungarian Foreign Ministry propaganda. But he continued working for Höttl and the SD. Korda carried on working for the Abwehr and in January 1942 transferred to the technical department.

Not all of the Budapest Abwehr's operatives were as ineffective as Götz. Like Rudolf Konitz, Richard Kauder (also known as Fritz Kauders and Richard Klatt) was an Austrian Jew, although his parents had converted to Catholicism. Born in Vienna in 1900, Kauder grew up in Sarajevo and Miskolc, eastern Hungary, where he learnt fluent Hungarian. He studied mechanical engineering then worked as a salesman in Vienna and Berlin. As the Nazi persecution of the Jews intensified, he moved to Budapest in 1938. There he became one of the legion of chancers, fixers and opportunists floating through the city's demi-monde, enjoying its nightlife and culinary and sensual pleasures. Using his well-honed eye for connections, opportunities and profit, Kauder flourished.

Kauder used his connections to become a fixer, obtaining visas and residence permits. Kauder's best source was an American diplomat called John J. Meily who was stationed in Zagreb, Croatia. Meily, like many American diplomats of the time, was naïve, with little, if any, sense of security. Kauders pretended to be Dutch and guided Meily and his wife on their shopping trips and visits to Budapest, helping Meily find antique weapons for his growing collection and changing money for him. As the two men's friendship grew, Kauders seems to have had easy access to Meily's office in Zagreb. He removed numerous documents, photocopied them and returned them – and gave the copies to the Abwehr. Meily was so trusting that he even gave Kauder a letter to hand to the American consul in Budapest. Kauder, naturally, copied it.[4] By May 1941 Kauder was in charge of the Abwehr station known as Schwert ('sword') in Sofia.[5] His contact name was Klatt, and he was known to the Abwehr as 'Jew Klatt'. In Bulgaria he resumed his dissolute lifestyle, spending the agency's funds like water, and soon became a fixture of the city's nightlife.[6] Kauder was eventually captured by the Allies. 'I was forced to work for the German Abwehr. I had to do it, because they could have arrested me and deported my mother',[7] he later claimed. However, Kauder's mother died in Budapest in 1943 and he continued to work for the Abwehr until the end of the war.

By the end of April 1941 many European Allied diplomats had left Budapest, or soon would. Their legations and embassies were closed and shuttered. But the United States was still neutral and its spacious legation, on Szabadság Square near Parliament, stayed open. The Americans also represented British interests and citizens still in Budapest. For many Hungarians, especially those who despaired of the country's ever-closer alliance with the Nazis, the American Legation was the last beacon of hope and civilisation. For the SD, the legation, and its personnel, especially the new Minister Herbert Pell, were key targets. Wilhelm Höttl launched an audacious operation inside the heart of the legation.

The legation had ordered a secure shredding machine known as the Wolf. The machine was built and delivered. The American diplomats duly fed their confidential papers into the Wolf, which shredded them and disgorged the fragments. Or so they thought.

In fact the papers were not shredded at all, but were later removed by a mechanic working for the Germans. Eventually the diplomats realised what was going on, but for a short while their confidential communications went straight to the Budapest SD bureau.[8] The Wolf episode was daring but only briefly productive. Höttl soon had a much more sophisticated operation running in the Dunapalota Hotel, on the Corso – one which would yield a much larger harvest of American intelligence.

Herbert Clairborne Pell, the new American minister, arrived in February 1941. Pell, like his predecessor, was not a career diplomat but a political appointee. A progressive Democrat, he was more sophisticated than Montgomery and was widely travelled. Fluent in German, he also spoke reasonable Italian. An internationalist, Pell believed that the United States was a force for good in the world, and should intervene when necessary. Pell had previously served in Portugal, whose capital Lisbon, like Budapest, had become a listening post and den of spies. There was some sympathy for Hungary among the American political elite. The country had suffered unjustly at Trianon – although the United States had not pushed for a more equitable settlement. Horthy's regime was seen as a buffer against the Nazis and a force for stability. Along with their Anglophilia, much of Hungary's elite was pro-American. Near the legation stood a statue of the American General Harry Hill Bandholtz. In 1919 Bandholtz was one of four Allied officers charged with supervising the withdrawal of Romanian troops from Hungary. One night in October, armed only with a riding crop and a very convincing manner, he prevented Romanian soldiers from looting the National Museum. Like the British newspaper magnate Viscount Rothermere, General Bandholtz had become a household name and national hero.

Pell too quickly became friends with Admiral Horthy, which greatly coloured his view of wartime Hungary. Pell became a fixture on the city's social scene, driving his Buick car around the city and organising frequent salons and dinners. Like Montgomery and Owen O'Malley, Pell was taken in by Horthy's claim that he was only a reluctant ally of the Nazis and was really pro-Allied at heart. In his reports to Washington, Pell glossed over the fact that by spring 1941 Hungary was a semi-police state, in lockstep with Nazi Germany. Instead, Pell described Horthy as 'universally respected as a good honest man and a patriotic Hungarian who does what he can to preserve the dignity and independence of his country. I think this opinion is justified.'[9]

Like Montgomery, Pell mixed mainly with the aristocracy and Budapest's social elite, many of whom were anti-Nazi, and so drew the erroneous conclusion that Hungary as a whole was opposed to the Germans. In fact, by spring 1941 a large section of society felt a dull resignation about the inevitability of being drawn into the war; a sizeable and influential group was actively pro-Nazi and eager to ally with Berlin as closely as possible to reclaim the lands lost at Trianon, while Hungary's Jews and a minority of intellectuals, left-wingers and liberals were anti-Nazi. Like Montgomery, Pell had a blind spot about Hungarian Jews. He claimed, 'there is naturally very little anti-Semitism in Hungary' and that 'the Jews were well treated'. It was only German pressure that forced the government to pass the Anti-Jewish Laws with which 'the majority of Hungarians had very little sympathy'.[10] It was true that German pressure had played a role in the passing of the Anti-Jewish Laws. But their easy passage through Parliament, with the outright support of the churches and few voices opposing the laws, showed clearly that many Hungarians were either indifferent to or supported the anti-Jewish measures.

10

Hungary Goes to War

Constant squabbling, outbreaks of hysteria and scenes of despair were daily occurrences. Even suicides had already occurred.

Alexander Szanto, on conditions in the Szabolcs Street internment camp in Budapest for Jewish refugees in July 1941.

'A State of War between Hungary and the Soviet Union', thundered the banner headline on the front page of *Újság* newspaper on Saturday, 28 June 1941. Two days earlier, fighter planes had bombed the Hungarian Air Force at Kassa (formerly Košice in Slovakia) and attacked a train. Eight people had been killed and more wounded in the 'outrageous attack', which was blamed on the Soviet Union. In fact, the Soviet Union had no desire to go to war with Hungary. Molotov, the Soviet foreign minister, had told József Kristóffy, the Hungarian minister in Moscow, as much. Relations between the two states were even warming up. In March Moscow had returned fifty-six flags that Russian soldiers had captured in the 1848 Independence War. Ilona Edelsheim Gyulai recalled in her memoir that Admiral Horthy had said repeatedly, 'We don't want to get mixed up in a war with the Soviets, it's not in our interests.'[1]

It is highly likely that the air-raid on Kassa was a German false-flag operation, organised with the pro-German Hungarian General Staff, to ensure Hungary joined Operation Barbarossa, the Nazi invasion of Russia. László Bárdossy, the prime minister, sat on Kristóffy's report about Molotov's reassurances and it was not circulated to either Horthy or the cabinet. Bárdossy, previously foreign minister, had been appointed prime minister after Teleki's suicide in April. Bárdossy did not share Teleki's Anglophilia and pursued a strongly pro-German line. Had Horthy known of Molotov's reassurances, Hungary might never have declared war on the Soviet Union. The course of Hungarian history – and the fate of its Jews – could have taken a very different turn. But Hungary duly declared war and 40,000 troops invaded Ukraine, the start of a campaign that would lead to utter catastrophe for Hungary.[2]

At first the Hungarian Army advanced swiftly, fighting together with German, Romanian and Slovakian troops at the Battle of Uman. That was a decisive defeat for the Red Army, with 100,000 soldiers killed or wounded and as many taken prisoner. Buoyed and confident, in August 1941 Bárdossy's government passed the Third Anti-Jewish Law. Clearly modelled on the Nazis' Nuremberg Laws, the legislation was focused on race, rather than quotas of Jewish employees. It was, notes Braham, 'by far the most openly and brazenly racist piece of legislation Hungary ever adopted'. The law introduced 'an exclusively racial definition of what constituted a Jew' as anyone with two Jewish grandparents or who was a member of the Jewish faith. However, anyone with two Jewish grandparents whose parents were Christian and who was born a Christian was not counted as Jewish.

The most shocking clause was that marriage and extra-marital sexual relations between Jewish men and non-Jewish women were now illegal – although only the Jewish partner faced criminal sanctions. This time the senior churchmen in the Upper House protested unanimously and strongly – partly because the law would classify many of their parishioners as Jewish, even if they were practising Christians. A compromise was reached that allowed the Ministry of Justice to waive the rules under exceptional circumstances. Beyond the immediate misery the new law caused, as Braham notes, it also had far-reaching psychological consequences. Hungary's Jews were now, officially, an alien implant, with whom Christian Hungarians could not have intimate relations. The Jews became the subject of 'a vicious propaganda campaign that associated them not only with the evils of Bolshevism, but also with the economic ills of the country'. The far right, ever more emboldened, demanded that Jews and other minorities should be 'resettled'.[3] A stream of new measures, restrictions and amendments added to the misery caused by the anti-Jewish laws and the draft for labour service.

Yet even as the war finally and irrevocably arrived, the columns of gloomy newsprint were studded with signs of the old Budapest, the city of art and literature, culture and dazzling nightlife, a cosmopolitan metropolis now half-hidden. Concerts on Margit Island would continue but would be restricted to the afternoon and daylight hours, reported one article in *Újság* the day that war was announced. A lyrical short story took up half a page under the latest political news. The third Hungarian National Film Week, due to take place on Margit Island, had been postponed until September, and would likely be in either Kassa or Kolozsvár (formerly Cluj in Romania) with the latest releases. Hungary had gone to war at the height of summer. A whole page of advertisements offered accommodation on the shores of Lake Balaton, including at the Rosenbaum pension in Siófok, 'Balaton's loveliest and most modern orthodox kosher pension'. There was more than a note of regret in the short, poignant article about Béla Bartók, the 'great Hungarian composer', who had now left Hungary to find fame and success in the United States, where he was now studying Indian folk music.

Compared to Jews in neighbouring countries, Hungarian Jews – those who could prove their citizenship – were still safe. In Serbia there were no strictly kosher lakeside guest-houses. Jews and Gypsies had been forced to register in late April and were already subject to severe restrictions, including a night-time curfew, forced labour and limited access to food supplies, and were forbidden from using public transport. In Romania in June the authorities themselves organised one of the bloodiest and most brutal pogroms of the war. On 27 June Marshall Ion Antonescu, the country's ruler, ordered the expulsion of the 45,000 Jews of Iași, a city in the north of the country close to the Soviet border. Overseen by the Romanian intelligence service, police and gendarmerie units and aided by German soldiers, a mob of locals rampaged through the city, pillaging Jewish houses, raping women and killing thousands of men, women and children on the spot, together with the few Romanians who tried to protect them. Many victims were beaten to death. Others were packed into a train for days until they died. Over 14,000 Jews were killed during and after the Iasi pogrom, a massacre mainly carried out not by German soldiers but by their Romanian neighbours.[4]

In Budapest, too, neighbours could prove dangerous. Early one morning in early July 1941, a knock on the door sounded at Alexander Szanto's flat. It was a detective. Now that Hungary was at war with the Soviet Union, the authorities were checking up on foreign citizens. The building's concierge, known as the *házmester*, had told the police that Szanto had recently arrived. The *házmester* usually lived on the ground floor of the apartment building so he could monitor residents' movements and report them to the authorities, if necessary. The detective was polite, examined Szanto's passport and left. Everything seemed to be in order – Szanto was a Hungarian citizen with genuine papers, a passport issued by the consulate in Berlin. He was married and running a small private language school, giving lessons in German, French and English. The business was flourishing. But he and his wife's comfortable existence was about to end.

Two days later the Szantos were summoned to KEOKH, the government department which regulated the status of foreigners. The KEOKH official informed them that every Jew whose citizenship could not be established without any doubt was to be immediately interned. Szanto protested that he was a bona fide Hungarian, which was proved by his valid passport. The KEOKH official shook his head. If Szanto had not been a Jew, the passport would be sufficient. But as he was a Jew, and had lived abroad for a long time, Szanto was now considered stateless. On a bureaucrat's whim, Szanto's entire existence had been upended, his legal persona invalidated. Much worse was to follow. The Kafkaesque nightmare then took a new twist. Szanto's wife Magda was now the wife of a stateless person, so she too was considered stateless.

Luckily, Szanto was able to call his lawyer before he and his wife were taken away to the synagogue on Rumbach Sebestyén Street, in the heart of District VII's Jewish quarter.

The neo-Moorish building, one of the city's most beautiful synagogues, was now a makeshift internment camp. There were two barracks in the courtyard – one for men, another for women – holding between sixty and eighty people, mostly men. The internees had either been denounced or caught in a raid. 'The KEOKH appeared to have gone wild', wrote Szanto. 'They organised formal people hunts, did patrols in the streets and the pubs, and dragged away at a moment's notice anyone of Jewish appearance who could not prove themselves beyond any doubt to be a Hungarian citizen.' A foreign name, an accent when speaking Hungarian – all of these were sufficient to be incarcerated. Luckily for Szanto, his lawyer was working hard to secure his release. The Ministry of the Interior refused to overrule KEOKH completely, but did agree to release Szanto's wife – albeit for three months and under police supervision.

Szanto was then taken to another, much larger internment camp on Szabolcs Street, at the far end of District XIII. There were two long barracks for men and a house for women and children. Hundreds of people were crammed into the camp. A patch of grass in the middle and some benches provided the only recreation. The site was guarded by two policemen and surrounded by a high barbed-wire fence. The physical conditions were tolerable but the uncertainty of the internees' status was exacting a high psychological price. Some had been held there for months, or even years. The most tragic were the children and young people who had become separated from their parents on their journey and were now alone. Jewish community leaders had asked to place these children in an orphanage, or at least organise a school, but Hungarian officials had refused both requests. The camp daily echoed to a cacophony of languages. Sephardi Jews from the Balkans spoke Ladino, while Hasidim from eastern Hungary chattered in a rapid-fire Yiddish. Other conversed in German, Polish and Hungarian.

Later that month the deportations from Szabolcs Street, and other internment camps in Budapest and around the country, began. The Jews were expelled to western Ukraine, now occupied by the Hungarians and the Nazis. It was clear to all what this meant. Every three or four days KEOKH officials appeared with a list of names and took away around a third of the inmates. Then the camp filled up again with new inmates and the process repeated itself. These were days of desperation, wrote Szanto. 'During these actions the camp inmates lived the whole time in the highest state of anxiety and despair. Everyone waited for when it would be his or her turn. No one could know anything precisely in advance, so no one was safe ... Pure accident, ignorance and the arbitrariness of the KEOKH officials played a big role.' Somehow the word spread outside the camp on the transport days. Relatives, friends and lawyers appeared at the fence to have fraught conversations and exchange snatched goodbyes. Most would never see their friends and loved ones again.

The lorries appeared with the KEOKH officials in the later afternoon or early evening. The inmates assembled on the grassy area and a KEOKH official read the names. The deportees gathered their few belongings, walked over to another corner of the camp and awaited their fate. Nurses sent by the Jewish community handed over packages of food and drink. Some of those called became hysterical and refused to board the lorries. They were violently dragged inside. Very rarely a lawyer managed to have his client released. Otherwise, records Szanto, once 'the lorries with their human cargo disappeared into the darkness of the night, then the remaining and temporarily reprieved camp inmates staggered back to their barracks in a state of complete nervous exhaustion. After a few days, the hideous theatre repeated itself.' After five weeks, Szanto was released.[5]

KEOKH was part of the Interior Ministry. Ferenc Keresztes-Fischer, the Anglophile interior minister, was a decent man, generally sympathetic to Jewish refugees and opposed to the deportations. But he was outnumbered by the pro-Nazi minister of defence, the chief of the general staff and others who argued that the Jews were merely being relocated to a part of Ukraine where they could make new lives. Bárdossy and Horthy authorised the expulsions. The Jews were forced into crowded freight cars for the journey to the border, which took between twenty-four and forty-eight hours. By late August around 18,000 people had been expelled. Most were Jews but their number also included numerous Roma who lacked the papers to prove their Hungarian citizenship. All were handed over to the SS and taken to the town of Kamenets-Podolsk. Many were attacked and robbed enroute by Ukrainian Nazi collaborators. On 27–28 August, together with the local Jews, the deportees were marched to a group of bomb craters and ordered to undress. They were then machine-gunned into the pits.

Just over 23,000 Jews and Roma were shot at Kamenets-Podolsk in the largest massacre of the early years of the war. By late summer 1941 the Einsatzgruppen had been active for weeks and reports had come back to Hungary of the massacres. A few survivors managed to return to Budapest. One, Lajos Stern, was part of a delegation to Keresztes-Fischer. He immediately stopped the deportations and seven trains were recalled.[6] Also among the survivors were the

Jews deported from Hungary in August 1941 marched through Kamenets-Podolsk in Ukraine on their way to their execution.

sister and husband of a Hungarian Jewish woman called Hansi Brand. Hansi and her husband, Joel, were active in the Zionist movement and were already experienced in bringing Jewish refugees over the border. They bribed a Hungarian intelligence officer to rescue Hansi's relatives. It took him several trips, but eventually he succeeded. Hansi's sister and her husband brought back terrible eye-witness accounts of the horrors they had seen: Jews forced to dig their own graves before being shot or buried alive. These accounts had enormous impact on the Brands and the other Zionist activists. They helped catalyse a much more organised rescue movement that would wield influence far beyond its small numbers when the Nazis finally invaded.[7]

Hungary's entry into the war had an immediate impact on daily life. The state became more intrusive and repression increased. Hungarian military spies were despatched to factories and industrial sites, to report back to the authorities on both production and the staff. Many of the board members of Ganz, the engineering combine where Károly Odescalchi worked, were Jewish. The firm had done its utmost to protect its Jewish directors and soften the impact of the Anti-Jewish Laws, records Károly in his memoir. One day the military spy demanded a meeting with the management to deal with what he called 'dangerous influences'. This was an employee called Torda, a bemedalled veteran of the First World War, of Jewish origins. Torda had said that he would not smoke another cigarette until Germany had lost the war. The military agent demanded that he be sacked. Károly refused, and declared that he himself was 'no friend of Germany'. The military agent then stormed out and said he would have Károly arrested. Károly managed to get a meeting with Pál Teleki, the prime minister, and ask for assistance. Eventually another board member made some calls to his high-level contacts and the military spy was transferred to another, smaller firm.

Hungary's attack on the Soviet Union had caught Herbert Pell by surprise. As late as 23 June he informed President Roosevelt that his Budapest contacts had reassured him that Hungary would not go to war. A week later he wrote, 'Things seem to be getting tighter and tighter. Hungary is right under the German power and cannot do anything.' But once Hungary entered the war it was clear that Pell's stay would soon come to an end. By the end of the summer the legation had closed and its bank account was frozen. Pell and his wife Olive were still living in their suite at the Dunapalota Hotel, formerly the Ritz, on the Corso. Olive was a keen and talented artist, and painted a portrait of Ilona and István Horthy in their wedding outfits. The hotel was a popular choice for rich travellers, but it was not secure. Its bars and cafés were watched by operatives of numerous intelligence services. Pell hired a personal housekeeper and assistant, a young Hungarian woman who served guests when Pell and his wife entertained and kept their living quarters clean and tidy. They trusted her absolutely. This was a mistake. The Pells' suite – especially now that the British and others had left – soon became a social centre for businesspeople, aristocrats and high-level politicians, keen to keep a connection to the West.

By autumn 1941 this irritated Wilhem Höttl, the local Nazi intelligence chief. Höttl decided Pell's salons, which were turning into an alternative power centre, had to stop. Höttl asked Reinhard Heydrich to ask the Hungarians to do something about the Pells. Von Ribbentrop, the German foreign minister, instructed the German minister in Budapest to raise the matter with the Hungarian authorities. The Hungarians received him politely but merely pointed out that however regrettable the situation was, there was little they could do. Hungary was at war with the Soviet Union, but the United States was still neutral. The two countries enjoyed diplomatic relations and Pell remained an accredited diplomat. From that moment, according to the intelligence historian Ladislas Farago, Heydrich ordered Höttl to place Pell under close surveillance. SD operatives followed his movements and Höttl also bribed the room-service waiters to watch and listen to the Pells' guests.[8]

Pell, aware that his time in Hungary was drawing to a close, began to review his files and destroy some of them. He tore them up and dropped the scraps into the waste-paper basket. Pell's trusted housekeeper, aware that this was valuable material, took it to her room and kept the shreds of documents. When Höttl tried to recruit her, she eagerly showed him the shreds of Pell's papers and agreed to became an SD asset. Höttl had hit the jackpot. He now had free access to the confidential papers of the most important neutral diplomat in Budapest. Whenever the Pells left their suite, the housekeeper worked with an SD technician to open Pell's filing cabinets and copy their contents. They included dozens of political and intelligence reports, and correspondence with President Roosevelt and Cordell Hull, the secretary of state. Höttl passed the Pell documents to his boss, Walter Schellenberg. 'The material provides abundant information about political and economic matters and of Pell's views of conditions in Europe', Schellenberg wrote to Heydrich, 'exactly as he communicated them to President Roosevelt and Secretary Hull personally and to the Department of State officially'.[9]

By December 1941 it was clear that Pell's time in Budapest was rapidly coming to an end. On 5 December Britain declared war on Hungary. Two days later Japan bombed Pearl Harbor. Finally, the United States was at war. On 11 December Bárdossy summoned Pell to his office. The American diplomat found Bárdossy 'almost in tears regretting that Axis solidarity obliged him to declare war on the United States'. The Germans pressed the Hungarians to intern Pell and his colleagues. They refused and Pell and his staff could still move freely around the city. Their suite, still a meeting point for those against the war and the Nazis, was soon awash with flowers. Pell was still a living symbol of freedom, democracy and a path not taken. Wherever he went he was surrounded by well-wishers, bemoaning that their country was now at war with the United States. Pell's Buick, which had become a symbol of America and something more, drew a large crowd wherever he drove it. The Hungarians politely asked him to use a government car instead. Pell finally sold the Buick to István Horthy.[10] Pell moved out of the Dunapalota Hotel in late December when von Ribbentrop, the German foreign minister, visited Budapest.

The Pells took a suite at the Palatinus Hotel on Margit Island. Before leaving the Dunapalota, Pell wrote an eighteen-page memorandum about Hungary, analysing its political and diplomatic situation. Incredibly, he left a draft on his desk. The housekeeper, who was paid for each document, quickly called her SD contact, who photographed each page.[11] Pell and his wife did not stay long at the Palatinus. On 16 January 1942 they and other American diplomats left Budapest by train. The station was jammed with well-wishers, uncaring that the crowd was also thick with Nazi intelligence operatives and their Hungarian collaborators, noting who was there. 'We organised a real demonstration when Herbert and Olive Pell left the country. We were not only seeing off friends but also wanted to make clear our opinion that it was madness for Hungary to declare war on the United States', wrote Ilona Edelsheim Gyulai.[12] An aide sent by Horthy presented Olive Pell with a large bunch of orchids, announcing it was a gift from the regent. The courage of the well-wishers was admirable. But as the train carrying the Americans pulled out, it took Hungary's last illusions with it.

PART TWO

Magyar Manoeuvres

Temetni, tudunk; we know how to bury people.

Hungarian saying

11

A Time of Dying

He was the only person we could trust; and this was why the country was behind him. With his well-known anti-German opinions he would stand his ground in carrying out Hungary's foreign and domestic politics.

Miklós Kállay, prime minister, to Ilona Edelsheim Gyulai
on the appointment of her husband, István Horthy,
as vice-regent in February 1942.[1]

The day after the Pells left Budapest a young Hungarian woman called Adél Visnovitz was also on a train, to Budapest's Déli ('Southern') Station. Visnovitz was a courier for SOE. Basil Davidson and György Pálóczi-Horváth had eventually relocated to Istanbul, from where they now ran the Hungarian SOE operation. Adél also lived in Istanbul but she had an Italian passport, so she easily obtained the Bulgarian and Romanian visas for the overland journey to Budapest. Fourteen microfilms had been concealed in her fox fur. So far her mission had gone very well. She had successfully delivered the SOE's codes and funds to a Serbian resistance group in Timișoara, northwestern Romania. The microfilms were for Imre Cserépfalvi, the owner of the Librairie Française.

The train finally pulled in and she alighted. Visnovitz walked over to the telephones. She looked around to see that she was suddenly surrounded by menacing-looking men. She was, they informed her, under arrest. Visnovitz was taken away and her belongings thoroughly searched. Hungarian counter-intelligence knew she was coming and even knew where to look. Eventually they found the microfilms. That same evening Cserépfalvi was arrested and sent to the Hadik barracks on Horthy Miklós Road. He was continually questioned and beaten. The interrogators repeatedly asked him about his and Pálóczi-Horváth's British connections. Cserépfalvi refused to talk about anything except his authors. After ten days he was released, forbidden from leaving the city and placed under intense surveillance.

Some time later Cserépfalvi and György Bálint were summoned to a special military court to be put on trial with Adél Visnovitz. The two men were freed, but Visnovitz was found guilty. She was sentenced to death, although the Hungarians did not usually hang women. Her sentence was commuted to eighteen years. In Istanbul Davidson was downcast, but still determined. He had a two-pronged strategy, outlined in a December 1941 memo: to create a sabotage, resistance and propaganda movement and to build up enough political support, especially among the middle class and ruling elite, to bring Hungary out of the Axis. The first was never a realistic option. There were very few Hungarians ready to engage in sabotage for the Allies. Hungary's governing class was never going to start blowing up its own railways or sabotaging power stations.[2] The second strand, focusing on political alliance-building and diplomacy to extract Hungary from the war, had more potential. That approach would soon garner substantial support among the governing elite.

By early January 1942 Hungary had been at war for more than six months. Its troops had initially been shocked and appalled at the massacres they had seen on the eastern front. But they too were becoming brutalised. Hungarian soldiers had carried out atrocities across northern Serbia. In Novi Sad they were preparing to carry out the biggest massacre of the war so far. Their prisoners, mostly Jews and Serbs, stood naked, shivering in terror by the riverbank. The guns were loaded, the ammunition readied. But at minus thirty degrees Celsius, the river surface was frozen. The gunners opened fire on the river itself. The ice shattered easily, the freezing water rushing and swirling freely over the riverside beach. The prisoners were ordered to strip and line up in rows of four. The men, women and children were shot into the Danube. So cold was the water that survivors begged the execution squads to finish them off. Once the news of the executions got through to Budapest, the order to stop was quickly issued. Over 3,300 people were killed in total at Novi Sad and other execution sites.

The reports of the massacres caused uproar in Budapest. Endre Bajcsy-Zsilinszky, the most prominent anti-Nazi MP, demanded an enquiry. He prepared a comprehensive report on the massacres, identifying those responsible, and passed it to Admiral Horthy. The government set up a commission of enquiry. Unfortunately its head was a secret member of the Arrow Cross. His report said the dead Serbs and Jews were 'Partisans'.[3] In the Royal Palace Ilona and István Horthy were shocked, ashamed and horrified. The massacre, she wrote, was 'too dreadful and too shameful' to cover up. The following month, though, brought rare good news. Miklós Horthy was now seventy-three, and needed to appoint a potential successor. His son, István, would stand firm against the growing power of the extreme-right and pro-Nazi bloc. On 19 February he was duly elected vice-regent, by acclamation, with thunderous cheers resounding around the Parliament. But in Berlin, among the Nazi leadership, István's appointment was greeted with anger. Goebbels sneered that he was 'even more pro-Jew than his father'. There was no German telegram of congratulations.

Dietrich von Jagow, the German ambassador in Budapest, wrote a long report attacking István as being pro-British, anti-Nazi and friendly with Jews, all of which was true. Von Jagow was recruited by von Ribbentrop as part of a cohort of Nazi former brownshirt officers to serve as diplomats in allied states in Eastern Europe. These ambassadors were much more aggressive and intrusive than traditional German diplomats, regarding themselves as semi-rulers over client states. Von Jagow worked closely with the extreme right and the pro-German faction in the general staff, plotting and threatening. From the moment of his arrival in Budapest in 1941, von Jagow continually pushed for ever harsher anti-Jewish laws, and then for the deportation of Hungary's Jews. That March Horthy asked László Bárdossy, who had manoeuvred Hungary into the war, to stand down. Bárdossy's replacement, Miklós Kállay, shared many of Horthy's political ideas; he too was a conservative patriot who attempted to steer Hungary away from Germany while protecting its Jews from the Nazis. The ultimate strategic aim was to get out of the war as soon as possible.[4]

As Kállay settled into office, Ilona started her nursing training. Like most aristocrats Ilona herself had never attended school and had been educated by governesses. In the classroom she panicked a little at first, but soon mastered the lessons. After a few weeks Ilona and her friends were sent to the Jurányi Street military hospital in Buda. Her first shifts lasted from 6.45 am to 2.00 pm, but as the casualties came in Ilona and her friends were given more and more duties. Some days she worked through the night until 7.00 am, after a full day of lectures. Meanwhile István Horthy joined the Hungarian Air Force as a reserve flight lieutenant, based in Szolnok, a city southeast of Budapest. Ilona qualified as a nurse and carried on with her gliding. She greatly enjoyed the sport and progressed quickly.

One day in June she took her examination and glided solo for fifteen minutes. Unknown to her, István was at the bottom of the hill, watching. 'When I landed he was there, waiting for me, and hugged and congratulated me. That was a happy moment I will treasure forever.' István left for the Russian front at the start of July. Ilona continued with her nursing and helped with the examinations for the volunteer nurses. She was accompanied by László Endre, the deputy lord lieutenant. Ilona did not like him. 'He gave me an unpleasant feeling even though he always behaved correctly and later I heard from others that he hated Jews ... I found his presence disagreeable.' Ilona's instincts were right. Endre had been a paramilitary leader during the White Terror. Endre was a sadist and virulent anti-Semite. In recent years he had unsuccessfully pushed for the Anti-Jewish Laws to be even more restrictive and curtail Jews' everyday freedoms. He was so obsessed with Jews that in 1942 he published a book called *A zsidókrol* (*About the Jews*), a hate-filled screed. But Endre's time was coming.

For Basil Davidson, spring 1942 brought more bad news. Lajos Nádas, one of his most important Hungarian agents, had been arrested in Győr, western Hungary, together with all his key contacts, including László Békeffi, the former cabaret master, Nádas's close collaborator Imre Márton and a woman called Irma Piesz. Nádas, a high-ranking official at the Győr power station, had been working for Ted Howe's Section D since the middle of 1940. His group planned to blow up an arms factory in Győr producing fighter planes for the Germans.[5] In response Davidson deployed yet another emissary: a Turkish diplomat called Satvet Lütfi Tozan.

Born in Bosnia, Tozan was a hugely rich financier and arms trader – and secret agent. His position as honorary Finnish consul in Istanbul gave him a diplomatic passport and an easy entry into the world of international intrigue. He lived in a vast Italianate mansion filled with fine works of art, its walls covered in walnut panelling, its ceilings bedecked with chandeliers. The house was famed for its secret hideaways, hidden staircases and a rumoured secret tunnel leading directly to the shore. Half-truths and stories about Tozan abounded. One said that he had survived a plane crash in the Black Sea and was then taken straight to the American Consulate, to share top-level intelligence about the resistance in Belgrade, gleaned from a German officer at a dinner party in Bucharest. Whatever the truth of such stories, Tozan was sophisticated, intelligent, impeccably dressed and well mannered, moving with ease among the spies and diplomats of wartime Istanbul.[6]

Bilingual in Serbo-Croat and Turkish, Tozan's network of contacts reached across the Balkans and Eastern Europe to Poland. He had been working for SOE for some time, mostly in Romania, with the codename of PANTS. Davidson and Pálóczi-Horváth drew up a mission plan for Tozan taking him to Sofia, Bucharest, then on to Budapest. Tozan and the wife of a Turkish diplomat in Bucharest would travel from Istanbul to Sofia by car. There he would meet a Finnish diplomatic courier. The courier would transport substantial sums in cash as well as gold and diamonds and then hand them over to Tozan, who would pass them to his contacts. There were numerous letters, several sets of secret codes to be handed over and radio transmitters for Bucharest and Budapest. In Budapest Tozan would hand over a letter to Imre Cserépfalvi, codenamed PIP. Tozan would communicate with SOE Istanbul in a secret code written in ancient Turkish. Everything was thoroughly planned and Tozan properly briefed. But this would be his first – and last – mission to Budapest.

Tozan left Istanbul at 6.00 am on 14 March. As he was also carrying a large quantity of tobacco for the Finnish Army fighting in Russia, he needed two cars to carry all his luggage. At first his Finnish diplomatic passport was invaluable. He passed through the borders smoothly, but he was in grave danger. Three days before his departure SOE in London had been alerted that the Germans suspected Tozan of being a British agent. But the telegram had not been passed in time to SOE in Istanbul. In Istanbul SOE eventually attempted to get word to Tozan via intermediaries, but failed. The Bulgarian and Romanian legs of his trip passed without incident. There were no problems at any of the borders, or on delivering the cash, diamonds and other material.[7]

Tozan arrived in Budapest on Saturday, 28 March and checked into the Hungaria Hotel on the Corso. He was under close surveillance by the Germans. The next day he dropped off the radio at the Turkish Embassy and went to Cserépfalvi's shop on Váci Street. The details of his visit are recorded in an account by Katalin Cserépfalvi, Imre's daughter.[8] Tozan showed Cserépfalvi his diplomatic passport and then said the pass-phrase: 'Greetings from Peter, who sends kisses to Pip and the children.' Cserépfalvi, already unnerved by his imprisonment at the Hadik barracks and the Adél Visnovitz affair, was even more unsettled by Tozan's arrival. Tozan then told Cserépfalvi that the Győr sabotage network had to be reorganised, and that he had brought Cserépfalvi a microfilm with instructions, new codes, a radio and money.

Cserépfalvi was extremely suspicious. He was sure that Tozan was an agent provocateur sent by Hungarian intelligence. Cserépfalvi advised him to go straight back to Istanbul then showed him out as quickly as he could. Cserépfalvi went to see his lawyer and told him what had happened. The two men agreed:

Tozan was an agent provocateur. Cserépfalvi had to report Tozan's visit to the authorities. Cserépfalvi went to the Hadik barracks and told them that a suspicious Turkish man had brought him a letter from Istanbul. He was told to report back the following morning.

Once Tozan was back in his hotel room there was a knock at the door. He opened it to see counter-espionage agents pointing their guns at him. They declared 'passport control' and searched his room. There was a rich haul. They found the letters to Cserépfalvi and other contacts in Tozan's cigarette case as well as the signal plan and codes for the radio transmitter that Tozan had dropped off at the Turkish Embassy. Tozan's failure to either hand over or properly hide these papers would have severe consequences. Tozan was arrested and brought to the Hadik barracks. There he was interrogated all night, and then he was taken to the military prison on Margit Boulevard.[9]

The next morning Cserépfalvi returned to the Hadik barracks. He was immediately arrested. So were his key contacts György Bálint, the *Pesti Napló* journalist, and Imre Kovács, the Peasant Party leader, who was also an SOE asset. Cserépfalvi was held at barracks for two weeks and then transferred to the military prison on Margit Boulevard. The officer questioning him was articulate, educated and knowledgeable. He explained that Cserépfalvi and his publishing operation had been under suspicion for years. His office and his apartment were searched and turned inside out. Documents, notes and correspondence were confiscated, right down to reminder notes on the back of envelopes. The officer accused Cserépfalvi of running his whole publishing business with British money, under the direction of Basil Davidson and György Pálóczi-Horvath, who instructed him what kind of subversive propaganda to spread. The officer told Cserépfalvi that all his publications and books had been carefully analysed. They contained coded messages which controlled the movements of secret agents. This was a fantasy but Cserépfalvi's fervent denials were ignored.

Things then moved quickly. Tozan, László Békeffi, Lajos Nádas and other members of his group were all put on trial together. Tozan had nothing to do with Nádas but the SOE connection was enough to group them together. Tozan, Lajos Nádas, Imre Márton and Irma Piesz were all condemned to death. But the Hungarians were unlikely to execute a foreign citizen of a neutral country, especially one with diplomatic status. Turkey interceded for him and Tozan's sentence was commuted to fifteen years' imprisonment. Márton was a highly decorated veteran of the First World War so his sentence was commuted to life. Piesz's sentence was reduced to twelve years. Several others received shorter sentences. But Lajos Nádas was hanged the same day.

Imre Cserépfalvi, György Bálint and Imre Kovács were charged separately with treason. They denied ever receiving money or instruction from SOE. The letters had been sent arbitrarily and without any consultation, they argued. All three were eventually released and the charges dropped. Kovács was released, and two weeks later so were Cserépfalvi and Bálint. Cserépfalvi and Kovács survived the war, but György Bálint was drafted to a penal battalion and sent to Ukraine, where he died in January 1943.

By spring 1942 it was clear that Hungarian counter-intelligence had a thorough knowledge of the SOE operation, its networks inside Budapest and its modus operandi. Yet despite the arrest of the previous couriers Davidson decided to despatch yet another operative to Budapest. Baroness Mary Miske-Gerstenberger was the wife of the Hungarian consul general in Istanbul. Born in Russia to a German father and British mother, she had long been an asset of the British intelligence services. Fluent in English, Italian, French, German and Hungarian, sophisticated, cosmopolitan, courageous and extremely intelligent, her ability to move with ease in international circles and her protected status as a diplomat's wife made her extremely valuable. She had met her husband, Baron Eugene Miske-Gerstenberger, in London. Baron Eugene was then posted to Trieste and Munich, where they stayed until the summer of 1941, when the baron was appointed consul general in Istanbul. Soon after they arrived von Papen, the Nazi ambassador, gave a dinner party to welcome them. Neutral Istanbul, with its glamorous nightlife and social scene, offered plenty of opportunities for the Baroness, codenamed FRUIT, to garner intelligence.

In early 1942 she executed a very successful intelligence-gathering mission while travelling through Bulgaria, Romania and Hungary. Miske-Gerstenberger was also despatched to Zagreb, the capital of the new Independent State of Croatia (known as the NDH), the Nazi puppet state carved out of Yugoslavia. She set up shop in the Hotel Esplanade, near the train station. The glamorous hotel was the centre of Zagreb's nightlife and usually crowded with high-ranking government officials and Nazi officers. Miske-Gerstenberger's task was to gather intelligence on the new Croatian government, its army and its diplomatic relations with Italy and Germany. In short, everything she could find. Once again, she moved with ease among the city's diplomats and spies, gathering valuable intelligence, which she passed back to London.

After being thoroughly briefed by Basil Davidson, Miske-Gerstenberger set off from Istanbul for Budapest at the end of April. She had memorised verbal instructions and had letters to deliver to the leader of the Social Democrats and influential editors. The letters were sealed between two sheets of cardboard and concealed in the back of a handbag mirror. These were delivered successfully. She and her husband then spent three weeks on his country estate in Kőszeg, western Hungary. But the baroness had long been under surveillance. The Miske-Gerstenbergers returned to Budapest, where her husband prepared to return to Istanbul. The Hungarian secret police quickly arrived and searched her and her possessions. They found more letters addressed to opposition figures. She was arrested and taken to the Hadik barracks where she was interrogated.

From there she was eventually transferred to the Conti Street prison, one of the city's worst. Incarceration here was often a slow death sentence. This was the darkest side of wartime Budapest. Conditions were atrocious, the warders brutal and the food meagre. Its cellars were torture chambers where prisoners, half-starved, were beaten senseless. Their screams echoed through the night as the jailers went about their work. One speciality was to beat prisoners' hands and feet so badly they could no longer walk and so had to crawl on their knees and elbows. Being female was no protection. Young women were also severely beaten. Her trial, she later recalled, became 'a test of strength' between the Foreign Ministry – and Kállay's peace group – and the pro-Nazi faction. In June 1942 Baroness Miske was found guilty of high treason and sentenced to death. The pro-Nazi faction had won, it seemed.

Soon after she was taken out with other prisoners to be shot. A reprieve came through at the very last moment. Her sentence was commuted to life imprisonment, after the intervention of Admiral Horthy. She was transferred to Márianosztra, a prison run by nuns near Szob in central Hungary. Conditions here were a form of torture. She was held in a tiny cell where a light was on day and night. She was forbidden to turn away from the light or hide under the blanket. There were ten to fifteen minutes a day of silent exercise in the prison yard. The food was atrocious: bread, water, cabbage soup and rotten beetroot. She stayed at Mária Nostra for more than a year. Eventually she was released in a spy swap – the only such exchange of the war – for a Hungarian diplomat in London who had been imprisoned for passing information to the Nazis.[10]

In Istanbul Basil Davidson was drastically reappraising the whole SOE Hungarian operation. All three couriers had been arrested. The results were disastrous. Their contacts, networks and operational procedures were now in the hands of the Hungarians and the Germans. The couriers' letters, he admitted in a report to Cairo and London in May 1942, 'did in fact mention a whole list of names, all of whom are now, we must suppose, under closest observation'. The plan had been to show the broad base of support for an anti-Nazi resistance movement. But it failed, and instead, 'we have told the Hungarian police exactly the people they ought to watch'.[11] There were no more SOE couriers to Budapest. Davidson was relocated to Cairo, where he was put in charge of SOE operations in Yugoslavia. In August 1943 he was parachuted into Bosnia. He linked up with Tito's partisans and fought with them for almost a year before narrowly escaping capture and being air-lifted out.

As for László Békeffi, SOE's cabaret impresario, he should have followed Imre Kovács's advice. Aranka Starosolszky was an operative for a new counter-intelligence department of the Hungarian intelligence service. Headquartered on Bajza Street in District VI, and created by Colonel Antal Merkly, the unit's task was to specifically target the SOE operations in Budapest directed from Istanbul. Békeffi had been released after the Nádas trial, but at the end of July 1942 he was on trial at the military tribunal, this time together with Starosolszky. She told the court that Békeffi had sent her to Istanbul with secret messages for Basil Davidson. Békeffi denied her claims, and said she had merely asked him to pay for her trip to Turkey. Both were found guilty. Békeffi was sentenced to twelve years, Starosolszky to two. She was quickly released. Békeffi was sent to the prison on Margit Boulevard. His conditions were comparatively comfortable and he even had a typewriter. The Budapest rumour mill said he was protected by Horthy himself. Békeffi was eventually sent to Dachau but survived the war.[12]

In Bajza Street Colonel Merkly was pleased with the result of a successful operation. The new department was thriving. It had agents and assets across the commercial and artistic worlds, all feeding a steady stream of intelligence. Among the most successful was Andor Grosz, the smuggler who was also working for the Germans and the Zionist movement as he moved between Budapest and Istanbul. Two years later, after the Nazis invaded, Grosz would take centre stage in a doomed attempt to save the remnants of Hungarian Jewry.

12

A New Spring's Hope Dies

I gather there are twenty or thirty thousand Jews out here who are completely at the mercy of the sadists. It makes my stomach turn; it's revolting.

István Horthy writing to his father, Admiral Horthy, about the Jewish labour servicemen on the eastern front.[1]

In August 1942 Ilona travelled to Kiev, in Nazi-occupied Ukraine, to treat wounded Hungarian soldiers. The train left from Nyugati Station on the Great Boulevard. A graceful construction of plate glass and steel beams, designed by Eiffel's studio in the late nineteenth century, Nyugati was a modernist centrepiece. Sunshine poured through the front as the crowd of well-wishers came to say goodbye, but the mood was subdued. The Second Army, deployed since late spring, was taking heavy casualties on the eastern front. The Nazis did not treat the Hungarians as equals. They deployed the Hungarian troops without consultation, and failed to provide proper supplies and ammunition. Bárdossy and the pro-German faction had achieved their wish, but the country was paying a high price. This train was going out, but others were coming in, filled with the dead and wounded, many of them maimed, missing limbs and wrapped in blood-soaked bandages.

The journey east was slow, with frequent halts and hold-ups. Ilona and her travelling companions, three right-wing MPs, spent their evening chatting and playing bridge. On the morning of the third day they stopped at Lvov, in Ukraine. The Nazis had occupied the city at the end of June. Thousands of Jews had already been killed by the Germans, with the enthusiastic assistance of Ukrainian militiamen. Ilona and her companions drove into the city. She did not know what had happened there, but she immediately sensed the atmosphere of fear and tension, and was horrified at what she saw: German soldiers leading columns of Jews, including women and children, out of the city. Their fate seemed clear. Ilona and the others returned to the train at lunchtime, and it set off towards Kiev. 'The atmosphere was one of extreme depression, and nobody asked to play bridge; everyone went to bed early', she wrote in her memoir.

Finally, at 10.00 pm on 15 August, after a four-day journey, the train pulled into Kiev Station. István was there, waiting for Ilona with a bouquet of flowers, at the start of a three-day leave. Their reunion had been carefully stage-managed; numerous war correspondents were there, their camera flashbulbs popping in the darkness, to Ilona's dismay. She was a private person and did not enjoy being in the public eye. The Germans had provided István with a Storch aeroplane and he had flown from the front with his batman, Gyuri Farkas. General Kitzinger, the Nazi military commander of Ukraine, made his villa available to Ilona and her husband. They spent the next three days there. Ilona and István had much to discuss and spoke freely. This was a mistake.

Ilona Edelsheim Gyulai, Admiral Horthy's daughter-in-law,
trained as a nurse and worked with the resistance to help Hungary
leave the Axis.

István's delight at seeing his wife was tempered by his gloomy mood. His experience at the front had convinced him that the war was lost. By then both the regent and the government wanted István to return as soon as possible – he should visit one or two units at the front, gladhand the soldiers and officers and then come home. Many questioned why the second-most-important person in the country was on active combat duty, flying sorties against Soviet fighters, in the first place. István agreed to return to Budapest, but also told Ilona that if she returned home before he did, to tell the regent that the Germans had irretrievably lost the war. István explained to Ilona that he could 'no longer see any way to do anything at the front or at home to extricate us from this predicament'.[2]

But he did have a secret plan, which he shared with Ilona. As soon as he returned to Budapest, he would fly to England or the United States to inform the Allies about Hungary's situation and the progress of the war, and try to find a way to extricate Hungary from Berlin's stranglehold. The details were all worked out, but those he kept to himself. István repeated his key point: it was no longer possible to help Hungary from the inside. The pro-German lobby, especially in the general staff, was convinced that the Nazis would win, and it was too powerful. Decades later, writing her memoirs, Ilona was incredulous that she and István could have been so careless and naïve to speak freely about such matters in the house of a Nazi general. 'How could it not have occurred to us – the outstanding engineer and the careful nurse – that our conversations would be bugged?'[3]

Ilona spent two days working at the Hungarian military hospital, then returned to the General's villa, where István was composing a letter to his father. The Hungarians had suffered 'fairly heavy' losses, he wrote. Hungarian forces should be concentrated, not replenished, or they would 'bleed to death in terms of men and equipment'. István also alerted his father to the terrible conditions of the Jewish labour servicemen at the front. This was a very different deployment to that of the previous year, when most stayed in Hungary. The labour servicemen were once again unarmed but completely at the mercy of their commanders, many of whom were vicious anti-Semites, drunk on their power of life and death.

The labour servicemen, many of them middle-aged, were poorly equipped to survive the coming Russian winter. Half-starved, they were put to work digging roads, trenches and fortifications and loading munitions. Sometimes they were forced to clear minefields with no proper equipment. Instead, they were forced to march over them. Some of the supplies were transported by horses. When the animals collapsed or died of exhaustion, the labour servicemen were ordered to replace them. The company commanders worked hand-in-hand with the SS and Nazi military police units. A few Hungarian commanders, wearying of their Jewish charges, simply shot them. Others forced them to climb trees and shout that they were 'dirty Jews', before firing at them for sport. A favourite amusement of some Hungarian guards in winter was to hose Jewish men down with water until they froze and became ice statues. The most sadistic were often the *Volksdeutsche*, Hungary's ethnic German minority.

The labour companies were also used by the authorities to disperse and break down the Jewish community's leadership. In April 1942 the Ministry of Defence even issued an order that between 10 and 15 per cent of labour companies were to be composed of Jews 'well known by their wealth or reputation'. Such Jews could also be recruited even if they were older than forty-two, the upper limit for being drafted. Not all the labour servicemen were Jewish. Communists and other leftists, interned in special camps for political detainees, were also drafted for labour service. They were given a yellow armband with a large black circle and placed in special punitive battalions, then sent to the most dangerous positions on the frontline. It is not clear exactly what István Horthy witnessed, but his anguish at the treatment of the labour servicemen is clear as he wrote to his father:

It's awful that this could happen even in the twentieth century … I'm afraid we will have to pay a heavy price for this sometime. Couldn't they be taken home to work there? Otherwise few of them will survive the winter.[4]

On their last afternoon in Kiev Ilona and István were driven to the airport. There he kissed her goodbye with surprising passion, considering they were in the company of others. István and his batman took their seats in his aeroplane and it sped down the runway before lifting into the sky. 'I watched it go', wrote Ilona, 'I could not take my eyes off it. Then there was just a tiny dot in the sky. I was still looking when there was nothing more to be seen … I had a strange feeling in my heart that I cannot easily describe. I have never been able to forget that moment.'[5] That strange feeling was, perhaps, a premonition. The news came through two days later, on 20 August, Hungary's national holiday. István's aeroplane had crashed. He had not survived. The next days passed in a daze of tears, shock and grief. István's funeral took place on 27 August in the main hall of Parliament. There is a phrase in Hungarian, *Temetni, tudunk*. Its literal translation would be 'We know how to bury people', but it has an extra layer, of sardonic affirmation, that when it comes to interning the dead, we Hungarians are experts. That day proved it well.

Ilona and Magdolna wore black, their faces covered by veils. István's body lay in a huge coffin covered with flowers. From Parliament the gun carriage transporting István's coffin moved slowly along the wide, stately Alkotmány Street to Nyugati Station, the route lined with soldiers standing to attention. Miklós Horthy, Magdolna and Ilona led the procession. The streets were crowded with everyday people, many sobbing or crying openly. Amid the sounds of grief, an air-raid siren howled. Nobody moved away. At Nyugati Station István's former colleagues at MÁV, the Hungarian railways, had lined the interior with black cloth, from floor to ceiling. As the carriage entered the station a band started playing the 'Hymnus', the Hungarian national anthem. Air Force servicemen lifted the coffin onto their shoulders and carried it into the main hall and onto the regent's train, the Turan, which had been readied for the journey to Kenderes, the Horthys' ancestral home. The train slowly moved out of the station to the sounds of gunfire and the national anthem. At every small station the railway workers formed a guard of honour, also holding lamps covered in black. Kenderes Station was draped in black cloth and from there the procession went to the Horthy family home. Church bells rang, prayers were said and István was finally laid to rest in the family crypt.

Was István Horthy's aeroplane sabotaged? The best answer, perhaps, is provided by the two questions detectives ask at a murder scene: who had the means and the motivation? The Germans, certainly, had both. Hitler, the Nazis and the pro-German faction in Budapest were enraged at his appointment, which blocked their plan to turn Hungary into a near-vassal state. As vice-regent, István was the second-most-important person in Hungary. István's final sortie was to escort a Hungarian reconnaissance plane, together with another fighter. There was no engagement with the enemy, the skies were clear, he was an extremely experienced pilot and there was no obvious reason why his aeroplane should have crashed. The cause of the crash was never properly established. The crash site was not properly sealed off and guarded, the wreckage of the aeroplane was not scientifically examined and the remains were dispersed. Some Hungarians even took pieces as macabre souvenirs.

At Kenderes a flood of condolence letters and telegrams arrived over the next few days. The one Ilona found most moving was from the diary of a nineteen-year-old man, whose heartfelt missive quoted the poet János Arany: 'How painful it is if flowers wither when they are still in bud, if a new spring's hope dies as soon as it is born.' The young writer – and János Arany – were more prescient than they knew. The Horthys had lost their son and Ilona her husband, but István's death was a decisive moment for Hungary's future. Apart from his father, István was the only national figure who could have united most of the country on a new path, out of the Axis and towards the Allies. 'He was in fact the head of the State, his father being incapacitated by old age and almost permanent illness', noted a report from the British

Embassy in Stockholm, which had excellent sources in the Hungarian émigré community. 'His removal was in the obvious interest of Hitler, who is now in desperate need of the unlimited direct command of Hungary's total resources in manpower and foodstuffs.' István's death would 'plunge Hungary into the worst confusion' and 'enable Hitler to turn Hungary into some sort of protectorate'.[6]

Budapest suffered two more losses that first weekend of September 1942: its naïve optimism and a literary titan. That Sunday the city woke up in shock, fear and righteous indignation. The rows of banner headlines in the Sunday edition of *Népszava*, the Social Democratic newspaper, clearly set out what had happened the previous evening: three waves of Soviet bombers, between thirty and forty aeroplanes, had attacked Budapest and central and northern Hungary. Seventeen bombs fell on Budapest and its surrounds, killing eight and wounding twenty-four. There was no damage to military targets.

A few pages along from the news reports, a long article mourned the death of Zsigmond Móricz, the great Hungarian realist playwright and novelist. A long-time editor at *Nyugat* (*West*) magazine, Móricz's prodigious output shone a harsh light on Hungary's stratified social class system, portraying in sensitive, sharply observed detail the lives of impoverished peasants and the once-grand nobility. His loss was keenly felt, one made sharper by the direction of some wartime Hungarian culture. Another article reviewed the new film, *Őrségváltás* (*Changing the Guard*). Its unsubtle storyline featured a young engineer whose career is stalled by the old-fashioned management of the factory where he works. By the end of the film he is the new boss, and clears out the old managers. The message was openly nationalistic and pro-German: a new era is dawning and a new generation taking power. For *Népszava*'s critic – his initialled byline, ironically, was S.S. – *Changing the Guard* was Hungary's first anti-Semitic film, full of anti-Jewish stereotypes. Eventually, the 'ugly Jewish capitalists' are replaced by 'nice Aryan capitalists'. The film was 'outstandingly educational', wrote S.S. with biting sarcasm, and simply had to be watched, but 'with the right kind of glasses'.

Yet apart from the air raids, and the grim news from the eastern front, life in the capital carried on as normally as possible. Between the reports of the war *Népszava* also carried advertisements for a new circus performance, the city's famed thermal baths, which were still open, numerous new films and theatre shows and a bitter mineral water named for the former emperor, Franz Joseph. There was enough to eat, although the quality of many processed goods and foodstuffs was definitely deteriorating. More and more ersatz products appeared on the shelf, including tea made from mulberry leaves, soy-bean sausages, fake chocolate and biscuits sweetened with carrots.[7] Those whose digestive systems struggled with the new products could find relief in Darmol, a popular laxative.

Hungary's Jews, traumatised by the loss of their menfolk on the eastern front and increasingly impoverished, lived day by day. The city was changing in front of their eyes. Budapest's streets, cafés and nightclubs were now crowded with strutting German officers. Another law, passed in March 1942, restricted Jewish land ownership and allowed the state to confiscate vast holdings. But unlike in neighbouring countries, Hungary's Jews, apart from those on the labour service, were safe. That same month the Slovak Nazi puppet government signed an agreement with Nazi Germany to deport its 89,000 Jews. In Nazi-occupied Serbia about 16,000 Jews, 90 per cent of the Jewish community, had been killed by May 1942. The men were shot, the women and children died a hideous death, locked in mobile gas vans and murdered by carbon monoxide poisoning.

In Budapest, and all of Hungary, Jewish schools, synagogues and cultural centres operated freely. There were no more mass deportations of refugees or grenade attacks at the Great Synagogue. Horthy and the government steadfastly refused Germany's increasing demands first to make Hungary's Jews wear Yellow Stars, and then to deport them. Jewish parliamentarians even continued to serve on various committees in the Upper and Lower House. Jewish communal life continued unhindered. When a group of

Jewish refugee children, smuggled out of Poland by the Zionist youth movement, arrived in Budapest during a Jewish festival they found it hard to believe what they saw. One wrote:

> How amazed we were to see Jews, dressed in holiday clothes, crowds of them, praying undisturbed. This was a sight we had long forgotten … In Dohány Street, where the Great Synagogue is, Hungarian policemen in white gloves were directing the traffic. Our feeling was that the war had not reached Hungary and the people, including the Jews, did not even want to know about it.[8]

Both houses of Parliament still sat, and opposition parties, both left-wing and conservatives, remained active. The censors were increasingly intrusive but daily newspapers still published and were critical of the government's pro-Nazi policies. Yet the blood price of Hungary's regained territories was becoming clear, both in bodies and moral corruption. Casualties were pouring in from the eastern front; the vice-regent was dead, probably murdered; and the country was now at war with Britain and the United States as well as the Soviet Union. Hungary's fate was now irrevocably bound to that of Nazi Germany. As far as the war was concerned, Hungary was not independent, or even autonomous, but a subjugated, junior partner. Far-sighted Hungarians realised that their homeland would not only lose the war, but would be harshly punished at any future peace conference.

Behind the scenes in Budapest, the pro-Allied diplomat László Veress had Kállay's ear and was consistently pushing for Hungary to reach out to the Allies and find some kind of accommodation. Kállay's determination to pursue a policy that always put Hungarian interests first would lead him into complicated ambiguities, so much so that his time in office was known for the *Kállai kettős*, or 'Kállay two-step'. His and Horthy's plan was to hand over as little food and military supplies to Germany as possible, protect their Jews from the camps, avoid being occupied by the Nazis and then somehow emerge after the war with enough goodwill from the Allies to keep the newly regained territories from Czechoslovakia, Romania and Yugoslavia intact. As Cartledge notes, 'Only the unique Hungarian capacity for self-delusion enabled these objectives to be seen as attainable.'[9]

Such delusions were quickly shattered on the eastern front, where temperatures had dropped to minus 35 degrees Celsius. By late 1942 the Hungarian Second Army was defending 160 kilometres of the frontline along the River Don, near the town of Voronezh. The Hungarian troops lacked proper winter clothes and sufficient weapons, munitions, anti-tank guns, air support and reserves. They were outnumbered by the Red Army three to one in men and ten to one in artillery. This was the catastrophe that István Horthy had predicted. The Soviet assault began on 12 January 1943. Buoyed by its increasing success at Stalingrad, the Red Army was unstoppable. After a week the entire Hungarian Second Army had been almost wiped out. Out of 200,000 soldiers and 40,000 labour servicemen, 100,000 were killed, 60,000 taken prisoner and 35,000 wounded. The Jewish labour servicemen, malnourished, weak and lacking any weapons to defend themselves, suffered the highest casualties, losing 36,000 out of 40,000 men. Yet they showed valour and determination. General Gusztáv Jány, the commander of the Second Army, wrote: 'Characteristic of the events of the last few days is that the Jewish labour service companies march in close order and in good discipline, whereas the so-called regulars give the impression of a horde sunk to the level of brutes.'[10] Unlike Hungary's Jews, Roma were allowed to serve in the army proper. Considered 'dispensable' by the authorities, they were conscripted in proportionately greater numbers. A large number fell on the eastern front and many were taken prisoner and held for years.[11]

Among the casualties was Attila Petschauer, the Jewish former Olympic fencer who had reported on the Prince of Wales's visit to Budapest in 1935. As an Olympian Petschauer should have been exempt from the draft for the labour service. But he was called up anyway and sent to the eastern front. For many years it was believed that he was tortured to death by Hungarian officers. The film director István Szabó, in his film *Sunshine*, shows a character based on Petschauer being forced to strip naked, climb a tree and crow like a bird, before being sprayed with water and freezing to death. Such incidents did take place, but recent research shows that Petschauer was taken prisoner by the Soviets on 14 January, then died of typhus in a POW camp.[12]

The catastrophe at Voronezh was a seismic shock. Hungary had a population of 9.27 million people. It had just lost more than 1 per cent of its citizens in a single battle, with another 1 per cent wounded or taken prisoner. There was barely a family in the country that was not affected. A wave of grief coursed through the city's churches and synagogues as they counted the loss of so many of their menfolk. Their grief was heightened, knowing that the bodies of their loved ones would never be returned for burial. Instead, they lay broken and abandoned in the icy mud and snow. The defeat at Voronezh followed the Soviet victory at Stalingrad, and the British victory at El Alamein and the Allied landings in North Africa. Hungary, it was clear, was now shackled to a country that would, eventually, lose the war. Encouraged by László Veress, Kállay set up a pro-peace group to leave the Axis and turn to the Allies. Its members also included Ferenc Keresztes-Fischer, the interior minister who had stopped the deportation of foreign Jews in 1941, and Antal Ullein-Reviczky, the press chief at the Foreign Ministry and a former ally of Basil Davidson. The 'Kállay two-step' was about to speed up.

13

A Marriage of Convenience

It is seen from S's statements that a sort of mutual aid society was formed between the Zionists and the Hungarian C.E. [counter-intelligence]. They helped each other but for different purposes.

British intelligence report on the interrogation of Samuel Springmann, a leader of the Vaada, the Budapest Zionist rescue organisation, May 1944.[1]

One day in early 1943 the leaders of the Hungarian Zionists gathered in a cosy flat near the city's zoo, home to Hansi and Joel Brand and their two children. The Brands and their comrades were now running a sophisticated cross-border rescue operation. They smuggled Jews out of Poland and Slovakia to Hungary, down through the Balkans and on to Palestine. They ran an extensive intelligence-gathering and secret courier network that reached from Switzerland to Tel Aviv and Istanbul, using members of both the Abwehr and the Hungarian intelligence services. Their detailed reports from debriefed refugees about the reality of the Nazi genocide were forwarded on to Jewish organisations in Switzerland and Istanbul. It was time to move on from ad-hoc rescue and smuggling to something more organised. The new organisation was known in Hebrew as the Vaadat Ezra ve Hazala, the 'Help and Deliverance Committee', or Vaada for short. The aim of the Budapest Vaada, as recorded in declassified British intelligence documents, was to:

co-ordinate all efforts to organise the escape from Poland and Slovakia to Hungary of Jewish refugees, their residence in Hungary and their onward transmission to Palestine and to control and allot the money, letters, food and papers coming in from Turkey.[2]

The Budapest Vaada was modelled on its equivalent in Istanbul, launched at the same time. The Turkish port city, like Budapest, was home to operatives of numerous Allied and Axis intelligence services. Istanbul's proximity to Palestine also made it a key hub in the communications and smuggling lines from the Yishuv, the Jewish proto-state, to Nazi-occupied and neutral Europe – especially Hungary.

The Zionists were determined, active and organised. All the main strands of Zionism, from Ichud and Hashomer Hatzair on the left, through the General Zionists in the centre, to the religious Mizrachi grouping and the Revisionists on the right, were represented, as well as the Jewish National Fund, which purchased land in Palestine for Jewish settlements. Theodor Herzl, the father of modern political Zionism and author of *Der Judenstaat* (*The Jewish State*), had been born by the Great Synagogue on Dohány Street. But most Hungarian Jews were not Zionists. They considered themselves patriotic Hungarians. Apart from the labour servicemen on the eastern front, the Hungarian Jews were safe. The Allies would eventually win, they believed, and their lives would return to normal. They had no desire to move to a hot, dusty strip of land where Jews and Arabs were already fighting. The traditional Jewish leadership, based at Síp Street, adhered to its tentative, legalistic approach, using its high-level contacts to lobby the authorities over the anti-Jewish restrictions – sometimes with success. But the Zionists, like their brethren in Palestine, had no patience for the old methods. For them, the outbreak of war and the news of the Nazi persecutions confirmed their belief that only Palestine offered a future for Hungary's Jews. And action, no matter how dangerous, was needed to bring them from Poland to sanctuary in Budapest.

The Vaada's five key personnel were its president Ottó Komoly, his deputy Rezső Kasztner, Joel and Hansi Brand and Samuel Springmann. Komoly, born in 1892, had served as the chairman of the Hungarian Zionist Federation. His father David had attended the first Zionist congress in 1897. A proud Hungarian patriot and civil engineer by trade, Komoly had served in the Austro-Hungarian Army in the First World War. Promoted to captain, he was wounded in battle. As a decorated war veteran Komoly was exempt from the Anti-Jewish Laws. He knew how to speak to Hungarian officials and used his status and network of establishment connections to relentlessly lobby for his co-religionists. Kasztner was younger, born in 1906 in Kolozsvár, a prosperous city in northern Transylvania. Kolozsvár and its surrounds were home to around 18,000 Jews, enough to support *Új Kelet* (*New East*), a Hungarian-language Jewish daily newspaper. Kasztner was a lawyer but worked as a journalist at *Új Kelet* for fifteen years. He was a polarising figure, a courageous but self-regarding and sometimes arrogant intellectual. He inspired strong loyalty among some but bitter dislike among others. For Joel Brand, Kasztner was 'quick and slapdash rather than reliable'. But he also had an 'uncommon facility for discovering the hidden links in a chain of events and when he really put his mind to something, he was able to achieve the almost impossible'.

Brand was a year younger than Kasztner, also from Transylvania. At the age of four his family moved to Erfurt, Germany. He dropped out of college and moved to New York for a while before travelling and working across the United States. He then went to sea, and roamed the world, possibly as an agent for the Comintern. Brand moved back to Germany but after the Nazis came to power he relocated to Budapest. To obtain a certificate for Palestine, Brand needed to be married. He chose Hansi Hartmann, a doughty businesswoman. They married in 1935 and had two children, although it was a union of friendship and convenience more than a love match. Hansi Brand was in love with Rezső Kasztner and their affair lasted many years. Although he was a committed Zionist, Joel Brand did not initially seem the type to actually relocate to

Palestine. He was a city-dweller with many friends, who loved Budapest's cafés, restaurants, bars and nightlife. Hansi opened a glove factory and Joel became its commercial representative.

Brand was in charge of the Zionists' Tiyul – Hebrew for 'trip' – network, which arranged the escapes from Poland and Slovakia and the passage across the border, often with the Polish and Slovak resistance. Once in Hungary, the refugees were supplied with false papers and safe houses. The illegal traffic operated in several different ways, according to a declassified British intelligence report, which provides fascinating detail about how Tiyul worked – and the appearance of a familiar name. One Tiyul channel saw Jews smuggled through Poland to hide-outs in Lvov in Nazi-occupied Ukraine. There, their clothes were changed for 'old peasant garments'. Using clandestine routes, a 'poor peasant woman' took the Jewish refugees to the Hungarian frontier, to be met by a member of Tiyul. In fact, the peasant woman was not very poor. She received 6,000 *pengős* for each Jewish refugee, around $1,000, a very substantial sum. At the border the Zionists had an 'invaluable helper' – Erzsébet Szapáry, who had worked with Caja Odescalchi. Erzsébet provided food, clothes and money and helped the refugees get past the authorities and any controls on the train. Once in Budapest the refugees were 'harboured, clothed and fed by youth organisations', while each was debriefed and checked to make sure they were genuine refugees. Thus numerous detailed accounts of life and death in the ghettos and the camps were sent on to the Jewish Agency, which organised emigration to Palestine, and the offices of the American Joint Distribution Committee, an aid organisation, in Istanbul and Switzerland, and to British and American Jewish leaders.

Samuel Springmann, described by Brand as 'a man of slim build and medium height, unusually quick and as sharp as a needle', ran the Vaada's courier network. Born in Lvov, then in Poland, in 1905, his family moved to Budapest the following year. He was an intelligent boy but suffered from ill-health. Springmann missed a lot of schooling but taught himself history, Zionism and Jewish culture. He set up a jewellery business in Budapest in his mid-twenties, which soon flourished. In some months he made thousands of *pengős*. The outbreak of war saw his shop become even more profitable. Gold and jewellery could be hidden, transported and easily sold – an attractive investment in uncertain times. Such expertise made him the natural choice to oversee the couriers that went back and forth to Istanbul, bringing correspondence, funds, jewels, gold and other valuables.

Springmann, the British intelligence report records, 'soon became known as a person to whom Jewish refugees, Zionist and non-Zionist could turn to for help'. He had a wide range of contacts in the Polish and Yugoslav consulates. Springmann obtained letters of recommendation for visas and also helped Jews to acquire visas and immigration certificates for Palestine. His house was often crowded with refugees whom he and Ilona fed and put up for as long as they needed. Springmann's best courier was his old schoolmate, Andor Grosz, the smuggler king of Budapest, who also worked for Hungarian intelligence and the Abwehr. Grosz recruited several Abwehr agents to his network as well as a Hungarian intelligence officer. Grosz had obtained a service passport identifying him as an official of the Hungarian Danube Navigation Company, which allowed him to move freely around Europe. He frequently travelled to and from Istanbul, bringing back large quantities of furs, ties, perfumes and cosmetics – all highly sought-after in wartime Budapest – unbothered by the authorities. Grosz also brought back gold, which he then sold for dollars on the black market. Springmann had his doubts about Grosz's loyalties and reliability. But his extraordinary ability to smoothly cross wartime frontiers was highly prized. He took out the Vaada's reports on the Final Solution to their colleagues in Istanbul and returned with messages, letters and funds.[3] As the British intelligence report records:

It would be more correct to say that it was Grosz's courier organisation as he took complete charge of the couriers themselves, who in most cases were only introduced to S. [Springmann] after they had done several journeys and in some cases were completely unknown to S. who invariably handed his correspondent [smuggling agent] to Grosz himself.

Grosz was a 'loose talker who was always boasting of what he could do for people and of the influence he held in high places'. But he delivered.

The Hungarian authorities were usually tolerant of the Zionists' activities, in part because of the bribes they received. At first the rescue missions were organised on an ad-hoc basis as individuals or small groups came across the border. As the war continued they became much more organised, often run in conjunction with the Polish resistance. The Zionists were allowed to open and fund reception centres. There were many cases of Hungarian soldiers helping refugees across the border, either for money, or out of idealism, while smugglers were also recruited. In 1943 and 1944, the British report records, 'there were cases of Government officials assisting in the illegal traffic of Jewish refugees; certainly frontier controls became much more lax'.[4] The Vaada also supplied Allied POWs who fled to Hungary with papers and safe houses.

The leadership of the Vaada (centre) Hansi Brand, Rezső Kasztner and Ottó Komoly, together with Zvi Goldfarb (far left) and Peretz Révész (far right), activists in the Zionist underground.

Life there, under very lax controls, was far preferable to being incarcerated in a Nazi POW camp.

Vaada leaders repeatedly warned their Jewish contacts and allies that the Hungarian Jews would share the same fate as the Jews in neighbouring countries if the Nazis invaded. They should obtain false Aryan papers and find an apartment in another name. Their warnings were mostly ignored. Such things would never happen in Hungary, their co-religionists insisted. Hansi Brand later recalled, 'They just couldn't accept it, because as long as they kept it away, they could just keep on eating, drinking, smoking, living a normal life like everyone else in Hungary and even when the men were taken to Russia with the labour service.'[5] By summer 1943 Springmann and his wife had decided to leave for Palestine. Working for the Vaada was exhausting, risky and nerve-wracking. He had done his bit, he felt. The problem was, he needed a Hungarian passport. Once more, Grosz came to the rescue, using his contacts at the Hungarian intelligence service.

The Budapest Vaada was also in close contact with its counterpart in Bratislava, known as the Working Group. Gisi Fleischmann and Rabbi Michael Weissmandel, its leaders, had attempted to negotiate with Dieter Wisliceny, who worked with Eichmann, and was in charge of the deportations from Slovakia. In the summer of 1942 Wisliceny was paid a bribe of between $20,000 and $50,000. Soon after, the deportations halted. The Working Group believed that the bribe had worked. In fact, the deportations had been stopped by the Germans after the papal nuncio in Slovakia, and Catholic bishops, had alerted the Slovak government that the Jews were not being relocated for labour but were being murdered en masse. The Slovaks had asked the Germans to inspect one of the concentration camps to see the truth of the matter. In response the Nazis had suspended the deportations.

The Working Group then began negotiations on an ambitious enterprise known as the 'Europa Plan'. Under the terms of the plan Wisliceny would suspend deportations to Poland in exchange for between $2 and $3 million, to be provided by Jewish organisations. The plan was never likely to succeed, because Jewish organisations in Allied countries could not send millions of dollars to Nazi Germany. The negotiations dragged on with Himmler's consent until the summer of 1943. The remaining Slovak Jews were deported to Auschwitz the following year.[6] The Europa Plan failed, but it was significant for Hungarian Jewry and the Vaada in two aspects. First, it showed that the Nazi leadership responded to the demands of its local allies when they asked for a halt in the deportations. Second, it showed that the Nazi leadership was susceptible to its own propaganda about the mythical financial power of international Jewry. After the Germans invaded Hungary the Vaada would exploit this in its own negotiations with the Nazis, with some success.

That January Satvet Lütfi Tozan was recovering in the Rókus Hospital, in Budapest's District VIII. Tozan had just had his gall bladder removed, even though it was perfectly healthy. This was a high price to pay to leave prison, but it had worked. A sympathetic Jewish doctor agreed to certify that Tozan needed an immediate operation. Tozan had his own room and was allowed visitors. After several attempts to delay the unnecessary procedure, Tozan was informed that if there was no need for an operation he would be returned to prison. The operation went ahead.

Even while convalescing the spymaster was back in action, setting up new networks from his hospital bed. Two senior Polish agents visited Tozan, Andrzej Sapieha and Marija Rzewska. Sapieha was a representative of the Polish government-in-exile and of General Bor, the commander of the Polish Home Army. Codenamed 'Tokaj' after Hungary's famous dessert wine, Sapieha, who had also been working with István Horthy, was charged with organising the Polish soldiers in Hungary and co-ordinating resistance activities. By now, early 1943, the first wave of Polish soldiers had long passed through Hungary en route to the Polish free forces. But more than 20,000 remained. The Home Army had set up a secret base in Budapest, codenamed Romek, in autumn 1939. Romek's task was to stay in contact with the government-in-exile in London, the headquarters of the Home Army and the resistance inside Poland. It also ran a courier service from Warsaw to Budapest and then on to London and channelled funds from London to the resistance. The Romek base also ran an illegal print shop, producing fake identity papers, flyers and leaflets for the resistance inside Poland. The question was what to do with the Poles who remained in Hungary. A new secret military organisation was set up in the Polish camp at Pesthidegkut, on the outskirts of Budapest, under the command of the Home Army. Its task was to prepare the Poles in Hungary to join the Polish resistance or assist the Anglo-American forces if they landed in Yugoslavia or northern Italy and fought their way into the Balkans.

A couple of months after Tozan's operation, the Hungarian authorities began enquiring about his health. Surely he was recovered by now and it was time to return to prison. Tozan was completely recovered, but now he was out, he intended to stay out. The hospital doctors were sympathetic and reported that while Tozan had made good progress after the operation, he was showing signs of irrationality and so needed to stay in hospital for further examinations. A psychiatrist then declared that Tozan was unfit to be returned to prison. That was good enough for a while, but Tozan needed to get out permanently.

Wilhelm Götz sat back, eyes closed, teeth gritted, as he waited for the blow that would break his leg. It was February 1943 and Götz, the Abwehr agent in Budapest who also worked for the SD, had been told that he would have to return to Germany for military service. Götz had been dodging his call-up for months. The man Götz had asked to carry out the task had drunk a bottle of Cognac, but was unable to wield an efficient blow. Instead, he opened a vein in Götz's leg. Blood gushed from the wound and Götz almost died. Thankfully, Tilde, his fiancée, arrived in the midst of the carnage. She called a doctor, who managed to staunch the flow.

The Abwehr in Budapest was a snake pit. Götz had not shied away from expressing his opinions about other Abwehr officials – and their corrupt business deals – who were now out to get him. It was imperative that he not be drafted. Andor Grosz persuaded

Richard Kauder, aka Klatt, who was now running the Abwehr station in Sofia, to give Götz a job in Istanbul. By summer 1943 Götz was back in the game. Colonel Merkly, the head of Hungarian military intelligence, arranged for Götz to send his reports back via the Hungarian military attache in Istanbul, which of course was a means of the Hungarians having access to Götz's intelligence. He was warned that British intelligence knew who he was, which was unlikely to be much of a revelation. It was widely assumed across the wartime Turkish city that every foreigner was a spy or agent for one intelligence service or another.

By summer 1943 Klatt had moved back to Budapest from Sofia. His Jewish roots were becoming increasingly problematic for his Abwehr colleagues. But General Szombathelyi, the Hungarian chief of staff, had no issues with this. Klatt relocated his operation from Sofia to Rózsa Street, in Budapest's District VI, operating under cover of an import-export firm. The office held one of his clandestine radio stations. Klatt had a second office in his apartment on Pannónia Street, a more upmarket part of town in the riverside District XIII. As long as he shared his reports with the Hungarians, Klatt could operate freely. Szombathelyi also arranged for Klatt, Wilhelm Götz and another operative to receive Hungarian passports. SOE documents record that Götz led 'a lazy, uneventful life' in Istanbul. He saw his sources once or twice a week, but otherwise spent his evenings drinking and playing cards, socialising with diplomats, businessmen and fellow spies and staying out till the small hours, before getting up every day at noon. However, Götz's Istanbul idyll – like that of so many others – would come to an end the following year.[7]

14

An Agreement in Istanbul

We Hungarians always have the talent to choose the wrong side, but to choose it when the failure is obvious, well this is no statesmanship but idiocy.

Dr Mária Mádi, diary entry for 10 October 1943.

Róbert Lichtenstein was fast asleep when the shouting began. The thirteen-year-old boy was on a scouting trip to the Hungarian countryside with his friends. Their scout group, Vörösmarty 311, was excluded from the national federation because of the Anti-Jewish Laws. But they still met each week at the synagogue on Frankel Leó Street, in Buda, organising regular hikes and overnight trips. The boys were suddenly woken up and told to run as the gendarmes were coming. That word was enough to instil fear: the gendarmerie was the often brutal paramilitary national police force. They quickly dressed and scattered. In fact, there were no gendarmes. It was an escape exercise, a drill to test and hone their ability to function under pressure. The scout leaders had even tested the local surrounds to make sure they were difficult enough for the boys to flee across.

For now, Hungary was calm. But worse times were coming – and scouting skills would help to navigate them. Robi, as he was known, and his friends learned Morse code, trekking and orienteering and honed their powers of observation with memory games. The group leader would place a number of objects on a table. They had a short time to memorise the objects and their position. They would then be covered up and the scouts would have to describe them and their placement. Their countryside hikes became more difficult. They practised how to traverse difficult terrain, manage without much food or water and carry a heavy rucksack. Some of the scout leaders talked about joining the anti-Fascist resistance. One of them had a connection with an official in a government ministry. 'Don't even think about it', he warned. 'You and all your group will be arrested.'[1]

The Lichtensteins lived a comfortable life at 18 Váci Way, a main road from Nyugati Station northwards out of the city. This was the edge of the area known as Újlipótváros, New Leopold Town, a middle-class quarter home to many Jewish families and a large synagogue. Robi lived with his father, Fülöp, mother, Erzsébet, grandmother, Katalin, and sister, Zsuzsa, in a homely flat with central heating. The family had a live-in maid. Fülöp and Erzsébet owned a shop nearby at number 10, selling fabrics and other fashion items, while Erzsébet also managed a small tailoring workshop. They went on holiday each year, to the Római Beach upriver on the Danube or to Lake Balaton. Once a week Katalin went shopping at the nearby market on Ferdinánd Square. Robi usually went with her. He was a keen reader, devouring everything from Isaac Babel's *Red Cavalry* to crime novels. Robi went to school at the Berzsenyi Dániel Gymnázium on Markó Street in District V. It was a highly regarded school, one of a few which still admitted Jewish pupils, albeit to a separate stream known as 'B' classes. Outside the classes the Jewish students were not separated from their peers and often shared the same teachers. Robi had been working at his parents' shop on Saturdays since he was ten. He enjoyed dealing with the customers and they liked being served by the quick-witted, friendly young boy.

Fülöp was away on labour service for much of the early war years. Thankfully he was not sent to Ukraine, but to Gödöllő, a small town northeast of Budapest, and could come home on visits. Robi had to grow up quickly and take over much of the running of the business – he had a sharper financial sense than his mother. He was soon dealing with the wholesalers and suppliers. He was missing a fair amount of school, but these were not normal times, and it was vital to make sure the family business kept running

Róbert and Zsuzsa Lichtenstein, two Jewish children,
lived a comfortable middle-class life in Budapest until
the Nazi invasion of Hungary.

smoothly. He bargained for the purchase price, and also set the
retail price in the shop. It was a substantial responsibility, but he
flourished. The school made a fuss about his poor attendance, but
he had always been a disobedient, rebellious boy, often breaking
the rules. In the times that were coming, these qualities would save
his and his sister Zsuzsa's lives.

Across the river, in the Foreign Ministry, Kállay and the peace
group were trying to make contact with the Allies and find a way
to leave the Axis. Hungarian envoys travelled to neutral countries
including Sweden, Switzerland, Portugal and Turkey to engage

with their Allied counterparts. The first attempts did not go well. Hungary's diplomacy was often amateurish, its security poor. Sending multiple envoys, instead of concentrating on one channel, sent different, confusing messages and greatly increased the chance of leaks and security breaches, which ocurred. László Veress, Teleki's former press attache, travelled to Lisbon in February and spoke with a British go-between. The reply from London was clear, the line decided at the January 1943 Casablanca conference: only unconditional surrender would suffice.

In March Veress set off for Istanbul, flying from Budapest airport on a JU-88 German aeroplane. This was a trickier assignment. Hungary's ambassador to Portugal was pro-Allied. But the one in Turkey was pro-Nazi, and so was not apprised of Veress's plans. Veress met György Pálóczi-Horvath, who had relocated to Istanbul and was still working for SOE. Veress and Kállay were not fans of Pálóczi-Horváth because of his leftist, pro-Soviet sympathies. Budapest had tried to have him removed from the negotiations but London stood firm. This was unfortunate as Pálóczi-Horváth was also a Soviet agent, reporting the details of the negotiations to Balankov, the Soviet commercial attache in Istanbul.[2] Veress and Pálóczi-Horváth met with two British SOE officers. Over fresh figs and Turkish coffee Veress outlined Kállay's offer. Hungary would not oppose Anglo-American or Polish troops if they reached the Hungarian border. At the same time Hungary would take 'positive action' against the Nazis. London's answer had not changed: only unconditional surrender would suffice. London demanded that Hungary send some high-ranking military officers to continue the discussions.

Veress was followed by Turkish intelligence throughout his stay. Back at his hotel room, Veress was relaxing when there was a knock on his door. Standing outside was a high-ranking SS officer. Veress thought he was about to killed or kidnapped. Instead, the SS officer asked Veress if he could take two carpets and his wife's jewels and valuables back to Budapest. Veress agreed. The SS officer was not the only person to use Veress as a courier. One afternoon another man knocked on his hotel door. He handed

Veress another carpet and gold coins for his daughter in Hungary, together with a large amount of money for a Jewish organisation in Budapest. Veress returned to Budapest by train, through Bulgaria and Yugoslavia, loaded with the SS officers' jewels, carpets and funds for the Jewish organisations. He had diplomatic credentials, so travelled with no problems.

Once home, Veress debriefed the prime minister personally. Kállay was taken aback by the demand for unconditional surrender and unwilling to send army officers to parley with the British – the higher reaches of the military were very pro-German. Like Admiral Horthy, Kállay dithered. He wanted Hungary to leave the Axis but was wary of German retaliation. Eventually Kállay agreed that Veress would continue his discussions with SOE by radio. He authorised Veress to speak in the name of the Hungarian government. Veress's plan was to get an offer from London which the government could not refuse, and present Kállay with a fait accompli. If only it had been that simple.

One day Veress opened his door to see the SS officer's elegant, beautiful wife smiling at him, together with an orderly. The orderly took the carpets downstairs and Veress handed the valuables to the wife. He expected her to leave, but she lingered. She gave Veress an even wider smile and looked past him at his apartment. Veress began to understand what was happening. Just to make sure her intentions were clear, she then stepped towards Veress. He stayed coolly polite and said goodbye. He had no intention of embarking on an extremely dangerous liaison and, in any case, his girlfriend Laura-Louise was due any minute. Veress had returned from Istanbul full of excitement and anticipation. His mission, if successful, would change the course of the war, save many thousands of lives – and Hungary itself. But the weeks dragged by and nothing happened.

The SOE–Istanbul line was not Hungary's only channel to the Allies. The Berne station of the Office for Strategic Services (OSS), the new American foreign intelligence service, was also a contact point. Formed in June 1942, the OSS was led by General

William J. Donovan, known as 'Wild Bill'. Donovan, a steadfast ally of Britain, was close friends with William Stephenson, the British spymaster based in New York. Like the SOE, the OSS was to carry out spying, subversion, sabotage and propaganda. The Berne station was headed by Allen Dulles, a scion of the American establishment. Dulles's patrician background was typical – wags quipped that OSS stood for 'Oh-So-Social'. After a successful diplomatic career, including at the Paris Peace Conference that had truncated post-war Hungary, he became a lawyer for Sullivan and Cromwell, a powerful New York firm, which had represented I.G. Farben, the giant Nazi conglomerate. Dulles developed extensive networks among anti-Nazi Germans and was also well-informed about Hungarian affairs.

His aide Royall Tyler knew Kállay well, spoke fluent Hungarian and had served as a financial adviser to the Hungarian government. Tyler's contacts had already asked him to start what he called 'non-binding informal talks' about changing sides. Dulles was enthusiastic about pursuing these leads.[3] Dulles forwarded the request to General Donovan. The Hungarians, he wrote, would never fight the Americans or the British. But they would fight against an invasion by the Romanians, Russians or Yugoslav Partisans.[4] But the talks with the Americans soon ran into the same problem as the SOE negotiations: the Hungarians believed they could arrange a deal purely with the Western Allies and cut out the Soviet Union. This was simply not possible. Dulles expressed his exasperation in mid-July.

> It is appreciated that there is on the part of these people a tantalising tendency to consider that they deserve special treatment because their table manners happen to be better than their neighbours, to say nothing of their irritating insistence on some deserved heritage from their history of one thousand years. It is my belief that these ideas should be knocked out of their heads if possible, and they be brought down to cold realities of the military necessities of the situation.[5]

Yet behind the scenes, London was adjusting its attitude. If Hungary really wanted to change sides, maybe it would be a mistake to simply repeat the Casablanca formula. In Berlin the Nazi leadership's network of spies and supporters kept it well informed about Kállay's secret diplomacy. In mid-April Horthy visited Hitler at Klessheim in Austria. He wore his customary white gloves so as not to have skin contact with people he disliked – especially Hitler. Hitler ranted about Hungary's attempts to contact the Allies. He demanded that Kállay be sacked and that Hungary's Jews be put into camps. Horthy refused. He then asked Hitler to refrain from 'interfering with his official functions'. The two men eventually parted with 'no trace of friendliness'. But the die was cast. Goebbels recorded in his diary that Hitler had 'deduced that all the rubbish of small nations still existing in Europe must be liquidated as soon as possible'.[6] A year later that process would be well underway.

Veress arrived back in Istanbul on 10 August. After almost a month, on the night of 9 September, Veress and two SOE officers set out from the coast on a motorboat, heading for the British ambassador's yacht, moored in Istanbul's bay. Hughe Knatchbull-Hugessen welcomed Veress and his escorts. The four men sat drinking beer from teacups. The ambassador laid out the preliminary conditions to accept Hungary's surrender. Hungary would reduce military and economic cooperation with Germany, withdraw its troops from the Soviet Union, aid Allied aircraft en route to bomb Germany and resist if Germany invaded. Hungary would then, at a given moment, place all her resources, including air bases, at the disposal of the Allies and receive an SOE mission to advise on the breakaway. Meanwhile Hungary would establish regular radio contact with London through SOE in Istanbul. The agreement would be secret until the Allied armies arrived. These terms, accepted by Veress, became known as the Istanbul Agreement. Soon after Veress returned to Budapest, again by train. His SOE contacts gave him two Morse code radio transmitters together with a book to code messages. The Budapest–London communication channel, via Istanbul, was now open.

In Bern the new Hungarian minister, Baron György Bakách-Bessenyey, suggested that the OSS despatch a mission to Hungary. Dulles enthusiastically endorsed this. Dulles recommended that three or four operatives should be used, ideally of Aryan origin.[7] But like László Veress, Bakách Bessenyey, codenamed 684 by the OSS, soon became frustrated. Kállay and his circle were simply unable to take decisive action. They were willing to accept an American mission but could not say where it could land or how such operatives could be brought across the border from Yugoslavia. Dulles cabled to Washington: 'The indecisiveness and slowness of his people have clearly disappointed 684. He has gone so as to intimate that he will finally resign unless they take more realistic action.' Kállay, not unreasonably, was also asking for proof that the Western Allies would defend Hungary against a German invasion, if the country changed sides.[8] This was not forthcoming.

By autumn 1943 Satvet Lütfi Tozan was living freely at the Palatinus Hotel on Margit Island. The Palatinus was not as luxurious as the hotels on the Corso, but it was a pleasant place, in the middle of the Danube. Tozan was much less likely to be noticed there.[9] Tozan's only restriction was that he had to report to the police from time to time and could not leave the country. In fact, he was making immediate plans to flee. Tozan believed, correctly, that the plans of Kállay's peace group to leave the Axis were not secret at all. Rather they were common knowledge, especially among diplomats and journalists – which also meant the Nazis themselves. A Nazi invasion of Hungary was inevitable, he believed. The only question was when. Tozan's freedom had cost a deposit of 100,000 *pengős* at the Military Court, and a new Mercedes car for Katalin Karády, István Ujszászy's lover.[10] Ujszászy was now one of the most powerful men in the country, promoted to general and head of the new Államvédelmi Központ (AVK), or State Protection Centre. He controlled the most sophisticated, well organised and ruthless intelligence service in Hungary's history. The AVK was a combined civilian and military agency, which oversaw all matters of state security and national defence. It was responsible for domestic and foreign counter-intelligence, surveillance, reconnaissance and investigations.[11] Its recruits included military and civil police officers, gendarmes and military investigators. The AVK was especially diligent in hunting down activists and officials of the illegal Hungarian Communist Party and other anti-war activists.[12]

Yet even as the AVK broke up left-wing networks, Ujszászy was also a key figure in Kállay's stuttering attempts to change sides. As Wilhelm Höttl, the Nazi intelligence chief, notes, 'In practice it was the Hungarian Secret Service which alone had the means of establishing unobtrusive contact with enemy countries. The principal confidential agent of the Regent and his Prime Minister was the Chief of the State Security Service – the counterpart of the German Gestapo.' After he was appointed head of the AVK, Ujszászy continued working closely with Colonel Gyula Kádár, his successor as chief of VKF-2, Hungarian military intelligence. By summer 1943 Kádár was even preparing the secret military details of how Hungary would change sides, like many expecting, or hoping, that the Western Allies would airlift thousands of soldiers to Hungary.

There was nothing secret at all about Ujszászy's affair with Katalin Karády. The actress and the master-spy were frequently seen in public at high-profile events. Many believed that such a liaison, in public, was completely inappropriate. The couple's appearance at a Red Cross concert had caused particular anger and criticism among high military circles. Ujszászy wore his military uniform while Karády was presented as his official partner and was greeted by a delegation of children. Karády was now at the height of her career. Between 1942 and 1943 she starred in fourteen films. She was public and outspoken in her solidarity with her Jewish colleagues. László Pusztaszeri, one of Ujszászy's biographers, notes that the spy chief even asked Admiral Horthy for permission to marry Karády. It was refused. Such a union was out of the question.[13]

Karády's sensual cinema performances, and her public anti-Nazism, raised the hackles of the nationalist right as well as many of Ujszászy's more conservative colleagues. Ujszászy's influence was behind Karády's career success, claimed Wilhelm Höttl. 'Újaszászy became her devoted slave. Asserting that she was one of the most valuable agents in the Security Service, he managed to furnish a princely apartment for her.' Colonel Kádár was also scathing about Karády, both snobbish about her working-class origins and sexist, claiming that she 'had no political opinions whatsoever'.[14] Kádár, like Karády's many critics, was wrong. When her Jewish lyricist, Gábor Dénes, was sent on labour service to Ukraine in 1942, she made such strident efforts to have him recalled that a court case was opened against her for violating the Anti-Jewish Laws.[15]

The AVK was also a channel to the West and Jewish organisations. Some time during the middle of 1943 Keresztes-Fischer, the interior minister, ordered Ujszászy to organise the rescue of Rabbi Aharon Rokeach, the leader of the Belz Hasidic community. Rabbi Rokeach was known as a 'miracle rabbi'. The mission began in Stern's restaurant, on Rumbach Sebestyén Street, in the heart of the Jewish quarter, by the Great Synagogue. Stern's was a very popular place with the Hungarian aristocracy and the artistic and theatrical communities, famous for its *cholent*, a heavy dish of beans and meat, slow-cooked overnight and served on the Jewish Sabbath. Miklós Horthy Jr. could often be seen there dining with his friends. Márton Stern, the owner of the restaurant, was a follower of Rabbi Rokeach.

One night three Hungarian Hasidic Jews met with an officer of Hungarian military intelligence – quite likely Ujszászy himself – to plan the rescue. Soon after, a Hungarian intelligence officer travelled to Bochnia in Poland, where Rabbi Rokeach and his brother Mordechai, also a rabbi, were hiding. The Hungarian officer instructed the two rabbis to shave off their beards and dress in the Soviet officers' uniforms that he had brought with him. The two men did as he bade. He then took their photographs and promised to return in a month with Soviet passports for them. He did return, although six weeks later, this time in a chauffeur-driven Hungarian official car, bedecked with royal emblems. The rabbis accepted their new papers. The story was that Aharon was a Soviet general and Mordechai was his aide. They had both deserted and surrendered to the Hungarian Army. Hungarian military intelligence was now bringing them back to Budapest. All the necessary papers, German and Hungarian, had been prepared, authorised and stamped.[16]

But in wartime Europe nothing was guaranteed. The most basic questioning by a suspicious Gestapo agent would immediately establish that Aharon and Mordechai were not, and never had been, Soviet Army officers. Confidence, the appearance of legitimate authority – and luck – were crucial. As the car approached the Polish–Hungarian frontier – now controlled on the Polish side by the Germans – and the passengers readied their false papers, the Hungarian officer said to Aharon, 'Sir, they tell me you are a miracle rabbi, so please pray for a miracle so we can get through the border without problems.' The car and its passengers passed into Hungary without problems. The brothers were taken to Budapest and registered as refugees. They lived freely over the next few months, but Aharon once again drew crowds of Hasidic Jews, seeking his advice, and drawing attention. In January 1944 Aharon was taken to see Péter Hain, formerly Horthy's detective, now head of the political police. Hain asked him to leave or he would be handed over to the Germans. The Rokeach brothers departed soon after. AVK agents helped them over the border to Romania, from where they took a boat to Palestine.[17]

For everyday Hungarians these were days of make-do-and-mend and ersatz foodstuffs. Black tea was replaced by herbal concoctions, while soya stood in for pork sausages. The shortages steadily worsened. Mária Mádi, a Christian doctor living and practising in Buda, kept a diary as a record for her daughter, Hilde, who had married an American and emigrated to the United States in 1941. Mádi, who came from a well-to-do family, spent part of her childhood in Leeds, England. She wrote in fluent English. Mádi enjoyed a busy social life and was well informed about current affairs through her many contacts and through listening to the BBC. Mádi was an unusual woman for her time – divorced and financially independent in a conservative society. Her diaries are a unique record of middle-class life in the wartime Hungarian capital.

The whole country was being encouraged to grow its own vegetables, she noted on 28 March 1942, and everyone was making plans to have their own potatoes, green beans, onions and so on. The problem was, there were no seeds available. By the end of May milk was rationed, with no milk or milk dishes available at all in cafés or restaurants. By 15 January 1943 there were numerous shortages of consumer staples, with 'very little' milk, and no butter, cheese or cream. Soap, meat, liver, kidneys, ham, salami, oil, liqueurs, perfume, cakes, crackers, tea and coffee were all unavailable. So were, from that day, cigarettes and matches. 'I could tell you still a long list of missing things and not have done with it', she wrote, while the situation was 'deteriorating all the time'. Two months later there were no stockings to be had. Pharmacies had a thriving new business selling liquid dyes, so pale-skinned customers could pretend their newly dark legs were covered by stockings. They then drew a crayon line along the leg where the stocking seam would be. Even if such luxuries were available, Mádi's salary would not allow them. She was paid 453 *pengős* on 1 April; after everyday outgoings were covered, she had 5 *pengős* left. By autumn 1943 the evenings were getting cold but she could only manage a small fire in the stove. A pair of leather shoes on the black market now cost 220 *pengős*. 'There is nothing else but to hold out with old and shabby things', she wrote on 13 October.

Although she was intelligent and sophisticated, with Jewish friends and acquaintances, Mádi also wrote about her irritation with several Jewish acquaintances, sometimes breezily perpetuating anti-Semitic stereotypes. 'You may remember in those years when you have been at home, how the Jews were everywhere in business, professions and pleasure-seeking. They really did not leave much space for us Gentiles. Of course, it was not right, but now they are chased out of the smallest living', she wrote on 19 June.[18] Yet Mádi also lamented the forced departure of the Jewish janitor of her apartment building, 'a very quiet good young man with [a] wife and beautiful little daughter of four or five years. Now they have to leave even this place. This again is not right and I am very sorry for them.' And when a Jewish family would ask for her help later in

1944, she would display extraordinary bravery and determination, risking her life for months. These contradictions only add to the value of her wartime chronicles. Mádi was not a saint, but she was a heroine. Her diaries show that even under extreme conditions there were choices to be made and opportunities to defy the Nazis and their Hungarian henchmen. In this, however, she was the exception.

15

A South African in Budapest

Intelligent, resourceful and a natural leader.

SOE report on Lieutenant Colonel Charles Telfer Howie.[1]

Lieutenant Colonel Charles Telfer Howie presented himself to the Swiss Consulate on Szabadság Square in central Budapest on 4 October 1943. The Swiss, based in the former US Legation, were the protecting power for the Allies. Howie, a South African, had been fighting with the South African forces alongside the British Army in North Africa when he was captured in June 1942. He did not look – or smell – like a senior officer. He had been wearing the same ragged, grimy clothes for a week, since he escaped from Stalag VIIIB in Germany (now southern Poland) with Tibor Weinstein, a Hungarian Jewish POW. After crawling through a tunnel, several nerve-wracking days travelling by rail and on foot through Germany and Austria on false papers, dodging the Gestapo and sleeping in the open, the two men finally crossed into Hungary and took a train to Budapest. Weinstein was elated to be home. But Howie wanted to travel to Yugoslavia and rejoin the war.

The secretary at the Swiss Consulate had worked at the Hungarian Embassy in London before the war and was helpful. Howie's best option was to walk a few blocks to the nearby Unitarian Church. Its head, Sándor Szent-Iványi, a courageous and principled man, was an anti-Nazi, very active in helping the Polish soldiers and other Allied POWs. Szent-Iványi, who Howie later described as 'a magnificent fellow', was very well connected with the Anglophile networks among the Hungarian elite. The

Szent-Iványis invited Howie to stay with them while he sorted out his arrangements. Howie moved into a small room at the back of the apartment.

The Szent-Iványis brought Howie meals and clothes – Count Gyuri Pallavicini donated an especially fine pair of trousers. Howie quickly settled in and orientated himself. The city's landmarks such as the Chain Bridge and the Parliament were an easy stroll away. Howie had long suffered from a stomach ulcer and a friendly doctor took him to a sanatorium for tests. Szent-Iványi recommended that Howie declare himself to the Hungarian authorities. The Hungarians were quite lenient with Allied POWs. Some escaped French POWs were even working as waiters at the Gellért Hotel. Szent-Iványi took Howie to meet Colonel Baló, who was in charge of the department dealing with POWs and internees.[2]

Colonel Baló was cordial and told Howie he could stay with the Polish soldiers at the Zugliget camp, in the Buda Hills. Conditions there were not luxurious but were certainly better than at Stalag VIIIB. Howie could leave when he wanted, accompanied by a guard. Howie readily agreed – this was far better than he had anticipated. He had his own room and could eat in a nearby restaurant. Countess Zofia Janina Radyszkiewicz, the wife of the Polish senior officer at Zugliget, spoke English and offered to help with anything he needed. She alerted the Polish resistance, who reported Howie's arrival to SOE in London. The only problem was the food, which was too spicy and irritated his ulcer. Jane, as Howie called her, lived with her mother and two twin sons, Andrzej and Bogdan, nearby. Howie was soon eating breakfast and dinner with them. It was bitter-sweet to be with her family; he was safe, warm and fed. But the domesticity made him long even more for his wife, Aldra, and five-year-old son, Craig.

Reuniting Jane's family had been an arduous, even miraculous process. She divorced her husband and lived in Warsaw with her sons. When the Nazis invaded her mother and boys had been away in the countryside. They were trapped behind Russian lines. Jane escaped to Budapest, where she met Magdolna Horthy, the president of the Hungarian Red Cross, whom she asked for help. Admiral Horthy instructed the Hungarian ambassador in Moscow to ask Stalin to let Jane's children go to Hungary. Stalin agreed. Everything was set for their journey in June 1941. But the Nazis invaded Russia and Jane was left in limbo, knowing nothing about the fate of her children. A year later, in July 1942, the Russians had pulled back from eastern Poland. A miracle happened: Jane was told to be at one of Budapest's train stations at four o'clock in the morning. After almost three years, she and her sons were finally reunited.

Over the next couple of months Howie's amiable guard took him to meet his friends and to the city's famed patisseries. Even in the midst of war, Hungarians still indulged their passion for cakes and sweets. After a while Howie was left to his own devices. As a declassified SOE report notes: 'By this time the subject was allowed to wander around where he wanted, accompanied when in town by a Hungarian escort who was very lax and eventually left him altogether.'[3] Howie had some money, but clothes were expensive and rationed. The Szent-Iványis obtained some coupons for him and Howie's guard took him to a tailor called József Kiss. 'The tailor astonished him by bringing out several up-to-date copies of the English *Tailor and Cutter* and asking him to choose the design he liked', notes Claerwen Howie, his daughter-in-law, in her account of Howie's time in Budapest.[4] The suit was a fine fit and as it was Hungarian-made, with Kiss's label on the inside of the jacket, helped Howie to appear less conspicuous. Howie also had a pair of brogues made by hand. The shoe-maker proudly showed him his visitors' book. It was full of British names – a glimpse of the lost world of pre-war Budapest.

Howie was better dressed now, but he was still quite conspicuous – tall, with a military bearing and obviously not Hungarian. He could not speak the language. Howie had come to the covert world through a round-about, unintentional route and was not sufficiently security-conscious. SOE documents record: 'Although HOWIE did everything in his power, he lacked training in our sort of work and as early as 1943 we received complaints from the Hungarians of his indiscretion and lack of security.'[5] As a POW Howie was entitled to the equivalent salary of a Hungarian officer but it took months to arrange. One day a Dutch officer and POW active in the resistance, Lieutenant Gerrit van der Waals, invited Howie to meet a Dutch businessman called Lolle Smit. He gave Howie 2,000 *pengős*, a substantial sum.

Smit was a spy for Britain and the United States. He had spent twelve years working in Berlin as head of General Motors before being recruited by Philips and moving to Budapest as regional director. Smit's name is little known in the annals of wartime espionage, but should be. The Dutchman was one of the Western Allies' most effective wartime agents. Smit, known as PETERS to the British and AD-420 to the Americans, used his high-level networks of business and political contacts to gather a stream of highly technical intelligence, much of it about weapons systems, which he fed back to London and Washington. According to one declassified US intelligence report, Smit had his own network of agents, including a source in Hermann Göring's office.[6] After the war Smit would be awarded high honours by both the British and the Dutch for his service to the Allied cause. Britain's citation to the Dutch authorities noted:

Mr Smit's personal reconnaissances – often undertaken in dangerous conditions – were appreciable factors in the estimation of enemy intentions and in the assessing of his strength.

At a later stage Mr. Smit was directly responsible for organising the release and for escape of interned Dutch and British prisoners of war several of whom probably owe their lives to him.

Mr Smit has worked throughout with utter disregard for personal safety and, needless to say, without hope of material reward. His sustained courage and dogged refusal to give way to despair, even in the darkest moments, were a spur and an inspiration to all in contact with him.[7]

Smit also worked with the Polish intelligence networks in Hungary and was in contact with British intelligence in Turkey. Through

Smit, Howie contacted the British Legation in Ankara, asking for instructions. Not every encounter Howie had was as friendly. There is an intriguing account in Joel Brand's memoir of an encounter with 'the highest-ranking British officer' in Hungary, a colonel. The officer is unnamed but was almost certainly Colonel Howie, especially as Brand was introduced to him by Tibor Weinstein. They met in a church. The colonel began with praise, telling Brand that the Zionists were the 'strongest underground movement in the country'. He had two initial requests: for the Vaada to help Allied POWs to get home, and to start 'active military operations'. The Vaada was happy to help move the POWs but it was extremely difficult to cross the Yugoslav frontier. The Partisans were not especially keen on the Vaada, fearing they would send women and children down the line. Active sabotage, though, was impossible, explained Brand. The Vaada was ready to engage the Nazis but not without allies. The Socialists and trade unions had no appetite for fighting the Germans. The Communists would only work on their own. In any case Hungarian Jewry's menfolk were almost all absent, on labour service. There was nobody available to form Partisan units and take up arms. The colonel then demanded that the Vaada hand over its Palestine certificates to him. Brand refused. The colonel threatened him with retribution after the war if he did not cooperate. Brand shrugged. There was no way the Vaada would surrender its precious certificates to an Allied officer. The two men met several times, but were 'never able to come to any agreement'.[8]

By autumn 1943 Hungary's peace proposal was being taken more seriously in London and Washington. The country was increasingly viewed as a potential ally. Kállay had relaxed censorship, recognised the Badoglio government in Italy, purged some pro-Nazi officials and ordered an enquiry into the Novi Sad massacre. He and Horthy repeatedly refused Germany's increasingly shrill demands to hand over Hungary's Jews. A memo from Frank Roberts, a senior Foreign Office official, written on 22 September, outlined multiple points in Hungary's favour: its Parliament functioned, and only the Communists and Nazis were banned; there was a flourishing Social Democratic movement with its own newspaper (*Népszava*), a Peasant Party and legal trade unions; and churches, the press and intellectual life were 'remarkably free'. Hungary, despite German demands, had not taken strong action against its Jews and those ethnic Germans who joined the SS lost their Hungarian nationality. Hungary's aim was to preserve its independence and keep the territories regained in Romania, Yugoslavia and Czechoslovakia.[9] By now Hungary had also reached a mutually beneficial agreement with the Allies over bombing raids against the Reich. Allied aircraft were allowed to fly over Hungary without being intercepted or shot at. They even gathered in formation in Hungarian air space before setting off for their targets. In exchange, the Allies did not bomb Hungary. 'Until the German invasion this agreement was kept by both sides', recalled Ilona Edelsheim Gyulai in her memoir, 'and benefited them as much as it did us'.[10]

But the Germans, aware that their influence was slipping, quickly applied more pressure wherever they could. In October 1943 Colonel Baló, who oversaw the Allied POWs, was replaced by Colonel Loránd Utassy, who was less easy-going. He ordered Howie to join the other Allied POWs held on Count Mihály Andrássy's estate in Szigetvár, southern Hungary. Count Mihály was Caja Odescalchi's second cousin. He and his wife, Mária, had been hosting fifty or so Allied soldiers since August 1943. Szigetvár was a picturesque, historic village nestling among lush hills in Hungary's wine country, close to the Yugoslav border. The Andrássys' country home stood inside the fort, next to a mosque, one of the few in Hungary that had survived the Ottoman era. Sultan Suleiman the Magnificent had died during the siege of Szigetvár in 1566 and some of his remains were buried nearby. Howie's conditions were comfortable: his large room had a stove in the corner and linen bed-sheets. There was plenty of food and less danger of arrest or a visit from the Gestapo. Howie went riding with Countess Mária and pheasant-shooting with her husband. But Szigetvár, no matter how pleasant, was a backwater – which was why he had been sent there. Howie was restless to get back to Budapest. After a while, the Andrássys returned to the capital and Howie went with them. He stayed for a few days at the Andrássy

Palace on the embankment. Howie asked Mihály to obtain a weapon for him and soon received a Steyr pistol.

Howie was introduced to the Pallavicinis, many of whom were related to the Andrássys and who were also anti-Nazis. Howie had dinner with Erzsébet Szapáry, Caja's cousin, and Colonel Gyula Tost, Admiral Horthy's aide-de-camp. The regent had almost certainly sent Tost to assess Howie as a possible contact point for the Allies. The Polish resistance had also been watching Howie. In December 1943 Erzsébet Szapáry brought Andrzej Sapieha, the representative of General Bor, the commander of the Polish Home Army, to meet Howie. By now Howie had returned to the Szent-Iványis' apartment. Sapieha asked Howie to set up a radio transmitter there to contact London. Howie agreed to do this, as reported in declassified SOE records: 'Subject became very friendly with SAPIEHA and commenced to do a great deal of work for these secret Polish groups, including sending radio equipment (from [LOLLE] SMIT's factory) to Poland and arranging for general supplies to Poland from Hungary.'[11]

By winter 1943 Hungary had been at war with the Western Allies for almost two years. Yet here was an Allied officer, living more or less freely, being fitted for suits and shoes, going to the opera, wandering the city as he wished, meeting whomever he liked, including known anti-Nazi aristocrats and a Dutchman working for American and British intelligence, running a clandestine radio station in downtown Budapest and organising POW escape routes, all while armed with a Steyr pistol. SOE records note that by December 1943 Howie had become 'a person of considerable influence in Budapest and was doing a great deal for POWs'.[12]

Yet numerous obstacles still prevented Kállay and Horthy from finally taking the decision to change sides. General Szombathelyi, the chief of staff, was a member of the peace group. But many of his high-ranking officers, drawn from Hungary's German minority, were still strongly pro-Nazi. If Hungary did change sides, then Germany would probably invade and some senior officers might fight with the Nazis. That said, much of the army was loyal to Admiral Horthy. Everything would depend on his reaction. A clarion call to fight the invading Nazis – who had led Hungary to disaster – would have a powerful effect. Hungary's biggest problem was strategic. If the Western Allies invaded the Balkans through Italy or Yugoslavia and reached Hungary, then it was conceivable that Hungary could join forces with the British and American armies and turn on the Nazis. Outside the pro-Nazi faction, there was a widespread hope that the British and Americans would soon arrive.

But Roosevelt was opposed to opening a new front in the Balkans. The Americans believed that it would be a distraction from the eventual landings in France. Allied operations in the Balkans would be restricted to commando raids, supplying resistance groups and bombing. Churchill tried again in November 1943, suggesting that British forces establish a bridgehead on the Dalmatian coast in Yugoslavia, before pushing forward into central Europe, but his own military leadership turned him down. All three Allied leaders – Churchill, Roosevelt and Stalin – met in Tehran in November. By then Moscow's opposition to a peace deal with Hungary had solidified. The second front could not be a means of the Western Allies liberating Central Europe and the Balkans. Meanwhile Kállay's plans were well known to the Nazi leadership. Berlin's fury at his policies was growing. An SS officer named Edmund Veesenmayer, who knew Hungary well, wrote a detailed report on the country. It named Hungary's Jews as 'enemy number one'. The Hungarian problem would be solved if Horthy's advisers were purged and the Hungarian leader made 'a soldier of the Führer'.[13] In other words, Germany should invade.

By November Samuel Springmann, the Vaada's courier maestro, was finally preparing to leave for Palestine. He handed over the details of his underground operation to Kasztner and Brand. Andor Grosz introduced the two Zionist leaders to Major József Garzuly of Hungarian military intelligence. Garzuly explained that he knew all about the Zionist courier and smuggling network from Budapest to Istanbul. He had a better offer. He would arrange for everything to be taken to Turkey and back by Hungarian diplomatic courier, so there was no danger of customs or other officials interfering with the transports. He would also manage the sale of the gold and dollars coming in from Turkey and their conversion into *pengős*, through the Hungarian National Bank. His price was a 10-per-cent cut on all transactions. This was an offer that could not be refused.

Kasztner and Brand agreed but Grosz was not very happy. He had previously handled the currency exchanges on the black market. Very sensitive communications and fund transfers were still handled by Grosz or a Swiss diplomatic courier, the safest option of all, who was moonlighting for the Zionists.[14] That same month Joel Brand held a conference at his house where it was decided to organise an armed resistance movement. Named the Hagana, after its equivalent in Palestine, the plan was to set up an armed wing to liaise with Jewish resistance groups in Poland and Slovakia and link up with Tito and the Yugoslav Partisans. Bunkers were set up across Hungary, where arms and food could be secretly hidden. Joel Brand's Tiyul group, which worked across the borders, arranged for Polish underground fighters to be brought to Budapest.[15] The Poles and Slovaks, who had experience of clandestine work under the Nazis, trained the Hungarians. Springmann and his wife finally left Budapest in early 1944. They travelled to Istanbul, where they spent two months. In early April they left for Palestine but Springmann was immediately arrested by the British on the Syrian border and sent to Cairo for interrogation. He and Ilona eventually arrived in Palestine in July 1944.

As autumn slid into winter Satvet Lütfi Tozan was also planning his exit. He had good relations with Branko Benzon, the NDH ambassador in Bucharest. Doubtless in exchange for a handsome bribe, Benzon came to Budapest and brought Tozan a Croatian passport in the name of Ivan Draganic. On the night of 30 November Tozan made his move. He packed up some of his belongings but spread other possessions around his rooms so the staff would not think he had left. The wife of a Turkish diplomat, travelling back by train, agreed to take Tozan's other luggage. Bezon was waiting at the station for Tozan, with tickets for both of them to Bucharest. The train was fifteen minutes late, minutes that Tozan later described as 'the gravest moments of my life'. Keleti Station, the gateway to the Balkans and Turkey, was closely observed. Had Tozan been recognised by the Hungarian or the secret police, he would have been arrested immediately. He took his seat and eventually the train slowly made its way eastwards through the flatlands of the Hungarian countryside to the Romanian frontier. A few hours later the two men arrived in Bucharest, where Tozan stayed as Benzon's guest. He was free.[16]

In Berne Dulles kept up the pressure to launch Operation Sparrow, the OSS mission to Hungary. The OSS operatives in Istanbul, like their SOE counterparts, were working with Ottó Hatz, the Hungarian military attache. They had been introduced to him by Andor Grosz. Grosz was serving an impressive array of different masters. As well as working for the Abwehr, the Hungarians and the Zionists, Grosz was now also an OSS agent, codenamed Trillium. Hatz, a former Olympic fencer, strongly disliked Grosz and the other Hungarian Jews in Istanbul. Nazi intelligence agents in Istanbul spread rumours that Hatz was pro-Allied, to ease his contacts with the SOE and OSS. In fact, Hatz was working for the Germans and had passed them details of Operation Sparrow. Dulles was repeatedly warned of this but decided to go ahead anyway.[17] Bakách Bessenyey, the Hungarian minister in Berne, assured him that everything was in place to receive the OSS mission. The key envoy could be in US uniform but should wear a trench coat to cover it. He should be able to speak German, if not Hungarian. 'It is preferable that the envoy be a sturdy American specimen, rather than one possessing any foreign traits', the Hungarians asked, which was understood to mean he should not be, or look, Jewish. Once the Americans arrived they would be taken to General Ujszászy, who was informed and prepared to receive the mission.[18] But the authorisation was painfully slow. The decision would eventually come, but far too late.

As 1943 drew to a close, László Veress radioed London that Budapest was ready to accept the SOE parachutists. He found a comfortable, secluded villa for them in Budapest. But his Christmas present was not what he hoped for: Hungary had not changed sides and was still fighting with the Nazis. It was small compensation perhaps that on 24 December Veress received an elaborate document, embossed with the seal of the Royal Crown: he had been appointed assistant press secretary at the Foreign Ministry. As for Howie, he spent the festive season in Szigetvár, working with other POWs on plans to receive the SOE parachutists who would land on the Andrássy estate. But now Britain prevaricated. The Russians again made it very clear that Hungary was in their zone of influence. The SOE mission to link up with Howie was cancelled. No Allied parachutists would float down to Szigetvár that winter and Howie would soon return to Budapest. There he would execute a new and perilous mission, which would take him to the very heart of Hungary's ruling elite.

PART THREE

The Last Days

Along the Danube Quay, where one strolled pleasantly under the lanterns in the pale summer nights in front of the row of world famous hotels – the Ritz, Bristol, Hungaria and Carlton - work detachments prepare for war. The coffee house habitues meet as usual at 5pm in the Negresco, then move on to the Dubarry or Hungarica bar around seven to have their customary 'Flip' or a good Tokaj – while Soviet aircraft indiscriminately drop bombs followed by flares into the city. For dinner the Soviet long-range artillery sends heavy shells into the city. The waiters serve on, nobody makes a fuss.

Werner Hannemann, German war reporter, autumn 1944.[19]

16

Operation Margarethe

His Highness has granted full powers to the government under his leadership in respect to all anti-Jewish regulations and in this matter he wishes to exercise no influence whatever.

Minutes of the meeting of the Hungarian Council of Ministers on 29 March 1944, after the German occupation of Hungary, as the first major batch of anti-Jewish decrees were passed and the plans for the deportations were drawn up. Admiral Horthy remained as head of state until 15 October 1944.[1]

The night of 13 March 1944 at Brindisi Airport, southern Italy, was filthy weather for flying. A gale howled across the runway, gusting sleet and hail. The five passengers shivered in their leather flying jackets as they struggled across the grass and stepped on board. Robert J. P. Eden, the British officer in command, was flying with four Jewish soldiers: Hannah Szenes, Reuven Dafni, Abba Berdichev and Yona Rosen. Born in Hungary, Romania and Yugoslavia, the quartet had been thoroughly trained by SOE and the British military. They were tense with nervous anticipation; finally their mission was underway. The plan was to parachute into Partisan-controlled territory in Yugoslavia. From there Hannah and Yona Rosen would cross into Hungary and organise Jewish resistance. Berdichev aimed to get to Romania. Dafne, who had been born in Zagreb, would work with Tito's Partisans. More Palestinian Jews would be dropped soon after to link up with them. Eden's mission was to help Hannah and Reuven into Hungary, then focus on getting Allied POWs, especially air crew, to the Yugoslav coast.

It was a gargantuan task for a young woman not yet twenty-three years old with no combat experience. Born in Budapest in 1921, Hannah had enjoyed a comfortable middle-class upbringing, typical of the assimilated Hungarian Jewish bourgeoisie. The family lived in a comfortable home on Bimbó Way in Buda with a governess and a maid. Hannah's clothes were laid out for her and her older brother Gyuri every morning. Her father, Béla, was a well-known playwright and novelist with several acclaimed works. Her mother, Katalin, was a homemaker. But Béla tragically died in 1927 from a heart attack, aged just thirty-three. Hannah had inherited her father's literary talent. She was a gifted poet and kept a sharply observed diary. Her first experience of anti-Semitism was

Hannah Szenes, a talented poet and passionate Zionist, left her comfortable life in Budapest to live on a kibbutz in Palestine. She trained with the SOE before parachuting into Yugoslavia.

at school. Aged sixteen, she was elected to the board of the Literary Society by her classmates. The election was declared invalid. 'This clearly indicated that they did not want a Jew – me, that is, to become an officer which hurts me very much ... it was a decided insult', she wrote in her diary on 16 September 1937.[2]

Such experiences – very common in late-1930s Hungary – and her passionate sense of justice and idealism helped to turn Hannah into an ardent Zionist. 'The only thing I am committed to, in which I believe, is Zionism. Everything connected with it, no matter how remotely, interests me. I can barely think of anything else', she wrote on 10 March 1939. Soon after graduating from high school that year she moved to Palestine, where she studied agriculture for two years. She then joined the kibbutz Sdot Yam, on the coast, where she worked in the kitchen and the laundry. But however committed she was to a Jewish homeland, she was still a very young woman, far from home. She was torn by doubt and guilt. Yom Kippur, or the Day of Atonement, is traditionally a time when Jews look back on the previous year and draw lessons for the next. On 30 September, the eve of the festival, in 1941 Hannah wrote of her doubts in her diary, and how she was thinking of her mother, Katalin, and brother, Gyuri. 'What's happening to them? Had I definitely known things would turn out like this, would I have left them? I think yes.' She could only ease her conscience with the hope that both would soon join her in Palestine.[3] Gyuri arrived in Palestine in January 1944. He and Hannah spent a joyous but poignant day together before she left for Egypt to commence her training. It would be the last time they saw each other.

Hannah's mission was a compromise. The Jewish Agency had requested that hundreds of Jewish soldiers be parachuted into Nazi-occupied territories to organise and carry out resistance. The British authorities in Palestine were in favour. London was not. Training a Jewish army would upset the Arab leadership in Palestine. But the War Office did allow a few dozen volunteers to work with the army, SOE and MI9, which organised the escape of POWs. Hannah and her group were trained in clandestine work, hand-to-hand combat, escape and evasion, parachuting and radio work. Each was promoted to officer status, to give some protection if captured, and they wore British Army uniforms. In theory they had a dual mission, to also help organise escape routes for Allied POWs. But for Hannah, the rescue of the Hungarian Jews was the overwhelming priority. Yoel Palgi, another Hungarian-speaking parachutist, had grown up in Cluj, Romania. He met Hannah after they had completed their training in Palestine and soon fell for her.

There was something enchanting, captivating in the way she sat, her long, pretty legs crossed, her hands resting gracefully on the little table. She was a soldier in the British Air Force and the blue-grey of her uniform matched her blue eyes. Her light-brown hair flowed in soft curls around her refined, elongated face; there was something delightfully harmonious about her.[4]

As the plane approached the dropping area the Germans opened up with anti-aircraft guns. Balls of fire rushed upwards, cutting through the night sky as the flak exploded around them. The crew opened the hatch. Eden jumped first, then the others. They all landed safely and a few minutes later Hannah sounded her whistle so they could meet. All were lucky to be alive. They had been dropped in a mountainous area, but heavy snow had cushioned their fall on the rocks, although Eden cracked his patella. They made their way to the house of a farmer, who put them up for the night.[5] But it would be almost three months until Hannah managed to cross into Hungary.

Where is spring, asked the *Népszava* columnist wistfully in the issue of Sunday, 19 March 1944. Like every Hungarian publication, the Social Democrat newspaper was subject to wartime censorship, but it was still publishing, a rare voice of liberalism in wartime Europe. Spring in Budapest usually had lots of signs: the shop window displays were changed, the ice-cream parlours reopened and winter coats were finally replaced. But none of those had happened yet. Instead, that March was as upended as a Budapest

April: one moment it wanted to snow, the next the sun was shining brightly. Sunday, 19 March was just four days after the national holiday on 15 March, marking the anniversary of the 1848 revolution. That uprising had been crushed and its leaders hanged by the Austrians. Lajos Kossuth, the leader of the brief period of freedom, had fled into exile. The newspaper carried several lengthy articles about Kossuth and his legacy. A quote from Kossuth recalled: 'The tyrant lives only for himself and living for himself loves to weaken the people, and to make them weak.' It was more telling than the editors had planned. By the time the newspaper went on sale the Germans had occupied Hungary. *Népszava* was immediately closed down. The newspaper would not publish again until late January 1945, after Budapest had fallen to the Russians.

The invasion also spelled the end of Operation Sparrow, which had finally gone ahead – with atrocious timing. On the night of Wednesday, 15 to Thursday, 16 March three OSS operatives boarded a Halifax bomber and parachuted into southwestern Hungary with a radio transmitter. Led by Colonel Florimond Duke, Operation Sparrow's aim was identical to that of the abortive SOE missions: to open negotiations with the government and engineer Hungary's defection from the Axis. None of the OSS officers could speak Hungarian, although at least one could speak German. After landing in a field the Americans buried their parachutes and radio set and walked to a nearby village. The locals greeted them with enthusiasm, believing that they were part of a much larger American force sent to liberate Hungary. The village ladies brought them ham, bacon, rolls and cakes – and served them hot tea and pálinka. Somehow word got back to Budapest and General Ujszászy that the Americans had arrived. After a while a man calling himself Major Kiraly, sent by Ujszászy, appeared.[6] Kiraly took the Americans to Budapest, where they were held in prison. They were well-treated and fed. The OSS men met Ujszászy on the evening of Friday, 17 March. The general had other matters on his mind, mainly the forthcoming and long inevitable German invasion. All the signs were there: troop movements, a build-up of forces on the Hungarian border, increased military chatter and activity. The OSS men wanted to speak to the foreign and defence ministers. Ujszászy told them that both men had left for Klessheim with Admiral Horthy to meet Hitler. They would be back in a couple of days. By then it would be too late.

Berlin knew all about Operation Sparrow. In Budapest, pro-Nazi officers in the Hungarian intelligence service had long been passing on the details of Ujszászy's shortwave conversations with the OSS to Wilhelm Höttl, the regional SD chief. 'I was well informed by Hungarian intelligence officers about all these negotiations and particularly about the liaison between Ujszaszi [Ujszászy] and the American colonel. I reported these happenings to Berlin. Now Hitler decided to act', Höttl recalled.[7] Höttl's intelligence, together with that provided by Ottó Hatz, the Hungarian military attache in Ankara who was also a German agent, helped make Hitler's mind up. Operation Sparrow, then, had exactly the opposite of its intended effect. Instead of extracting Hungary from the Axis, it infuriated Hitler, helped trigger his plan to invade Hungary and so helped turn the country into a Nazi puppet state.[8]

In Yugoslavia Hannah Szenes wept tears of grief, rage and frustration when she heard of the German invasion. She asked Dafni, 'What will happen to them … to the million Jews in Hungary? They are in German hands now and we're sitting here.'[9] It took ten days for Hannah and her companions to fight their way through German-controlled territory with the Partisans to their headquarters. When they arrived, the Partisan commander asked them to remove their Palestine patches from their uniforms. The Nazis had spread their propaganda that the Jews had caused the war, so it was better not to draw attention to their origins. Hannah, Dafni and the others were upset about this, but agreed. Between themselves they spoke Hebrew. When the Partisans asked what language they were speaking, they replied that it was Welsh. But Hannah's determination to cross the border did not waver.

Admiral Horthy arrived at Hitler's castle at Klessheim, Austria on the morning of Saturday, 18 March 1944. He was accompanied by General Szombathelyi, the chief of staff, and the foreign and defence ministers. The supposed reason for the meeting was to discuss Horthy's request to withdraw Hungary's troops from Ukraine and the general military situation. The actual reason was to ensure Horthy and the Hungarian leadership were out of the country when the Germans invaded. The Hungarians were virtually held hostage until the evening. Horthy's train eventually left Salzburg at 9.30 pm for the overnight journey. It would be his last meeting with the Nazi leader.

The invasion commenced in the early hours of Sunday. The Wehrmacht and the Luftwaffe quicky took control of the borders and strategic assets such as airports and railway stations. The Wehrmacht was not allowed to interfere in the Jewish question. That was the responsibility of several hundred Gestapo and SD agents under the command of Ernst Kaltenbrunner and a separate SS unit under the leadership of Adolf Eichmann. Kaltenbrunner, the head of the RSHA, was an Austrian lawyer who had joined the Nazi Party in 1931. A fanatical Nazi and Hitler loyalist, Kaltenbrunner had helped set up Mauthausen concentration camp near Linz, which would over the next few months receive large numbers of Hungarian Jews. Six foot four inches tall, his face scarred from student fencing duels, Kaltenbrunner was an intimidating, physically imposing figure. Eichmann, another Austrian, was less charismatic – and would eventually be famously described by Hannah Arendt, the German Jewish philosopher, as a bland bureaucrat who embodied the 'banality of evil'. But there was nothing banal about Eichmann. His sustained determination to murder Hungarian Jewry would drive his every decision.

Eichmann was a former salesman who had joined the Nazi Party and the SS in 1932. He quickly became an expert on Jewish issues, travelled to Palestine in 1937 and even learnt some Hebrew and Yiddish. After the Anschluss he moved to Vienna and took charge of Jewish emigration. Within two years nearly 100,000 Jews had left Austria legally and several thousand more illegally. After the RHSA was established in 1939 Eichmann was appointed head of the Department for Jewish Affairs. By 1942 there was no more talk of emigration. The Einsatzgruppen were massacring hundreds of thousands of Jews, Roma, Communists and others across Nazi-occupied Europe.

In January 1942 the Nazi leadership met at Wannsee and decided on the Final Solution. Europe's Jews would be corralled into ghettos, transported to camps and either gassed on arrival or be worked to death for German industry. Eichmann's department was responsible for implementing this. The Holocaust demanded detailed planning, logistical expertise and liaison with local authorities. By the time Eichmann arrived in Budapest the model had been finely honed. Eichmann was the Third Reich's pre-eminent expert on solving the Jewish question speedily and efficiently. As Braham notes, 'Eichmann was at the prime of his life. The prospects of liquidating Hungarian Jewry at lightning speed must have enticed him, for they were the last large relatively intact Jewish community of Europe.'[10]

Adolf Eichmann, a fanatical Nazi and central figure in the Holocaust, was determined to annihilate Hungarian Jewry.

Horthy's train stopped just outside Budapest on the morning of the invasion. Dietrich von Jagow, the German ambassador, appeared with his replacement, Edmund Veesenmayer. A career SS officer and fervent anti-Semite, Veesenmayer had served in Zagreb and Belgrade, where he had pushed for the strongest anti-Jewish policies. After lengthy periods in Hungary, he was now regarded as an expert. Already a close friend of Himmler, as Hitler's Reich plenipotentiary Veesenmayer was now immensely powerful. Péter Hain, Horthy's personal detective, who eight years earlier had accompanied the Prince of Wales on his visit to Budapest, then introduced Horthy to Ernst Kaltenbrunner. Hain was a traitor – a double agent who had been working for the Nazis since before the war.

Horthy was met by prime minister Kállay at the train station when they arrived in Budapest. He briefed Horthy as they drove to the palace. Twenty-two parliamentarians had been arrested and the police headquarters had been seized, together with the Astoria Hotel. The choice was ominous; the Astoria in downtown Pest was a short walk from the Great Synagogue and the headquarters of the Jewish community on nearby Síp Street. There were already German sentries at the palace gates but the car passed through into the courtyard. Once inside the building, Horthy convened the Crown Council. Kállay resigned. There were scattered shots here and there, but no real resistance against the Germans. Endre Bajcsy-Zsilinszky, the courageous anti-Nazi politician, opened fire on the Gestapo when they came to arrest him and was wounded. Bajcsy-Zsilinszky was taken into custody. Soon after the invasion a detachment of SS troops came to Kállay's residence at 6.00 am to arrest him. His guard managed to hold them off while the whole family escaped through a network of secret tunnels. Horthy gave the family sanctuary under his protection. The Turkish ambassador sent his car for Miklós Kállay, who moved into the embassy's residence. From that day the Turkish Embassy was surrounded by German armoured vehicles and lit by floodlights at night.[11]

The OSS men were woken at dawn on the morning of the invasion and brought to Ujszászy. They handed over their cipher pads and radio set and returned to their cells. Thankfully, they were in uniform, so the Geneva Conventions applied and according to the laws of war they should not be shot as spies. But the laws of war were no guarantee of anything where the Gestapo was concerned. The Americans were eventually handed over to the Germans and taken to Belgrade to be interrogated by Luftwaffe intelligence. Their story was that they planned to join the Partisans but had landed in the wrong place and so were captured by the Hungarians. It seemed the Luftwaffe believed them. They were put on a bus to be transported to a normal POW camp when the Gestapo appeared. The Americans were swiftly hauled off. Difficult times followed. The OSS men were moved around between Belgrade, Berlin and Budapest for continual interrogation until late June, when they were finally transferred to Colditz, the 'escape-proof' camp for high-value prisoners. All three survived and were eventually liberated by American troops in April 1945.[12]

On Monday afternoon, the day after the invasion, László Veress met his girlfriend, Laura-Louise, at Nyugati Station. His role as Kállay's envoy and his SOE contacts made him one of the Nazis' most wanted – Kaltenbrunner himself demanded his detention. Veress was exhausted from lack of sleep and stress. He had been fast asleep in the middle of the night on 18 March when the call came from the Foreign Ministry: get to the office as soon as possible. There were no taxis, so he ran up the steep streets of Castle Hill. Once inside the building the strong smell of burning was everywhere. Kállay had ordered that his office's papers and the secret files of the Foreign and Interior Ministries were to be destroyed, together with any codes. Veress spent the rest of the night incinerating the contents of the safes and filing cabinets. By the morning he was covered in soot, but the job had been done.

He then went home and packed a small bag very quickly. The SS had already appeared at the Foreign Office and he expected them to arrive at his apartment any minute. Veress's plan was to flee to his parents' house in Sepsisszentgyörgy, in Transylvania, and then somehow join the Partisans in Yugoslavia. But he had no idea when the next train was leaving and Nyugati Station was filled with SS and Nazi soldiers, watching for those people trying to leave the country. Veress still had a diplomatic passport, but that was now a danger rather than a protection. Thankfully, he was in time – the last train left in a few minutes. He and Laura-Louise hugged and quickly kissed goodbye. Veress boarded at the last moment as the guard sounded his whistle.

Later that day Laura-Louise went to Veress's flat, a brave if not foolhardy act. She wanted to check if he had left any incriminating papers there or other evidence of his contacts with the Allies. The Orion radio was still on, the remains of his breakfast on the kitchen table and the ashtray was full of cigarette butts. For a moment she was overwhelmed and lay down on the brass bed. Surely László would appear at any moment, call her 'Lolly', his nickname for her, and they would have coffee and cakes then go for a walk along the Danube, hand in hand. The sound of armoured vehicles outside suddenly brought her back to reality. She found his codebook, hidden in the laundry basket, and put it on the bookshelf – it was safer to hide it in plain sight. There were drafts of a coded message to SOE on the table. She tore them, mixed them with left-over food, poured water on top then turned them into a mulch. After packing up some clothes, she walked out with a suitcase and an oriental rug under one arm. Even more bravely, she returned the next day. The lock was broken and the door closed with an SS seal. She broke the seal, reasoning that the Nazis were unlikely to return so quickly, and went inside. The flat had been ransacked, the radio stolen and the mattress sliced open. Laura-Louise realised that she also needed to get out of Budapest. The Gestapo would likely have a file on her as well. She and her daughter, Dalma, quickly left to stay with friends in Transylvania.

17

Head of State in Absentia

A day in Yugoslavia was more dangerous than a year in
Hungary.

> Edmund Veesenmayer, German minister and
> Reich plenipotentiary in Budapest.

Countess Eduardina Zichy Pallavicini learnt that the Nazis had
invaded when her maid brought her breakfast tray in and informed
her that there were soldiers posted all over the Castle district. It
was not unexpected – other friends had already reported troop
movements at the border. Edina, as she was known, was Caja
Odescalchi's sister-in-law – her brother, György Pallavicini, was
married to Borbála Andrássy, Caja's sister. Born in 1877 into one
of Hungary's most influential aristorcratic dynasties, Edina lived
in style and luxury in a historic house built around a courtyard on
Werbőczy Street in the Castle, near the former British Legation
and residence. Edina's father Eduard had been a pillar of the
ruling establishment: a banker, businessman and member of the
Upper House of Parliament. The Zichys' extensive domestic staff
included cooks, maids, a footman, a driver, a laundress and a
stable-master for the eight horses. Edina was a well regarded
writer and translator and for ten years served as the editor of a
popular women's magazine. She had become a household name
in 1923 when her husband Rafael sued for divorce, accusing
her of having a lesbian affair with Cécile Tormay, an extreme
right-wing anti-Semitic writer and editor and close ally of
Admiral Horthy. The case scandalised and fascinated the country

– especially as Rafael had bugged Edina's bedroom and shared extraordinarily salacious details of their married sex life in court. The legal battle lasted four years but each court hearing refused Rafael's request for a divorce.[1] Twenty years later their mutual anger had long faded. They remained legally married, and were now simply friends. The previous day Edina and Rafael had enjoyed lunch together at the Gellért Hotel. Rafael had even brought her a small cigar to enjoy at the end of the meal, a safely scandalous gesture.

A sensitive and perceptive observer with a fine eye for detail, Edina was fluent in English, Italian, French, Spanish and German. She kept a diary from March 1944 to November 1945, written in English. A devout Catholic with a strong moral core and sense of social responsibility, Edina despised the Nazis and their Hungarian allies. The world of the Hungarian aristocracy was small and close-knit. Edina was close friends with Magdolna Horthy and had easy access to both the Regent and his wife. Edina's account of the spring and summer of 1944 and the subsequent siege, never before published, is a vivid and evocative portrayal of wartime Budapest, with unique insight into life, death and decision-making at the core of Hungary's ruling elite. The Gestapo's sweep through the city on 19 March had caught many of her friends. 'All this day one heard nothing but news of people having been arrested. Many of our friends left for the country', she wrote.

Two days later Edina went to see Magdolna Horthy with her son, Nandor. She found her in a terrible state, depressed and sobbing that her husband had been betrayed by accepting Hitler's invitation to Klessheim. Just before eight o'clock in the evening Horthy himself arrived, looking grim-faced. He explained that 'they' had accepted his conditions, so he had to name a government. Edina asked what these conditions were. The Germans would guarantee Hungary's sovereignty, leave within ten days and not force the Reichsmark to replace the *pengő*. Edina enquired who 'they' were – did that mean the army or the Gestapo? Horthy was indignant, replying, 'What Gestapo? There was no question of it.' 'The Gestapo which has arrested some of your ministers and most of our friends', she replied. There were few people in Hungary able, or willing, to confront Horthy with such sharp, uncomfortable truths. Horthy looked away. The footman soon announced that supper was served. Edina and Nandor left soon after. Hungary was finished, she told him.

The next day Horthy swore in the new prime minister and his cabinet. General Döme Sztójay was Hungary's former ambassador to Berlin. Pro-Nazi and of limited intelligence, he was an acceptable choice for Edmund Veesenmayer. Andor Jaross, the new minister of the interior, was a veteran extreme-right politician and a virulent anti-Semite. Together with his two key lieutenants, State

Countess Edina Zichy Pallavicini was a conservative-minded, devout Catholic and a staunch anti-Nazi.

Secretaries László Endre and László Baky, Jaross quickly began to implement plans for the extermination of Hungarian Jewry. Both Endre and Baky had taken part in the White Terror as part of the Szeged group of ultra-nationalists around Horthy in 1919 and 1920. It was Endre, well known for his virulent anti-Semitism, who had so unsettled Ilona Edelsheim Gyulai the previous year. Endre soon became one of Eichmann's most important allies. He so impressed him that Eichmann later joked that Endre 'wanted to eat the Jews with paprika'.

When Jaross asked Endre if he would be responsible for the Jewish question, Endre presented him with a thick file containing all the necessary draft laws.[2] The work had already been done. Baky, too, was consumed with hatred for Hungary's Jews. A former MP for the Arrow Cross, he left to join the Hungarian National Socialist Party and had long been an agent for the SD, the Nazi intelligence service. Unlike the Nazis, Endre and Baky did not bother with euphemisms like 'resettlement' or 'Special Treatment'. Baky declared after his appointment: 'I will make my job dependent on the final and total liquidation of left-wing and Jewish mischief in this country. I am sure that the government will be able to accomplish this overwhelming task which is of enormous historical importance.'[3]

Eichmann and his fellow SS officers stayed at the Astoria for a few days before setting up their headquarters at the Majestic Hotel on Sváb Hill. The Majestic was actually a block of serviced apartments, where residents were provided with meals and laundry if requested. Joel Brand had kept an apartment there but quickly fled after the Nazis arrived. For his residence Eichmann seized a large villa with spacious grounds at 13b Apostol Street in Buda. The owner, Lipót Aschner, an innovative Jewish industrialist who was the head of Tungsram, was immediately sent to Mauthausen. Jaross moved quickly to reorganise the police force. The political police department was renamed the State Security Police – Hungary's version of the Gestapo – and placed under the command of Péter Hain. Horthy's personal detective finally received his reward for his long and faithful service to the Nazis.

The section dealing with Jews was moved to the Majestic Hotel, one floor above Eichmann's office. The Hungarian Gestapo soon emulated its German namesake, not least in its plunder of Jewish wealth and artworks. Wilhelm Höttl's steady stream of intelligence about Hungary had proved most useful. The Nazis arrested not only prominent Jewish industrialists and bankers, but Christian politicians, journalists, civil servants, opposition figures and the governor of the National Bank. Ferenc Keresztes-Fischer, the pro-Allied minister of the interior, was arrested on 20 March and later deported to Mauthausen. So were Mihály and Gabriella Andrássy, with whom Howie had stayed at Szigetvár. With the liberal and aristocratic opposition decapitated, Hungary's Jews had lost their natural allies. There was nobody to stand up for them.

Horthy remained head of state – but he stayed silent as former allies, opponents and friends disappeared. Horthy's continued presence in the Royal Palace was crucial for the success of the Nazi takeover. Just by staying in place, he pacified the population and legitimised the Nazi occupation and the puppet Sztójay government. As Braham notes, Horthy's presence also placed the 'entire Hungarian state apparatus' in the hands of the Nazis, specifically Eichmann and his key Hungarian allies: Interior Minister Andor Jaross and his officials László Endre and László Baky. Horthy's continuance in office assured the maintenance of law and order and 'generated the development of a quisling spirit in the country'. After the war Vilmos Nagy, Kállay's defence minister, wrote in his memoir that had Horthy resisted, the country would have followed his leadership – and Hungary would have been seen after the war as a victim of the Nazis instead of as a willing ally.[4]

Horthy claimed in his memoir that after the occupation he was initially powerless. 'For a long time I was helpless before German influence, for, in Budapest and its vicinity, I lacked the means to check or thwart the joint actions of the Germans and the Ministry for Home Affairs.'[5] This is not true. Horthy had both the means and the stature to do so. He had ruled Hungary since 1920, an impressive record during a very turbulent era. For all his flaws, Horthy had kept Hungary unified and stable. Unlike

Czechoslovakia or Poland, the country still existed in a meaningful sense. For this he was immensely respected. Horthy could have rallied the anti-Nazi forces. Instead of going to the Royal Palace on the day of his return from Austria, he could have gone to the radio station and broadcast a clarion call to the nation to resist the Nazi occupiers. He could have simply refused to cooperate with the Germans, refused to form a new government and issued orders for the army to resist. He could even have shot himself, as Teleki had. It is true that much of the army high command was pro-Nazi, but most of the soldiers were Hungarian patriots, not German sympathisers. The Hungarian public would have listened to such a clarion call. But it was never made.

Horthy's other sin was also one of omission. By early 1944 it was clear that the Germans would sooner or later invade. Horthy had received reports in January that the Germans were concentrating troops on the border and around Vienna. When the Hungarians asked why this was happening, the Germans were dismissive, saying it was a purely German matter and that Vienna was a transport junction for the Balkans.[6] More precise intelligence came through around 10 March. József Antall, the senior government official dealing with the Poles, was warned by his Polish contacts that the Germans would soon occupy Hungary. Antall in turn informed Keresztes-Fischer, the interior minister, and his military contacts. Antall and his colleagues began calling their Hungarian and Polish contacts and advising them to flee, while destroying important or incriminating paperwork.[7] Their rapid, efficient response was in sharp contrast to that of Horthy and Kállay, who failed to act decisively or prepare a resistance plan.

The experience of other countries showed that when the Nazis met resistance to their plans to deport local Jews, they backed down. In Nazi-occupied Denmark the local authorities kept control over the legal system and police forces – rather like Hungary. But when the Nazi round-up began on 1 October 1943 there were barely any Jews to be found. A nationwide rescue operation had ferried 8,000 Danish Jews and their relatives to Sweden. The Danish authorities, including the police, simply refused to cooperate with the Germans. The churches and the royal family protested against the Nazi measures. Unlike Hungary, Denmark even protected its stateless Jewish refugees. When several hundred refugees – without Danish citizenship – were eventually deported to the Theresienstadt concentration camp in Czechoslovakia the Danish authorities continually demanded information about their living conditions and whereabouts. Most of them survived.[8]

Bulgaria's record was more mixed, but also showed that national leaders had room for manoeuvre. In March 1943 Bulgarian police and soldiers deported 11,000 Jews from territories they had occupied in Macedonia and Thrace. Almost all were killed in Treblinka. The Bulgarian government agreed to next deport 8,000 Jews from Sofia, the Bulgarian capital. But news of the planned deportations caused uproar. Opposition politicians, intellectuals and priests protested. After an intervention from the Metropolitan of the Bulgarian Orthodox Church, Tsar Boris cancelled the deportations in May 1943. About 20,000 Jews were then expelled from Sofia to the provinces, with males forced to work in forced-labour camps. But almost all of the Bulgarian Jewry survived. At the end of the war the community was still around 50,000 strong, the same as its pre-war level.

The contrast with Hungary is sharp. Kállay cowered in the Turkish Embassy. Horthy stood back and gave the Sztójay government a free hand. He signed most legislation adopted by the new government, except the torrent of anti-Jewish legislation which was issued by ministerial decree and so did not require his signature. After the war both Veesenmayer and Baky were put on trial – Veesenmayer at Nuremberg and Baky in Hungary. Veesenmayer stated: 'Horthy himself told me that he was interested only in protecting those prosperous, the economically valuable Jews in Budapest, those who were well off. The others could be sent to Germany for labour.' Baky claimed that Horthy had told him:

The Germans have cheated me. Now they want to deport the Jews. I don't mind. I hate the Galician Jews and the Communists. Out with them, out of the country. But you must see, Baky, that there are some Jews who are as good Hungarians as you and I ... I can't allow these to be taken away. But they can take the rest.[9]

Years later, Eichmann gave a long series of interviews to *Life* magazine. He recalled:

It was clear to me that I, as a German, could not demand the Jews from the Hungarians. We had had too much trouble with that in Denmark. So I left the entire matter to the Hungarian authorities. Dr. Endre, who became one of the best friends I have had in my life, put out the necessary regulations, and Baky and his Hungarian gendarmerie carried them out. Once these two secretaries gave their orders, the Ministry of the Interior had to sign them. And so it was no miracle that the first transport trains were soon rolling towards Auschwitz.[10]

On the afternoon of 19 March Himmler telephoned his officials in Budapest to ask about the incarceration of prominent Hungarian Jews. The answer did not please him. Two hundred people with Jewish-sounding names were quickly picked at random from the telephone book, arrested and sent to Mauthausen. Meanwhile, two members of Eichmann's unit, Hermann Krumey and Dieter Wisliceny, appeared at the Budapest Jewish community's headquarters at 12 Síp Street. Both were experienced mass killers. Wisliceny had worked on the deportation and murder of Jewish communities in Slovakia and Greece. The two SS officers ordered the community leadership to gather the next day at 10.00 am.

The Nazis knew that the Jewish Councils, known as the Zsidó Tanács in Hungarian and Judenrat in German, were key to organising the genocide. The councils were to be composed of community leaders and rabbis. They were responsible for the execution of the Nazis' orders, including instructions for deportation and as for housing and conditions in the ghettos. As Braham notes, 'The Nazis assigned a crucial role to the Jewish Councils, turning them into involuntary accessories to German crimes.'[11] The role of the councils remains one of the most contested, controversial and sensitive aspects of Holocaust history. Their defenders argue that they were powerless and operating in conditions of abject terror. By carrying out the Nazis' orders and negotiating with them when possible, the councils protected their communities as best they were able for as long as they could. Their critics dismiss such arguments. They accuse the council members of collaboration in the slaughter of their own communities, sometimes to save themselves and their families. In Budapest the Jewish Council would play a central role in the catastrophe of the Hungarian Jewry, so much so that there were attempts to put several surviving members on trial after the war for collaboration.

The Jewish leaders met at Síp Street the next morning. After asking the Hungarian authorities for advice, they had been told to obey the Germans' orders, so they obediently did. Some of the Jewish notables brought small bags, assuming they were about to be deported. Krumey told them that from now the Germans would have complete control over all Jewish matters. But they were not to worry – nobody was going to be arrested or deported or even lose their properties. Instead, they must establish a Jewish Council. All members would receive a special immunity certificate. Life would continue as normal, even religious life. The Council was to prepare detailed reports on the organisations, structure and holdings of the Jewish communities. The Council's responsibility was to keep the community calm and stop any signs of panic and hysteria. The Jewish leaders were so desperate to believe him that some took his words at face value. The issuance of 250 immunity certificates, signed by the German and Hungarian police, also helped.

The Central Council of Hungarian Jews was formed on 21 March. It had eight members, representing the main strands of Judaism: Orthodox, the more modern Neolog, Status Quo and the Zionists. The Central Council would rarely meet in full. Power rested with Samu Stern, the president of the Pest Jewish community, who often took ad-hoc decisions as he saw fit. Stern was the natural choice. He was a successful, prosperous businessman who knew Horthy well, and had intervened with him several times on Jewish affairs. Stern was a counsellor of the Hungarian Royal Court, a cautious, legalistic establishment figure, well connected to the aristocratic and conservative political elite.

On 23 March, four days after the German invasion, the first censored issue of *A Magyar Zsidók Lapja* (*The Journal of Hungarian Jews*) appeared with an appeal from the Jewish Council. Its placid, obedient, reassuring content could have been written by Eichmann himself. Everyone should work and carry out their duties, while Jewish religious, social and cultural life would continue. Nobody would be arrested for being Jewish. No Jews could travel in or out of Budapest or change their address without permission – all such requests must be submitted through the Jewish Council. 'We emphasise the need for strict and conscientious adherence to all these regulations. Only by following the rules can it be possible for everyone to pursue his civilian life within the permitted framework.'[12]

Five days later, Samu Stern summoned the leaders of the provincial Jewish communities to Síp Street to set up a new national organisation for Hungarian Jewry. Most returned home to follow Sándor Leitner, the leader of the community in Nagyvárad, northern Transylvania, returned home to follow Stern's placatory, calming line. Samu Stern and other Jewish leaders met Eichmann at the Hotel Majestic at the end of the month. By now it was clear that Krumey's promises were all lies. A stream of new anti-Jewish edicts were being issued. Non-Jews were forbidden from working in Jewish households, Jewish lawyers, civil servants, journalists, actors and theatre workers were dismissed, while car ownership had to be declared. Stock and commodity traders were dismissed. Thousands of Jews had been arrested, many to be interned at a makeshift concentration camp at Kistarcsa, on the northern outskirts of Budapest. Built for 200 political prisoners, it soon held 2,000 people. The media, now German-controlled, were pouring out a stream of hateful anti-Jewish propaganda.

The Germans had started issuing demands for goods and requisitioning property. The Jewish leadership was eager to cooperate, believing this would buy German goodwill. When one of Eichmann's officials asked for a piano, he was offered eight. He replied that he simply wished to play the instrument, not open a shop. German demands ranged from hundreds of mattresses and blankets, buckets and brooms, to luxury items for officers such as silverware, paintings and cars. The arrival of the Germans triggered an immediate bank run by Jewish customers, desperate to withdraw their funds and empty their safe deposit boxes. The next day, after a request from the Germans, Hungarian banks limited all withdrawals to 1,000 *pengős* and sealed safe deposit boxes. When the endless German demands for goods – from kitchen furniture to Old Master paintings – could no longer be met, the Nazis and their Hungarian allies simply plundered whatever they needed or wanted.

The Yellow Star was to be compulsory from 5 April. Eichmann explained to Stern and the others that the stars must be uniform, factory-made and issued by the Jewish Council. László Endre would handle the matter of fabric supply. Each star should cost three *pengős*. When the Jewish leaders responded that there were many poor families with children who could not afford that much, Eichmann replied that rich Jews could pay for them.[13] That same day László Endre gave a radio interview, assuring his listeners that the new anti-Jewish regulations were just the start of the solution of the Jewish question in Hungary.[14] On 5 April, Rezső Kasztner and Joel Brand of the Vaada met with Wisliceny and others to open negotiations. Wisliceny said the price for saving Hungary's Jews was $2 million, with an immediate down payment of $200,000 in *pengős*, to be paid at the black-market rate, around 6.5 million *pengős*. Kasztner then went to Samu Stern and other Jewish Council leaders. Believing, wrongly, that such tactics had worked in Slovakia, the Jewish leaders agreed to raise the money. A couple of weeks later, 3 million *pengős* were delivered, then another 2.5 million on 21 April.

But by then it was clear that the Nazis' promises were worthless. The Jews of eastern Hungary were already being forced into ghettos. The money poured into the Hotel Majestic and the trains, crammed full with Hungary's Jews, were soon en route to Poland. Throughout the next months, Stern and the Jewish leadership believed they could play for time. But there was no time. Aided by his Hungarian henchmen, Eichmann knew exactly what to do and how to do it. The Jewish Council's role was to help maintain order and calm among its fearful co-religionists – which it did with a tragic degree of success.

18

A Wave of Arrests

Society ought to do something, one cannot just submit to everything.

Edina Zichy Pallavicini, 6 April 1944.

In the early hours of 19 March, as news came through of the German invasion, several Polish Red Cross workers rushed to the Andrássy Palace and began burning documents. Throughout the war the palace had remained a centre of Polish and anti-Nazi resistance, home to the Polish Co-ordinating Committee, the Polish Red Cross and the Polish Medical Centre. With the support and tolerance of the Hungarians, the Polish organisations had strengthened and grown over the years. The Poles had their own schools, community groups, social and medical services, and even a newspaper, *Wieści Polskie*. Polish POWs lived comparatively freely at the Zugliget camp. The resistance ran a courier service to London and Poland and a clandestine radio network. Henrik Slawik, the president of the Polish Co-ordination Committee, worked with József Antall, who remained in a senior position at the Ministry of the Interior.

Within a few hours the Poles' highly effective system of mutual aid and humanitarian support, carefully nurtured over several years, was destroyed. Berlin's agents had prepared extensive dossiers on the Polish organisations. The Gestapo knew almost everything when they arrived: the names, aliases and addresses of the Polish leaders, the structure and activities of their organisations, even the aliases the Hungarians had given the Poles.[1] The SS and Gestapo immediately occupied the Andrássy Palace. Polish medical staff and patients were shot dead.[2] The Gestapo and the SS raided every Polish organisation, including the Polish library and the offices of *Wiesci Polskie*. Hundreds of Poles were arrested. Many were summarily executed or sent to Mauthausen. Unfortunately, officials at KEOKH, the government office that controlled foreigners resident in Hungary, had not destroyed its lists. These were captured by the Gestapo and led to a fresh wave of arrests. A catastrophic error by Edmund Fietowicz, the representative of the Polish government-in-exile in London, also cost lives. Fietowicz had been called at 5.00 am by a contact in the Hungarian Foreign Ministry, warning that the Germans had crossed the border. Fietowicz should destroy every document then disappear. Unfortunately, he was still in his office in the afternoon when the Gestapo arrived – together with many documents which he had packed up rather than destroyed.

József Antall was also burning documents at dawn. He too was arrested on the day of the invasion and sent to the prison on Fő Street in Buda. Antall was one of hundreds of prisoners rounded up, including Hungarians, Poles, British and French. He was a category-one prisoner, the most serious, held in solitary confinement. Antall was not allowed to talk to other prisoners or receive books. His cell was searched every week. He was imprisoned for weeks and regularly interrogated, but stuck rigidly to his story: he had only helped the Poles with humanitarian and welfare assistance. He knew nothing about escape routes or soldiers fleeing to Yugoslavia. Henryk Slawik listened to Antall's warning and went into hiding near Lake Balaton. Slawik was one of the Gestapo's most wanted. He knew many details of the relationships between the Poles, their Hungarian protectors and the Hungarian ministries with whom they worked.

Erzsébet Szapáry took refuge in the Turkish Embassy, where Miklós Kallay was still hiding. On his last evening of freedom Erzsébet's brother, Antal, had dinner with Edina Zichy Pallavicini. He was 'very nervous', hoping that his position in the Red Cross and connection to Ilona Horthy would save him from arrest. They did not, and he was sent to Mauthausen. Some of those detained in Budapest were later released and their accounts of their treatment were 'horrible', wrote Edina. The prisoners were constantly threatened with machine-pistols, were not allowed to move and had to stand or sit facing the wall for hours. The main problem was that there was no one person or office to apply to for news of the prisoners and to bring them clothes and food. 'Now people disappear and you did not know where to', she wrote. Yet even in these times, her sense of duty endured. 'In spite of feeling as if we were doomed and there is no way out of this impasse, life has to go on and one must attend to all one's obligations as if everything were all right', she wrote on 21 March. Three days later Margit Keresztes-Fischer, the wife of the former interior minister, held a meeting of her welfare committee. She had once been surrounded by hangers-on. But now that her husband had been sent to Mauthausen, nobody attended. A few days later Edina went to see her, and found her 'very much astonished at my coming'.

Colonel Utassy moved quickly to protect the POW camps that were now holding British, Dutch, French and Polish soldiers. He issued an order that all the camps were to be sealed off and placed under the protection of the Hungarian Army. Utassy knew Lieutenant General Hans Greiffenberg, the German military attache in Hungary. Colonel Utassy asked him to ensure that the POWs were treated correctly. Greiffenberg, who later became the Wehrmacht commander in Hungary, was helpful. He persuaded the SS that there was no need to send the Allied POWs to Germany. For the moment, the POWs were reasonably safe.

As József Antall burnt his papers, Sándor Szent-Iványi woke Charles Howie and told him the Germans had invaded. Howie quickly packed his few possessions and his radio set and crossed the river to Buda. He knew he was high on the Gestapo's arrest list, but luckily they looked for him at another Unitarian building and did not arrive at the flat until Monday. That gave Szent-Iványi vital time to destroy his documents. He went to the Ministry of Defence and reported that Howie had escaped. This was recorded but meant that as Howie was no longer a registered POW, he had no salary or ration coupons. When the Gestapo finally arrived, Sándor himself had gone into hiding.

With nowhere else to go, Howie went to Jane Radyszkiewicz's house near Zugliget. Jane bravely agreed to hide the Polish radio set and let Howie stay for a short while. But as word came through that numerous Poles were being shot on sight or arrested by the Germans, Jane asked Truus Harff, a Dutch lady who lived nearby, to host Howie. Truus was already hosting Jane's mother, and agreed. Jane knew that she was certainly on a list as well, and would soon be visited by the Germans. Once she had moved Howie, Jane called Colonel Merkly of Hungarian intelligence. Merkly said he had told the Nazis that Jane was working for him, and her name was not on the arrest list. But there was no guarantee this would work in the long term. Howie was safe, at least for now. The Harffs lived in a large villa, shielded from the road by a hedge. Howie moved into the basement. But it was a very different life to his time at Zugliget, with his friendly Hungarian guard. It was extremely dangerous to leave the house. Life at the Harffs' was boring, nerve-wracking and lonely, leavened with guilt at the knowledge that he was endangering both Jane and the Harffs.

One day in late spring Howie was sitting on the terrace reading when two men in civilian clothes arrived. They rang the bell and asked to speak to Jane, who was visiting her mother. Howie quickly made his way to his hiding place in the roof. The two men entered the house and told Jane they had come to arrest her. She asked them to call their superior and make sure they were in the right place. At that moment an air-raid siren sounded. Telephone calls were forbidden during an air-raid. The two men searched the house. Thankfully they failed to find Howie's razor – which Jane had hidden in her pocket – and checked everyone's papers. Eventually they left. Howie spent some of his days writing up a long report of recent events, which he buried in the garden. But he knew he could not stay at the Harffs' for much longer.[3]

*

Now that Hungary was occupied by the Germans, its understanding with the Allies was over. British and American bombers raided Hungary repeatedly at the start of April. The bombs mainly hit transport hubs and industrial sites such as the Manfred Weiss works on Csepel Island in southern Budapest. Ferencváros in District IX, a working-class quarter of Budapest, was badly hit. Ilona Edelsheim Gyulai was called to help with the many casualties. She gathered some of István's clothes to give away. It was hard, but she forced herself. 'I wondered why it hurt so much to let them go. It was as if they were a part of Pista, his clothes still contained the essence of his personality.' When Ilona was not nursing, she took refuge with her son, István, during air raids in the huge network of tunnels under the Royal Palace. Miklós Horthy had asked that if the air-raid sirens sounded all family members should head back to the palace and shelter underground. Ilona could not always do this – she only left her patients once they had been led into the hospital shelter. Once, on the way back from the hospital, she saw a raid on the Pest side. She was transfixed. 'I could see the planes and the falling bombs and hear the loud explosions. I was surprised not to find it at all frightening; in fact I have to admit it was fascinating sight.'[4]

The Nazis used the air raids to force the Jewish Council into a new level of collaboration. They immediately demanded that the Council requisition 500 apartments for bombing victims. If the Council failed to provide the apartments, the authorities would pick them themselves and kick the Jewish residents out, with their belongings. Those thrown out of their homes had to leave behind adequate bedding, furniture, linen, kitchenware and so on for the new inhabitants. Requisition units were formed of two Jewish representatives, a policeman and a Christian teacher. As soon as the first requisition units were despatched a new order came through for a further 1,000 apartments. Eventually, 1,500 apartment keys were gathered and deposited at City Hall. All of this caused extreme distress to those Jews who had, with barely any notice, been thrown out of their homes. These dispossessions were merely a foretaste of what was to come.

By now it was clear that the Yellow Star was the first stage of separating Hungary's Jews from their homeland and Christian neighbours. Enough Polish, Slovak and other Jewish refugees had made their way to Budapest and reported on the tragic fates of their communities. What followed – ghettoisation, transportation and extermination – were well known to a good part of the Hungarian Jewish leadership. Yet still they continued to obediently do Eichmann's bidding, unwilling or unable to believe that a similar fate could occur to Hungary's proudly patriotic and loyal Jews. The Council ordered their co-religionists to wear the Yellow Star in all public places and workplaces. The star was to be sewn on firmly, clearly visible and uncovered by scarves or collars.

Mária Mádi watched, appalled, as the state turned on its Jews. 'They are sick with shame and fear', she wrote in her diary on 31 March. 'They may be set out for any brutality.' The following day she recorded that a Jewish neighbour, Erwin Natyler, had died suddenly. Natyler had been ill, but Mádi believed that he had committed suicide. His manservant found him dead in his chair, his Bible in his lap. Natyler 'would not survive the Yellow Star and other humiliations. An honest man passed away with him.' The anti-Jewish measures were causing a pro-Jewish reaction, she wrote on 2 April. Parallel with the official anti-Semitic propaganda, 'a real philosemitic wave' was arising. People were switching off the radio when the propaganda began, 'and do whatever they can for Jews and try to be extremely nice to them'. For others, the Yellow Star signalled open season on Budapest's Jews. Police and Arrow Cross thugs soon stopped random Jews in the streets and ran spot checks on the stitching. If the star was too loose and they could force a pencil behind it, or it was the wrong kind of yellow or shape, or conformed to any imagined infraction, the Jewish person wearing it was arrested and interned.[5]

More anti-Jewish regulations soon followed. Jews were forbidden from wearing school or military uniforms, using public baths or swimming pools, or eating in restaurants, cake shops or cafés. Jews were required to list and declare the current value of all their property by 30 April and were only allowed to withhold goods worth 10,000 *pengős* – by then worth around $300. Nothing valuable, such as rugs, paintings or silverware, could be included in that sum. All Jewish-owned shops and firms were closed and their stocks and goods were inventoried. Jews could not buy veal or pork and were only allowed 100 grams of beef or horsemeat a week and 30 grams of sugar a month. 'It is a new blow everyday', wrote Mária Mádi on 22 April. 'Yesterday it was their business, today it is their rations ... Don't think me sentimental because I am so terribly sick of these things. It is true, I am very sorry for my friends, but the chief reason is this state of lawlessness we are living in. It is only a matter of time and these things may happen to us.'

At the prison on Fő Street József Antall was interrogated every two or three weeks. The interrogators insisted that the Poles had already explained that he was deeply involved in the military escape routes. All Antall had to do was admit his role and explain how it worked, and he could go home. He knew this was a lie and also that it was crucial that he did not change his story. As Antall and his colleagues had diligently burnt the Interior Ministry records, there was no way for the Gestapo to prove that he had been working with the Polish resistance. One day he was allowed out into the inner courtyard for exercise. The prisoners were moving in a circle, in the centre of which sat the prison director, watching. Some were moving very slowly as they had been tortured. Others were jogging. Among the walkers Antall saw his closest colleague, Henryk Slawik, who had been caught by the Gestapo. The other strollers included the editor of *Népszava*, Endre Bajcsy-Zsilinszky, the opposition MP who had opened fire on the Gestapo and Lipót Baranyai, the former governor of the National Bank, who had been in contact with Allen Dulles in Berne.

Antall joined the runners. As he passed Slawik he quickly asked what he had told the Germans. Slawik answered when Antall passed by the second time: nothing, you only helped with social and welfare issues. You knew nothing about escape routes. After that the two men continued communicating by tiny written notes. They were passed back and forth at mealtimes by those working on the kitchen detail. Eventually the Gestapo brought Antall and Slawik together in an interrogation room. Slawik had been beaten and tortured but gave nothing away. He stuck to his story: Antall had worked solely on welfare and humanitarian issues. It worked. Antall was eventually released. Antall recalled in his memoir that he did not like running, but that run in the courtyard of the Fő Street prison brought a great prize: his life. But Slawik lost the race. He was sent to Mauthausen, where he was executed in late August. His wife, Jadwiga, was caught by the Gestapo and sent to Ravensbrück. Somehow Krysia managed on her own at Lake Balaton and was eventually reunited with her mother, who survived.[6]

Away from Síp Street and the Jewish Council, wartime Budapest steadily adjusted to the new order. The Jews were cowed and terrorised. Much of the anti-Nazi political elite was either imprisoned, deported to Mauthausen or other camps or in hiding. Mádi's friends, and others, may have rallied around their Jewish acquaintances, but most Hungarians were not involved in any kind of resistance activities. Everyday people went to work, kept their heads down and tried to provide for their families. Restaurants, cafés, theatres, nightclubs and cinemas stayed open. The black market thrived. In Budapest, like every city at war, every luxury was available for those with money and connections. The café and restaurant terraces were open once more, often filled with SS and German Army officers spending freely. The churches were crowded on Sundays, although most priests had little, if anything, to say about the Jews. But the lack of resistance did not mean that the Germans were universally popular. 'Working men are grumbling against Gerry's arrival and plundering', wrote Mádi on 2 April. 'Shops – except for German soldiers – are rather empty, business is killed.'

The Nazi occupation of Hungary was a unique construct. The façade and illusion of independence was crucial for Germany. Edmund Veesenmayer was immensely powerful but he was Germany's representative, not a governor like Hans Frank in Poland. Hungary retained its own currency and a government with some powers. The Nazis needed Hungary's cooperation. Hungary's supply of foodstuffs and other goods and secure passage for oil coming northwards from the Balkans were vital. Admiral Horthy remained as head of state. He was rarely seen in public and adopted a low profile but for many Hungarians was a calming, reassuring presence that legitimised the occupation. The Council of Ministers met regularly to pass legislation. The Nazis especially needed Hungary's cooperation in implementing the Final Solution. The three key figures organising the anti-Jewish drive and deportations were Andor Jaross, the interior minister, and his henchmen László Endre and László Baky – all Hungarian, not German, officials. The Gestapo added a new layer of fear, but Hungary had long had its own secret police. Hungarians well knew to be careful about what they said to each other and whom to trust.

Edina Zichy Pallavicini was watching the lack of resistance with mounting horror and frustration. She wanted to fight back, to 'start some line of action against the arbitrary imprisonment of so many people and the ill treatment and deportation of the Jews that has been starting everywhere', she wrote on 6 April. That evening she went to visit Magdolna Horthy. She tried to persuade Magdolna that her husband should resign and not stand by as such 'horrible laws' were being enacted. If he did not have enough power to oppose the Germans, then at least he should not cooperate and 'allow such notorious Nazis like Endre and Baky to occupy responsible and important posts'. A few days earlier Edina's son, Nandor, had met Admiral Horthy to bring important news: he and some others had access to a small aeroplane hidden in the countryside. They could fly him, or Miklós Kállay or Count Bethlen, to a neutral country to form a government-in-exile and start political action against the Nazis from abroad. None of these three took up the offer. Magdolna explained to Edina that they were continually watched and their telephone was tapped. They sent messages out through one of the footmen. Horthy himself appeared later that evening, looking 'tired and dejected'.

Numerous publications had been closed down, but *Pesti Hirlap*, a city newspaper, was still publishing, albeit under firm

Nazi control. The front page of Saturday, 14 April's edition had a lengthy report about British air raids on Budapest. Other articles covered the importance of knowing the black-out rules, Easter in Jerusalem and new regulations governing Jewish-owned pharmacies. Beyond the war Budapest was still a city of culture. Music lovers could listen to performances of Beethoven or Mozart. The Scala Cinema was showing the much-anticipated *Machita*. Katalin Karády's new film had premiered a couple of days earlier to great excitement. Despite her known liberal and pro-Jewish sympathies, Karády remained enormously popular among many Hungarians – apart from those on the far right. She was the country's most glamorous actress, whose fine-boned face and smoky voice were instantly recognisable, although by the time *Machita* opened she had given up acting, in protest at the treatment of Jews in the entertainment business.

The newspaper's critic, doubtless aware of Karády's sensitive public profile, gave *Machita* a mixed review. He praised its restrained story-telling and attractive camera-work but opined that Karády's male co-stars delivered better performances than the female lead. Karády played a classic role – a seductive nightclub dancer and spy, sent by a hostile power to Hungary to obtain the plans for a new anti-aircraft gun. She has three engineers in her sights; two fall quickly for her charms. But the third, György, proves stubbornly patriotic and resistant, although he eventually succumbs. They travel together to hand over the plans to Machita's contacts. Then the tables turn: Machita realises she has fallen for György. She refuses to give the documents to her fellow spies. They shoot her and she dies in György's arms.[7]

Such melodrama aside, the film had a powerful resonance for what was about to unfold. Karády, her lover, General Ujszászy, and his colleague, Colonel Kádár, were all now in grave danger. Berlin ordered that the two spy chiefs be made to pay for their treasonous attempts to make Hungary change sides – and especially for their key roles in Operation Sparrow. Veesenmayer had called for Ujszászy and Kádár to be immediately arrested. Both men and Karády were taken into custody at dawn four days later.[8] Karády was brought to the Gestapo headquarters at the Mirabell Hotel on Sváb Hill in Buda, close to the Majestic, where Eichmann had his offices. She was taken to a room on the third floor, locked inside and left there for hours with nothing to eat or drink. At five in the afternoon she was taken to the office of Otto Klages, a high-ranking SS officer and the head of the SD in Hungary.

Karády explained who she was, that *Machita* was now playing, with posters for it all over the city. Klages was not interested. At first he sounded reasonable. He asked her where her secret radio transmitter was. Karády replied she did not have one. Klages asked her about her left-wing friends. Karády replied that she did not deal with politics. Klages screamed abuse at her and punched her in the face. Karády was then taken to the police station on Zrinyi Street, in District V. There she was put into a filthy cell that was infested with bed-bugs. Within a few minutes she felt them crawling all over her body. After five days there without food she was covered with bites. Her skin itched and burned. She could no longer stand.

On the eighth day she was taken back to the prison on Gyorskocsi Street, where she was again held alone in a cell. Warders held up her up as they fed her soup as she was too weak to hold the bowl. Karády was then taken to Klages again. He screamed more insults at her, punched her in the face and kicked her repeatedly. She was taken back to Gyorskocsi Street prison, where she was held for weeks. There she was starved, beaten, had her teeth knocked out and was threatened with execution. Shots rang out every night as prisoners were killed in the courtyard. Thanks to a sympathetic cleaner Ujszászy managed to smuggle letters to her in the prison. One day Klages and two other Nazi officers searched Karády's cell and found the letters. She was taken back to the Mirabell Hotel. Klages and the two other officers held her by her hair and dangled her out of the window. By now Karády was skin and bone. She fainted.

Ujszászy and Kádár had better protection. Their incarceration angered Horthy. The imprisonment of Hungary's two most important intelligence officers by the Germans was a national humiliation. Admiral Horthy repeatedly demanded that the two men be released. Eventually, in June, Ujszászy and Kádár were set free. Ujszászy was taken into Hungarian protective custody and sent to a Hungarian Army hospital. He was in poor mental shape after his captivity, made worse by the Allied air raids. After one especially intense bombing he suffered a nervous collapse.[9] Karády stayed imprisoned for about three months. When she was finally released her flat had been stripped of its carpets, paintings and furniture. She had to report to the police once a week and was vilified in the press. But she was alive.[10]

19

Warnings Ignored

I insist, I do have a right to live and I want to live!!! Not
marked, not with a star.

Judit Ornstein's diary entry, April 1944.

Judit Ornstein spent much of 13 April, the day of the heavy air raid,
sheltering in the cellar of the Jewish children's home where she lived
on Damjanich Street, not far from the City Park. Judit was born in
the small town of Hajdúnánás, in northeastern Hungary, in 1926.
She had moved to Budapest the previous year to train as a dental
technician. The Hajdúnánás community was typical of provincial
Hungarian Jewry, with two synagogues and a thriving middle class
of doctors, shopkeepers and businessmen. Judit's father, Lajos, was
a businessman but had lost his job because of the Jewish laws and
instead worked as a bookkeeper and financial adviser. Her mother,
Frieda, was a highly intelligent woman and a homemaker. Judit had
three young brothers, Zoltán, Tibor and László, and one older sibling,
Pál. The Ornstein home was not especially well-off financially, but
it was rich in literature and culture. Pál had been living in Budapest
since the start of the war, studying at the Rabbinical Seminary on
Rökk Szilárd Street. He had a fine time, exploring the city and the
Buda Hills with his friends. Like many of his fellow students, Pál
was not especially religious but the seminary offered an easy way to
gain a higher education, as the universities were closed to Jews. The
seminary was not far from Judit's workplace and they met often.
They went to the cinema together and Pál often visited her at the
home, sharing the Friday-night Shabbat dinner.

On 29 March, ten days after the Nazi invasion, Judit had started keeping a diary. Her chronicle, written in the form of a 'Dear diary', is an evocative first-hand record of events in 1944, written from the perspective of a perceptive and sensitive young woman with a rich literary talent. It took Judit a while to settle. She shared a dormitory with eleven other girls and at first they were not especially welcoming. But Judit was a warm and outgoing person and soon made friends. She became especially close to Klára néni, Auntie Klára, who ran the home and who quickly became a substitute mother for the homesick young girl. Judit's first entry was a copy of a letter she had sent to the rabbi who served the home. The air raids which intensified after the Nazi invasion had led Judit to 'ponder the prospect of death more and more', but thanks to the teachings of the rabbi, and Maimonides, a medieval Jewish scholar, she was 'starting to make friends with it'. Judit may have had a girlish crush on the rabbi, as his picture stood on her night table. She noted the introduction of the Yellow Star on 5 April and the festival of Passover, a few days later. The Seder, the festive meal, took place at the home without any disturbances. But Judit missed her parents intensely, thinking of her mother, Freda, lighting the Passover candles and her father saying a blessing over her three little brothers.

The air raid of 13 April – as the Hungarian newspapers reported – was heavy. Sitting in the cramped, dark cellar as the bombs exploded above ground, Judit was assailed with overpowering waves of emotions: fear of dying, immense love for her family, a terrible homesickness mixed with relief that her family was safe from the bombs. 'Above us, the thundering music of cannons. My God! My fervently beloved Father and Mother! You are my every thought. My dear little Laci, Zoli, Tibi! The thought that you are at home fills me with joy, my dear little brothers.'[1] A few days later, on 16 April, Judit wrote in her dairy again, her entry full of the surging emotions that shaped the life of a teenage Jewish girl in Nazi-occupied Budapest.

Well, yes, we are 'Jews!' We are stamped with a star but I can assure you, we are 'proud Jews'. Despite it all, we have found a small place where we can breathe freely: this is the 'small courtyard'. Here I feel at home, as if I were playing with my brothers. Around me the trees are blossoming: next to me is 'new life'.

Like Hannah Szenes, Judit was also a talented poet. In 'To the Deadly Spring', she writes of the joy and pain of spring in wartime, when 'golden sunshine' penetrates her soul, even though she is in pain everywhere.

> *But you, spring sunshine,*
> *Break through the pain,*
> *You turn souls to gold,*
> *Shine, go on shining!*

The poem ends with a haunting plea from her shelter during an air raid.

> *I hugged you tightly to me*
> *When we sat in the cellar's dark side*
> *From the evil of man, trying to hide*
> *Above us, cannons thunder and churn*
> *My God, please let Joy and Peace return.*

At the end of the month Aunt Klára had bad news. All books by Jewish authors had to be surrendered for destruction. 'Barbarism, barbarism that reaches to the sky? Don't you hear it, my God', wrote Judit on 30 April. At the beginning of May the young rabbi who had been serving the home was called up for labour service. For a while Judit's brother, Pál, took over at the Friday-night dinners. He and his fellow students even managed to graduate that month, in a ceremony attended by the Hungarian minister of education. Pál had thought about running away or obtaining Aryan documents. One of his peers had gone underground, obtained false papers and posed as a Protestant minister. Pál had a certificate from the Ministry of the Interior that he was exempt from the labour service. When he was called up for the labour service he attended and presented the document. For Jews in Budapest in 1944 it was always a mistake to answer official summons. The officer tore up the paper. Pál was conscripted. He said goodbye to his younger sister, neither knowing that they would never meet again.

The Hungarian Holocaust was organised in concentric circles. The ghettoisation and deportation began in the outer regions, then moved steadily into central Hungary. The final stage would be the deportation of the 250,000 or so Jews of Budapest, the largest surviving community in Europe. For the Nazis it was vital that the trains north to Auschwitz did not pass through areas where Jews were still living, otherwise the transports might have sparked panic. The German invasion rapidly dispelled the illusions of the Jewish leadership that they were somehow safer than the Jews of neighbouring countries. Their secondary set of illusions, that they had allies, was also quickly vapourised. Their friends in the conservative-aristocratic group that had previously exerted power and influence were immediately targeted by the Nazis. Leading figures such as the interior minister, Ferenc Keresztes-Fischer, were arrested and sent to Mauthausen. The leftist opposition and trade unions were shown as powerless. There was no workers' movement ready to stand in solidarity. Admiral Horthy simply stepped aside and turned his face to the wall, completely abnegating his responsibility as head of state.

But perhaps most shocking of all was the response – or lack of one – of the Jews' Christian friends and neighbours, especially in the provinces, to the deportations. Most non-Jewish Hungarians did not know about the reality of Auschwitz. They likely believed the official lies that the Jews were being relocated for physical labour. But even if that were true, their lives were being cruelly uprooted, their communities destroyed. Harsh penalties for hiding or helping Jews also acted as a strong deterrent. But while there were individual acts of kindness and bravery, most Hungarians simply watched passively as the Jews were taken away, while some supported the deportations wholeheartedly. The three Anti-Jewish Laws may indeed have reduced some of the German pressure to deport the Jews before March 1944. But combined with the relentless anti-Jewish propaganda drive, which was rooted in the White Terror of 1920, they successfully reconfigured Hungary's Jews in the national consciousness as something external and alien. Their departure would be no loss and generally was not viewed as one. Once László Endre issued his appeal on 15 April for 'every honest Hungarian' to help implement the anti-Jewish decrees with full force, the denunciations poured in. Between 30,000 and 35,000 individuals denounced their Jewish neighbours and acquaintances during the Nazi occupation. Péter Hain, the head of the Hungarian Gestapo, investigated 7,000 cases and arrested 1,950 Jews. About half, mainly the richer ones, were handed on to the Germans.[2] The readiness of many Hungarians to cooperate amazed the Nazis. This was the highest number of denunciations in any country that they had occupied.

By the end of April news was coming into the Jewish Council about the start of the ghettoisation in eastern Hungary. Tens of thousands of Jews were crammed into unsanitary conditions with barely any food or water, many living outside, for days on end. On 27 April the Council wrote to Andor Jaross describing the 'extremely grave and critical situation'. In Ungvár, eastern Hungary, 20,000 Jews were crammed into a brick factory and lumber yard. Children, the sick, the elderly and pregnant women were all in danger, the Council said, asking the authorities to provide proper facilities, and to allow Council representatives to be deployed. The Council then wrote to Eichmann about the horrors unfolding inside the ghettos: women were raped while midwives brutally examined young girls, shoving their fingers into their vaginas to check if they had hidden their jewellery inside their bodies. The procedure was degrading and extremely rough and painful. The midwives' gloves were not disinfected and the same pairs were worn while they penetrated dozens of women in sequence. For Eichmann none of this was new or shocking. Everything was going to plan.

Yet even as the Jewish Council sent its pleading missives to the Hungarian authorities, it assisted them in rounding up prominent Budapest Jews. The Germans and Hungarians presented the

Council with a list of hundreds of journalists, lawyers and 'unreliable' Jews. Everyone named was to report to the Rabbinical Institute on Rökk Szilárd Street, supposedly for labour service. The classrooms were emptied and straw pallets were installed for the prominent Jews to sleep on, recalled Pál Ornstein, Judit's brother, in his memoir. He and the other fifth-year students were allowed to stay and mix with the prisoners. The students could move freely around the city and often took messages from their prisoners to their families.[3] The Jewish Council drafted the summons and instructions to bring a blanket, three changes of underwear, shoes, a spoon, a metal cup and food for three days. Those who did not turn up were sent a reminder, with the warning that 'failure to appear could incur the gravest consequences'. When some recipients went to Síp Street to ask what it all meant, officials assured them it was only labour service – and not turning up would mean grave consequences for their families. Those who dutifully reported were not sent on labour service. They were sent to the makeshift concentration camp at Kistarcsa, just outside Budapest, and from there to Auschwitz, in some of the earliest transports. Those who did not turn up often survived. Even the Gestapo did not have the means of tracking down hundreds of people. When some Council employees proposed not cooperating or even sabotaging the drive, Zoltán Kohn, the executive secretary, refused, saying such actions would endanger the entire Jewish Council.[4] A dark joke was soon circulating among Budapest Jewry.

Kohn is woken at 4.00 in the morning by a loud knock on the door.
'Who is it?' he asks.
'Get dressed, it's the Gestapo', a voice answers.
Kohn breathes a sigh of relief. 'Thank heavens for that. I thought it was the Jewish Council.'

It is possible that some Jewish Council members believed that those who reported to Rökk Szilárd Street were being sent on labour service. There was no shortage of cognitive dissonance and denial, not just at Síp Street but across Hungarian Jewry, in the spring and summer of 1944. Who knew what about the camps and the gas chambers, when they knew it and when and where they shared that information remains highly contested, even today. Contemporary accounts and documents give different versions. But it is possible to draw some broad conclusions. The Hungarian Jewish leadership and the Vaada had for years been extremely well informed about the fate of Jews under Nazi occupation. Information came in from the BBC, Voice of America and Kossuth Radio, Hungarian-language broadcasts from Moscow. Zionist emissaries moving between Budapest, Bratislava and Istanbul brought back detailed accounts of the death camps, as did numerous Jewish refugees and camp escapees. In addition, Hungarian soldiers had reported back with horror the activities of the Einsatzgruppen on the eastern front. Braham notes:

> By late summer 1941, the Hungarian Jewish leaders had solid information not only about the extermination of the Jews deported from Hungary, but also about the mass executions carried out by the Einsatzgruppen and their local henchmen … as well as about the first experimental use of gas vans.[5]

In April 1943 Bronislaw Teicholz, a Jewish refugee from Lvov, met the Hungarian Jewish leadership. Teicholz's parents and all eight of his siblings were killed by the Nazis. Teicholz was fighting with the Partisans when he was captured by the Hungarians and brought to Budapest and interned. He escaped and joined the Polish underground. Teicholz explained how the Nazis used the Jewish Councils to ensure the Jews remained submissive and walked calmly to their own deaths. He predicted what the Nazis would do if they invaded and warned the Hungarian Jewish leaders not to cooperate. His pleas fell on deaf ears. The Hungarians explained that such things could never happen in Hungary.[6]

Unwarned and uninformed by the leaders, until the deportations began in mid-May most Hungarian Jews knew nothing or very little about the fate of their co-religionists. Many believed, or chose to believe, that they were being sent to labour camps. 'Incredible as it may seem today, it is a telling fact of history that, before the second half of May 1944, Hungarian Jewry had no idea of the horrors of the extermination camps of the details of the deportations', wrote Ernő Munkácsi, the secretary of the Jewish Council, in his memoir, *How It Happened*, an invaluable first-hand chronicle of the destruction of Hungarian Jewry. 'The Jews buried their head in the sand, convincing themselves that whatever they could not see could not exist ... while all the Jews of Europe might perish, no harm could come to us in Hungary.'[7]

The clearest account of the mass murder was written by Rudolf Vrba and Alfred Wetzler, two Slovak Jews who managed to escape from Auschwitz in early April 1944. Vrba and Wetzler were both long-term prisoners with jobs as clerks. They could move around inside the camp and had a thorough understanding of its inner workings. Preparations were complete for the arrival of the Hungarian Jews. A new rail line was built from the local train station straight to a ramp inside the camp. There inmates were to be selected either for the gas chambers or slave labour. Prisoners of different nationalities always brought their own food, packed away in their luggage. The suitcases were opened and stripped of valuables and food. Dutch Jews brought supplies of cheese. Greek Jews brought olives and halva. By spring 1944 the SS officers were joking about the forthcoming arrival of 'Hungarian salami'.

Vrba and Wetzler arrived at the Jewish community offices in Zilina, Slovakia, on 26 April. They were questioned at length and in great detail. A forty-page report, known as the *Auschwitz Protocols*, was then typed up in German. The report, which included architectural drawings, described the structure and layout of the camp, from the kitchens to the hospital and gas chambers, to the process of selection, to tattooing, gassing and cremation. Newly arrived inmates were told they were being taken to the baths. Two men with white smocks gave each prisoner a towel and a bar of soap. The prisoners were squeezed into the gas chamber, barely fitting in so everyone had to stand up straight. The SS often shot into the crowd to force those in front further inward. When everyone was inside, the door was locked shut from the outside. There was a short pause, then the SS men, wearing gas masks, went onto the roof, opened the valves and sprinkled the Jews with a dust-like preparation emptied from tin cans.

The whole process took three minutes. The screams began. The prisoners rushed for the door. It was a hideous death, choking, agonising and drawn-out. The dying soiled themselves and vomited. Nobody survived. The door was opened, the gas chamber ventilated and the Sonderkommando, specially selected prisoners, took the bodies out on flat trolleys to the crematoriums, where they were burnt. The four crematoria, operating at full capacity, could burn the bodies of 6,000 people a day.[8] Hundreds of Jewish communities, some many centuries old, quickly vanished in the smoke stacks. In March 1943 43,000 Jews arrived from Thessaloniki, the cosmopolitan centre of Sephardic Jewish life in Europe. Many Greek Jews spoke Ladino, Judeo-Spanish, and could trace their lineage back to the expulsions from Spain in 1492. Just over 38,000 were immediately gassed. Many of those selected for slave labour quickly died of disease. Apart from a handful of survivors, the Jews of Thessaloniki vanished forever. Nowadays there is barely any Jewish life in the city. The same fate awaited the Hungarian Jewish communities outside Budapest.

The *Auschwitz Protocols* were incontrovertible evidence of the Nazi genocide. Exactly when the Jewish Council in Budapest received a copy remains contested. It seems likely the original German version arrived at Síp Street, probably brought by Rezső Kasztner of the Vaada, at the end of April, with the first Hungarian translation being completed in Budapest around two weeks later. Jewish leaders who survived the war such as Samu Stern, Fülöp Freudiger and Rezső Kasztner make vague or contradictory references to the report in their memoirs or ignore it.[9] It is unclear who Kasztner showed the document to. It may be that not all of the Council members were informed of its existence. Ernő Munkácsi, the secretary of the Jewish Council, writes in his memoir that Council members did not receive a copy of the *Protocols* until the second half of May, and then via the Swiss Embassy, where the Jewish Council had a powerful ally.

Carl Lutz, the Swiss Vice-Consul who would later help save thousands of Jews by issuing protective papers, was a courageous and determined anti-Nazi. Lutz and his wife Gertrud, who would play an important role in the rescue operation, lived in Owen O'Malley's former residence on Werbőczy Street in the Castle district. Lutz was in close contact with Rezső Kasztner and Ottó Komoly of the Vaada. Perhaps the spirit of O'Malley, Caja Odescalchi, Krystyna Skarbeck and Basil Davidson still lingered in the courtyard complex. Lutz certainly acted with a bold courage that they all would have appreciated. Lutz changed the name of the Budapest office of the Jewish Agency, which organised emigration to Palestine, to the Emigration Department of the Swiss Embassy.

Lutz then persuaded the Hungarian authorities to grant the new 'department' diplomatic immunity and moved its office into the basement of the embassy on Szabadság Square. Lutz gave Swiss protective passports to Rezső Kasztner, Ottó Komoly and

Carl Lutz, the Swiss Consul, with his driver Charles Szluha, on the Buda embankment, across from the Parliament building. Lutz was a central figure in the neutral diplomats' Jewish rescue operation.

Miklós Krausz, the director of the Jewish Agency. He also gave Swiss identity documents to the young Zionist activists who were setting up safe houses and smuggling Jews across the borders.

Even if the Jewish Council leaders finally received copies of the *Auschwitz Protocols* later in May, they still did not act decisively. Faced with a detailed, credible account of the coming fate of Hungarian Jewry, they continued to adhere to their legalistic policies of placating the Nazis and preventing panic. Munkácsi notes in his memoir that copies began to be made in 'the greatest secrecy'. Valuable time was wasted translating the document into Italian, to send a copy to the pope, even though there were plenty of German speakers at the Vatican.

The former British Legation on Werbőczy Street was taken over by the Swiss and became a crucial centre of the Jewish rescue operation.

After the war, survivors accused the Vaada leadership, especially Rezső Kasztner, of keeping silent about Auschwitz to protect its negotiations with Eichmann. The anger at the Vaada, and the accusations – which still continue – are misplaced. The Zionists represented a small minority of Hungarian Jewry. The Vaada could comfortably fit in one room. Three of its most important leaders – Rezső Kasztner, Joel Brand and Samuel Springmann – were not even from Budapest. They had almost no domestic following and their names were largely unknown to most Hungarian Jews, especially outside Budapest. The Vaada had no radio station or newspaper. The leaders of the Jewish Council, such as Samu Stern and Fülöp Freudiger, in contrast, commanded immense respect. They did have a newspaper, which they used to instruct their fellow Jews to follow orders and stay calm, with catastrophic consequences.

In fact, unlike the Jewish Council, the Vaada and the Zionist movements did send envoys to try and warn the Jews outside Budapest not to move to the ghettos or get on the deportation trains. The emissaries advised those who could to flee to Budapest. It was almost impossible to hide in a village or small town but it was possible to live underground in the capital. The Zionists could help with money, false papers and accommodation. Such suggestions were usually met with bemusement or anger, recalled Lea Komoly, daughter of Ottó, many years later. Even the young Zionists' own parents did not believe them, asking, 'Why are you telling us such horror stories?' The Jews in the provinces said that they were not afraid of going to work, and insisted that they would stay together.[10]

In some places the enraged Jewish leaders threatened to hand the envoys over to the police. Even if the envoys were believed, the young Jewish women said they would not leave their siblings, mothers and grandmothers to their fate.[11] For most, the idea that the Jews in the countryside were all about to be murdered en masse was impossible to process. Zsiga Léb, a Zionist from Kolozsvár, lived in Budapest and tried to warn his friends and relatives. 'The worst part is that the people simply won't believe what is hanging over their heads', he told the Vaada. 'I told everyone I could reach to get away from the ghetto and to flee to Romania, or to go underground with false papers. One out of a hundred followed my advice.' Leb's own uncle angrily denounced him as a 'blasphemer'.[12]

20

Mission Impossible

Blood for goods.

Adolf Eichmann's proposal to exchange Hungarian Jews
for trucks and commodities.

At 8.00 am on 25 April Joel Brand met Josef Winninger at the
Opera Café on Andrássy Way. Winninger was an Abwehr agent
and one of Samuel Springmann's Vaada couriers. Winninger told
Brand that a car would arrive in an hour to take him to the Hotel
Majestic. Brand would be meeting Adolf Eichmann, whom Brand
knew as the architect of the Holocaust, and the man in charge of
the Final Solution in Hungary. Not surprisingly, this news made
Brand very nervous. It was his birthday – his last, he now thought,
certain that he would not return. Brand called Kasztner, Komoly
and his wife Hansi. They all said the same thing: he had to go to
the meeting.

A black Mercedes arrived on time and an SS officer opened
the door for Brand. It sped through the city to Sváb Hill. The SS
guards at the Majestic saluted Brand and led him to Eichmann.
It was the start of one of the most bizarre episodes of the war.
Brand knew the Majestic well. Before the Nazi invasion he had
lived there, in the very apartment that was now Eichmann's office.
It no longer felt like a home from home. Brand would come back
from the encounter, but that morning would shape the rest of his
life. Eichmann fixed him with a cold stare. Brand tried to not let
his nervousness show. Eichmann, he recalled, was about forty years
old. 'He might have been an office clerk in a business firm. Only his

eyes were unusual. Steely blue, hard and sharp, they seemed to bore through me.' Brand was completely in Eichmann's power. With a single word he could be despatched to Auschwitz – but presumably Eichmann wanted something.

He did. Eichmann said: 'I expect you know who I am. I was in charge of the "actions" in Germany, Poland and Czechoslovakia. Now it is Hungary's turn', Brand recalled in his memoir after the war. Eichmann then offered his terms, which had been authorised by Himmler. The Nazis would exchange 1 million Jews for goods, to be used only for civilian purposes or against the Soviets. The Jews could come from anywhere: Hungary, Poland, Czechoslovakia, wherever they could be found. Brand tried to think on his feet. He protested that the Hungarian Jews no longer had any goods. Their businesses and factories had been confiscated. Eichmann spoke with the 'clatter of a machine gun'. He was not interested in Hungarian goods. Instead Brand, and the Vaada, should use their contacts with the Allies and then come back with a proposal. Brand paused while he thought this over. The whole conversation was incredible, unimaginable. But it was happening. Brand told Eichmann that he would need to go to Istanbul. Eichmann agreed, but Hansi and their children would remain behind, as hostages.[1] Soon after Joel took Hansi to the Majestic to meet Eichmann. Hansi would represent Joel while he was away. Eichmann agreed on the condition that Hansi telephone him every day with an update, especially if there was news from Joel.

Several days later Brand was summoned back to the Majestic. This time Eichmann was accompanied by Otto Klages, the SD chief. Klages was a complex figure. He had brutally beaten Katalin Karády, but over the coming months was often helpful to the Vaada, especially to Hansi Brand. He once spent a night talking with Kasztner on the roof of his house, watching an Allied air raid. Some thought Klages was sympathetic to the Jews, but it was more likely that he was, like many Nazis in the summer of 1944, a cynic and an opportunist. An alibi that he had helped the Jews would be most useful after the war, so Klages aligned himself with Eichmann's bizarre plans to negotiate with the Vaada.

Brand's second visit to the Majestic was even more surreal. Eichmann passed him a parcel from Switzerland which the Nazis had intercepted. It contained over $50,000 and a large pile of letters in Hebrew, Yiddish and Polish. Brand could keep everything but should inform Eichmann if there was any information of interest. Brand told Eichmann that he could leave for Istanbul at once but he had no merchandise to offer, only money. Eichmann shook his head. He was not interested in money, only goods. Grotesque bargaining followed. The terms were one army truck for 100 Jews. The trucks could also be filled with tea, coffee, soap and other commodities, which would boost the deal. In addition, Eichmann assured Brand, the trucks would only be used on the eastern front, never against the Western Allies. If the offer was accepted, Eichmann would close down Auschwitz and bring 100,000 Jews to the border. 'A thousand trucks for every hundred thousand Jews. You can't ask for anything more reasonable than that.'

Brand returned home unsettled but also elated. Perhaps there was a way to save the last Jews of Europe. He met with the other Vaada leaders. They looked through the letters. One in particular highlighted the powerlessness of the Hungarian Jews. Nathan Schwalb, a Zionist delegate living in Switzerland, had written suggesting that the Vaada unite with the Hungarian opposition, Liberals and Social Democrats and organise a partisan movement. He sent a list of politicians to recruit, and promised substantial funds from the Allies if this went ahead. Brand and the others despaired. Every person on the list had either been arrested or was in hiding – with the help of the Vaada.

On 15 May Eichmann summoned Brand to the Majestic for the last time. The deportations were starting, with between 10,000 and 12,000 Jews a day being sent to Auschwitz. Brand asked him as a gesture of goodwill and seriousness to stop or delay the trains. Eichmann refused. 'It is up to you, Herr Brand, to get the matter settled with all speed and thus avert this danger.' Eichmann's revolver lay on the table. Brand's eyes drifted towards the gun. Eichmann saw this and smiled. 'Do you know, Brand, I often think how glad some of your people would be to bump me off. But don't be too optimistic, Herr Brand.' Brand's departure was set for the next day. He would be accompanied by Andor Grosz, who had been intriguing in the background since Eichmann had first raised the idea of the 'Blood for Goods' deal. That same day Eichmann left for Auschwitz, to ensure that the camp was ready to receive the transports of Hungarian Jews that would soon be arriving.

Grosz had his own mission, which had been authorised at the highest levels of the Reich. Before Grosz left he was briefed by Klages, who had two sets of instructions for Grosz, as declassified British intelligence documents reveal. The first was that Grosz was to shadow Brand everywhere he went to ensure that he carried out Eichmann's mission. If Brand could not get the trucks and other goods, he was to bring back enough money from Turkey to pay the ransom for each Jew that the Germans allowed to leave Europe. Klages would take 10 per cent of these funds. In addition Brand, together with the Istanbul Vaada and the American Joint Distribution Committee, would launch a propaganda campaign praising the new, more humanitarian policies of the Nazis. The demands were preposterous, but no more than the original idea of Blood for Goods.

The second set of instructions concerned Grosz's separate mission. Grosz was to arrange a meeting in any neutral country between high-ranking British and American officers and senior SD commanders. The meeting would discuss the terms of a separate peace between the Nazis and the Western Allies. This meeting would be arranged through the Zionists and/or a wealthy Czech Jewish businessman called Alfred Schwarz, who lived in Istanbul and was already known to Grosz. Schwarz had his own network of anti-Nazis in wartime Istanbul and ran couriers to the neutral countries for the resistance. But Schwarz's network had been penetrated by the Nazis, which may have been why Klages recommended that Grosz work with him.[2]

The Allied officers could meet with any high-ranking SD officer they liked, except Himmler himself, who obviously could not leave the Reich, explained Klages. If the Istanbul line did not work, then Grosz and Brand were to try and open a channel to the Allies through Jewish organisations in Switzerland or Lisbon. If Grosz and Brand did not come back their families would be killed and all their goods confiscated. The Jews in Europe would then be 'treated in a manner never witnessed before', whatever that might mean, while Grosz would eventually be found and brought back to Germany to be executed.[3] Grosz later told Brand: 'The Nazis realise they have lost the war and they know no peace will be made with Hitler ... The whole of your Jewish business was just a side issue.'[4] If the mission succeeded, however, the deportations would stop, the ghettos would close and the Jews be allowed to leave Europe for Palestine or North Africa. Grosz was told that in Vienna he would be given a briefcase. It would appear empty but had documents concealed inside. Grosz should give the briefcase to Schwarz in Istanbul. The passphrase was to tell him that he received the case from 'an unknown fat man'.

The whole mission was to take place in conditions of the strictest secrecy. It seemed another example of the high farce that sometimes characterised Nazi espionage operations. But it was deadly serious. It was crucial that the Hungarians knew nothing of Brand's and Grosz's mandates. Brand and Grosz left the next day. They were driven to Vienna, spent two nights there, then flew to Istanbul. Grosz duly received his briefcase. En route, the aeroplane stopped twice in the Balkans. Grosz, true to form, had a gift or chit-chat for every airport official that he met. Grosz was met by his wife at the airport but there was nobody to receive Brand, who also had no entrance visa. Eventually, after Grosz paid a bribe, Brand was allowed to enter Turkey. Schwarz came to collect the briefcase, which Grosz handed over with the passphrase about an 'unknown fat man'. Brand spent the next days with the Istanbul Vaada, clearly outlining the fate of Hungarian Jewry, the realities of Auschwitz and Eichmann's demands. Their lacklustre response made him despair.

Sándor Leitner, the leader of the Orthodox Jewish community and president of the Jewish Council in Nagyvárad, northern Transylvania (now Oradea in Romania), had attended the Jewish

Council's meeting at Síp Street at the end of March. By early May, as the Jews of Nagyvárad were forced from their homes into the city's ghetto, he saw the worthlessness of the Jewish Council's reassurances. Leitner's lengthy, detailed report on the fate of his community is one of the most detailed eyewitness accounts of the savagery and unbridled sadism of the ghettoisation and deportation, and the central role of the gendarmes. Nagyvárad's ghetto, which was split into two sections, was then the largest in Hungary. From early May around 27,000 Jews were incarcerated in the main ghetto near the main Orthodox synagogue. Between ten and fifteen people were crammed into each room, terrorised, starving, lacking water and medical care. But the true horror began on 10 May, when Jenő Péterffy, a lieutenant colonel in the gendarmerie, took control. Péterffy issued a set of rules called 'Discipline in the Ghetto'. Any Jews leaving the ghetto would be summarily executed. Jews must stand at attention and be bareheaded in front of any Hungarian or German officer.[5] The ghetto must be silent from early evening to early morning. It was soon echoing to screams of agony and terror.

Péterffy commanded a special unit of forty gendarmes, working with local police. The unit set up a torture chamber inside the nearby Dreher brewery, known as the 'mint' for the valuables it produced. There the gendarmes gave full vent to their blood lust. They stripped their victims naked before beating and whipping them, or torturing them with electric shocks, sometimes in front of their families. Such was the humiliation that some committed suicide. The torturers of Nagyvárad were not rogue officers or criminal chancers, but state officials, acting by government decree. They enjoyed their work. Each prisoner was beaten by four to five gendarmes at a time, notes Leitner, 'rushing at him, shoes, clothing, underwear would soon be torn from him, two of them would beat the heels, two others the hands, arms and other parts of the body and the head would not be spared'. Leitner asked one of those who had been tortured with electric shocks to describe the process. A cable was tied around the victim's left wrist, while a piece of iron, which delivered the charge, was pressed into the 'head, heart, sexual organs, thigh, shank, heel'. The pain was unbearable, said the victim. 'My brain turns out, my heart leaps into the throat.'

One day Leitner saw an elderly man limping forward, his face swollen from beatings, barely able to stand on his feet. It was Leitner's father, and he rushed to help him. Leitner's mother was also taken away but returned soon after. Leitner asked her where she had been. 'You know, my child, they treated me with an electrical apparatus', she replied. Leitner asked if she had suffered great pains. 'Yes, but it will pass away. You know, my child, they have maltreated me in vain. I have told them, that I was not informed about fortune matters. Even if they kill me they will not be more informed.'[6]

On 18 May two VIP visitors arrived: László Endre, wearing Hungarian national costume, and Desiderius Nagy, a high-ranking official in the Finance Ministry. He met with the gendarme commander Péterffy and Deputy Mayor László Gyapay. Leitner wrote:

Alas, the prominent foe of Hungarian Jewry, who undertook to carry out the orders of the SS hangman, who distinguished himself in the noble competition of anti-Semitism, Mr Ladislas ENDRE has condescended to come to us, who were standing on the deepest level of human fate, in order to feast his eyes on our suffering. He surely got good reports from his bailiffs, Peterfi [sic] and Gyapay, as his face shone with satisfaction.

Péter Hain, the head of the Hungarian Gestapo, was also satisfied with Péterffy's work. Jewish wealth worth around 41 million gold *pengős* was confiscated. Leitner noted sarcastically that the results were a miracle, and that 'the state revenue gained by torturing of Jews amounts to much more in a few days, than tax collection in some years by ordinary methods'. In fact, that revenue came at a high price. In Nagyvárad, like every Hungarian city, town and village, the Jewish community was woven into the fabric of everyday life and the city's thriving economy. Factory owners, artisans, doctors, teachers, businessmen and women, shopkeepers – all these lived and worked peacefully and side by side with their Gentile neighbours and customers. It made no sense whatsoever for any country, especially one struggling through a long war, to expel and murder 5 per cent of its population, many of whom were highly economically productive. The money and jewellery confiscated by the gendarmes was meagre compensation for the massive financial and social damage caused by the deportations.

Soon after the ghettoisation, Gyapay, the deputy mayor, wrote to Döme Sztójay, the prime minister, highlighting the severe impact of the drive against the city's Jews. Hundreds of shops and businesses and 5,000 apartments had been confiscated and now needed to be registered and evaluated. Thousands of locals, previously working for Jewish-owned businesses, were now unemployed. Businesses which had been taken over by local officials were now paying their employees less than their former Jewish owners had. The flow of raw materials to factories had virtually ceased, while artisans had piles of goods ordered by Jewish customers and were unable to sell them. Jewish employers had been paying allowances to the families of men serving in the army, which had now stopped. Gyapay naïvely requested that Sztójay set up a special commission to deal with 'the insurmountable difficulties' caused by the removal of the city's Jews.[7]

Sztójay's opinions were irrelevant. What mattered were Endre, Baky and Eichmann – for whom everything had gone to plan. Returning from his tour, Endre declared, 'The population in all cities and communities has hailed the government measures with genuine delight ... the population has rejoiced and has frequently supplied means of transportation to speed resettlement and get rid of all the Jews.'[8] The savagery of the gendarmes in Nagyvárad was not the exception but the rule. Across Hungary, Jews were starved, imprisoned, tortured and beaten to death with impunity. Those who had held high positions, such as judges, lawyers or prosperous businessmen, often triggered a special rage and were punished for their effrontery for daring to pretend to be loyal Hungarians. The Jews' neighbours then gleefully plundered their former homes and businesses, helping themselves to furniture, bedding, artworks, cutlery – anything that could be removed.

The last deportation train left Nagyvárad on 3 June. The procedure was well honed. Gendarmes told the Jews that they were going north to work on the *puszta*, the Hungarian plain. They robbed the Jews of their last items of jewellery. They forced them into cattle trucks, where they were jammed inside. There was a bucket for a toilet and no food or water. Some of the elderly died on the journey. Others lost their mind or committed suicide with poison. The journey took three days. When the train arrived at Auschwitz the Jews, dazed, starving, exhausted, ravaged by thirst, spilled out of the wagons onto the ramp. The young and strong were selected for labour and the rest were sent to the gas chambers. Leitner escaped to Budapest and survived. Nagyvárad's Jewish community, and those of its surrounds, were no more.[9]

Endre's visit to Nagyvárad was part of a wider tour of the ghettos in the region. He was very pleased with what he saw. After his return to Budapest Endre gave an interview to the pro-Nazi newspaper *Új Magyarság* (*New Magyardom*). Hungary, he explained, was defending itself by 'ridding it of the Jewish poison, a self-defence which will end Jewish predominance', while the local populations were greeting the anti-Jewish measures with 'genuine delight'. The measures against the Jews 'were always carried out humanely and with consideration for moral factors. Really no harm is befalling them.'[10] Between 15 May and 7 June, a total of 92 trains carrying 289,537 Jews left eastern Hungary and adjoining areas.[11] Most were killed on arrival at Auschwitz. As the historian István Deák notes, the deportation 'was probably the smoothest administrative operation in Hungarian history'.[12]

Ten years earlier Endre had demanded that travelling Gypsies be incarcerated in camps and sterilised. That had not happened, but the Hungarian state also turned on its Roma citizens. As early as 1942 municipal authorities in Esztergom, just north of Budapest, had ordered all local Gypsies and anyone living with them into a closed camp. They were only allowed to leave to work, and were forbidden from walking on the Danube promenade or sitting on park benches. By summer 1944 the much harsher methods used to solve the 'Jewish question' were deployed against the Roma. Across Hungary a network of forced-labour camps for Roma, guarded by the gendarmerie, were set up. Exact numbers are not known but thousands were relocated into ghettos. The gendarmes oversaw the procedure with their customary cruelty. They surrounded the Gypsy quarters then force-marched the inhabitants to a collection centre, where they were disinfected and had their heads shaved and any good or valuables stolen. Some Roma people were relocated to the site of former Jewish ghettos. Like the Jews, they were starved, deprived of medical care and subjected to violence and terror, before being used as slave labour. Those who tried to escape and were caught were beaten to death on the spot. Others were sent on to concentration camps in Germany.

21

Exodus

I do not think that the history of the world can serve us with another instance when 250,000 people in a city moved house or were forced to share their home with others in all of eight days. Yet this is precisely what happened between 17 June and 24 June 1944, in Budapest, the 'citadel of civilisation' and capital of a nation formerly celebrated for its 'chivalry'.[1]

> Ernő Munkácsi, on the forced relocation of
> Budapest's Jews to Yellow Star houses.

On Sunday, 14 May, as the first deportation trains to Auschwitz were being prepared, Judit Ornstein sat in the courtyard of the children's home watching two children do some gardening. Their joyous play and laughter brought back poignant memories of her own happy childhood. Even under Nazi occupation, life at the home continued, with all its childish intrigues and jealousies. Friendships and alliances formed and dissolved as often as the girls' crushes on the boys they knew. Sometimes they covered for each other so that romantic assignations could take place without the staff knowing. Aunt Klári, somewhat exasperated by Judit's adoration of the rabbi, told her that she would drive out her 'infatuation'. Judit was indignant. 'Well, there is really no need for that! After all, am I not a self-respecting girl? Or at least that is what I have to be', she wrote. And anyway, as Judit told her diary, 'there is no one who awakens in me a feeling that says I am a Girl and the person in front of me is a Boy. Now only a friend or Pál can be by my side.'

Even so, Judit was very pleased that the rabbi had managed to attend the Friday-night dinner a couple of days earlier. Everyone around the table had to sing or recite a poem. One of the girls sang Judit's favourite song, from Bizet's opera 'The Pearl Fishers', and another that Judit's father Lajos loved. 'It was heavenly, hearing them together', wrote Judit. For a moment the war and the Nazis seemed far away. Until the air-raid siren howled and everyone had to go done to the cellar. 'Is it always going to be like this from now on?' she asked. These days were becoming more and more difficult. A couple of days earlier Judit had received a letter from Lajos. 'My father's picture as a soldier is also here before me, my mother's is in my heart, and the sweet laughing face of Laci is also smiling at me', she wrote. But the news from home was not good. The town was preparing the ghetto for its Jews. 'Oh will I ever see them again?' she asked. Judit could not know that the Jews of Hajdúnánás were forced into the town's ghetto on that very day. In the meantime, she promised herself and Aunt Klári that she would be 'conscientious and rational: an orderly person'. She tried to console herself with the thought that she was with her family mentally.

Not far away from Judit, David Gur was posing as a model in the attic of an apartment building on Bethlen Square, in District VII's Jewish quarter. He spent his days there with Shraga Weil, a Slovak Jewish refugee. Weil had studied art in Prague and was a talented painter. The attic housed the young Zionists' forgery workshop, which Gur ran. The artist's studio was a cover. The walls were bedecked with drawings and paintings. The most important painting was a half-finished portrait of Gur – if anyone knocked on the door, Gur quickly stripped off his shirt while Weil moved over to the easel and continued painting his portrait. Gur, who was born Endre Grósz, came from Okány in eastern Hungary and changed his name after the war. His father was a wood merchant. The family was assimilated and Gur went to a Protestant school in a nearby town. Gur was an intelligent boy who in more normal times would have gone to university. But that route was closed. He arrived in Budapest in 1943 at the age of seventeen and took a job as a trainee draughtsman. He joined Hashomer Hatzair, the most left-wing of the Zionist movements. His rapidly developing and increasingly precise skills of drawing and penmanship would soon help to save many lives.

David Gur, dressed in an Arrow Cross uniform. The Zionist activists sometimes dressed up as Arrow Cross gunmen. They rescued Jewish prisoners and launched surprise attacks on the Arrow Cross, killing as many as they could.

The Nazis and the Hungarians were extremely bureaucratic. They kept records of everything, from the books by Jewish authors that were handed in to be pulped to the names of residents in each Yellow Star house. They issued a stream of orders and regulations. This system of control was built on top of existing mechanisms. Hungary's highly centralised bureaucracy and its rigid system of official permits predated both the German invasion and the Horthy regime. Citizens' movements were controlled and monitored by the police. The power of officialdom to regulate lives was deeply engrained in the national consciousness. Each time someone moved house they had to fill in a police form with their details. One copy was kept by the person, one by the police and one handed to the building superintendent.

Yet conversely, this created a space for the Zionist resistance to operate. They could now engage in a kind of asymmetric warfare. With the right papers – or the right fake papers – and enough confidence, the activists and those they sought to save could navigate the deadly new officialdom. When the first refugees arrived in the early years of the war the Zionists bought fake papers from the Budapest criminal underworld. These were expensive – an identity card or residence permit cost 60 *pengős*, more than a week's wage for an average worker. The answer was to make their own. The starting point was the electoral register, which was open to the public. That information was enough to apply for copies of baptismal certificates, birth certificates and other important papers. From that an entire false or stolen identity could be documented. The operation grew rapidly into a full-scale forgery workshop. Gur's workshop moved frequently, trying to stay one step ahead of the authorities. It would soon be supplying documents not just to Jews, but also to high-ranking Communists and other members of the resistance.

László Endre and Péter Hain were drawing up their plans to intern all the Jews of Budapest, prior to their deportation. This was a more complicated endeavour. There was no single site in the city, or anywhere in Hungary, where more than 250,000 people could be concentrated. Hain and the SS had initially favoured setting up a ghetto mainly in Districts VII and VI, where large numbers of Jews lived. But substantial numbers of Christian Hungarians also had homes there and did not want to leave. The decision was taken to relocate all of Budapest's Jews to designated residential *csillagos-házak*, [Yellow] Star Houses. The first stage in this laborious and complicated operation was to register the places where the Jews already lived and evaluate their suitability for designation as a Yellow Star house. József Szentmiklóssy, the designated municipal official, had good relations with the Jewish Council. He was appalled by the plan and initially offered to resign. But the Council decided that it would be better to have an ally implementing the relocations. A total of 2,639 buildings were marked as Yellow Star houses.

With the register completed, the order could now be issued for the Jews to leave their homes and move into the Yellow Star houses. The order was issued on 16 June. They had eight days to relocate and began to move in to their new residences. Budapest's Jews were running around the city to their friends, looking for rooms to move into, wrote Mária Mádi. 'It is stated that they can take all their furniture with them but how, when a family gets one room in the best case. Furniture left behind will be "disposed" [of] later. Organised robbery.' One friend of hers, Klára Forrai, ended up squeezed into a single room with her two teenage sons and fourteen other people. Many Christian inhabitants of buildings designated as Yellow Star houses appealed. István Bertényi, a close friend of László Endre, wrote asking him to reclassify his apartment building at 42 Pozsonyi Way in District XIII, a middle-class, mainly Jewish area, as a Christian house after it had been listed as a Yellow Star house. Addressing Endre, one of the most powerful men in the country, as *kedves Lacim*, 'my dear Laci' – the diminutive for László – Bertényi outlined how his building had just eleven Jewish inhabitants, while the high-rent apartment house opposite, at 53–55, only had Jewish inhabitants. 'You were so kind when we last met, and you suggested again that you would gladly help, if it was needed.' It only needed a word from Endre to fix everything, Bertényi wrote on 20 June.[2] The archive does not include a reply, but Jaross and Endre usually ruled in Christian petitioners' favour. Thus 800 buildings were removed from the register, reducing the available space by almost a third. Even more chaos ensued. Some Jews had to move out of their new homes and relocate again.[3]

Many Jewish men were away on labour service as Budapest's housing crisis unfolded. Husbands, father and brothers were unable to help or protect their families as the news came through of the forced relocations. Their anxiety and frustration are evident in their letters home. Ignatz Katz, the former wrestler and sports reporter, had been called up again for labour service. He was deployed to Bácskertes (now Kupusina in northern Serbia) when he learned that his wife Ilona and the rest of his family had to move to a Yellow Star house. 'I am very worried about you', he wrote on 20 June, advising Ilona to 'go to a place with a good [air-raid] shelter'. Ignatz wrote again the next day, 'I was very affected all week by your situation but cannot help, only by being with you in spirit. Write when all of you are settled, who lives where.' Clearly aware of the growing danger for Budapest's Jews, he emphasised, 'Don't walk around in the streets.'

The process of moving and the Jews' new living conditions were regulated with Teutonic precision, down to the tiniest detail. The Yellow Star sign on the building had to be 30 cm in diameter on a black background. Generally, each family was allocated one room, unless it was less than 25 m² in size or the family was larger than four people. No Jewish family could ever occupy more than two rooms. Conditions were at least better than in the ghetto in Nagyvárad and other provincial towns. Budapest's Jews were allowed to bring most of their personal possessions with them. Those left behind were to be placed in one room of their original flats. There they would be inventoried, before the room was sealed. The utility meters would be read and the figures recorded. The Ministry of Finance would be responsible for the safekeeping of the Jews' stored goods. It was a gargantuan, vindictive undertaking, an almost surreal waste of time, manpower and resources in the middle of a war. Budapest's Jews lived in 10,000 buildings. About 28,000 apartments had to be emptied. The last day for the relocation was Saturday, 24 June, when biblical scenes unfolded across the city. Munkácsi wrote:

On that day Budapest turned into an unprecedented, bustling scene, with the children of Israel hauling all their belongings, basic furniture and household objects, handcarts, wheelbarrows or – if they had no access to such conveniences, in bundles on their back to the 'designated houses'.[4]

Alexander Szanto, the Hungarian Jewish man who had returned to Budapest from Berlin and narrowly escaped being deported in 1941 to Ukraine, was also on labour service. He was luckier than Ignatz – he was stationed in Gödöllő, a small town outside Budapest. Generally, the nearer the labour servicemen were to Budapest, the easier were their conditions. The true horrors unfolded on the Ukrainian front.

The officers in charge of Szanto's company were usually open to a bribe. Several of the group managed to return to Budapest on the day of the move to the Yellow Star houses to support their families. It was extremely stressful, Szanto wrote after the war:

> [We] helped our wives and parents to rescue the most urgent belongings from the apartments, to stow them on urgently procured handcarts or other makeshift vehicles.
>
> All this had to be done in a great hurry. Valuable objects were hidden with non-Jewish friends, distributed, buried or placed in some shelter that was thought to be safe. I was on my feet all day, carrying pieces of furniture, pushing trolleys, hurrying up and down stairs, negotiating with janitors, accommodating the family, visiting friends and acquaintances, trying to secure a hiding place for the threatening future.[5]

Once Budapest's Jews were finally relocated, a new slew of regulations was passed to restrict their already rapidly shrinking freedoms. Jews could only leave their houses between 11.00 am and 5.00 pm. No guests were permitted. Jews were not permitted to speak to other people across the street through windows. A responsible person must prepare a list in triplicate of all Jewish residents, with their name, age and sex. One copy must be kept by the door on protected display and the other must be available for inspection. The building superintendent must check the list every day against the people in the building. Anyone missing must be reported immediately. Air-raid shelters should be physically segregated, with separate areas for Jews and non-Jews. Jews could only travel in the last tram carriage. Jews were forbidden from going to parks or promenades. Hungarians had brought the world numerous inventions: the ballpoint pen, invented by László Bíró, the safety match, the telephone exchange, Vitamin C and more. Now its bureaucrats had conjured up something unique in the annals of anti-Jewish persecution: the ghetto-in-a-building. Not surprisingly, many Jews believed they would soon be deported. Some slept fully clothed and kept a bag packed at all times.

Charles Howie was also on the move, although his new hosts seemed unlikely candidates to hide an Allied POW. Béla Kővári, the owner of 149 Bimbó Way, a comfortable residential street in Buda overlooking the city, was a captain in the Hungarian police. He shared his home with Georgina Kress, known as Gin, and her German husband, Róbert. Howie's former host Jane knew Gin, who had offered to help out some time before. Gin's husband, Róbert, said he was an anti-Nazi, while Howie thought that Béla Kővári realised that the Germans had lost the war, so was looking for an alibi after the Allied victory. Even if that was the case, all three were still taking a dangerous risk and could be executed for hiding an enemy officer. Howie moved in during early June 1944, transported at Jane's request by an official car supplied by Colonel Merkly, Jane's protector in the Hungarian intelligence service. Howie was pleased with his new home. The one-storey house was set back from the street and his room was at the rear, with its own entrance.

Lieutenant Colonel Charles Telfer Howie, a South African army officer and escaped POW, negotiated with Admiral Horthy in secret and tried to persuade him to change sides.

Jane brought food most days but life on Bimbó Way was rather different to the Harffs' family villa. Gin was in her mid-thirties, a stylish dresser and very attractive. Her husband was frequently away and she was having an affair with a Hungarian government minister. There were other dalliances as well. But overall, Howie found her charming, intelligent and 'fiercely loyal' to those close to her. Howie was bored and lonely. The main danger was from Allied air-raids, which were now increasing in strength. The noise was horrendous as the anti-aircraft gunners fired continually at the bombers. At night Howie could see the line of tracer bullets cutting through the darkness. One day he heard an enormous noise and watched an American bomber twist and turn, its engines howling before it crashed. Two parachutes slowly descended earthwards.

Yet after a while Howie thought he began to be noticed. The house was searched by plainclothesmen several times. Once, when the Gestapo arrived, Howie had to hide in Gin's wardrobe, which was full of her perfumed dresses. The smell pricked at his nose but he managed not to sneeze. Meanwhile Gin, who seemed to almost enjoy the danger, kept her cool. She joked with the Gestapo men and served them drinks. They departed soon after. In July another British POW appeared. An RAF officer called Reginald Barratt brought Howie pipe tobacco and greetings from the escape committee at Stalag VIIIB, his former POW camp. Barratt had also been living on the Andrássy estate in Szigetvár, together with Tibor Weinstein, the Hungarian who had escaped with Howie. After the Nazi invasion they had attempted to get to Yugoslavia but had been caught by the Germans. The two men were then sent to Germany and interned at Stalag VIIIB, but had escaped again.

Meanwhile, the plan to liberate Hungary was taking shape. Prime Minister Kállay gave Howie a radio transmitter to make contact with the Allies. The country would be invaded by Allied paratroopers. They would unite with the Hungarian Army and take over key military installations while the population rose up against the Germans. One evening later in July a large black Mercedes with official insignia on its sides and a blue light on the roof pulled up outside the Kőváris' house. Howie's time in Hungary was about to enter its most important – and dangerous – phase. Howie sat down inside the car to be greeted by Miklós Horthy Jr., known as Niki.

Miklós Jr. was Admiral Horthy's last surviving child and had returned from serving as Hungarian ambassador in Brazil. Niki too was an anti-Nazi, the head of the Kiugrási ('Exit') office. Supposedly concerned with the affairs of Hungarians living outside the borders, it was actually gathering information about anti-Nazi groups with the aim of supporting their activities and finding a way for Hungary to leave the Axis. 'It formed a link between the Regent and the illegal organisations', recalled Ilona Edelsheim Gyulai in her memoir, and also worked with Jewish communal leaders.[6] Niki told Howie that his father was waiting for him at the Royal Palace. Did he want to meet him? Howie did, and the car set off for the short drive to the Palace.

Admiral Horthy received Howie with his aide, Colonel Tost and Count Bethlen, the former prime minister who was in hiding from the Nazis. Horthy spoke to Howie in excellent English. His was a similar tale of woe to Kállay's failed attempts to extricate Hungary from the Axis the previous year. Horthy wanted to change sides but the demand for unconditional surrender made things very difficult. The two men met several times, record declassified SOE documents.

> During these meetings 'H' [Howie] pressed Horthy to surrender immediately to the Russians but Horthy could not make up his mind, partly as 'H' put it, because his honour would not permit him to stab his country in the back and partly because he still felt that he had everything to gain and nothing to lose by postponing the evil day as long as possible.[7]

No decision was taken, but Horthy and Howie agreed to meet again. But if the Horthys knew about Howie, so did others. Jane learned that the Bimbó Way house was being watched. And Gin

and Jane were not getting on – Gin was becoming possessive of
Howie and his resistance work with the Poles. Howie's instincts
had served him well and kept him alive. It was time to leave the
Kress house, he sensed. In late July Howie and Andzrej Sapieha,
the representative of the Polish Home Army, moved into the Royal
Palace, into the apartment of General Lázár, the commander of
Admiral Horthy's bodyguards. The two men were comparatively
safe but sequestered. The Palace was full of German spies and they
could not risk being seen.

Howie wanted action. He attempted to organise a resistance
cell to start executing Hungarian collaborators. Declassified SOE
records report: 'He frequently tried to organise such a group but
it failed owing to the apathy and fear of the population.' The first
target was Péter Hain, the head of the Hungarian Gestapo. 'It took
two months to find six Hungarians who were willing to do this
and by that time the plan was not feasible and had to be dropped.'
One evening Colonel Ujszászy and General Vörös, the chief of
the general staff, came to talk about the radio equipment the Poles
needed. The Hungarians were not very cooperative – Howie later
wrote that Vörös did not believe he was an Allied officer. Ujszászy
was highly suspicious of him. But the real problem was the same
as ever: Horthy could not act decisively and change sides. As the
SOE document records:

'H' said that Horthy always listened to the last people to see
him, and as the Germans naturally saw him oftener than 'H',
he allowed himself to be swayed by them.[8]

The time was coming when Horthy's wavering would be
irrelevant. Soon Hungary's fate would be decided in Berlin, not
Budapest.

22

A Dirty Business

Her eyes no longer sparkled. She was cold, sharp, her reasoning now razor-edged; she no longer trusted strangers.

Yoel Palgi, Palestinian Jewish parachutist,
on Hannah Szenes, May 1944.

High in the mountains of Yugoslavia, Hannah and her comrades' time with the Partisans stretched into weeks. There was no way to cross the border safely. It was under continual surveillance. In early May, two more Palestinian Jews arrived: Yoel Palgi, who had known Hannah in Palestine, and Peretz Goldstein, who was also from Transylvania. Palgi immediately saw the difference in Hannah: 'She was the first to suspect the Partisans of unwillingness to help and of misleading us.' Yet she remained determined to enter Hungary. By mid-May Hannah could wait no longer. Palgi and the others were still unsure. Palgi tried to dissuade her but she would not listen. It was impossible to oppose her, he later recalled.[1] Hannah decided to make her own way to Budapest, set up a network and then meet Palgi and the others there at a later date.

She said goodbye on 13 May. It took her and her Partisan escorts twenty-six days to reach the border, dodging Nazi-German patrols and outposts. Finally, on 9 June, Hannah crossed into Hungary with two members of the Jewish underground called Kallos and Fleischmann and Jacques Tissandier, a French POW. As dawn broke the group decided that Kallos and Fleischmann would go ahead to scout a nearby village. Hannah and Tissandier would remain in the reeds, hiding by the riverbank.

After three hours with no word, and the appearance of German soldiers, it was obvious that something had gone wrong. Hannah and Tissandier buried their radio transmitter. Catastrophe had indeed struck, an event which remains inexplicable.

Kallos and Fleischmann, both armed, were stopped and questioned by two Hungarian policemen. They produced their papers, but the policemen asked them to go to the station. Fleischmann's hand slipped into his pocket, readying his Beretta. One of the policemen then said they should walk another hundred metres, then let the two men go. Fleischmann relaxed. But for some reason Kallos drew his gun and shot himself in the head. The policemen swiftly arrested Fleischmann then found the radio set's headphones in Kallos' pocket. The Germans and Hungarians immediately launched a massive dragnet and soon found Hannah and Tissandier. They pretended to be lovers, rolling around in the reeds. It almost worked. But headphones meant a radio set, somewhere. Hannah and the others were taken in for questioning. For two days she was beaten on her palms and soles of her feet, but she refused to talk. Any doubts vanished once the transmitter was found.

Hannah was put on a train to Budapest and taken to the Hadik barracks on Horthy Miklós Road, where so many British agents had been held. There the serious torture began. She was stripped, beaten and had her hair pulled out and her teeth knocked out. But she still refused to talk. Hannah's mother, Katalin, knew nothing of this. On the morning of 17 June a detective appeared at her front door to politely escort her to the Hadik barracks. Katalin was nervous, but arrests in those days were frequent and often inexplicable. The main thing was that Hannah and Gyuri were safe in Palestine. Once inside the prison she was questioned by a man called Rózsa. The interrogation was long and detailed, examining every aspect of Hannah's life. Katalin read her statement and signed it. Rózsa then told Katalin that her daughter was in the next room. Years later she recalled, 'I felt as if the floor were giving away under me and clutched the edge of the table with both hands. My eyes closed ... I was completely shattered, physically and spiritually.'

Four men then led Hannah into the room. Her hair was a filthy tangle, her eyes were blackened and there were welts across her cheeks and her neck. Hannah collapsed into her mother's arms, crying and asking her to forgive her. Katalin was horrified but also mystified. What was her daughter doing here, back in Hungary, when she had been safe in Palestine? Rózsa then broke the two women apart and sent Katalin home. Soon after she was arrested, this time by the Gestapo. She was taken to the German prison that was based in the prison on Gyorskocsi Street. An SS officer slapped her hard around the face and she was taken to her cell, shared with twelve other prisoners. That night she tried to kill herself by slashing her wrists with a stolen razor blade but was stopped by another prisoner. The following morning Katalin was taken with about forty prisoners to the Gestapo prison on Sváb Hill. En route the other prisoners pushed postcards through the vehicle's air vents, in the hope that passers-by might forward them on to relatives. But Katalin was not questioned.

Her prison life settled into a dull routine. Her cell became more and more crowded. Eventually there were twenty prisoners in a space designed for six people. The prisoners could receive parcels once a week. The highpoint of the day was the ten-minute walk around the prison yard – which often became a chance to meet friends and acquaintances Katalin hoped had escaped. Then on 23 June came news: as Katalin was being taken for interrogation another prisoner muttered that Hannah was also being held there. Mother and daughter managed to meet the next day in a bathroom. Katalin was overjoyed. At last she could hold her daughter and kiss her. Hannah looked much better. The marks of the beatings had healed and her hair was clean. She did not appear to be mistreated. Hannah explained her mission, that she was now an officer in the British Army. She told her mother, 'I'm reconciled to my fate. But the thought that I have needlessly involved you in all this is unbearable.'[2]

In Istanbul Joel Brand was languishing. His mission seemed to be going nowhere. He had clearly informed the Vaada there about the fate of the Jews in Nazi-occupied Europe, the destiny of the surviving Jews of Hungary and the terms of Eichmann's offer. But he felt as though he was speaking into the wind. The Zionists in Istanbul were dutiful and honest – perhaps too honest – but they lacked any sense of urgency. Like the Jewish Council in Budapest, the Istanbul Vaada was slow and ponderous, fretting about permissions and legalities. Brand could not help but compare its bureaucratic approach to the focus, courage and determination of his comrades at home. 'They had not looked death in the face day after day as we had done in Budapest, and they had not, like us, lived dangerously. In Budapest we had left the frontier of legality far behind us. We knew the risks we ran, but we were determined to play for the highest stakes.'[3]

While Brand tried to rouse his fellow Zionists in Istanbul to action, Hansi took over the negotiations with the Nazis. She went to the Majestic Hotel to introduce herself and other Vaada leaders, including Rezső Kasztner, to Eichmann. Hansi understood that the Vaada's negotiations were based on a giant bluff. The Vaada was highly skilled in rescue operations, organising safe houses, forging documents, compiling reports and sending them abroad. But it did not represent anyone of real importance. It had no political or diplomatic power. Its leaders were barely known among most Hungarian Jews. And its international links – as Joel was discovering in Istanbul – were not proving very fruitful. But Eichmann and the SS, she realised, could know nothing of this. They actually believed that there really was an international Jewish conspiracy, that the Zionists' power and influence reached around the world.

That belief had to be reinforced, right down to the way she and the others conducted themselves at the Majestic. It was a place of terror, where with just a word from Eichmann they could all be taken into the basement to be tortured or sent to Auschwitz. He spoke sharply with Hansi, as he had with Joel. But they could never let their fear show, Hansi told the others. All they had was their dignity. They had to show Eichmann that they were 'not poor trembling Jews but partners in the negotiations', someone the Nazis would 'want to do business with'. Kasztner too shook in his first meeting with Eichmann, Hansi recalled many years later. 'When we came out, I told him that we had nothing left but to show we are not afraid of them.' Kasztner lit up a cigarette on the street. Hansi said, 'You didn't expect the SS to offer you a cigarette, did you?'[4] Hansi did not let her stress and fear show, but it was still there. 'Every evening we went to pieces and during the night we tried to build ourselves up again, so we could go into the street again and look like human beings again.'[5] Eichmann and the SS did not torture Hansi. But the Hungarians did. Hungarian intelligence had discovered Brand's mission to Istanbul. They were furious that such machinations were taking place without their knowledge. Hansi and the other Vaada leaders were arrested.

For David Gur Hansi Brand's arrest was a disaster. They had relocated the forgery workshop to the Brands' flat, believing that it would be a safe place and that the Brands' high-level connections would protect them. Everything was still there, packed into a single suitcase: all their forms, stamps, ink, chemicals and tools. Now it was all lost, or so Gur thought. He visited the flat, followed at a short distance by a comrade carrying a loaded revolver who waited outside the building while Gur went inside. Joel Brand's mother, who also lived there, had hidden the vital suitcase under her bed. Nobody had looked there when her daughter was arrested. She pulled it out and handed it over. Gur relocated the workshop to a safe house on Darázs Street in Óbuda, on the other side of the Danube. It was a quiet residential area and not especially Jewish.

The Hungarians severely beat Hansi with rubber clubs, hitting her around her face and beating the soles of her feet, trying to get her to talk. Why, they demanded, had the Germans sent Joel and Andor Grosz to Turkey? What was their mission? Hansi did not reveal anything, fearful that if she spoke the mission would be compromised and abandoned. After several days the Germans discovered that she had been arrested. They quickly ordered that she be released into their custody. Hansi was taken to Otto Klages, the head of the SD. Klages was outraged, or pretended to be, that a woman could be beaten so badly. Hansi arrived at lunchtime.

Klages invited her to share his meal, which she accepted.[6] She could not stand properly for weeks, and had problems with her feet for many years afterwards.

Hansi Brand and Rezső Kasztner's negotiations with Eichmann did bring some results: 600 holders of Palestine immigration certificates would be allowed to leave Hungary – although not for Palestine. A special train arrived in Budapest on 10 June carrying 388 Jews from the ghetto in Kasztner's hometown of Kolozsvár who were saved from deportation. The passengers were moved to the Institute for the Deaf on Columbus Street, just north of the City Park. This was one of the safest places in Hungary for Jews, as Braham notes. Known as the 'Privileged Camp', it was guarded by five SS officers. The list of 388 was drawn up by the Vaada leaders with Zsigmond Leb, the former president of the Kolozsvár Orthodox community. Places were supposedly reserved for those who served the community or were widows and orphans of labour servicemen. Predictably, the allocation was chaotic, as local Jewish leaders, Hungarian officials and Germans pushed for their favoured candidates to be included – often after being bribed. These notables and others would be allowed to leave Hungary for a neutral country on a special train.

Kasztner continued pushing Eichmann for further concessions, offering him jewellery, foreign currency and the equivalent in *pengős* of 5 million Swiss francs for 100,000 lives. At this time the Nazis urgently needed slave labourers for farms and factories in and around Vienna. Eichmann agreed that between 18,000 and 20,000 Jews from the countryside, including Debrecen in the east and Szeged in the south, could be sent to Strasshof in Austria to work, some of them children and the elderly. This deal was probably Kasztner's greatest achievement. Another account, by Andreas Biss, who was also involved in the negotiations, claims that it was his close relationship with Otto Klages that enabled the deal and Himmler's cooperation. It is impossible to definitively judge. What is known is that about three-quarters of those sent to Austria survived the war and many were treated quite humanely by the Austrian farmers and villagers.

Meanwhile the Vaada had to find the *pengő* equivalent of 5 million Swiss francs, plus $1,000 a head for those supposed VIPs on the special train. The Vaada auctioned 150 places on the train – triggering chaos as its office was mobbed by crowds of frantic Jews trying to obtain a place. Fülöp Freudiger, the Orthodox leader and member of the Jewish Council, bribed Dieter Wisliceny to bring his favoured Orthodox Jews to Budapest. Several members of the Council found places for their families, who were escorted to Budapest by the SS. The final collection of monies and valuables was brought to the Majestic Hotel on 20 June, and delivered to Kurt Becher, an SS officer. Over the coming months Becher would become a central figure in the fate of Budapest Jewry, negotiating several financial deals, all the while reporting to Himmler, while making sure to substantially enrich himself. Becher would navigate these difficult currents with skill, and become close to Kasztner – a relationship that would shape and doom Kasztner's post-war life.

Kurt Becher arrived in Hungary in March 1944, supposedly to buy horses. Becher was comparatively young, born in 1909 to a modest background. A keen horseman, he joined the mounted division of the SS in 1934 and was later trained in the Totenkopf ('Death's Head') unit of the SS, which served in the field or as concentration camp guards. Becher was sent to Poland, where his unit, operating behind the advancing German Army, killed thousands of Jews, Partisans and Communists. After the war he claimed that he had personally not killed any Jews, and was only an 'administrative officer'. Administrative tasks in such a place can only be imagined and Becher received a medal for his service on the eastern front. Certainly it was there that he first learned the techniques of robbing and looting. Like Eichmann and Klages, Becher held the rank of *Obersturmbannführer* in the SS, equivalent to lieutenant colonel. Despite his bloodstained past, it seems he did not share Eichmann's manic determination to murder all of Hungary's Jews. As the chief of the SS's economic department in Hungary, he took a more pragmatic approach, fuelled by self-interest more than Nazi racial ideology. Becher's job was to extract as much of the Hungarian Jews' wealth as possible for the SS and Himmler. If that meant allowing them to live, then so be it.

Becher was married with four children, but in Budapest he had an impressive array of lovers. As well as his main mistress, Countess Hermine von Platen, he had two other paramours. Becher had a taste for luxury which he easily and quickly indulged. He moved into the spacious villa and offices of the richest Jewish family in Budapest, at 114 and 116 Andrássy Way, and lived there in comfort with von Platen. The Weiss/Chorin/Kornfeld dynasty owned and ran the Manfréd Weiss steelworks and armaments factory on Csepel Island, in the south of the city, Hungary's most important industrial concern. Manfréd Weiss had been ennobled by Emperor Franz Joseph for providing supplies to the Austro-Hungarian Army. The dynasty's grandees often socialised with Horthy – they were his type of loyal Magyar Jews, not unsavoury 'Galician types'. Manfréd's daughter, Edit, was one of the first influential Hungarians to work with the Poles at the outbreak of the war. Some of the family converted to Christianity – but they retained their connections with the Jewish community. Edit also worked with the Red Cross, advocating for Polish Jews who had sought refuge in Hungary.[7]

Directed by Himmler, Becher moved quickly. Immediately after the invasion the SS and Gestapo swept through Budapest looking for the key Weiss family members and employees. The most important director, Ferenc Kelemen, was arrested and tortured at the Gestapo headquarters at the Astoria Hotel. The head of the family, Ferenc Chorin, fled to a rural monastery. But he telephoned his home a few days later, not knowing that the house had been taken over by Becher and the line was tapped. Chorin was located and arrested, held at the prison on Gyorskocsi Street, sent to Vienna and then brought back to Budapest. Chorin was allowed to live at home under house arrest. Becher soon made it clear what the terms of the deal were: the Weiss dynasty would hand over the steelworks to the SS, in exchange for safe passage for the family to a neutral country. The Weiss dynasty had been caught up in a power struggle between Himmler and his rival Hermann

Göring. Göring had his own economic empire, the Hermann Göring-Werke. Himmler wanted the same for himself. The Weiss steelworks were a good place to start. The Weiss industrial empire reached around the world, including into the United States. US intelligence was concerned that the Weiss holdings' international links would provide a very effective cloaking mechanism for shifting Nazi economic assets into neutral countries.

A series of complicated negotiations followed between Becher and Chorin, with fanciful arrangements about trustees, share ownership and percentages of the turnover. The new incarnation of the company was to be supervised by two SS officers, one of them, naturally, Kurt Becher. The deal had to be kept secret; from the Hungarians, who would strongly object to a strategic national asset being handed over to the Nazis, from the German Foreign Ministry, the SS's rival and from Edmund Veesenmayer, the Reich's minister in Budapest. At this time Becher and his staff were also engaged in much smaller scale blackmail. They extorted large sums from Hungarian Jews to avoid wearing the Yellow Star and forced Jewish craftsmen and artisans to produce goods for the SS – while the Jewish Council paid their salaries. But the real prize was the Manfred Weiss works.

On the evening of 17 May Ferenc Chorin, his wife, Daisy, and other family members, including Thomas de Kornfeld, the grandson of Baron Manfred, were taken to a villa closely guarded by the SS. Decades later, de Kornfeld recalled that fateful evening when the family signed away its assets for their lives. 'We were assembled at four p.m, at nine p.m. we signed and at ten p.m. we were out. There is nothing anybody could have done for, to or about it.' As for Becher, 'He was well educated, courteous, a gentleman who kept his word. He was polite and businesslike.' De Kornfeld and the other family members were taken to Vienna, where they stayed for several weeks, living on a train in sleeping cars. De Kornfeld recalled that they were treated as German VIPs, guarded by the SS.[8]

Eventually forty people travelled to Switzerland and Lisbon, including Edit Weiss and Thomas de Kornfeld. Other relatives and the family's lawyer were kept in Budapest as hostages, to ensure that those freed stayed silent. It was an impressive achievement by Becher: he had obtained control of one of the most important industrial complexes in Europe for the SS and Himmler without a shot being fired – right under the noses of the Hungarians and Veesenmayer. After the deal was done Veesenmayer telephoned Albert Speer, the Nazi armaments minister, and complained that he had been put in an impossible position as the Weiss steelworks were technically the property of the Hungarian state.[9]

Why did Becher even bother negotiating? He could have sent the Weiss family to the camps or had them shot and simply taken the steelworks. The Nazis usually had no such qualms. The main reason is that Germany still needed Hungary as an ally. The country was occupied by the Nazis but retained its own head of state and government. The Hungarian state administration was vital for the smooth-running of the deportations. The illusion of independence was important. The Weiss dynasty was close to Hungary's ruling circles. The tactics that were applied in places such as Poland, of murder and outright theft, had to be adjusted. The Hungarians were enraged when they discovered what had happened. But the deal was done.[10]

Becher's other key negotiation was also successful. The Vaada VIP train left Kelenföld Station in Budapest late in the night of 30 June. In later years it became known as 'Kasztner's Train', which annoyed Hansi Brand. It had not been one man's project, but a collective effort, she recalled. Hansi had organised the food; others had helped in many ways. Eichmann had authorised the departure of 1,300 people. The day of the departure, there had been an air raid. In the chaos another 384 extra Jews sneaked on board and stowed away, including two men on labour service whose train had stopped nearby. The train was halted for three days on the Austrian border. At one stage it seemed it was going to pass near a place called Auspitz in Czechoslovakia, which caused panic. In the end the group was taken to Vienna, then Linz, arriving in Bergen-Belsen on 8 July. There they were placed in a separate VIP camp, where they were reasonably treated, with supplies of food and medicine. Several hundred passengers were freed and allowed to travel to Switzerland during the summer, and the remainder in December 1944.[11]

The second half of May was a difficult time for Joel Brand. He had visa problems with the Turks and his permit to remain was renewed from day to day. There was no sign of Moshe Shertok, the head of foreign policy for the Jewish Agency in Jerusalem. The sense of wasted time was unbearable. Across Hungary trains crammed with thousands of Jews were leaving for Auschwitz every day, but nothing was happening. Grosz informed Brand of a new plan; they were wasting their time in Istanbul. They would cross the Turkish frontier to Syria and then travel on to Palestine and deal with the Jewish Agency directly. Brand reluctantly agreed, even though he was travelling into British territory on a German passport. Grosz left Istanbul on 1 June, Brand on 5 June. He and another Vaada delegate took the train to Aleppo in Syria.

When the train stopped in Ankara, Brand met two comrades from the Zionist movement. They warned him that the British wanted his mission to fail. They wanted to entice Brand and Grosz onto British territory so they could arrest both men. Brand ignored the warning and decided to carry on, feeling he had no other option. The warning was correct. Both Brand and Grosz, who was travelling with his wife, Madeleine, were quickly detained by the British once they arrived in Syria. Moshe Shertok did come to meet Brand in Aleppo but could not gain Brand's freedom. Brand was interrogated and then sent to Cairo for more questioning. For a while he was held in the same place as Samuel Springmann. Brand was decently treated but miserable and frustrated, cut off from his family and Budapest and unable to achieve anything. His mission had failed and he was held and interrogated for months.

Finally, on 5 October he was released. Together with a British officer, he took the night train which then ran from Cairo to Jerusalem. Madeleine Grosz was on the same train but had no news of her husband. Brand stayed in Palestine and did not return to Budapest during the war, but he lived freely. Andor Grosz fared less well. The British remained highly suspicious of his connections with Hungarian intelligence and the Nazis. The smuggler king of Budapest had finally been trapped. He languished in British custody until the end of the war.

23

Summer Salvation

I left feeling awfully sorry for them, but more sorry for the country and the nation.

Edina Zichy Pallavicini after visiting Magdolna and
Miklós Horthy, 10 July 1944.

The banned books by Jewish and foreign authors met their fate in mid-June. Schools, libraries and companies in possession of such works had to compose an inventory. Five copies of the inventory were to be submitted to the government. Now that Hungarian culture was being reconfigured on Nazi lines, there were plenty of more suitable works available. *Magyar Világhíradó* (*Hungarian World News*), the state newsreel for early June 1944, showcased the national book festival. The narrator excitedly reported how enormous crowds browsed a wide selection of books. One discussed in great detail a nineteenth-century blood libel in the village of Tiszaeszlár, in eastern Hungary. Another was entitled *Élettér: Új Európa* (*Lebensraum in the New Europe*). A Hungarian translation of Henry Ford's *The International Jew* was also displayed.[1]

The next edition of *Magyar Világhíradó* showed the destruction of the books. The film footage shows a procession of horse-drawn carts, piled high with hundreds of bundles, being unloaded and unpacked. Each book is then hurled into a giant concrete mill and crushed by a wheel weighing several tons. Jewish culture – like the Jews themselves – was being reduced to a formless mass. Mihály Kolosváry-Borcsa, a high-ranking official, threw the first two books into the mill: a collection of poems by József Kiss and Franz

Werfel's *The Forty Days of Musa Dagh*, set during the Armenian genocide. 'It is only now that we are seeing the true reality of the poisoning effect of this literature that is so far from the Hungarian soul, has done to the Hungarian soul', he declared. The country's soul had indeed been poisoned, but not by Jewish and foreign authors. Once the books were destroyed they were sprayed with water and turned into pulp, to be processed into paper. The former owners – excluding Jews – were then compensated to the value of the scrap paper, based on their inventories. The destruction of the books was also reported in *Pesti Hírlap*. The story was on the same page as the list of Yellow Star houses, spread over ten columns, covering Budapest's fourteen districts. A total of 447,637 books were destroyed that day – just a few thousand more than the 430,000 Hungarian Jews who were being deported to Auschwitz.

The painstaking, methodical planning of the gathering and crushing of the books deftly illustrated the psychotic hatred of Endre, Baky and their circle for Hungary's Jews. For Eichmann, Edmund Veesenmayer and the other SS officers, the Jews of Hungary were the same as any other nation: *Untermenschen*, 'sub-humans'. They would soon meet the same fate as the Jews of Poland, Greece, Slovakia – everywhere the Nazis had conquered. For Jaross, Endre, Baky and their allies, the existence of Hungary's Jews was a personal affront. The rage, fury and blood lust that they had felt during the White Terror had never faded. But now it could be acted on. Yet even as they sought to destroy Hungarian Jewry, they remained obsessed with it.

Zoltán Bosnyák, one of Hungary's most notorious anti-Semitic hate-mongers, was an advisor to László Endre. Bosnyák now ran the Hungarian Institute for Researching the Jewish Question, an official state body. Housed in the Union Club on Vörösmarty Square, by the historic Gerbeaud café, the Institute's mission was to 'study the Jewish question in a systematic and scientific manner' and inform the Hungarian public. The Institute had its own newspaper, *Harc* (*Struggle*), modelled on the Nazi publication *Der Stürmer*, spewing hate-filled articles and grotesque cartoons.[2] Speaking at the Institute's launch the previous month, László Endre declared that the government had decided to 'bring about a final solution of the Jewish question within the shortest possible time given the present circumstances'.[3]

Endre also had the power of life and death over individuals. A word from him or a scrawled mark on a file would decide their fate. Endre's surviving letters from the spring and summer of 1944 detail the pleas of those hoping for sympathy or a shred of humanity and to be spared deportation. But unless the correspondent was requesting that a house marked for Yellow Star status be reclassified as Christian, or had a very powerful protector, they were refused. Sometime in June 1944 Döme Sztójay, the prime minister, wrote to Endre about the case of Mrs Jenő Schwarczer, who had been interned, ready for transport to Auschwitz. Mrs Schwarczer had converted to Christianity thirty-two years earlier and married a

Hungarian Jews being rounded up in 1944 in front of smiling bystanders. Most Hungarians stood aside and watched as their Jewish neighbours were taken away.

Christian, so should not be deported. Endre agreed and wrote back that he had arranged for her to return home. One ardent admirer even sent Endre a two-page closely typed poem, entitled 'All to the Ghetto', a psychotic screed calling for Hungary's Jews to be rounded up and 'blasted by fire'. He would get his wish.[4]

Judit Ornstein did not write in her diary for three weeks, from 18 May to 10 June. At one stage she had to register with the authorities and prepare to be relocated under the regulations for the Yellow Star houses. But then the order was rescinded – the children's home itself became a Yellow Star dwelling. News was filtering through of the ghettos and the deportations, not just to the Jewish Council, but among the whole community. Judit despaired of the fate of her family, writing on 10 June:

> Back home, they have locked the gates of the ghetto and the Jews have vanished into the medieval twilight. I can almost see before my eyes the broken figures of my Father and Mother, but they smile at times. And the children, oh the children, the children are not so small that they can rise above this barbarity.

Four days later she received a card from her brother, Pál, who was worried about his girlfriend, Anna. Thankfully, Pál had not been sent to Ukraine. He was in Várpalota, south of Budapest, building an airport runway. That morning there was another air raid and Judit and the girls took shelter in the basement. When they emerged at noon the city was wreathed in smoke from burning buildings. Judit's turbulent emotions embody the pain, rage and confusion of Hungarian Jews at their betrayal by their country. 'Forgive me, God', she wrote:

> While my heart ached for my fellow human beings, I also felt a bit of joy mixed in with the pain. I can explain it. My dear, good Mother is in the 'Ghetto' with my three little brothers. My father is 'serving his country' as is my brother

Pali. This is the Twentieth Century. 'You', decayed world, barbarian humanity! Let me live – or destroy me. Or treat us like animals.

Two days later she wrote:

There is again something terrible brewing in the air. Am I happy now? Hmm, can one be filled with joy for having our house marked as a Jewish house and at the same time hundreds and thousands of people losing their homes? This is the much praised culture of the twentieth century.

More anguish was to come. At midnight on 19 June Judit was on night duty at the home. She had just received a postcard from her father Lajos who was still on labour service. He was alive but her mother and three younger brothers had been deported. She wrote:

Is it possible, my Dear Mother, that I will never see you again? Will I never be able to sit in your lap again, my one and only Good Father? Will I never embrace you again, my dear little brothers? You will think of me, won't you Lacika?

Such news was too much for anyone to bear, let alone a young girl far from home and her loved ones. The next day she poured out her heart again:

I am at home, am I? Really? My father's postcard means the collapse of a world for me. The sword has fallen and swept away what was in its way, the ghetto. Mother and the children have moved on like migrating birds, but not with the freedom of birds. I have no one left, just my free thoughts.

The sign on the door of Lieutenant Colonel László Ferenczy's office on Semmelweis Street, near the Astoria Hotel, said 'Moving Company'. László Endre had his office in the same building. As the gendarmerie commander in charge of the deportations, Ferenczy was extremely proficient at his job. Hungary was usually a slow, bureaucratic state where decisions often were shunted sideways or kicked into the bureaucratic hedgerows. But not where its Jews were concerned. Ferenczy was born in Transylvania in 1898, to an average middle-class family. He fought in the First World War and was awarded two medals for bravery. He joined the gendarmerie after the war and rose up the ranks, serving for a while at the Horthys' summer residence. After the war, his aide Captain Leó Lulay described him as an 'extremely taciturn distrustful man ... impatient, impulsive and extraordinarily tight-fisted ... narrow-minded with a rather limited intelligence'.[5]

But for Ferenczy and Endre, the biggest prize, the Jews of Budapest, was yet to be moved. Several factors began to work against the final planned stage of the Hungarian Holocaust: logistical, diplomatic and strategic. Numbering between 250,000 and 280,000, depending on the status of converts to Christianity, they were now crammed into just over 1,800 buildings. It would be impossible to deport them quickly, let alone in secret, as the Nazis preferred. Dragging this many people from their homes, including women, children and old people, in full view of their neighbours, corralling them into holding camps and then forcing them onto trains would demand large numbers of gendarmes and German soldiers.

There would also be substantial diplomatic fall-out. By the second half of June the Jewish Council had finally started to distribute copies of the *Auschwitz Protocols* to their government allies, Church leaders and contacts abroad. Copies arrived in Switzerland, where numerous international Jewish organisations were headquartered. They informed Allied diplomats, who sent urgent reports back to their governments. The Swiss newspapers wrote in detail about the ghettoisation and deportations, and the reports were picked up by the Western press. Horthy still hoped that Hungary would somehow be liberated by the Western Allies. The stream of negative foreign press coverage unsettled him. Pressure also came from István Bethlen, the pro-Allied former prime minister. In a long memorandum to Horthy, Bethlen called for:

an end to the inhuman, stupid and cruel persecution of the Jews ... which has besmirched the Hungarian name before the eyes of the world and which has given rise to the most loathsome corruption, robberies and thieveries, into which, unfortunately, a considerable part of the Hungarian intelligentsia was also drawn.[6]

The strategic situation had also changed. The Western Allies were advancing through France after D-Day on 6 June and Soviet forces were steadily moving towards Hungary. It was clear the Germans were losing the war. Budapest was still home to a substantial contingent of neutral diplomats, including Angelo Rotta, the papal nuncio, who were repeatedly protesting about the deportations. Rotta, who had been posted to Hungary in 1930, was the dean of the Budapest diplomatic corps. A central figure in the neutral diplomats' rescue work, he used his moral and religious authority as the Vatican's representative with courage and determination. 'The ambassadors of neutral foreign countries showed up at the Ministry of Foreign Affairs one after the other', records Munkácsi, 'hardly a day passed without one paying a visit to protest'. The Vatican had received a copy of the *Protocols* in late April 1944 but had so far stayed silent. Pope Pius XII, like Hungary's Church leaders, had said little in public about the Nazi persecution of the Jews. Like them, he focused his efforts on aiding Jews who had converted to Catholicism. But on 25 June the pope finally took action and personally called on Horthy to stop the deportations.[7] The next day President Roosevelt passed an ultimatum to Horthy via the Swiss Legation. If the deportations were not stopped Horthy would be tried as a war criminal after the war. Four days later King Gusztav of Sweden also pressured Horthy to stop the deportations.

The protests and warnings had an effect. On 26 June Horthy ordered that the deportations be drastically curtailed, Baky and Endre be fired and the gendarmerie be forbidden from taking part in the deportations. Yet no concrete steps were taken to ensure that this happened. In response, Ferenczy and his henchmen speeded up the remaining transits. Thousands of Jews from southern Hungary were rapidly entrained and sent to their deaths. Across the outskirts of Budapest, in Újpest, Kispest, Csepel Island, Békásmegyer and other places, the Jews were rounded up. Baky and Endre then conjured up an elaborate scheme for a coup. The gendarmes would gather on Heroes Square, an iconic plaza at the top of Andrássy Way, on 2 July for a flag dedication ceremony presided over by Magdolna Horthy. They would then be given three days' 'leave' – time to be used for reconnaissance of the Yellow Star houses. Thousands of gendarmes duly flooded Budapest's streets, strutting confidently, sending a wave of terror through Budapest's Jews. Their deportation was scheduled for 6 July. The detailed blueprint for the operation was drawn up by Colonel Jenő Péterffy – the same torturer and murderer who had commanded the detachment in the Nagyvárad 'mint'.[8] Gendarmes from Nagyvárad were to be deployed to assist in the Budapest deportations.

But the protests and threats from the pope, neutral countries and President Roosevelt had unsettled Horthy. As Munkácsi notes, doubtless the West's most effective message was delivered on 2 July by the US Air Force: the first massive, daytime bombing raid against Hungary targeting industrial sites and transport infrastructure. More than 5,000 civilians were killed.[9] The air raid also devastated much of Andrássy Way and the side streets leading off it. Edina Zichy Pallavicini visited a few days later to see the destruction. 'Lots of villas of our friends were damaged: the Geist villa, Walkos, Gladys Széchenyi's, the Pallavicini house, Bethlen villa etc', she wrote on 7 July. The American air raid, Baky and Endre's planned coup and the defiance of the gendarmes finally roused the regent to action.

The day after the air raid Ilona Edelsheim Gyulai went in the afternoon to see the bomb damage at Keleti Station and the surrounding areas. She was now head nurse at the Szikla Hospital, treating those injured in the bombings, often working with a group of Jewish doctors. The hospital had been set up in the caverns under the Buda Castle. It treated patients regardless of religion or nationality. When Ilona returned to the Royal Palace she had a visitor: Sándor

Török, a member of the Jewish Council and leader of the Association of Christian Jews in Hungary – the converts. Török was Ilona's most important contact in the Jewish community. During the summer of 1944 Török telephoned her most days, under the code-name of Bardocz, the bookbinder. If Török said that the job was finished it meant he had something important to tell her. Ilona did not discuss anything important over the telephone, suspecting that the Palace telephones were bugged by the Gestapo.

Ilona had a number of high-level contacts gathering and sharing intelligence. Soon after the start of the deportations she had set up a small group of trusted 'conspirators', including Papal Nuncio Angelo Rotta, Red Cross officials, religious leaders and Edina Zichy Pallavicini. Ilona passed the information they gathered to her father-in-law. Sometimes she intervened directly, as when a government official demanded that the Jewish doctors with whom she worked at the Szikla Hospital be sent to the front. Ilona informed the official that if he persisted she would go straight to Admiral Horthy and have him sacked. He immediately backed down.

Török had brought Ilona a copy of the *Auschwitz Protocols*. It had an immediate impact. 'Somehow I sensed straight away that every word of this account was true, that it was not written for propaganda purposes but was a matter-of-fact account of the horrors they had experienced and which the human mind could barely comprehend', she wrote. Ilona gave a copy to Magdolna Horthy, who promised to pass it immediately to the Regent. In her memoir Ilona rejects claims that Horthy already knew about the realities of Auschwitz and the fate of those deported. 'In my judgement this is impossible, because when we discussed the Auschwitz records [*Protocols*] in the evening after reading it, he certainly would have told us if he had known earlier about it already or if someone had told him such things.' For Ilona, it was 'perfectly clear' that the *Protocols* made Horthy stop the deportations.[10]

Whatever the final catalyst was, Horthy acted decisively. The flag-dedication ceremony on Heroes Square was cancelled. Horthy ordered General Károly Lázár, the commander of the loyal Home Guards, to commission Colonel Ferenc Koszorús, the commander of the First Armoured Division, to stop Baky's coup attempt. Colonel Koszorús was a highly regarded officer who had served with distinction on the eastern front. His division was stationed in Esztergom, thirty miles north of Budapest. Horthy summoned Colonel Koszorús on the evening of 5 July and gave him his orders: the gendarmes must be expelled from the city and by force if need be. There was no time to waste. Baky and Endre had planned to begin the deportation of Budapest's Jews the next day. Colonel Koszorús ordered his division to enter the city. The armoured column began to move from Esztergom towards the capital. They far outnumbered and outgunned the gendarmes, who were only armed with rifles and pistols.

Meanwhile, in the early hours of 6 July, General Lázár summoned the two gendarmerie commanders who would oversee the deportations from their hotel rooms to the Royal Palace. They were brought in official cars, flanked by motorcycle officers with sidecars, their outriders armed with sub-machine guns. General Lázár then gave them their orders: withdraw their units immediately from Budapest or face the full force of the army. They accepted their instructions. By 7.00 am the loyalist First Armoured Division had taken control of the city, sealing off the roads and deploying their units at strategic sites, with their guns primed. At 11.00 am Horthy summoned more gendarmerie commanders to the Royal Palace. He was blunt in his condemnation:

You have betrayed my confidence and become political playthings. Perhaps against your will. I order all gendarmerie units to leave the capital today by 4.00 pm. I do not wish to see a gendarme in Budapest. In order to ensure calm I have summoned army units to the capital.[11]

There was no resistance. Baky ordered the gendarmes to leave the city. The coup was over before it started. Horthy's action came too late to save the Jews from the outskirts of the city, and a further 24,000 were deported between 6 and 8 July. But the remaining Jews of Budapest were saved, for now.

Edina Zichy Pallavicini was watching events with mounting rage and frustration at Horthy's passivity. Yes, the gendarmes had left, but the situation remained deeply unstable and dangerous. On 10 July she visited the Horthys at the Royal Palace. Magdolna was once again downcast. This passive approach achieved nothing, Edina believed. When Horthy appeared Edina told him that if he could not get rid of Baky and Endre, he ought to shoot them himself. But Horthy was incapable of such decisive action.

Sitting in his office at the Majestic Hotel on Sváb Hill, Adolf Eichmann was enraged at Horthy's expulsion of the gendarmes. Without the gendarmes Eichmann was powerless to deport Budapest's Jews. The regular police and the Hungarian Army would follow Horthy's orders, not the Germans' instructions. There were not enough Gestapo and SS officers to round up 250,000 people and force them onto trains. The German Army was busy in the east as the Soviets advanced. Meanwhile in Berlin, Heinrich Himmler, Eichmann's ultimate boss, was watching carefully as Allied armies advanced on Germany from both east and west. By now Himmler was considering the prospect of a separate peace with the Western Allies. The deportation of Hungary's Jews would not help this cause. But if the Jews were saved, for now, their lives remained immiserated. The Yellow Star was still compulsory. They remained confined to Yellow Star houses, controlled by a plethora of petty, spiteful regulations. Their food rations were steadily reduced. Most could no longer work as they were only allowed out between 11.00 am and 5.00 pm. Their businesses had been closed or appropriated. Their assets remained frozen. The gendarmes were gone but Arrow Cross militiamen still patrolled the city streets, brutalising and terrorising their victims.

Not only Himmler and Horthy had begun to see the writing on the wall. Budapest's Jews gained an apparent new ally: Lieutenant Colonel László Ferenczy, the gendarmerie commander formerly in charge of the deportations. The mass killer of the countryside Jews now remodelled himself as the saviour of the Jews of Budapest. The Jewish leaders were naturally divided about Ferenczy's overtures. Ferenczy repeatedly tried to put the blame for the deportations on the Germans, although the central role of the gendarmerie was by now well known to the Jewish leaders. On the other hand, Ferenczy had approached the Council. The Jews of Budapest were still alive and needed every ally they could get. Ferenczy remained a very powerful figure. A series of meetings followed, veering on the grotesque. Ferenczy even visited Samu Stern at home, in what Munkácsi described as 'a scene of farcical horror' as he 'politely entered and took a seat in great decorum'.[12]

The power struggle between Eichmann and Horthy ramped up a level. Soon after Baky's coup failed, columns of German tanks and armoured vehicles roared down the main streets of the city, in a very public reminder of their power. For now Eichmann had lost the war; the Jews of Budapest were still there and still alive. But he quickly won a significant battle. On 14 July, five days after Horthy had announced the end of the deportations, around 1,500 Jews interned at the Kistarcsa camp outside Budapest and the National Theological Institute on Rökk Szilárd Street were entrained and sent to Auschwitz. The Jewish Council quickly went into action, alerting its allies in the churches, neutral diplomats and the regent. Horthy summoned Jaross and ordered him to stop the deportation. The train was only at Hatvan, around thirty miles from Budapest. It was stopped and the prisoners returned to Budapest. Eichmann was enraged. Five days later every member of the Jewish Council was summoned to the Majestic Hotel early in the morning. They were held all day incommunicado while SS officers made polite conversation about nothing in particular. Meanwhile a Gestapo unit, working with Baky, was at Kistarcsa. The telephone lines were cut. Most of those on the previous transport were entrained again. The Jewish Council members were finally let out at 7.30 pm. By then the train from Kistarcsa was out of Hungary, en route to Auschwitz.[13] Buoyed by their success, Eichmann and his Hungarian allies quickly sent another 1,500 Jews held at an internment camp in Sárvár, western Hungary, to Auschwitz. That was the final deportation of the summer.[14]

*

As the air raids ravaged Budapest, Robi Lichtenstein had a new job. He and his family had been relocated from their flat on Váci Way to a smaller apartment in a Yellow Star house nearby at 18 Kresz Géza Street. The four of them lived in one room. Conditions were much more crowded and the regulations were oppressive, but unlike their relatives in the countryside, they were all still alive. Robi and his sister Zsuzsa had already had the first of several narrow escapes. When the Nazis invaded their parents had thought about sending them to the small town of Abony, southeast of Budapest, where Fülöp's brother Zsigmond was the town baker. Robi spent much of each summer working at the bakery. One of his earliest happy memories was of breaking open a fresh loaf and deeply inhaling the wonderful smell. Zsigmond and his family had been deported to Auschwitz. One daughter survived.

The area around Váci Way and Kresz Géza Street was hit heavily in the bombings – it was very near to Nyugati Station, a prime target for the Allied air raids. Robi now worked as a salvager, helping to clean and sort the rubble on the bomb sites. The teams were divided by floors; one group took out bathroom fittings, sinks and bathtubs from the apartments. Anything salvageable was removed. Robi was sent to work on the roofs. It was dangerous work as they, or the buildings, could collapse. But as he scampered along the tops of the apartment buildings, he did not feel scared. Instead he enjoyed the view of the city and the sense of freedom. High above the streets, nobody cared that he wore a Yellow Star.

24

Neutral Rescuers

> The undersigned representatives of the neutral powers accredited to Budapest have learned with painful surprise that the deportation of all the Jews of Hungary is to be started soon. We also know, and from an absolutely reliable source, what deportation means in most cases, even when it is masked as labour service abroad.
>
> Letter of protest from neutral diplomats in Budapest
> to Admiral Horthy about the planned deportation of the
> city's remaining Jews, 21 August 1944.

The handsome young Swedish diplomat was causing quite a stir at the von Bergs' dinner table. Ten years earlier Patrick Leigh Fermor had stayed at Tibor and Bertha's home at 15 Úri Street in the Castle district. Tibor and Bertha had since divorced, but still shared the same house. Bertha now lived upstairs with her half-sister Countess Erzsébet Nákó. Raoul Wallenberg had arrived in the city a couple of days earlier on 9 July 1944. Tibor, who had strong family connections to Sweden, had quickly invited him over. Per Anger, a Swedish diplomat stationed in Budapest, was also a distant cousin of Tibor's. Wallenberg was thirty-one and already knew the city well, having made numerous business trips there during the war. He had enjoyed himself, partying with the city's social elite. Even in wartime Budapest's hedonistic spirit still lingered.

Wallenberg is the best known of the cohort of courageous, determined neutral diplomats who saved tens of thousands of Jews in Budapest during the last months of the war. The Swede was the only neutral diplomat to be sent to Budapest specifically to save the remnant of Hungarian Jewry. The Swiss Carl Lutz, the Italian/Spanish Giorgio Perlasca, the Papal Nuncio Angelo Rotta and other neutral envoys were already in the city when they became rescuers and issued protective papers. Wallenberg had originally been recruited by Iver Olsen, the Stockholm representative of the US War Refugee Board (WRB). The WRB had been set up by President Roosevelt in January 1944 to rescue Jews and other victims of Nazism. It worked with the American Jewish Joint Distribution Committee and the Zionist rescue networks, supplying them with funds and other assistance. The WRB already had representatives in neutral countries including Sweden, Turkey and Switzerland. The WRB representatives were in prime position to gather intelligence, which they sent back to Washington. They used spies, forgers and money-launderers to save Jews and help resistance movements. As the United States and Hungary were at war, the WRB could not send an American to Hungary. But a Swede was permitted.

The evening at the von Bergs' went well. Erzsébet was clearly intrigued by Wallenberg. But the attraction was one-way. The twenty-two-year-old countess was short and stocky, not his type. But she was vivacious and engaging and had a wide circle of connections across the city. Per Anger suggested to Erzsébet that she work as Wallenberg's secretary. She readily agreed. She soon became indispensable to his increasingly complex rescue operation – and fell in love with Wallenberg.[1] The Swedish diplomat soon grew to admire and appreciate Erzsébet's talents as a secretary. But he had no romantic feelings for her. Another young woman would soon catch his eye – which would later cause some tension.

Per Anger had rented a villa on Minerva Street in Buda, from where he had already given out several hundred Swedish protective passes, declaring that the holder was under Swedish protection. This innovative manoeuvre, rooted in the arcane concepts of extra-territoriality, diplomatic immunity and neutral protecting powers, had proved surprisingly successful, which was why Anger needed Wallenberg to work with him. The Minerva Street villa was mobbed every morning by Jews desperate to obtain one of the passes, brandishing real or imaginary Swedish connections. At the start the operation had just over a dozen key workers. But within a month the organisation had forty employees and was continually expanding. It was divided into seven sections: reception, registration, accounts, archive, correspondence, housing and transportation. The applications were piling up – there were around 4,000 to be dealt with and about 600 more arrived each day.[2]

One day in September 1944 a new recruit arrived: an eighteen-year-old boy called Gábor Forgács. His father, Vilmos, the manager of the Orion electronics company, was one of the earliest recruits and a central part of the operation. Gábor had escaped from labour service. He had not been sent to Ukraine, but was working in a coal mine. Every day he walked seven kilometres to work, dug coal for ten hours, then walked back again. He was fed but lost a lot of weight. Vilmos had sent his son a Swedish passport. But Gábor was not sure about drawing attention to himself by presenting it to the overseers. In any case the work, while extremely tough, was not dangerous. Nobody was torturing or executing them. On 6 September Gábor and some of the others were put on a train and told they were going to the front in Serbia. The train passed through Budapest, where Gábor jumped off. He went home. The next day Vilmos took him to Minerva Street and he started work as a messenger.

The young boy's recollections give a vivid picture of the day-to-day workings of the rescue operation. Wallenberg had two assistants: Erzsébet Nákó, who wore colourful outfits matching her exuberant personality, and Mrs Falk, who dressed in conservative business suits. The three key male workers – Gábor's father, Vilmos, Hugo Wohl and Pál Hegedűs, always wore business suits and ties. Wallenberg himself dressed formally but in a more American style, wearing button-down shirts. But the real head-turner was Berber Smit, the daughter of Lolle Smit, the head of Philips and an Allied intelligence agent who had worked with Colonel Howie and numerous other Allied POWs. The Smits' house was now under Swedish protection. Lolle had left Budapest in June but his family was still in Budapest. Berber was tall with "lightning-green eyes", coffee-coloured skin, a winning smile and a shapely figure. Gábor Forgács was entranced. "She was wonderful, a miracle," he recalled many years later. Wallenberg asked Berber out on a date. By the next month, the two were a couple.[3]

Wallenberg's arrival in Budapest was noted in several capitals including Moscow. He was a scion of the most powerful banking dynasty in Sweden – whose operations were closely watched by numerous wartime intelligence services. Jacob and Marcus Wallenberg, his father's cousins, ran Enskilda Bank, the most powerful bank in Sweden, which controlled a good part of the Swedish economy. The two brothers played a smart and very lucrative game – keeping good relations with both Allied and Axis powers. Jacob looked after the German connection, while Marcus worked with the Allies. Iver Olsen of the War Refugee Board, who sent Wallenberg to Budapest from Stockholm, sent regular reports back to Washington about the Wallenbergs' and Enskilda's business operations. He was not a fan. In February 1944 Olsen reported his impressions of Marcus Wallenberg:

> Although he is considered to be strongly pro-Allied in sympathy, the implications of this sentiment are obscured somewhat by the fact that he handles all United Nations business, while his brother, Jacob, is equally entrenched in the Axis end. In other words, the Stockholm Enskilda Bank has its position pretty well hedged.[4]

The Wallenberg family name doubtless helped open doors for Raoul. It would also, ultimately, doom him.

Hannah Szenes's mother, Katalin, was not the only inmate that Hannah knew at the Gyorskocsi Street prison. Yoel Palgi finally crossed into Hungary with Peretz Goldstein, another Jewish parachutist from Palestine, later in June. From Pécs, in southern Hungary, Palgi and Goldstein took a train to Budapest without problems. This is because they were being watched by Hungarian intelligence. Palgi went several times to the Great Synagogue to look for Hannah, as they had agreed, but there was no sign of her.

He went to the Jewish Council on Síp Street and also met with the Vaada, including Hansi Brand. She asked Palgi whether he had brought a plan with him, setting out what should be done to save the Hungarian Jews. Palgi pulled something from his pocket and presented it to her. Hansi was incredulous and started laughing. The parachutists were all brave, but their mission was futile. Why had they come? What could they achieve? There was no armed resistance movement in Hungary and nor was there likely to be. And the two men were clearly being watched – Hansi noticed several Hungarian intelligence agents hanging around nearby. More, Palgi and Goldstein were endangering the delicate negotiations with Eichmann about the VIP train and the transport of the 20,000 Jews to Austria that were now moving to fruition.

Kasztner decided that as Palgi's presence was known to the authorities, he should present himself to the Nazis as an emissary from the Istanbul Vaada, bringing its response to the Brand mission. Palgi agreed and in the meantime went to stay with Hansi at the Brand family apartment. It was a comfortable home with plenty of books and a decent cognac. But that night there was an air raid and a bomb exploded nearby, shattering the windows and blowing Palgi out of bed. The next day was a Saturday. That morning Hansi took Palgi to the Hotel Majestic. But Eichmann was not there, nor was Klages. They found two other SS officers to whom Palgi spun his story. It seemed to work. One of the SS men agreed to give Palgi a paper that he was working for the Gestapo and told him to come back next week to collect it. Beneath the civilised conversation and cigarettes the Majestic was a place of violence and terror. Palgi saw a Jewish prisoner who had been whipped and beaten being dragged along the corridor. But he freely walked out of the building, stunned at the ease with which he, a Hungarian Jew and British officer, had entered and left the Gestapo headquarters. The air raid was still going on in the south of Budapest, so Palgi went for a walk. Sváb Hill was one of the most scenic parts of the city, renowned for its hiking trails and fresh mountain air. It was a warm, sunny day and young couples strolled along the paths. The whole experience was surreal.[5]

Back in the city Palgi decided to model himself a disguise. He bought an elegant blue suit, shaved off his moustache and changed his hairstyle. He practised walking with a different gait. It was to no avail. He was arrested two days later by the Hungarian secret police. Palgi's protests that he was under Gestapo protection were worthless. He was savagely beaten. Goldstein gave himself up, also at the urging of Kasztner. The Hungarians were on his trail and would soon find him anyway. Kasztner doubtless believed that he could use his connections to arrange for both Palgi and Goldstein to be released later. This was a miscalculation. The Vaada's connection and influence were with the SS and Eichmann's group. The Nazis would rescue Hansi Brand from the Hungarians as she was working for something that was also in Himmler's interest. But the parachutists were not. The Hungarians were already enraged about the Brand mission. The Hungarian Jews, and their wealth, were the property of Hungary, not Germany. Palgi and Goldstein were brutally interrogated, before they were imprisoned on Gyorskocsi Street.

Once inside the prison, Palgi heard repeatedly about the 'Palestinian girl' inmate. Hannah was held three floors above him in solitary confinement. They managed to communicate by flashing messages to each other with their mirrors. June turned into July. Most days Hannah was taken to the Majestic to be questioned. She sometimes held up paper letters at the window of her cell to send messages to the other prisoners. Hannah used her daily journeys to gather information from other prisoners with whom she was transported and from the guards, who now knew her. As the weeks ground on, her conditions eased. On 17 July, her birthday, Katalin managed to get a jar of marmalade to her cell. Hannah wrote a thank-you letter, which arrived the same day. There were a number of child inmates at the prison and Hannah was able to play with them and make dolls and toys from rags and string for them. One of the female warders even brought her a chair to stand on to make it easier to communicate with her mother through the cell windows. Hannah made more and more dolls. She sent some paper dolls of a young couple to her mother. Katalin wrote back: 'Though I have always dreamed of the day you would present me with grandchildren, for the time being these substitutes will do.'[6]

The interrogations, however, did not stop. Hannah could not tell the Germans the details of her code-book as she had deliberately left it on the train to Budapest. But she had admitted that the radio was hers. She was tortured. She spoke of none of this with her mother. Instead, Hannah suggested that her mother learn Hebrew as she had plenty of time on her hands. Hannah sent her mother Hebrew lessons each day. After a while Hannah's interrogations changed. They became less violent. It was clear she was not going to talk. For the Germans Hannah was a curiosity. A place in Palestine was highly prized and hard to obtain. This courageous, daring young Jewish woman had made a new life there but had come back to Hungary to rescue her people. The Germans were intrigued by her and her life in Palestine.

On 26 June, partly as a result of foreign pressure after the publication of the *Auschwitz Protocols*, the Hungarians agreed to authorise the emigration of 7,800 Jews, most of whom were sponsored by the Swiss, with several hundred under Swedish protection. The registration of the emigrants was to be organised by the Palestine Office, under the leadership of Miklós Krausz, who worked in the basement of the Swiss Legation under the protection of Carl Lutz. Krausz was an effective organiser and interlocutor with Hungarian officialdom. But he was not popular with his fellow Jews. He was secretive, uncommunicative, unwilling to work with others and often cantankerous. Krausz was unable to delegate, so one room of his office was always jammed with supplicants, waiting hours to see him. He was exempted from having to wear a Yellow Star, which greatly increased his safety and freedom of movement. Krausz understood the potential power and influence both of the neutral countries and of bureaucracy. Whether under the Austro-Hungarian Empire, during the Horthy era or now under the Nazis, Hungarian officialdom had a near-mystical reverence for forms garnished with signatures and stamps.

Even made-up documents, if they looked official enough and were flourished with enough confidence, could work wonders – and in wartime Budapest they did.

The Hungarian government had agreed that 7,800 individuals could leave. Krausz and the other Jewish leaders decided that this actually meant permission for 7,800 families to emigrate. This would demand extensive paperwork. Each Palestine certificate was numbered, to prevent duplication. Carl Lutz advised that this process should take place away from the Legation. A new premises was acquired at 29 Vadász Street in District V, a short walk from the Legation, known as the Glass House. Its owner, Artúr Weisz, was in the glass business. The new office opened on 24 July and was given Swiss diplomatic status, meaning it was legally Swiss territory. The Glass House would soon become one of the most important sanctuaries in Budapest. Numerous young Zionists working there were given Swiss and Hungarian identity papers and were exempted from the Yellow Star regulations. They could move freely around the city and sleep where they liked.

The Zionists turned the Glass House into the headquarters of the Jewish resistance, using it as a base to produce and distribute forged documents, rescue Jews from prison camps inside Hungary and smuggle them out to Romania, Slovakia and Yugoslavia. This caused considerable tension with Krausz and Weisz, who believed such activities endangered their activities, which were tolerated by the authorities. Within a couple of weeks a Swiss collective passport had been compiled for 2,200 people, complete with Hungarian exit and Romanian transit visas. By now word had spread among Budapest's Jews about the Glass House. Every day the site, like the Swedish Minerva Street villa, was mobbed by hundreds seeking protective papers.

The deportations had stopped but Budapest's Jews were still living in a state of fear and anxiety. The departure of Fülöp Freudiger, a leading member of the Jewish Council, only increased their nervousness that a new catastrophe awaited. Freudiger and his family fled to Romania in early August, disguised as Romanians, with the help of his Nazi contact Dieter Wisliceny. Many were furious that the Orthodox leader abandoned his community in their hour of need – an anger that simmered for decades. Eichmann took revenge for Freudiger's escape. On 18 August the Gestapo arrested three leading members of the Jewish Council, Samu Stern, Ernő Pető and Károly Wilhelm, together with their families. Munkácsi, who had also been slated for arrest, avoided the pick-up. After strong protests by Admiral Horthy, Stern and Wilhelm were released the next day. Pető was released on 21 August.

Once released, the SS ordered Pető to compile a list of all Council members, staff and volunteers. The Nazis' demand for the details of the Jewish Council personnel triggered a fresh wave of panic and terror. By now everyone knew what lists meant. The Jews' fears were well founded. Eichmann had not given up. The gendarmes were gone but the Germans and their Hungarian allies had drawn up a detailed plan to deport the Jews of Budapest. Between 50,000 and 60,000 'Galician infiltrators' would be handed over to the Germans. Jews on labour service and their families would not be deported. Other Hungarian Jews would be placed in work camps in the countryside. They would stay in Hungary. Any Jews that were deported were to remain alive. The several thousand Jews who were authorised to emigrate to neutral countries such as Sweden and Switzerland would be allowed to leave.[7] Lieutenant Colonel László Ferenczy showed the Council leaders the planned timetable. The Jews would be taken from the Yellow Star houses, then to settlements outside the city, from where they would be deported. The whole operation would last from 27 August to 18 September.

The Jewish leaders quickly responded. They lobbied their allies among the neutral diplomats to take action. They readily agreed. A group of envoys, including Papal Nuncio Angelo Rotta and Swedish, Portuguese, Swiss and Spanish diplomats sent a strongly worded note to the Hungarian government, demanding that the deportations be stopped finally and for good. Any more deportations, the diplomats wrote, would 'deal a death blow to the reputation of your country'.[8] The Nazis' new deportation plans were quickly leaked to the wider Jewish community, 'intensifying the already rampant panic to the point best described as an endemic frenzy that threatened to break out of control at any minute', records Munkácsi. Terror turned to hysteria and back to passive acceptance. The emotional roller-coaster was unbearable. One moment the Jews were safe, then doomed, then safe again and doomed once more. It was impossible to live like this. As the deportation day approached, it was an hour of 'utter despair', when some waited apathetically and others succumbed to 'sheer madness'.[9]

August 15 was Judit Ornstein's eighteenth birthday. She had received eighteen red roses from her friend, Gyuri, who was a year younger. The two of them had spent a lot of time together. Gyuri had fallen hard for Judit but she only wanted to be friends, even close friends, but nothing more. It seems another boy called Jóska had won her heart. Gyuri, though, was persistent. Even after Judit explained to him that she was not romantically interested, he still professed his love, writing her short stories, sending her letters and asking for a photograph. Judit admitted that she was flattered. 'I cannot say I wasn't pleased. After all, one is happy when one is loved. But I wasn't filled with the same joy as he felt when he sent them.'

The roses were not the only birthday gift. Judit also received an amulet, Bizet's opera *The Pearl Fishers*, a handkerchief, a fountain pen, a handbag, a first-aid kit for the shelter and book covers. But the best present was a long letter from her father Lajos. Her thoughts that day were of home. Judit longed so much for her mother she imagined that she heard her voice. Her diary entry is almost unbearably poignant. 'Bits of sounds wafted in from afar on the August breeze. The sound came in from the Waldsee or from Vienna. It was my mother's voice. My Mother, you thought of me and you thought back to your eighteenth birthday.'

Judit's mother and her three little brothers were all dead, turned to ashes. The Jews of Hajdúnánás had been deported to Debrecen in mid-June and from there most were sent to Auschwitz. It is impossible to know if Judit suspected their fate, but her yearning was as powerful as ever. 'They will come home. I know they will come home. It is always the best that comes after the worst and it is high time for that ... I think of Dad so often. I will write to him now. It makes me feel so good to do so', she wrote on 20 August.

25

A Time of Alibis

I wonder where they took my little brothers?! No one answers
me and I am again living in a fog.

Judit Ornstein, diary entry, 3 September 1944.

August 23 was a hot summer day, although there was a slight breeze,
recorded Mária Mádi in her diary. The air-raid sirens sounded all
morning. Her clinic now operated in a state of perpetual alert
– 'everybody, patients, nurses and my clerk were ready in any
moment to run to the shelter, although nothing happened'. The
sirens, the air raids, bomb damage and non-stop anxiety were a
part of everyday life, but were also immensely wearying. 'You may
imagine how tired people must be, day and night alarms and sitting
for hours in the shelter seems to be a part of the daily routine.
Serves them right.' Mádi's former partner in her medical practice
came to visit, with 'bad news from her husband'. She gave Mádi
a detailed, well-informed account of the train from Kistarcsa that
Horthy had ordered to be returned – and how a few days later,
the SS had raided the camp, overwhelmed the Hungarian guards
and deported the inmates again. 'Since then', noted Mádi, 'no news
about these people'.

But outside Hungary the news of the war was very cheering.
Mádi was still listening to the BBC, although this was now highly
illegal and dangerous. The US Army was charging towards Paris and
would soon liberate the city. 'The end of the war is in sight, really, if
they can keep up this pace', she wrote. But the really big news – at
least for Hungary – came through at 11.00 pm that day: Romania

had made peace with Russia and joined the Allies. 'This will mean either total collapse or an entire isolation of Germany herself.' Mádi's predictions were correct, but would take far longer than she, and many others, believed. King Michael I had led the coup, toppling Marshall Ion Antonescu, the Romanian prime minister and staunch ally of Hitler. King Michael immediately accepted an armistice with the Allies and declared war on Germany – and thus on Hungary as well. Romania's turnaround was a hammer blow to the Axis. Vital supplies of oil and foodstuffs were now lost as well as control of supply lines. An army of 1 million soldiers was now fighting with the Soviets against the Germans. Border clashes quickly erupted on the Hungarian–Romanian frontier. But here was a potential model for Admiral Horthy, if he could finally conquer his aversion to breaking his gentleman's promises to Hitler and act decisively.

For a moment, it seemed he could. That same evening Colonel Kudar of the AVK summoned Howie to see Horthy. Discouraged by Ujszászy's suspicions and near hostility, Howie had moved out of the Castle back to the Harff family home. Horthy asked Howie if the Western Allies could be contacted by radio. Howie said it was possible and suggested that Andzrej Sapieha and his team be used. The Poles and Howie then moved back into a disused wing of the Palace. Colonel Tost, Horthy's adjutant, brought them food and overlooked their security. The Poles sent two messages on Saturday morning, 26 August, asking for terms in Horthy's name. But the transmissions to London usually took place on Mondays and Thursdays, with a different, less powerful transmitter, so the Poles were not optimistic that the signal was picked up in London.

It was picked up in Budapest, loud and clear, by the Germans. Veesenmayer, the Reich plenipotentiary, warned the Hungarians that if the transmissions continued the Germans would shell the city. All further radio transmissions were cancelled, although a courier was sent to Switzerland to try and open a channel there. Howie and the Poles were immediately taken out of the city to a cottage by Lake Balaton, next to the Kudar family's holiday home. The Poles tried repeatedly to contact London using three different radios, but with no success. And the Gestapo were on their trail. After a few days Howie and Sapieha were taken across the Danube into Slovakia, then finally moved to Szigetszentmiklós, a pretty town on the Danube south of the capital.

The day after King Michael's coup Horthy met with Veesenmayer. He informed him that the Jews of Budapest could be transferred to camps inside Hungary but there would be no more deportations abroad. Eichmann conceded defeat. He asked his superiors in Berlin to recall his unit. On 25 August Himmler instructed the SS in Budapest that further deportations from Hungary were forbidden. The Russians were advancing steadily towards Hungary and now they had the Romanian Army on their side. This was no time to annoy the Hungarians. The Jews of Budapest could be dealt with later, once the Soviets had been beaten back. None of this was known to Budapest's Jews. Panic rose to new levels.

On the morning of Saturday, 26 August, the day when the deportation was supposed to start, thousands mobbed the Jewish Council offices on Síp Street. The furious crowd accused the Council of abandoning them. Inside the Yellow Star houses some packed bags, ready for the journey they had so long feared and anticipated. Some prepared to tear off their Yellow Stars and escape. Others set up makeshift guard units, ready to fight the gendarmes when they appeared. If they were going to die, then at least they would die fighting. At the children's home on Damjanich Street Judit Ornstein, Aunt Klára and the other staff and children prepared to be deported. The gate would be locked at eight o'clock in the evening and they would be transported out later that night, they believed.

The Jewish Council leaders returned in the early afternoon from a meeting with Lieutenant Colonel Ferenczy. The rumours of deportation were false and the situation was no worse than a week or two previously, they declared. Nobody was going anywhere against their will. The panic subsided. The Jews of Budapest 'flocked into the streets, wondrously relieved to still be around', notes Munkácsi. At Damjanich Street Judit and the other Jewish children celebrated. Aunt Klára had promised that if the rumour of impending deportation was not true and they were still at home that evening, they could bring out the gramophone and have a little party. 'Well it wasn't true. And we did bring it out', wrote Judit.

Further cheering news followed on the night of 29 August. Horthy finally sacked Döme Sztójay as prime minister and appointed General Géza Lakatos, the former commander of the Hungarian forces in Ukraine, in his stead. Horthy did not take Edina Zichy Pallavicini's advice and shoot László Baky and László Endre, the key officials behind the deportations, himself. But he did sack them and numerous other pro-Nazi officials, including Mihály Kolosváry-Borcsa, the book crusher. General Lakatos was tasked with boosting production, defending the frontiers, preserving peace and order, reestablishing Hungarian sovereignty, extricating Hungary from the war and stopping the persecution of the Jews.[1] Conditions eased quickly – Budapest's Jews were allowed greater freedom of movement including permission to attend synagogue during the coming New Year and Day of Atonement. On 10 September Horthy met with his most important advisers and officials, including General Lakatos, the former prime minister István Bethlen, the foreign and defence ministers and several generals. The decision was taken: Hungary would have to stop fighting immediately.

An envoy, Colonel Ladomér Zichy, was despatched to Slovakia, to make contact with the Slovak Partisans and then Moscow. Meanwhile a smaller problem remained. Count Bethlen was wanted by the Nazis. There were fears that news of his presence in the Castle might leak, Ilona recalls in her memoir. It was decided to shave off his distinguished moustache to make him less recognisable. Unfortunately, that left a very noticeable white patch of skin above his upper lip. Luckily Ilona remembered that István, her late husband, had a sun-lamp. She covered Bethlen's face with a towel and shone the sun lamp on his upper lip until it darkened. He was then smuggled out of the palace, back to his safe house in the country.[2]

*

For many Hungarian officials August 1944 was a month of rapid calibration and sudden desire for an alibi. Ottó Komoly, the president of the Vaada, was finding all sorts of doors that were previously closed suddenly opening. Now the Germans were losing the war numerous Hungarian officials were keen to show that they had helped the Jews. Of the Vaada leaders Komoly had the best connections to the Hungarian ruling elite, as well as good relations with the remnants of the liberal and left-wing opposition and members of the clergy. Komoly's diary, which survived the war, is studded with brief notes of intriguing assignations. On 21 August he met Leó Lullay, the gendarmerie captain and deputy of László Ferenczy. Like his superior officer, Lullay wanted to present himself as a saviour of the Jews, working to stop any further deportations. Komoly was well aware of the central role of the gendarmerie – and Ferenczy most of all – in the destruction of provincial Hungarian Jewry, but if there was advantage to be gained by Lullay's volte-face, he would use it. The two men met at the Pilvax Café, Komoly noted, to 'establish we're comrades'. The next day Komoly was in contact with Tibor Kóródy, an MP for the Arrow Cross, who was turning against the Germans. Two days later, Lullay and Ferenczy were warning the leaders of the Jewish Council to go into hiding in case the Germans targeted them.[3]

By now Komoly had joined the Jewish Council but in the eyes of many Jews it had been eclipsed by the Vaada. Apart from Komoly, many of the Council's leaders were faded, discredited figures. Fülöp Freudiger had rescued his chosen rabbis then fled to Romania. Samu Stern, the president, was a near-broken man. Although some Jewish attacks on Samu Stern were 'unmerited', wrote Komoly on 29 August, he also 'expressed his concern that Stern's qualities, attitude and manner do not match today's requirements'. Still, Komoly did his best to smooth over the rancour and in-fighting that still plagued the Jewish leadership. Komoly was dealing with the Hungarians, while Hansi Brand and Kasztner were negotiating with the Nazis. Brand's mission had failed, but it never stood a chance. But the VIP train had saved almost 1,700 people, while thousands more had been sent to Austria to work instead of Auschwitz to be gassed.

The Vaada's continuing attempts at deal-making were at least a mechanism and a means of engagement to try and stop the Nazis' attempts to resume the deportations. A further complicated set of negotiations was unfolding in Switzerland between Kasztner, Kurt Becher and Saly Meyer, who represented the American Jewish Joint Distribution Committee, a relief organisation, also involving substantial sums of money.

Spurred on by the success of the Glass House and the Swiss protective papers, a new drive was launched to protect Jewish children. Thousands had been left on their own or with relatives. Their fathers were on labour service, and their mothers had been deported. In early September Friedrich Born, the delegate of the International Red Cross, set up a new section, known as 'Department A', headed by Komoly. Funded by the American Joint, Section A soon became one of the largest rescue operations in wartime Budapest, headquartered on Mérleg Street in District V, near the Corso and the Chain Bridge. Department A was soon operating 52 children's homes across the city under Red Cross protection, where 550 workers cared for 5,500 Jewish children. Conditions were austere, with between five and ten children sleeping on mattresses in each room. The children did not leave the building. But they were clothed, fed and safe, for now. Later that month, on 15 September, Komoly met with Miklós Horthy Jr. to talk about dismantling the anti-Jewish measures. The son of the regent opened their discussion with a startling monologue:

> I was born and brought up an anti-Semite. Unimaginable for me to marry a Jewess, contaminate our blood. Then I entered the commercial world, found difficulties, e.g., getting export licences, but with Jewish help it became possible … What I foretold happened – mistakes everywhere, including the Jewish question. It should not have gone the way it has.

By now Komoly was involved in drawing up plans for the composition of the first Hungarian government after the defeat of the Germans. As for Miklós Horthy Jr., Komoly describes him as 'a well-intentioned disjointed thinker, who needs powerful advisers'.[4]

For the citizens of Budapest, both Jewish and Christian, the autumn of 1944 was a time of watching and waiting. The Jewish families' menfolk, away on labour service, garnered what news they could and tried to comfort and support their wives, sisters and children with their letters home. By the end of August Ignatz Katz and his comrades had been redeployed to Zombor (Sombor) airfield in northern Serbia. Ignatz had written to his wife Ilona and other relatives through the summer, with words of advice, snippets of news and requests for food and cigarettes. Their letters and packages arrived from Budapest, although sometimes the written notes became greasy from the food. Ignatz was talking to priests about converting to Christianity, perhaps joining the Reform Church. The weather was warm, and he was very sunburned. He understood that the end of the deportations in early July meant a reprieve for the Jews of Budapest. 'I think the situation has improved a lot and will continue to do to do so', he wrote on 23 July. But Ilona should not go to their haberdashery shop and she should be careful moving around the city. It seems that both were well aware of the deportations from the countryside. 'What you write about the relatives, we have information that they would be brought back. Regarding the future, be calm it will be all right.' Ignatz wrote again at the end of August, trying to reassure Ilona. 'Be calm, don't fret, everything will come in its time, we will yet be happy.'

But the war was everywhere. General Lakatos, the prime minister, gave what he hoped would be a rousing speech, reported *Pesti Hírlap* on 5 September. Hungary's full readiness for war must now be evident on the domestic front. Individual interests and concerns, comfort and luxury would all have to be supressed for the common good and every aspect of life devoted to the war. There would be no more tolerance of Budapest's nightlife. This was a time for everyone to do their duty – when the existence of the nation was being decided. Those 'tasteless and soulless' people who were still enjoying themselves would quickly find themselves in new jobs, where they would learn about the meaning of work. Advertisements praised the new austerity products. Two smiling children were shown happily drinking mugs of the enticingly named *Családi kávépótló*, 'family coffee substitute'.

At the Gyorskocsi Street prison conditions steadily eased. Hannah's interrogations slowed, then stopped completely. Prisoners began to be released. Her mother Katalin's cell was far less crowded. One moonlit evening she walked over to the window and looked across the courtyard. Years later she recalled how Hannah was 'silhouetted against the half-open window wearing her light-blue dressing gown, her hair softly framing her lovely face. It seemed to me her soul was mirrored in her face at that instant.' Katalin lay on her bed and sobbed.[5] On 1 September Hannah was moved into a cell next to her mother's. They walked together in the exercise yard and could sometimes hug in the corridors.

Ten days later Yoel Palgi and Hannah were told to pack their belongings. They met in the corridor of the prison. Palgi recalled: 'She looked so young and lovely, though very pale. She skipped lightly down the steps, wearing a raincoat and carrying a black case – as if she had just returned from a journey and was stepping off the train.' Both were taken to one of the military prisons. There the warders were friendly and welcoming, even shaking hands with the prisoners. Palgi asked permission to speak to Hannah. The last time the two comrades had spoken was in May, at a campfire in Yugoslavia with the Partisans. So much had happened since. They talked through everything: how the mission had gone wrong, Kallos's suicide, the headphones in his pocket. Perhaps their mission had been doomed from the start. The next day they were driven off again. Hannah was taken to the Conti Street prison. She smiled at Palgi and gave him a thumbs-up as the van drove away. He never saw her again.

Katalin Szenes was sent to Kistarcsa. No longer a transit camp for those en route to Auschwitz, the regime there was now easy-going, with few restrictions. There were no limits on letters or parcels and visitors were sometimes allowed. But Katalin had no news of Hannah and did not know where she was, and whether she was still alive. Katalin was finally released at the end of September. When Katalin got home she learned that a lawyer called Nánay had offered to represent Hannah if her case went to trial – he already represented Yoel Palgi and Peretz Goldstein, who were still incarcerated. Finally, in early October, Katalin was allowed a ten-minute visit with Hannah. She looked well but her cell was cold and she needed warm clothes. Katalin was working every contact to try and get Hannah released, especially among the Zionists. She met with a young man called Groszman, who made promises, but nothing happened. Groszman was powerless: the man to see was Rezső Kasztner. But Kasztner was never available. Katalin visited his office repeatedly and finally, on 12 October, she was allowed in. She met Ottó Komoly – he said he did not even know that Hannah was in Hungary. Komoly reassured her that they would do everything to get Hannah out. In fact either Katalin, or the Vaada, or both, should have informed the Swiss, who represented British interests, that British POWs were being held by the Hungarians in harsh conditions and tortured. Carl Lutz, who represented British interests, was a powerful ally of the Jewish community and would likely have intervened. But it seems this did not happen.

That autumn it was clear that the last days were approaching, a prelude to the final showdown with the Germans. But would the Hungarians fight with the Russians against the Nazis, or with the Nazis against the Russians? 'By mid-September, everybody realised that the game was nearing its conclusion', wrote Munkácsi. 'This gave rise to the widespread premonition that the murderers and traitors would not surrender without a fight, but force a bloody and fearsome confrontation to the end.' Some Jews disappeared from the Yellow Star houses, tore off their own Yellow Stars and obtained false papers in the name of Christians from the countryside. They found an increasing number of Christians in the city willing to hide them. Some sought an alibi for the post-war era, while others acted out of simple humanity.

For Alexander Szanto and his fellow labour servicemen, conditions eased somewhat. The company mostly worked in the fields, bringing in the harvests or repairing roads, although there was never enough to eat. They passed through towns and villages where the Jewish communities had vanished. 'The numerous, once flourishing communities in the province[s], looking back on a centuries-old proud history, had disappeared,' he later wrote. Szanto was well informed about the process: first the ghettoisation, then the deportation. 'Women and children, the old and the sick, everyone was dragged into the wagons, no exceptions were made'. Now only the Jews of Budapest were left and what would be their fate? 'Would these Jews – among them our family members – also be deported or would the liberation, the end of the war come sooner? It was a race against time.'

Occasionally Szanto met labour servicemen who had returned from the Ukrainian front, skeletal, half-starved figures who told terrible stories of sadistic Hungarian officers, brutality and deprivation. One favourite pastime was to make the labour servicemen climb into trees and make animal or bird noises. The men were sprayed with icy water and often used as target practice. Szanto's company was relocated to Jászberény, a small town 80 kilometres east of Budapest. There he saw one of the strangest sites of the war. In one part of the barracks was housed a group of labour servicemen who were either physically or mentally handicapped. Some were lame or crippled, while others were deaf-mutes. Several had gone insane. The Budapest Jewish community had repeatedly asked for the men to be released so they could be housed in communal institutions but the bureaucracy moved very slowly. Each day the men were allowed out for a while in a certain area. Szanto and the others tried to help as much as they could, and give them food, medicine and cigarettes from their own meagre supplies. 'It was a ghostly, gruesome sight as they moved along the walls, between them nervous patients twitching, epileptics in convulsions, the mental patients were running around in circles and others were squatting on the floor'. Eventually, the men were released. Later that year

Szanto managed to escape and return to Budapest for good. He and his wife Magda posed as non-Jews with false papers and survived the war.[6]

Allied bombers pounded the capital as the Russians advanced, sometimes turning whole buildings into dust and rubble. The Jewish Boys' Orphanage was hit by a bomb and completely destroyed. On 3 September Judit Ornstein finally received a postcard from her brother, Pál. The relief was indescribable. She had not heard from him for three months.

It looks like a card that has been washed by a storm but the important thing is that it is his writing. He is alive and he is going to come home. My intensely loved older brother, Pali! In my happiness at receiving your card, I don't even know what to write.

Her older brother was alive, but Judit was utterly haunted by the fate of her mother and little brothers, her anguish repeatedly detailed in her diary entries. Not knowing their fate was unbearable. That same day she wrote a heartfelt message to her mother, imagining her on the deportation train.

It was summer, and the sun beat down like a madman, but you were only granted a tiny bit of it, only a few rays penetrated into the ghetto. You were locked in, surrounded by a fence ... They just put you into wagons with your three little boys and took you where it pleased them. My dear Mother, I cannot possibly imagine what was going on in your mind. I only feel the weight of its unspeakable pain. And this is still with me. I don't know if you are still with your children, or whether fate has cut your paths from each other. But I believe, and I know that you will return home together ... Mother, Dear Mother, don't leave me alone. Write, give me a sign that you are alive and come home. Your little girl is waiting for you and her heart aches so for all of you.

Judit Ornstein as a young girl with her brothers Tibor, Zoltan and Pál. Tibor, Zoltan, their youngest brother Lászlo and their mother Frieda were all killed in Auschwitz.

A week later some good news came at last. Judit received a photograph from her father Lajos on labour service, showing him together with his work group. He looked 'very good' in it. Judit longed to see him. That was not possible but she wrote back the next day. Like many Hungarian Jews Judit's loyalties were now in turmoil. Her homeland had turned on her and her family. Zionism seemed ever more appealing. Where was her homeland now, she wrote on September 11. 'I can only call that place my "homeland" where I am not just a tolerated person. In that case, Hungary is not my homeland. My homeland is far, far away and that's where I long to be. My homeland is Palestine.'

Two days later she wrote a diary entry to her friend, Joska. She had hurt her foot and was reading a book by the Austrian Jewish writer Stefan Zweig. It was hard going, with many difficult words, but she was determined to persevere. She reminded Joska of a rainy afternoon they had spent playing ping-pong together. 'Do you think we will ever meet again? I just think you must think of us sometimes, but we will never meet. The siren has just gone off!!!'

Her prediction was correct. The children and their helpers rushed down to the cellar but Judit moved more slowly because of her bad foot. One of the teachers came back to get her. The children's home took a direct hit. Both she and Judit were killed. Judit's diary was later found in the wreckage of the building.

26

A New Year's Promise

Never before had they felt the truth of this prayer and the nearing of the days of judgement as they did on that day.

Ernő Munkácsi, on the service for Rosh Hashanah, the Jewish New Year, at the Great Synagogue in September 1944.

Tears streamed down the face of the congregants as they intoned the Rosh Hashanah prayers. The emotions surging through the aisles of the Great Synagogue, once a symbol of a prosperous, integrated community, were almost palpable. The Jewish communities of the provinces no longer existed. But perhaps 200,000 Jews – more if converts were included – were still alive in Budapest, the largest community in Europe. 'How many shall pass away and how many shall be born, who shall live and who shall die', sang the cantor, his voice reaching to the very heavens. It was an extraordinary spectacle for a country still occupied by the Nazis. The curfew had been eased for the Jewish holidays. Thousands of worshippers had gathered at Dohány Street and the nearby synagogues, even though the air raids were ever-present and there were no shelters nearby. Some of the congregants were optimistic. Yes, they were still living in Yellow Star houses and wore the same badge on their clothes. But it was clear that the Allies were winning. Perhaps the new year would mark the start of a new era, when they could tear off their Yellow Stars and return home. The brief interregnum of a more normal life would last until mid-October.

Soon after the Jewish New Year, Colonel Zichy, Horthy's envoy to the Russians, returned from Slovakia with good news. Stalin's terms for an armistice were acceptable. Hungary would remain free and independent, the Romanian Army would stop outside Transylvania and only the Russians would enter Hungarian territory. A referendum would later decide the fate of Transylvania. There was enough there to start negotiations. Horthy organised a delegation, including Géza Teleki, the son of Pál Teleki, to go to Moscow. The three-man delegation split up and crossed surreptitiously into Partisan-controlled territory in Slovakia, where Stalin's aeroplane came to collect them. There was already a shortwave radio transmitter above Colonel Tost's apartment in the Royal Palace. It now served as the secret link between Budapest and Moscow.

Even if Stalin was making accommodating noises, Horthy and his government had not given up on Hungary being liberated by the Western Allies. By now it was a pipedream, but still one with profound appeal. On 20 September Colonel Kudar came to collect Howie from his hideout in the countryside and brought him to the Palace. There he met Niki Horthy and Ilona Edelsheim Gyulai. The three of them talked at length. Howie, Ilona recalled, 'seemed a decent and trustworthy man'. Admiral Horthy's plan was now that Howie would fly out with General István Náday, the commander of the First Army, to Italy. There they would ask for an armistice and for Western Allied armies to occupy Hungary. Howie's mission was to happen under the highest levels of secrecy and he was shut away in Tost's quarters. Ilona brought his meals. Each time she was served lunch or dinner she packed it up in a mahogany food container, gave the food to Howie, then returned with empty plates. The palace servants, she thought, would wonder at her newfound appetite.

Horthy's plan had a fifty-fifty chance of success, Howie thought. The first problem was that all the airfields were under German control. The second was how to fly an enemy aircraft into Allied territory without being shot down. János Majoros, the captain, set the departure for 22 September, when cloudy weather was predicted – useful to hide from German fighters in pursuit. Howie met Horthy for the last time just before his departure. Howie proposed that Horthy focus on negotiating with the Russians. But Horthy still argued that the priority was to get Western Allied troops into Hungary. Howie's final request was for protection for Jane, who had provided him with sanctuary. Ilona arranged for her and her sons to find refuge at a convent in Buda. The boys were renamed Anna and Marie and dressed as girls, to their huge embarrassment. But they were safe.

The weather on the day of departure was cloudy, as the forecast had predicted. The Heinkel's engines were already running once Howie and General Náday arrived at the airfield. The aeroplane took off without problem and there were no German fighters in pursuit. As the Heinkel approached the Italian coast the pilot told the radio operator to signal using a code Howie had agreed. But the radio was dead. They were now in low cloud with no means of communication. Majoros wanted to fly on to Benghazi in Libya, but Howie insisted that they head for Allied headquarters in Naples. Majoros tried to land at Foggia, on Italy's east coast. He circled over the airfield and fired flares to indicate that the Heinkel was in distress, waiting for the landing lights to be switched on. Nothing happened. He fired more flares. The airstrip remained in darkness. The only option now was a forced landing – always a danger with a Heinkel as the fuel might explode. Majoros told his passengers to brace, raised the undercarriage and crash-landed the Heinkel in a field.

It was a remarkable feat of flying. Nobody was hurt and everyone disembarked. A few minutes later American airmen arrived and took Howie and the Hungarians to a nearby US airbase under armed escort. There Howie explained to the senior officer what their mission was. From there Howie and General Náday were taken to Bari in southern Italy, then on to Allied headquarters at Caserta. At first the Allied commanders were incredulous. A South African colonel, fighting with the British Army and living underground in Budapest for a year, had just crash-landed in Italy with a Hungarian general, bringing a plan for Allied parachutists to invade Hungary so the country could change sides. The two men's story seemed fantastic. But after a while their identities were confirmed. Perhaps a year earlier, when László Veress and the British ambassador to Turkey had first thrashed out terms of surrender, the Hungarian proposals might have led to something. But now they were far too little and too late.

There was no fighting yet on the streets of Budapest, but the war was everywhere. Sometimes it sounded as a continual low hum as shopkeepers shook their heads in regret at their lack of stock or variety, smiling regretfully as they intoned *Sajnos, nincs*, 'unfortunately there isn't any' of whatever the customer asked for. At other times it was an ear-splitting howl of the air-raid siren, then a body-shaking blast as the bombs exploded, shattering buildings, windows and people. As the Russians steadily advanced Soviet planes now joined the Allied raids on the city. A bomber crashed somewhere near Mária Mádi's apartment on 18 September, knocking out the tram service. 'You cannot imagine how the whole life of the city is paralysed', she wrote in her diary. 'No traffic, no shopping, no postal service, no telephone, no work done and much damage.' Mádi had planned to send some money to a relative, buy cigarettes and shop for food. But all that was impossible. The newspapers that usually appeared at noon were still not on sale at five o'clock in the afternoon. People were 'exhausted, exasperated', but still believed that the only remedy was for the Germans to hold out against the Russians. Mádi was no fan of the Russians, but understood that the coming Soviet invasion was the only way to get rid of the Nazis. She was scathing about those who failed to grasp this. 'Again, I can tell you, what I have already told you already several times, there is no hope when the bulk of the population is so dumb.'

The coming showdown between Hungary and the Germans was ever more evident. Horthy ordered the arrest of the Arrow Cross leaders but his loyalist gendarmes were unable to bring them into custody, as they were under Nazi protection. Emil Kovarcz, the terrorist leader soon to play a central role in the *Götterdämmerung* about to unfold across Budapest, was ensconced in a villa on Pasaréti Way.[1] Ferenc Szálasi was hosted by Karl Pfeffer-Wildenbruch, the commander of the SS forces in Budapest. Such weakness showed

Horthy's regime was entering its end. Adolf Eichmann was also back in Budapest. Hitler was well aware of Horthy's plans for an armistice and to change sides. The defection of Germany's only remaining ally – all the others had changed sides – could not be allowed to happen. Which was why Hitler's favourite commando was wandering around Hungary wearing a business suit with a Baedeker guidebook in his hand, posing as a Mr Wolff as cover for his reconnaissance missions.

Otto Skorzeny was a tall, imposing SS officer, with a long duelling scar down his left cheek. After serving on the eastern front, where he was wounded by shrapnel, he was recruited by Walter Schellenberg, the high-ranking SD officer, to train soldiers in paramilitary and behind-enemy-lines operations. In September 1943 Skorzeny led a daring airborne operation to rescue Benito Mussolini. His mission now was to take control of the Hungarian capital so that the Arrow Cross could take power and send Admiral Horthy into exile.[2] Even for Skorzeny this was a formidable military operation. The Royal Castle was heavily defended on a densely built-up hill with tanks, bunkers and machine-gun nests. There was nowhere to land gliders. The defenders would have a clear field of fire on any assault on the roads leading up to the Castle, while parachutists would be picked off in the air. There had to be an easier way to bring down Admiral Horthy than a full-frontal assault. Thanks to Wilhelm Höttl, there was. Skorzeny, the SD and the SS launched Operation Maus, a sneering jibe at Miklós Horthy Jr.'s first name.

Around this time Admiral Horthy charged István Ujszászy with a new task: build a popular anti-Nazi front. Katalin Karády had used her underground contacts to arrange meetings for him with left-wing groups and the small but active Communist resistance. It was an ironic mission for Ujszászy. As chief of the Hungarian secret police he had spent years hunting the Communists. His officers had arrested numerous activists and imprisoned them. Some had even been executed. Now he had to make an alliance with them. Ujszászy met with László Rajk, an influential Communist leader. They discussed plans to arm the workers so they could take control of the factories, roads, bridges and railways. The weapons would be distributed by General Bakay, the loyalist commander of the Budapest Army Corps. Like many of Horthy's initiatives and ideas, nothing came of it. Outside the working-class areas of Budapest, the Communists had very little support.

For Wallenberg, too, the September easing of restrictions and the release of prisoners made his work easier. The Kistarcsa and Columbus Street camps were handed back to the Hungarians. While no Jews had been relocated from Budapest to the countryside, 5,000 Jews (such as Robi Lichtenstein) had been drafted for digging and cleaning up after air raids. There were plans to issue a total of 4,500 protective passports, of which 2,700 had been given out. Choosing who would receive the life-saving papers was an agonising task. Around 100 people were now working for Wallenberg's department. A job at the Legation was highly prized – employees received a card from the Interior Ministry. Both they and their families were exempted from wearing Yellow Stars and from being drafted for labour service.

The constant air raids were making rescue work more difficult. But the real problem was the success of the safe passes. With a piece of paper with the right stamps and frankings being able to save the life of a family, many took desperate measures to try and obtain one. Shady characters were promising things they could not deliver, wrote Wallenberg, in a report to Stockholm on 29 September, which was obtained by the Americans:

> It has been known that several persons who were not employed at the section, among others some simple lawyers, who took advantage of the Jews' position of distress and sometimes took very great renumeration for the purpose to handle a request for passports. These claimed that they had relations among certain members of the staff.

Some of these people had been reported to the police – but it seemed that such behaviour was not actually illegal.[3]

A Swedish Schutz-Pass (Safe-Pass) issued by Raoul Wallenberg's office. Such a piece of paper could mean the difference between life and death.

Wallenberg, like all the neutral envoys engaged in rescue work, understood that for his operation to keep working, he needed allies and contacts. The worsening food shortages meant that entertaining in restaurants was becoming ever more difficult, so he invited his contacts to his home. As a neutral diplomat he had access to food and drink. And as the Russians advanced, many of his guests doubtless judged that a good word from a Swedish official might be quite useful when the Red Army arrived. Wallenberg was living in an eighteenth-century house on Ostrom Street, on the hill leading up to the Castle District, not from the von Bergs' house on Úri Street. It was an elegant place, with chandeliers and marble statues in the garden, rented from Aurél Balázs, a Jewish businessman and judge. Raoul had met his son Aurél Jr. on his previous trips. He now employed him as one of his drivers.[4]

The same day that Wallenberg submitted his report on the situation of the Jews, he wrote a letter to his mother about a charismatic SS officer he had recently met: Kurt Becher. Becher, who had brokered the handover of the Manfred Weiss steelworks, was ever more adept at manoeuvring between the Jewish leaders, his fellow Nazis and his boss Heinrich Himmler. Always on the lookout for deals, he saw that the neutral diplomats' rescue operation offered all sorts of potentially profitable opportunities. Wallenberg told his mother:

I have arranged now some very nice dinners at home for various officials who are important for my operation. A few days ago I had invited a very interesting creature from the higher ranks, namely Himmler's representative. Unfortunately he was delayed by work at the last moment and was unable to come. He is a very entertaining man, who by his own account, is planning to shoot himself in the near future.

There were plenty of people committing suicide in Budapest in autumn 1944 and their numbers would soon soar. But none of them were or would be Kurt Becher. It was more likely that Becher's rival, Adolf Eichmann, jealous of his line to Himmler, might arrange an accident for him. Despite Becher's past on the eastern front, the SS officer and Wallenberg seemed to get on socially. They were both sophisticated, intelligent people who in another world might have been genuine friends. Both had worked in the export business, had traded in horses and disliked Eichmann.[5]

The Germans were well informed about Horthy's plans to change sides and began their counter-offensive. The telegrams from the Hungarians in Moscow, updating Horthy and his allies, began arriving on 5 October. Each time Palace radio operators sent a transmission back, a German aeroplane flew overheard. Horthy and his loyalists did not seem to understand the determination of the Germans to keep control of Hungary and nor did they take adequate security measures. The Germans swiftly decapitated Hungary's loyalist military leadership. General Bakay was not going to distribute arms to anyone. On 10 October his car pulled up at the Dunapalota Hotel on the Corso in thick fog. He was snatched by the Gestapo and sent to Mauthausen. The commander of the Danube flotilla was arrested next. But much of the Hungarian military leadership did not need to be arrested. They were traitors – more loyal to Nazi Germany than their own commander-in-chief. Perhaps sensing Horthy's weakness, the Soviets then changed their terms. They included the immediate withdrawal of all Czech, Slovak and Romanian territories occupied since 1937 and the immediate declaration of war on Germany. It was all or nothing and there would be no more negotiations.

Tension rose day by day as the Germans grew more confident. The Palace defences were reinforced. The regent had forbidden Ilona and Niki Horthy to leave the Palace. Unable to work as a nurse, Ilona began to prepare to flee. She packed vitamins for her young son, István, and made a belt to hide her jewellery. Ilona also helped with coding and decoding the flurry of telegrams back and forth to Moscow. Hungary accepted the preliminary ceasefire conditions. Admiral Horthy ordered the First and Second Armies to be withdrawn behind the River Tisza in the east of Hungary – well within the 1920 borders. The next day a telegram arrived from the Hungarians in Moscow, confirming that the delegation had signed the preliminary ceasefire. The Russian advance was halted for one or two days while Hungarian troops withdrew to Budapest. They were needed there to reinforce the Hungarian forces against the Germans. Meanwhile, rumours swirled of an impending coup by the Arrow Cross and the SS. Veesenmayer, who was well informed about Hungary's secret diplomacy, asked to see Horthy on 13 October. Horthy refused. Ilona, Niki Horthy and Colonel Tost, Horthy's aide-de-camp, composed a long telegram for the Hungarians in Moscow with details of the deployment of the SS, Gestapo and armoured units.

The next day Horthy gathered his close confidants, including General Lázár, commander of his guard, and his family: Magdolna, Ilona and Niki. He informed them that the following morning, 15 October, he would announce the ceasefire in a radio broadcast. That night General Lázár sealed off the Buda Castle area with barricades and mined the roads. Nobody was allowed in or out. Finally, it seemed that in just a few hours, Hungary would leave the Axis and join the Allies.

27

A False October Dawn

We were all mad with joy.

Edina Zichy Pallavicini on hearing Horthy's broadcast that
Hungary was withdrawing from the war, 15 October 1944.

Ilona and Niki Horthy stayed up almost until dawn on 15 October.
Perhaps it was fatigue, or bravado, or a combination of both
that led Niki to make a terrible mistake. Just after 9.00 am he
departed with his bodyguards to meet an envoy from Marshall
Tito, the commander of the Yugoslav Partisans, at the Danube
Port Company office nearby on Eskü Square. Niki Horthy had
previously used this connection to contact Tito through one
of István Ujszászy's agents, called Marti. But unknown to the
Horthys, Marty was also working for the Nazis. Operation Maus
was in motion, commanded by Otto Klages, the Budapest SD
chief. The SD was waiting.

Niki was suspicious enough to arrive with bodyguards and a
security detail, whom he deployed in the other rooms and on the
roofs of neighbouring houses. Once he was inside the building a
group of Germans burst in, screaming at him to put his hands up.
He drew his revolver but was immediately hit on the back of the
head with a rubber-and-metal club. More blows followed. He was
handcuffed and dragged away into a waiting van. German soldiers
had been deployed to seal off the block and prevent his escape.
Niki's security detail opened fire on the Germans. A gun battle
ensued. The Germans threw hand-grenades at Niki's car, killing
the driver and wounding one of the bodyguards. There were few

casualties but Otto Klages was shot in the stomach and later died of his wounds. The van holding Niki went straight to the airport, where an aeroplane took him to Vienna. From there he was put into another vehicle. An SS officer looked inside at him, and said, '*Horthy Schwein*', 'Horthy pig'. His journey that day ended at Mauthausen.

Once word got back to the palace that Niki had been kidnapped, Ilona and the regent decided not to tell his mother, Magdolna. Instead, Ilona pretended that Niki had travelled south that morning. Horthy had prepared a lengthy announcement to be broadcast on the radio. Hungary, he said, had been forced into the war by German pressure, but only wanted to repair the injustices of Trianon. Germany had broken numerous promises and arrested many Hungarians, including the interior minister. It had repeatedly lied and violated Hungarian sovereignty and had dealt with the Jewish question inhumanely. A list of other German betrayals and broken promises followed with the declaration that Horthy had informed Veesenmayer that 'We are asking our enemies for a ceasefire and will cease hostilities against them. From today Hungary regards itself as being at war with Germany.' All soldiers serving in the Hungarian Army should uphold their oath of loyalty to their commanding officers and the regent himself.

Incredibly, the same misbegotten sense of honour that had prevented Horthy from changing sides in 1943, or from following Colonel Howie's advice to simply surrender to the Russians that summer, now demanded that he notify Veesenmayer in advance that Hungary was changing sides. The German plenipotentiary was due at noon. Thus on the one day, more than any other during the war, when it was vital for Horthy to take control of events, vital hours were lost. Instead of ordering his statement to be broadcast and the loyalist troops to deploy and take control of the city that morning, Horthy was sitting around, waiting for Veesenmayer. Ilona's job was to sit outside the room and eavesdrop on the conversation. Once Veesenmayer was informed that Hungary was withdrawing from the Axis, she was to go to another room and give the order for the regent's proclamation to be broadcast. But why was this meeting taking place at all, she wondered. What was the point of telling Veesenmayer? 'Correct procedures are all very well, but they do not work with villains', she recalled in her memoir.

Eventually Veesenmayer arrived. Horthy was furious with him and protested volubly about Niki's abduction. Veesenmayer at first said he knew nothing about it. A loud bang echoed through the room as Horthy flung down a German cartridge container that had been found at the scene. Veesenmayer said that Niki had been arrested for working with the enemy. Horthy replied that he had asked the Russians for a ceasefire. Veesenmayer turned pale. Ilona had her signal. She stood up and went into the next room and gave the go-ahead. Eventually, after some back-and-forth with General Lakatos and others, Horthy's statement was broadcast – but not in its full, original form. The previous day, without Horthy's knowledge, Lakatos had removed the sentence that Hungary was now at war with Germany.[1] At the time Ilona knew nothing of this. She – like almost every Hungarian apart from the Nazis' allies – felt a great sense of relief, 'as if a great heaviness had been lifted from me ... It was good to hear the Nazis' despicable acts listed openly'. She thought of her late husband, István, and how pleased and proud he would have been to hear his father's proclamation.

Edina Zichy Pallavicini was having lunch alone in her country home near Aba, southwest of Budapest, when the news came through. She had already relocated a good part of her furniture and favourite paintings there. It was a relief to be away from the city and the ever-more-intrusive presence of the Nazis. There were days and evenings, sitting in the garden, enjoying the fresh and local food, when she could almost forget the war for a few moments. One of the housekeepers rushed in crying that Edina must come to the kitchen and listen to the radio as the regent was speaking and there would be peace. She caught the end of the broadcast, with Horthy's statement listing German perfidy and treachery and the news that an armistice had been signed with Russia. By then the kitchen was packed with the gardener, the gamekeeper and the coachman, all giving thanks that the war was over. There would be no more air raids and everyone would come home. Edina then went for a walk to think through what she had just heard. 'So Horthy had come to his senses at last and broken with our nefarious allies. It was the last hour indeed and ought to have been done long before – however – better late than never', she wrote. Their joy – that of much of Hungary – was short-lived.

Horthy and his allies had laid out an elaborate plan to take control of the army and resist the Nazi counter-measures that they knew would follow the broadcast. A coded order was to be broadcast to the First and Second Armies, telling them to go over to the Soviets. After the Germans had abducted General Bakay, the commander of the Budapest Army Corps, his replacement General Aggteleky had taken over. Hearing that Niki Horthy had been abducted, Aggteleky placed the Budapest garrison on full alert. The Germans then occupied Gellért Hill. Aggteleky ordered his troops to recapture the area, but the order was never carried out. Instead, General Iván Hindy, who had gone over to the Germans, burst into Aggteleky's quarters with several soldiers, pulled out the telephone line and locked Aggteleky in.

Hindy then countermanded all of Aggteleky's orders and confined the Budapest garrison to their barracks – in the name of Aggteleky. The soldiers, confused but obedient, did as they were ordered. All of this happened by 11.00 am. By the time Veesenmayer met Horthy the Germans already had full control of the city – with barely a shot fired. A coded order for the First and Second Armies to change sides was supposed to be issued. The orders were destroyed by officers at the general staff headquarters and never sent. The Germans also took control of the radio station. They broadcast a fake notice, supposedly from General Vörös, the chief of staff, that the regent had only been talking about negotiations for a ceasefire and everyone should keep fighting as they had been. General Dálnoki Veress, the commander of the Second Army, was arrested at gunpoint by German troops and handed over to the Gestapo. General Béla Miklós, the commander of the First Army, managed to evade those looking for him, cross the frontline and go over to the Soviets – but without his troops.[2]

Ilona writes in her memoir that even at this stage, there was still a chance to outwit the Germans. Her account of these tumultuous hours differs from that of Wilhelm Höttl, but on this they were agreed. Höttl wrote that Horthy and his allies wasted 'precious hours'. The German Legation on Úri Street in the centre of the Castle District was completely surrounded by Hungarian troops, with only intermittent communications to the outside. The roads were mined and there was no way out. The Germans could have been held hostage until the Nazi forces withdrew from Budapest. 'Horthy or any determined general could certainly have overcome the weak German forces, but the Hungarians wasted the short time at their disposal', wrote Höttl. By sheer fluke a group of Tiger tanks on the way to the eastern front were waiting in a goods yard in Budapest. The SS commander for the city immediately drove them around Budapest. Faced with this display, Horthy finally surrendered.

Horthy's broadcast had brought joy and relief, most of all to Budapest's Jews. Many tore off their Yellow Stars and walked freely on the streets. The nightmare, they believed, was finally over. But it was only just starting.

At the Hadik barracks Horthy's speech caused joyous uproar. Captain John Coates and Lieutenant Gordon, two British SOE officers held there, were called into the office of Colonel József Garzuly, the head of counter-intelligence. Garzuly shook the two men's hands, gave them sweets and said they were free. What would they like to do now? Coates had been dropped into Hungary with two Hungarians, Lieutenant Gordon – whose real name was Gelleny – and Lieutenant Thomas, on 13 September. They had landed near Pécs, in the south, and were captured by the Germans within three days. SOE missions had continued through the spring and summer of 1944 without much success.

Operation Dibbler had the SOE's usual ambitious but unrealistic aims. They included contacting and organising local resistance groups, planning military sabotage, opening escape routes to Tito's Partisans and running reconnaissance missions further into Hungary to gather intelligence. But there was no large-scale resistance network in the area. Mihály Andrássy, whose family home at nearby Szigetvár had provided a base for Allied POWs, was now in Mauthausen. The failure of Hannah Szenes's mission illustrated that the sensitive border region was always on high alert and kept under surveillance. The Hungarians had been expecting Coates and his team. A previous British operative had been captured and forced to send out messages under duress.

The SOE officers had first been interrogated in a local village by Hungarian counter-intelligence and the SD. Coates had been tortured with electric shocks. The clips had been attached to his toes. The pain was excruciating. When his interrogator, a Hungarian called Csongor, said they would next apply the clips to his penis, Coates gave them his cover story: they were not spies, but had come to help the Hungarian resistance. From there the three SOE officers were taken to Pécs, where they were held in the military prison. Coates carried on with his cover story, which was clearly nonsense. In his report on the mission Coates later noted, 'My declaration that we had come to help Hungarian partisans took a lot of justification since it was obvious to any child that there were no partisans anywhere near PECS [*sic*] and that there never would be or could be.' After a while an SD officer also questioned Coates, but there was no more torture. But Csongor ordered more electric shocks for Lieutenants Gordon and Thomas, who were also severely beaten.

The SOE officers arrived at the Hadik barracks on 4 October. Conditions there were better than in Pécs. Coates and his two comrades were just the latest of a stream of British agents and officers to be incarcerated there since the start of the war. Coates's post-mission report provides fascinating detail about the inner workings of the prison. The prison was in the basement of the building and had about twenty cells, most of them for two people. There were warm showers, although the beds were infested with fleas and lice. Four guards – a sergeant, a corporal and two ordinary soldiers – watched over the prisoners. They were all 'extremely friendly'. The other prisoners included British, Russian and American airmen who had been shot down during the bombing raids, Russian parachutists, Yugoslavs, Slovaks and Jews. There were also Hungarian political prisoners, including a fighter pilot called Mátyás Pirithy who was an anti-Nazi. Pirithy, who had flown with the Finnish Air Force in the 1940 Winter War against the Russians, had many influential relatives. He was a privileged prisoner, allowed to have visitors, and did everything he could to help the British captives, bringing them food and news of the outside. Major József Garzuly, who had worked with Andor Grosz and aided Colonel Howie, was also friendly and supplied the three men with books and newspapers.

Immediately after Horthy's statement was broadcast the prison officers began burning the records, including the SOE officers' statements and interrogation reports. In answer to Garzuly's question, Coates said they wanted to leave. But they stayed another night, which was a mistake, as by the next morning the Arrow Cross had fully taken power. More interrogations followed from the SD, but on 4 November Garzuly arranged for all three SOE officers to be moved to the camp at Zugliget, where many Polish soldiers were still held. He also gave them the addresses of two safe houses in Budapest. Even after the Arrow Cross coup, conditions at Zugliget were still comparatively lax. The Polish soldiers had papers allowing them to move around the city. Some lived elsewhere in Budapest. 'The camp', noted Coates, 'was run on extremely haphazard lines'. A stream of other POWs passed through, including other British, Russian, Romanian and American officers on their way to other camps. Coates and the others were safe for the moment, but began to plan their escape. The Dutch and Polish POWs ran an escape line. Coates met the Poles every day for 'English lessons' as cover to plan their break-out.[3]

As the Arrow Cross forces and their SS allies took over the city, Ilona and her relatives moved into the cellars. The Germans launched reconnaissance missions during the night, clearly preparing for an attack on the Royal Palace. Around four o'clock in the morning Ilona decided to take refuge at the house of Angelo Rotta, the papal nuncio. They left just before dawn. It was a very short distance to the residence on Dísz Square, she recalled in her memoir, 'but it seemed endless'. Ilona covered her son's body with hers, in case anyone opened fire. Rotta was away but his deputy, Monsignor Verolino, ushered them into a large room. Ilona had been born on this square, at number 12. She looked at her family house through the window, watching a column of German tanks rumble past. Half an hour later German soldiers arrived. They looked at the Horthys but said nothing, and posted guards on the door. Skorzeny's troops had arrived and General Lázár had surrendered the garrison. There were a handful of casualties on both sides but the deal had already been done.

Admiral Horthy was taken to Gestapo headquarters, in the palace formerly owned by the Hatvany family of Jewish industrialists, nearby on Werbőczy Street. He gave the ceasefire order. The situation was hopeless, it was now clear. That evening Ilona and Magdolna were taken to see him. He had terrible news: Gyula Tost, his aide-de-camp, was dead. He had shot himself in the head. Ferenc Szálasi, the Arrow Cross leader, had visited, twice, strutting in to greet Horthy with a Nazi salute, asking to be appointed prime minister. Horthy had refused. Later that day Horthy was allowed to return to the Palace. The SS troops had wrecked everything, he wrote in his memoir: 'Every cupboard and drawer had been forced open. Everything that was movable and looked valuable had been taken, from my wife's jewellery to the money the staff had saved.' There was a moment of grotesque comedy when he went to his bathroom to collect his toiletries: a German solder came out, wearing his bathrobe. General Lakatos and Veesenmayer arrived. They presented Horthy with a written notice, ready for his signature. It said that he was resigning and appointing Szálasi as prime minister. Horthy indignantly refused, until Veesenmayer made it clear that Niki's life depended on his agreement. Veesenmayer gave Horthy his word that if he signed,

Niki would be freed and able to join the rest of the family. Horthy signed.

Soon after General Lakatos arrived with Veesenmayer, who told Ilona that the whole family would be travelling to Germany the next day, on 17 October. The next time Ilona looked through the window, Dísz Square was full of Arrow Cross militiamen, wearing their armbands with the movement's symbol: a green arrowhead cross on a white background, encircled by a red border. Angelo Rotta arrived at noon. Ilona wanted to go back to the Palace and pack but Rotta advised against this. Instead, Monsignor Verolino went there, together with the nanny, Ila. They returned a while later with two suitcases, having gathered what they could. The Palace was swarming with SS soldiers who had plundered the family's possessions. Even the clothes drawers were empty. The SS troops were under the command of a brutal, frightening-looking officer with a scar down one side of his face, wearing the regent's jacket and sitting at his desk: Otto Skorzeny. His troops had also occupied the prime minister's residence and arrested any Hungarian ministers they could find.

The Horthys left Budapest the next afternoon from Kelenföld Station, accompanied by their staff, two officers, Veesenmayer's deputy and Skorzeny himself. The train sped through Hungary without stopping until it reached Vienna late at night. There Horthy ran along the carriage, shouting in German, '*Wo is mein Sohn, wo is mein Sohn*, where is my son?' in a state of great distress.

Admiral Miklós Horthy de Nagybánya, Regent of Hungary, had ruled his homeland for twenty-four years. No other European leader had stayed in power for so long. The date of 15 October marked the end of an era and of an old-fashioned social system that had proved surprisingly durable but unable to resist a determined simultaneous assault from within and without. Like so many of his compatriots, Horthy had been forced onto a train and deported by the Germans, to call vainly for his loved ones. The next day the family was taken to Schloss Hirschberg, in Bavaria. Ilona managed to scribble a note and hand it to a Hungarian railway worker, for her sisters, letting them know that she was alive and well. The note arrived. Niki Horthy remained in Mauthausen and was later transferred to a VIP section of Dachau. He survived the war and was eventually reunited with his family. But Admiral Horthy would never see Hungary again.

28

The Gates of Hell

We are in the hands of utter lunatics and they have all the
weapons.

Edina Zichy Pallavicini, in the evening of 15 October 1944.

Admiral Horthy was largely brought down by Wilhelm Höttl and
Otto Skorzeny, but decisions he had taken decades ago helped
ease the Arrow Cross to power. The party had been sporadically
banned and suppressed but its illegal terrorist wing still existed.
Ferenc Szálasi now appointed Emil Kovarcz as the commander
of all Arrow Cross forces. Kovarcz had long been waiting for the
opportunity for more bloodshed. Twenty-four years earlier he had
led the murder squad that had killed Béla Somogyi, the editor of
Népszava, and his colleague Béla Bacsó during the White Terror.
The militiamen had been prosecuted by the military authorities but
were released and then pardoned by Horthy. Kovarcz joined the
gendarmerie then served as an instructor at the military academy
and as an Arrow Cross Member of Parliament. In 1940 he was
prosecuted for his involvement in a bomb attack on the Dohány
Street synagogue but he fled to Germany, returning with the Nazis
in March 1944.

The killing frenzy began as soon as Szálasi took power, followed
by a blizzard of anti-Jewish decrees and announcements. Gangs of
green-shirted Arrow Cross militiamen rampaged through the city,
storming into Yellow Star houses, murdering dozens of Jews and
looting at will. Groups of Jews were herded onto the Chain Bridge
and Margit Bridge, and then shot into the Danube, the first of

many of thousands who would meet their deaths this way. All of Budapest's Jews were sealed inside the Yellow Star houses for ten days. They could not go shopping, see a doctor or bury their dead. The leaders of the Jewish Council went into hiding. One, Miksa Domonkos, eventually managed to contact László Ferenczy, the gendarme colonel in charge of the deportations who had courted the Jewish Council that summer, seeking a post-war alibi. Ferenczy, true to form, had now switched sides again. 'The Jews finally got what they were asking for', he declared. Domonkos had to organise the food supply for the public kitchens and the Jews in internment camps. He donned his Hungarian Army captain's uniform, made sure to exude an arrogant self-confidence and claimed to be issuing orders in the name of Ferenczy. Domonkos even managed to free several members of the Jewish Council from Arrow Cross captivity. As Braham notes, 'His air of authority and commanding manner were such that the Nyilas [Arrow Cross] who periodically appeared at Council headquarters thought he was in fact a representative of the Hungarian armed forces.'[1] This ruse, of wearing a Hungarian uniform and adopting a fake official persona, would be used by the Jewish resistance with considerable effect during the months to come.

Events over the next few days also highlighted the soft but effective power of the neutral diplomats. Underneath its murderous intent and practice, the Arrow Cross leadership was deeply insecure. The Szálasi regime was kept in power by the SS, but hungered to be seen by its fellow Hungarians and the world as a legitimate government. The role of the neutral states and the Red Cross here was crucial. When several thousand Jews were rounded up and interned in the Great Synagogue on Dohány Street and the nearby house of worship on Rumbach Sebestyén Street, the neutral envoys protested vociferously. The Jews were released. Three days after the coup, Gábor Vajna, the virulently anti-Semitic new minister of the interior, issued a decree that foreign passports or letters of safe conduct were no longer valid. Nor were conversions. All Jews, whatever their professed religion or nationality, were members of the Jewish race and would be treated as such. The neutral states, the

Vatican and the International Red Cross immediately threatened to sever all relations with Hungary. Vajna's order was rescinded.

Eichmann arrived back in Budapest on 17 October and quickly reached an agreement to transfer 50,000 Jews to Germany while the others would be deployed on forced-labour projects around the city. The offices of the Jewish Council at Síp Street were mobbed by those desperate for news of their relatives or seeking ways to avoid being mobilised. The Council tried to reconstitute itself but could not operate under the Szálasi regime. At its last meeting at the end of October Samu Stern and another member were arrested by the SS and taken to Eichmann's villa on Apostol Street. Stern was released and went into hiding for the rest of the war. Several officials and community leaders were later arrested and killed. Even Eichmann could sometimes be negotiated with, but the Arrow Cross were fuelled by fury and hate, wanting nothing more than to torture and kill Budapest's Jews, or work them to death, as rapidly and as efficiently as possible. Many of the militiamen were sadists and psychopaths, delighting in their bloodletting. When the Jewish labourers were marched over the Horthy Miklós Bridge, just downriver from the Gellért Hotel, the Arrow Cross gunmen would shoot anyone slow or struggling into the river. So many Jews were being shot into the Danube that the police were called out to stop the slaughter. The Russians were advancing and the boom of their guns echoed around the city. But the nearer they advanced, the more frenzied became the Arrow Cross, doubtless aware of their likely fate once the Red Army arrived.

At the start of November all remaining Jewish property was confiscated by the state. Jews were only allowed to retain their wedding rings, medicines, other personal items and a small amount of cash. More call-up orders followed, for Jewish women aged between sixteen and fifty who could sew, while those women between sixteen and forty were press-ganged for labour service. The Budapest police chief issued an order that every building superintendent, known as the *házmester*, had to ensure that no Jews registered in a Yellow Star house had gone into hiding. Christian houses were also to be searched in case any Jews were hiding there.

The *házmester*, like his equivalent in Paris or Berlin, had long been a liaison point between the residents and the authorities. Some were helpful but many were snitches, informing on the building's inhabitants. The superintendent controlled physical access to the building and locked the front door in the evening. Tenants did not have their own entrance keys. The superintendents now exerted enormous, potentially life-changing powers. They guarded the entrances to the buildings and ensured that Jews were only allowed out at their allotted hours. The eleven o'clock Jewish exodus to the shops and the market soon became a feature of city life. A cartoon published in August in *Egyedül Vagyunk* (*We Stand Alone*), the Arrow Cross newspaper, showed two well-dressed men standing in the street. One asks the other what time it is; his friend gestures behind, where a stream of people are crowding out of a Yellow Star house. 'Just look over there', he says, 'It's exactly eleven o'clock'.

Some of the concierges, from poor villages, were hostile to the urban middle-class Jews over whose lives they now exerted so much power. The Phoenix House building complex, which was under Portuguese protection, covered an entire city block in District XIII. Portuguese status might provide some protection against the Arrow Cross. But everyday life was another matter. Antal Szalay, the manager, had been in charge since 1930. He was an unpleasant, authoritarian figure who made life difficult for the Jewish residents and turned the anti-Jewish regulations into a very profitable business opportunity. After 15 October it became very difficult for Jews to obtain food. Supplies were already short as the front drew nearer and the Russians advanced. By the time the Jewish shoppers reached the market there was little left. It was anyway extremely dangerous to venture into the city, where the Arrow Cross gangs prowled at will, beating and sometimes shooting Jews on a whim, or taking them to their headquarters to be tortured. Thus market traders sometimes came up to the Jewish houses to sell their goods inside the courtyard. At the Phoenix House Szalay bought up their goods, and then resold them to the Jewish tenants at a much higher price. He forbade Jews to receive parcels and also set up a kitchen in the air-raid shelter exclusively for family members and those who would pay to use the stove. Szalay's wife accepted money, paintings, silver cutlery or other goods.

A few metres away, 24 Pannónia Street was under Swedish protection. There the building manager openly threatened new arrivals that 'here the Swedish embassy has no right to command. Here I am the commander, and if you cause problems to me I will hand you all to the Arrow Cross units.' Not surprisingly, he received a weekly bribe of 400 *pengős*, twice the usual monthly salary. The superintendents were already charged with carrying out a daily headcount of the Jewish residents and had to inform the authorities if anyone had gone missing. The superintendents knew their buildings inside-out, their secret places where someone could hide and the ages of the tenants. A word from them that a Jewish person was within the age range for an Arrow Cross round-up would be enough to have them taken away. Others led the Arrow Cross to their Jewish tenants' hiding places. Not all were malevolent. Some of the superintendents used their powers to help – keeping watch for Arrow Cross patrols when they left the house, or bringing back food supplies.[2]

Later in October, some days after the Arrow Cross takeover, it seemed that Robi Lichtenstein's luck had run out. At 5.00 am gendarmes, police and Arrow Cross militiamen stormed the Yellow Star building on Kresz Géza Street where the Lichtensteins were living and ordered Jewish men aged between sixteen and sixty to gather in the courtyard. They were told to be ready to leave in an hour and bring food. The men were to be deployed in slave-labour companies digging trenches and building fortifications in southern Budapest, to where the Russians were advancing. Robi was taken to a sport arena in Újpest, in the north of the city, together with his neighbour and family friend Artúr Schwarz. The authorities had demanded fit and healthy men who could carry out labour. Robi was still only fourteen, while Artúr Schwarz was elderly and partly lame. But the gendarmes did not care. They were Jewish and male and that was enough.

The gendarmes and the Arrow Cross men treated their prisoners savagely. A demon had been unleashed – the savagery of the deportations across the provinces in the early summer was now unfolding across the capital. There was shooting, shouting and beatings, but the situation at the Újpest arena was also chaotic, which was in the prisoners' favour. Robi was sitting with Artúr as night fell. Artúr told him to wait until the right moment and then run as fast as he could. Robi waited until the guards were distracted and not looking in his direction. He said goodbye to Artúr and sprinted as fast as had ever done in his life. Robi made it out but the stadium was more than an hour's walk from the Yellow Star house on Kresz Géza Street. It was night now, well past curfew. Somehow, he made back to his family. There were tears of relief when he knocked on the door. Miraculously, Artúr Schwarz also came back the next day – he had been released because of his bad leg.

Soon after the Arrow Cross takeover the Lichtenstein family moved again. They were relocated to the Palatinus House complex of apartment buildings. The complex stood on the corner of Pozsonyi Way and Katona József Street, right by the Danube. This area, where many buildings were under Swedish, Swiss, Spanish and other neutral protection, was known as the International Ghetto. The family's living conditions at the Palatinus were much worse than in the previous Yellow Star house. Seven of them were crammed into a small room two metres wide. Fülöp, Robi's father, had escaped from labour service and made his way home to Budapest. They shared the cramped space with Artúr Schwarz and his wife. Each of the Lichtensteins' moves, from their original home to the Yellow Star house and now to this single room, had further impoverished them. Their universe was steadily shrinking, or rather was being shrunk for them. The concerns of the earlier war years – Robi and Zsuzsa's progress at school, the state of the family businesses, trips to Lake Balaton, which restaurant to go to on Saturday night – all these now seemed like a dream, one from another world.

All that mattered now was food. And it became Robi's job to find it. He was street-wise and understood danger. Those scouting trips to the countryside, the scout leaders yelling 'Gendarmes' in the middle of the night, had helped hone his instincts. So had his time on the bombed-out roofs. He needed to get back to Váci Way, where the family had lived at the start of the war. There, at number 8, was a Christian couple called Szilágyi. They had been regular customers at the shop – childless themselves, they were always happy to be served by Robi. Fülöp cut off a section of a gold chain and gave it to Robi. The plan was to swap the gold chain for some bacon with Szilágyi. Fülöp's chain was one of the several pieces of jewellery the family still had. In April Jews had been required to surrender their jewellery and valuables. This presented a quandary – to surrender nothing would draw attention. The Lichtensteins, while not especially prosperous, were not poor either. But to surrender everything would leave them nothing to bargain with in times that were getting ever darker. On 27 April Fülöp handed in what he hoped was sufficient: one gold ring, one gold watch, one pair of gold pearl earrings, six small pieces of gold weighing between three and five grams, and a couple of other items. He was issued with a stamped, official receipt. Robi and Fülöp also hid a box of valuables in the building's cellar – which they recovered after the war.

It was a straight fifteen-minute walk to Váci Way along Katona József Street, but every step was fraught with danger. Robi, like all Jews, was only allowed out at certain times. And now he was on the street without a Yellow Star on his coat. This was extremely dangerous – if he was stopped by an Arrow Cross patrol and they discovered he was Jewish he could be shot on the spot, or taken to the headquarters on Szent István Boulevard. There was another potential hazard: the *házmester* at 8 Váci Way was an Arrow Cross member. His son had gone to the same school as Robi. When Robi and his family still lived nearby they had been scared of him. Building managers were now even more powerful – acting as a part of the state. Robi made his way along Katona József Street as fast as he could. The plan, pre-arranged some time earlier, was for Robi to meet Szilágyi in front of a small kiosk that stood on the corner of Katona József Street and Váci Way. Szilágyi was there – and he and Robi made their exchange. Robi made it back with the bacon, and later repeated the trip.

At the start of November an Italian businessman called Giorgio Perlasca finally became a Spanish citizen. He immediately joined the neutral diplomats' rescue operation. At first glance Perlasca seemed an unlikely saviour of Budapest's Jews. Born in Italy in 1910, in his twenties he had been an ardent fascist, serving with the Italian Army in East Africa. During the Spanish War he volunteered for the Italian Foreign Legion, which served with Franco's forces. By the early 1940s Perlasca was working for the Italian government, procuring food supplies across the Balkans for the Italian Army. Mussolini and Hitler were close allies but Italian fascism differed from Nazism. Unlike Nazism, at least in its early years, it was not based on blood but belief and ideology. It was a fusion of nation and state, not race and state.

It was in Belgrade that Perlasca first became aware of the human cost of the Nazi racial laws. He saw that the city's Jews completely disappeared, as did the Gypsies. One day the violinists playing in the restaurant where he dined were no longer there. He asked the owner where they had gone. The owner explained that they had been taken away – for being members of an inferior race. In Hungary, though life was very different, Perlasca had done business with Jewish firms and they had gone out together in the evenings with no restrictions. The Gypsy violinists had still serenaded their customers. He had enjoyed his time in the wartime capital, where for those with money and connections, the war could seem quite far away.

Life became more complicated in September 1943, when Italy declared an armistice. Perlasca was no longer a citizen of a friendly state but an enemy one. However, as an official with the Italian Trade Commission, he had diplomatic status. Perlasca remembered that Franco's government had pledged that anyone who fought in the Spanish Civil War on the side of the victorious Fascists could always ask Spanish diplomats for help. He went to the Spanish Legation on Eötvös Street, in District VI, a short walk from where Andrássy Way crossed the Great Boulevard at Mussolini Square.

THE GATES OF HELL

The Spanish diplomats were agreeable, but the process would take a little time while Madrid ran its checks.

But when Hungary was invaded by the Nazis there was no more room for ambiguity. Perlasca was interred from early April until 13 October. Conditions were comparatively comfortable and he was treated as an Italian diplomat. The internees were properly fed and given cigarettes, small luxuries and even pocket money. But Perlasca, sensing perhaps that this idyll could not last, escaped. In any case he had no desire to be a prisoner any longer, no matter how well treated. He procured fake papers authorising him to go back to Budapest for medical treatment. That day a Swiss diplomat arrived to check on the internees. Perlasca persuaded the Swiss visitor to take him back to Budapest. After the Arrow Cross coup Perlasca hid for a few days then finally returned to the Spanish Legation on 1 November to ask for his Spanish passport. They remembered his request, which had been authorised. He formally became a Spanish citizen. The Hungarian authorities immediately informed him that as he had no right to reside in Hungary with his new passport, he had to leave the country within fifteen days. Perlasca would stay for six months, one of Budapest Jews' most steadfast and courageous allies.

By then Spain, like the other neutral powers, was issuing protective papers. Angel Sans Briz, the chargé d'affaires, had persuaded the Hungarian government to let him grant Spanish passports to 200 Hungarian Jews of Spanish descent. Once agreed, he immediately extended that to 200 families. In fact there were very few Sephardic Jews in Budapest – as there were few Swedish Jews. Like Wallenberg, Lutz and other neutral diplomats, Sans Briz also placed the buildings where the Spanish-protected Jews lived under extra-territorial protection, as well as children's homes and hospitals. Unlike the Swedish and Swiss Legations, the Spanish operation had a very small staff. Only one employee was dealing with the protected Jews and he was completely overworked. Perlasca offered to help, for free.

Sans Briz quickly agreed and appointed Perlasca as a member of the Spanish Legation. The Hungarian Foreign Ministry issued him with a diplomatic identity card. But 200 families was not enough, Perlasca knew. After adding some more official Spanish stamps to his diplomatic passport to make it look more impressive, Perlasca went to the Arrow Cross Foreign Ministry. He was accompanied by Zoltán Farkas, the Legation's lawyer. Farkas, who was Jewish, would be Perlasca's most valuable adviser, helping him navigate Hungarian officialdom. Now the bluff began, and it had to be executed with complete confidence. Perlasca explained that there were many more than a few hundred Spanish Jews in Budapest. There were also thousands of Hungarians living in Spain. If the Hungarian government wanted good relations it must show willingness and flexibility, he explained, his voice stern. The Arrow Cross official asked if this was a threat. Perlasca smiled and said that, yes, it was. They agreed that there would be no limit on the number of people but the number of protected houses would not be increased.

Giorgio Perlasca, an Italian government official, proclaimed himself Spanish consul-general and saved thousands of Budapest Jews.

29

Death March

God rot those gendarmes, wherever they are, deep in the ground.

Mrs János Rostás, one of several hundred Roma deported to Germany from Kispest, November 1944.*

Hannah Szenes's trial for treason began on 28 October. She pleaded 'not guilty' and delivered an impassioned speech, about how Hungary was her native land, which she loved, but which had turned against her, against all its Jews. Her voice rose with passion as she declaimed against the traitors who had sold out Hungary to the Nazis. They had brought calamity on their homeland, not her. Finally, she implored the judges to not add to their crimes by finding her guilty. For they too would eventually be judged. The judges looked at each other. This fiery, impassioned young woman, who had been imprisoned for almost five months, was not what they were expecting. And perhaps her words hit home: Hungary under the Arrow Cross was a lawless, murderous place. The war was lost and there would indeed soon be trials of those responsible for the catastrophe. Hannah's lawyer had already reassured her that the sentence did not matter: the war would soon be over and she would be freed. While the judges conferred, Hannah and Katalin could briefly meet and embrace in an ante-room. Soon after, the word came from the judges: they

* Mrs Rostás adopted the traditional form of using her husband's first name, rather than her own.

were unable to reach a verdict. Sentencing had been postponed for eight days.

As the Russians advanced and American bombers pounded the city, the Arrow Cross state began to collapse. The Conti Street prison, where Hannah was held, was evacuated and she was transferred to Gyorskocsi Street, where Yoel Palgi was still interred. Katalin was unable to visit Hannah at the end of October because of the frequency of the bombing raids. Eventually when she could get to the prison, on 2 November, she was told to ask a Captain Simon for a pass at his office at the Hadik barracks. There she was told that Simon would be away until 7 November. Katalin arrived on that day to find the barracks being emptied out. Trucks were leaving stuffed with books, files, office equipment and prison officials.

Simon was not there – unknown to Katalin, he was at the Gyorskocsi Street prison. That morning he walked into Hannah's cell and asked her to come with him. He informed her that her sentence had been decided: she was to be executed. This was not true. But for some reason Simon was determined to see Hannah die. It was his decision and his alone. Simon asked Hannah if she wished to plead for clemency. She refused. She was given an hour to write her last letters and taken to the prison yard. There she was strapped to a post. She refused a blindfold. The firing squad took aim and fired. The shots resounded around the prison. Many of the inmates were puzzled – there was usually a routine before an execution, a bugle was sounded, the execution yard readied. Everybody knew when a fellow prisoner was scheduled to die. But the word soon spread that Hannah had been shot. Many of the prisoners were in tears. Palgi became hysterical when he heard.

Simon then returned to his office at the Hadik barracks to find Katalin waiting for him. He told her that Hannah had been found guilty of treason and sentenced to death. The sentence had already been carried out. For a while Katalin could not speak. Why, she asked in her anguish, had she at least not been permitted to see her daughter before her death? Simon said that Hannah had not wanted to. Katalin was later given Hannah's possessions. She had written a letter on a scrap of paper:

Dearest Mother,

I don't know what to say – only this: a million thanks, and forgive me if you can. You know so well why words aren't necessary. With love forever.

Your daughter,

Hannah[1]

Stunned and grieving, Katalin made her way home, to a house full of memories. But the agony of the Jews of Budapest was entering a new and even darker phase. The death march to the Austrian border was about to begin. Thousands of Jews were relocated from their forced-labour sites and assembled in Óbuda, at the Újlaki brickworks. They were guarded by Arrow Cross militiamen, who beat and tortured them, robbing what meagre possessions they had managed to save until then. A dossier sent to the Red Cross headquarters in Geneva by Friedrich Born, the Red Cross representative, included a first-hand account of the atrocious conditions at the site. The buildings had roofs but no walls. Between 5,000 and 6,000 people, including the elderly and young children, were crammed together without space to lie down. There were no sanitary or medical facilities. Families were in great distress as they were split up. When the author of the report saw a group of children being led away, he asked a guard where they were going. The guard replied that they were going to be turned into soap.[2] Others held there committed suicide. A small group of Christian doctors volunteered to treat the prisoners.

The gendarmes also turned on Budapest's Roma. After the Nazi invasion some Hungarian Gypsies were deported to Auschwitz, joining those from other occupied countries. When the Roma from across the Reich arrived the families refused to be split up and to follow the SS's orders unless they could stay together. About 23,000 Roma and Sinti [Roma of German background] people passed through a separate area of Auschwitz known as the Gypsy or family camp. Many died from disease, harsh labour, maltreatment and starvation. Others were gassed. Children perished in hideous medical experiments carried out by Dr Josef Mengele and other SS doctors. Mengele, who was fascinated by twins and by the Roma, once sewed young Roma twins together, connecting their blood vessels. It took them three days to die. In mid-May 1944, the SS tried to round up the inmates of the family camp and send them to the gas chambers, to make room for the new arrivals from Hungary. In one of the least known but most courageous episodes of the Holocaust, the Roma fought back ferociously. Using knives, stones, pieces of wood, anything they could find, they launched themselves at the SS guards, punching, kicking and beating them with their makeshift weapons. Stunned by the fierce resistance, the SS retreated. The priority was the arrival of the Hungarian Jews. A few thousand Gypsies, they decided, could wait. The SS returned in August, this time determined to succeed. The family camp was destroyed, the families violently broken up and the adult men sent to camps in Germany. Almost 3,000 men, women and children remained at the camp. All were gassed on 2 August.

Mrs János Rostás had just turned eighteen years old when she was rounded up with her family on the morning of 3 November. Her husband, János, had been taken for forced labour. She lived with her parents and seven siblings in Kispest, on the outskirts of southeastern Budapest. The Jews of Kispest had been deported at the end of June, on one of the last trains to Auschwitz. But the Roma were still there. The family lived in poverty, sharing a small part of a house. None of the children went to school. The police burst in, screamed at the family to get dressed, stole their meagre belongings and took them to the local police station. About 200 of Kispest's Roma inhabitants were taken away, including many of Mrs Rostás's relatives. From there all of them, including the children, were marched to Óbuda, a journey of around ten miles.

They were held at the brickworks for about two weeks in appalling conditions with barely any food. Like the Jewish prisoners, the Roma suffered continual beatings and abuse. From Óbuda they were deported to Germany. When she asked the gendarmes for water, they replied, 'Go, stinking Gypsies, you're all gonna die here.' Mrs Rostás was held in a series of camps including Dachau. She was stripped, given a uniform and had her head shaved. She was forced to work as a slave labourer, washing the outside of the camp barracks, and to sleep on the ground without even a blanket. Many of the prisoners died, including numerous friends and relatives. Near dead from starvation, she survived on raw potato peelings. She and her father managed to survive and return to Budapest. Her husband, János, lived through labour service and also came home. But the family they had dreamed of was not to be.

In February 2000, at the age of seventy-three, Mrs Rostás gave an interview to the Hungarian historian Ágnes Daróczi and recounted what happened to her:

I had no children because they gave us those injections … so that we do not reproduce. All the young ones. Huge injections, like this. Sometimes they gave us injections every week. I myself got three or four. That's why I have no children. Never one born. I could never overcome it, not until this day.

László Endre had first called for Hungary's Gypsies to be sterilised in 1934. More than six decades later, long after his death, his dark legacy lived on.[3]

By mid-November 1944 the von Bergs' house on Úri Street had become a central base of the rescue operation. It was placed under Swedish diplomatic protection. The deep cellar was used to store funds needed for bribes, the detailed records of the accounts and for hiding Jews. Erzsébet Nákó, always efficient and organised, was in charge of the archive. She was also deeply in love with Wallenberg and tormented by his affair with Berber Smit. The lovers used to meet in Pál Hegedűs's flat near the Chain Bridge, according to Gábor Forgács. Around this time Erzsébet finally snapped, flashing her nails and declaring to Wallenberg that 'You cannot do this with me.' Such human drama aside, the Wallenberg operation had to feed those under Swedish protection. Twice a week Gábor was part of a team bringing food supplies from the warehouse owned by the Stühmer food company on Szentkirályi Street in District VIII to the International Ghetto. The nerve-wracking four-kilometre journey across the city sometimes took two hours. The group usually had no protection, only the official passes authorising their movements. But in Budapest that winter of 1944 no papers were a guarantee of safety, especially when food was in such short supply. 'We were like horses, pushing this carriage filled with flour, sometimes with eggs and bacon, without any guards and the soldiers staring at us', recalled Gábor. Occasionally Vince Görgey, a high-ranking Arrow Cross journalist, provided security. Görgey helped himself to the provisions – which he could later sell – and in return ordered several gendarmes to escort the Wallenberg group. [4]

Raoul Wallenberg, the son of a Swedish banking dynasty, saved the lives of thousands of Jews in wartime Budapest – sometimes personally confronting Nazi officers.

Wallenberg's operation set up a new department: a security service, charged with finding and rescuing Jews under Swedish protection who had disappeared. After the Arrow Cross coup the rescue operation had relocated to a substantial apartment building at the start of Üllői Way, by the Grand Boulevard, that had been owned by a Hungarian–Dutch insurance company. Many of the staff lived there, with their families. Wallenberg took over the large executive office, which boasted a Persian carpet, fine furniture and a large safe. The security service had its own apartments, with separate telephone lines. Its operatives, who were sometimes armed, worked in shifts around the clock. Wallenberg despatched frequent missions to the Újlaki brickworks in Óbuda to find and rescue Jews with Swedish papers, sometimes appearing himself, as did Carl Lutz.[5]

After two or three days at the brickworks, the Jews were despatched on foot to the Austrian border. Living in the open with no food or medical help, proper clothing or footwear, the ragged, starving prisoners were in no condition to make such an arduous journey at the start of winter, let alone engage in hard labour. Those who could not march were shot on the spot. The Arrow Cross guards hit the marchers with truncheons, whips and rifle-butts. Sometimes they tossed hand-grenades into the crowd. The road westward was soon lined with corpses, which was doubtless the intent. Some had been shot by the Arrow Cross guards; others had died of cold, beatings, hunger and sheer terror. Others took poison and committed suicide. Reports of the horrors soon reached Budapest. The neutral powers did what they could. Wallenberg and Miklós Krausz of the Palestine Office met on 22 November at the Swedish Legation, with representatives of the Swiss and Portuguese Legations. Together with Papal Nuncio Angelo Rotta and Friedrich Born, they sent envoys to the border to rescue those with protective papers.

Even the SS were appalled at what they saw on the road. Such scenes of horror were not only distasteful but would likely ensure harsh punishment after the war. Waffen-SS General Hans Juttner met Kurt Becher in Vienna. Becher told him that he had seen columns of Jews marching to the frontier, which had 'made a strong impression on him, since the terrible exhaustion of these people was apparent at first sight'. Juttner did not believe Becher's descriptions, until he saw for himself. The two men drove back to Budapest the next day, passing the marchers going in the other direction. 'The first columns, which had been on the march for several days, made a truly terrifying impression and confirmed Becher's statements of the day before.'[6] Those who survived the eight-day journey were put into a lice-infected barracks at Hegyeshalom on the border. Typhoid and dysentery raged through the prisoners. Some of the women prisoners gave birth. The babies were immediately attacked by lice and died within a few hours. One SS officer placed a Jewish woman about to give birth under a spotlight and watched as she went into labour, saying he was curious about the process. Katalin Szenes, Hannah's mother, was taken on 14 November. The march began on Alkotmány Street, near Parliament, and continued to the Margit Bridge and across into Óbuda. More and more people joined along the way and it began to rain, soaking their clothes and meagre bundles of possessions. Katalin walked as she was told, still numb with grief after the execution of her daughter and spent the night at the brickworks.

The Jews left at dawn the next morning, marching four abreast in groups of 100. Most were convinced they were being sent to Auschwitz or other death camps. They spent the night in some huts and the next morning began marching again. They passed through a village where the local people stood and watched. A few women ventured out with glasses of water. The second night they spent in the open in a field, surrounded by barbed wire. Katalin watched a young woman and older man die, hearing their death rattle from the poison they had taken. The field was full of corpses the next morning. The following day they slept in a stable. It stank of human excrement that was piled up everywhere. Soon after that, in the Danube town of Komárom, there was an air raid. Katalin and several others pulled off their Yellow Stars and ran for their lives. They knocked on the door of a nearby house, praying that the owners would let them in. They did, thus saving their lives. Katalin and the others managed to hitch a ride back to Budapest. There she obtained false papers from a friend and went into hiding.[7]

Katalin Szenes was not the only one to escape. The marchers far outnumbered their guards, which was why they used such terror and brutality to keep them under control. For those with enough physical strength and courage, there were sometimes opportunities to flee. Lili Taub was taken on the death march with her neighbour, also called Lili, from their homes on Csengery Street, in District VI. Lili lived with her four-year-old daughter, Zsuzsa. Her husband, Elemer, was on labour service. Lili had planned in advance what to do if she was deported and Zsuzsa was left behind. She somehow got a message to Christian friends who lived on the outskirts of the city. Lili's friends came to fetch Zsuzsa after half a day.

The two Lilis both had fake Christian papers. After they escaped from the death march, they were helped somewhere in the countryside by a local man who hid them under the straw in his horse-drawn carriage. They travelled some distance but were later caught by the Germans. Their Christian papers did not protect them. Zsuzsa's mother watched with horror as her friend was brutally interrogated. Each time she gave an answer the German did not like he slapped her hard around the face. Lili could not face such violence and pretended to faint. Her captors threw a jug of freezing-cold water over her. Somehow the two women got away and made their way back to Budapest. After being away for two months or so, Lili returned home and was reunited with Zsuzsa. She refused to wear a Yellow Star. The mother and daughter moved to a flat in District VIII, where both pretended to be Christians. By late 1944, the city was under continual bombardment and they spent most of their time in the cellar. Like her mother, Zsuzsa had to learn the Lord's Prayer, behave like a Christian and recite the Christian prayers. Both survived. Lili's husband, Elemer, was liberated from one of the concentration camps but died of typhus on the way home.

As the Russians advanced, the Szalási government was evacuating Budapest and relocating to western Hungary. Debrecen, the country's second city, 200 miles east of the capital, and Szeged, on the southern border, had been liberated in October. By early November the Red Army had reached Budapest's eastern suburbs around Vecsés, just twelve miles from the city centre. Yet Szálasi and his ministers still found the time and resources to issue new regulations classifying Hungary's Jews into six categories. The two most important were that the 15,000 or so Jews holding foreign protective passes had to relocate to the area around the riverside Szent István Park in District XIII, by Pozsonyi Road, by the afternoon of 20 November. Anyone who failed to relocate would be arrested and put in a labour camp. At the same time, thousands of other Jews, known as *kölcsön-zsidók*, or 'Loan Jews', were to be given to the German government supposedly for slave labour. The deportations started again, from Józsefváros Station.

Conditions inside the International Ghetto, once a comfortable middle-class area, were now grim. More than 15,000 Jews were living in apartments that had previously housed fewer than 4,000 people. They slept on the staircases and in attics or cellars. Some two-room apartments were now home to fifty people.[8] Despite the many flags of neutral nations adorning the fine 1930s apartment houses, the International Ghetto was not safe. It was very near the Danube into which the Arrow Cross delighted in shooting Jews. Even in the protected houses there was no safety. The Arrow Cross gangs raided, supposedly to check papers. In fact some of those with protective papers were carrying fakes. The Zionist resistance had set up a sophisticated printing and distribution operation. Unfortunately sometimes mistakes crept in. One batch of protective passes had the word 'Susse' instead of 'Suisse'.

Those living in the houses around Szent István Park without an international protective pass were kicked out. Some were marched to the Újlaki brickworks in Óbuda and sent on to Hegyeshalom. Others were relocated to Yellow Star houses in the other Jewish quarter around the Great Synagogue. The great trek to and from the protected houses recalled the scenes of June when all the city's Jews had been relocated to the Yellow Star houses. But this relocation was far worse. Arrow Cross gangs rampaged around the city, robbing, beating and torturing their captives. Some of the Jews were taken to the Arrow Cross house at 2 Szent István Boulevard, conveniently located by the Margit Bridge and the start of Pozsonyi Way. The building, known as the House of Correction, was an especially savage place of terror. Many of those taken there did not leave alive and were tortured and beaten to death in the cellars.

The Russian onslaught on Budapest drove the Arrow Cross to new depths of savagery. The boom of shellfire echoed across the city, but the streets around the Pest side of the Danube resounded to a different noise, especially at night: the crack of rifle and pistol shots. Gangs of Arrow Cross, often feral teenagers, raided the main ghetto and the International Ghetto, arresting anyone they pleased before taking them down to the riverbank. Before the prisoners were murdered, they were forced to take off their shoes and coats, which were then gathered up to be sold in the market. The usual method of execution was to tie three people together, stand them on the bank of the Danube, then shoot the person in the middle in the back of the head. The dead body would then drag the other two into the water, who would then drown. Sometimes one or both of the bound Jews managed to escape and swim downriver, where Wallenberg's people waited to fish them out.

A number of Budapest Jews, including many children, found sanctuary with their Christian neighbours. Their motives were varied: some Hungarians loathed the Nazis and the Arrow Cross and acted out of humanitarian concerns. Others sought an alibi for when the Russians arrived. Whatever the reason, hiding Jews in Budapest in the winter of 1944 took steadfast courage: discovery would likely mean execution for everyone in the flat. In addition, the fugitive Jews needed to be fed. By winter 1944 food supplies were getting scarcer and scarcer, thanks in part to the Germans, who were plundering Hungary's livestock and crops and sending them back to the Reich. The most challenging mission of all was hiding Jewish children, as Mária Mádi was learning. No matter how many times a child, even a teenager, was told that it was vital that they stayed silent, children were innately noisy, especially once they stopped being terrified and relaxed in their new home. Irene Lakos arrived at Mádi's flat with her seven-year-old nephew, Alfréd – 'Fredi', in the diary – on 17 October 1944, two days after the Arrow Cross coup, asking for refuge. The two women were already friends and neighbours. Irene's brother, László, Alfréd's father, had been sent on forced labour somewhere outside Budapest. His wife, Rózsa, tried to bring him some food but was caught travelling without a Yellow Star and was arrested. She somehow managed to call a friend and ask them to look after Alfréd. Rózsa was sent to Auschwitz, where she was murdered.

Mádi took Irene and Alfréd in, even though her apartment only had one bedroom and was across the street from the Germans' radio station. Her diary entry for that day is laconic, that when she got home she 'found guests waiting for me'. Mádi's wide network of friends and acquaintances brought her ever-more-disturbing reports of events in the city. On 23 October she wrote about a ghastly ocurrence at 5 Szent István Boulevard, near the Margaret Bridge. The area was an Arrow Cross stronghold with one of the most notorious torture centres across the road at number 2. The previous Monday the house superintendent's son-in-law, an Arrow Cross man, and his friends ordered all Jews living in the building into the cellar. They were then locked in, with short breaks, until Thursday night, when they were finally allowed back into their flats. 'I suppose you ask me, why did not somebody report the case to the police?' wrote Mádi.

The danger aside, the sudden arrival of two flat mates, one of them a small child, meant a very different life for someone who was used to living on her own and was quite set in her ways. 'My friend here with me is absolutely tactful. We do not disturb each other in the least', she wrote on 24 October. 'But with the poor child it is more difficult. I can hardly stand him. He gets on my nerves.' The next day new regulations confirmed the death penalty for spreading non-official news and for hiding Jews. Mádi was self-aware enough to know that she struggled with her feelings about Jews. She was an anti-Nazi, and was risking her life. But she was also a creature of her time, who had absorbed and internalised some of the widespread prejudices of Horthy-era and wartime Hungary. 'The more I am attached to my Jewish friends, there is a certain Jewish type I hate', she wrote on 28 October, 'and the best joke is this seven-year-old child is just the worst type, who I try to save'. Yet the same night she stayed up until 1.30 am, talking with Irene, about the loss of her relatives, noting, 'these times are weighing heavily upon her'.

The next month brought more danger. The announcement on 8 November that building superintendents and janitors were now ordered to search apartment blocks for Jews in hiding meant even more power for the *házmester*. 'The child with us here is difficult and his naughtiness may mean death for us all. I have to confess, I am a bit nervous', she wrote that day. Mádi made a hiding place for Irene and Fredi, behind a large mirror. But it would not be sufficient if the flat was properly searched. When the janitor arrived to inspect the water meter a day earlier than agreed, Mádi did not let him, as she was not prepared. Yet she was also learning to manage Fredi and his fears. By late November the sound of war was relentless. At first Fredi was terrified of the thunder of the artillery and the explosions that shook the building and the windows. Mádi cleverly turned the cacophony of war into a game, saying that the Russians guns were far too lazy and did not fire enough. When the city fell silent, she complained loudly that there was not enough shooting. Once it started up again, she pretended to be very happy, so Fredi joined in the fun.

30

To the Ghetto

In this life-and-death struggle, which may decide the fate of the Hungarians for centuries to come, all of us must make sacrifices.

Gábor Vajna, Arrow Cross interior minister,
ordering Christians to leave the area of the newly
established Budapest ghetto, 29 November 1944.[1]

Jenő Galántay was angry and indignant. The official notification arrived on 14 November. Jenő and his family had to move out of their comfortable apartment at 62 Akácfa Street. The thoroughfare ran through Budapest's Jewish quarter in District VII and would soon be in the heart of the planned Jewish ghetto. The Galántays were Christians and had many friends among their Jewish neighbours. They were a cultured, middle-class family, with a summer house at Lake Balaton and a home full of books and music. Jenő managed the ensemble at the Opera House and his wife, Margit, was a homemaker. The Galántays had three boys, Eugene, at seventeen the eldest, Ervin, who had just turned fourteen, and Tibor, who was four. As soon as the letter arrived Jenő put on his medals from the First World War and marched over to the municipal administration to protest. He was a decorated veteran and an officer in the reserve, he said, and it was an outrage to force him and his family from their home. It was no to avail. These were national, political decisions. The municipality had no say – power now rested with the Arrow Cross. 'A green-shirted lout curtly informed me that that the ghetto will soon be delineated', Jenő told his family when he returned home.

He called up his contacts in the military, everyone he could think of who might be able to help. Nobody could.

The checkpoints around the Jewish quarter went up quickly. Two days later Ervin had to show his residence papers to be allowed past the police and Arrow Cross control on Dob Street and go home. But apart from the checkpoint, and the large numbers of Arrow Cross men on the streets, life continued almost normally. The streets were crowded with Orthodox Jews, while in one courtyard rows of Jewish women were sitting hunched over sewing machines, making sheepskin jerkins for the army. The local brothel was still in business. Red lights illuminated a row of windows on the mezzanine floor in a nearby apartment building. A young woman called Ervin to come over. She snatched his cap and lifted her top up to show him her breasts. Ervin was a hormonal teenage boy and highly interested in girls – but was completely flustered. In any case brothels were forbidden for soldiers in uniform. He threatened to call the police. She threw his cap back and swore at him in return.

Ervin was a military cadet at the army academy in Kőszeg in western Hungary. But as the Russians advanced he was allowed to return home to Budapest to help bring his mother and little brother back from Balatonkenese. Arriving home he saw an elderly Jewish man standing at the building entrance with a Yellow Star on his coat. He seemed frightened of Ervin, until they recognised each other – Pali *bácsi*, Uncle Pál, was a childhood friend of Ervin's father. Uncle Pali had come to leave his valuable violin in his care – he was about to be deported to Theresienstadt. Once everyone was back home, Ervin signed up. War, he was sure, was going to be a great adventure. *Boy Soldier*, Galántay's diary-cum-autobiography, covers the period from November 1944 to February 1945. It is a unique first-hand account of life and death on the frontline with no detail spared – from the perspective of a boy barely old enough to be able to handle a weapon. Ervin was fluent in German but wanted to join a Hungarian unit. There were not many openings for a fourteen-year-old but on 19 November he joined the Vannay Battalion. The new formation was not an Arrow Cross militia and was incorporated into the Hungarian Army. But László Vannay, its commander, was a fervent anti-Semite. A veteran of the White Terror, he had served with Pál Prónay. In 1926 Vannay had taken part in the attack on Vilmos Vázsonyi, a pioneering Jewish leader and former justice minister. Vázsonyi was beaten so severely that he later died. Vannay was fined just 48 *pengős* for the attack.[2]

At the start of the war Vannay had organised commando raids against the Czech forces in Slovakia. Vannay was close to Emil Kovarcz, the veteran Arrow Cross terrorist and murderer who was now minister for total mobilisation. Vannay told Kovarcz that he could raise a battalion of 600 men for the defence of the capital, specialising in close-quarter urban combat. Many of those recruited were firefighters and sewer and postal workers who had an intimate knowledge of the city's hidden passageways, tunnels and culverts. Kovarcz agreed that he could go ahead and gave Vannay authorisation to seize whatever he needed. The high politics of the battalion were way over the head of Ervin. His concerns were fighting for his country, and girls. Vannay was courteous to Ervin when they met, asking him questions about himself and his family. For Ervin he had 'an impressive moustache' and spoke 'slowly with a raucous voice'. Ervin asked for accelerated combat training. Vannay smiled at the young boy and said for the moment he would have a desk job.

The Galántays, who had many Jewish friends, were patriotic Hungarians but not Arrow Cross sympathisers. Jenő was incredulous that while Russians were 'knocking at our gates' the authorities had nothing better to do than move tens of thousands of Jews into the ghetto and thousands of Christians out. As well as being inhumane, it was an epic waste of time, manpower and resources. Ironically, Vannay took one elderly Jewish couple under his protection. Roth *bácsi*, Uncle Roth, was an expert stamp cutter who moved into the battalion headquarters with his wife. The Vannay Battalion needed to be able to produce their own papers. Uncle Roth set up a document forgery operation, producing fake *laissez-passers*, and Arrow Cross and other documents. He and his wife, Rózsa, had no choice about being in 'protective custody' but were reasonably treated. Rózsa ran the laundry and the kitchen in the building across the street from the battalion headquarters.[3]

By late October Ignatz Katz and his fellow labour servicemen were back in Hungary. After three days of walking north they arrived in Nágykőros, fifty-five miles southeast of Budapest. 'Apart from being tired, I am fine and I hope you are too', he wrote to his wife Ilona on 15 October, the day of the Arrow Cross coup. Later that month they were relocated to a brick factory in Dunaszekcső, in the far south of Hungary. 'I am fine. Write about yourselves, lots of kisses', Ignatz wrote on 28 October. Such terse notes – all of which were subject to military censorship – could provide only meagre comfort. By 9 November Ignatz had been relocated again to Balatonkenese on the eastern shore of lake Balaton. A few days later he was back in Budapest, at the Albrecht barracks on Arena Way, finally in the same city as his family. Ignatz sent a postcard home on November 24, asking for winter clothing, long trousers, a coat and other items. He could not meet any of his loved ones, but they, or someone else, could come to the barracks' gate and deliver the clothes for him. Ignatz's anguish and anxiety for his family under the Arrow Cross terror is clear, even in the brief notes that were permitted. 'You cannot come in here but send a sign of life with someone', he wrote.

That postcard was the last sign of Ignatz's life. No more followed. Even now, more than eighty years later, his final days and the precise details of his fate remain unknown. Some Jewish men on labour service at sites such as the Albrecht barracks and other places in the city were handed over to the Nazis by the Arrow Cross, as 'Loan Jews' for slave labour or worse. Ignatz may have been deported from Józsefváros Station to a concentration camp, or sent to the front to work on fortifications, where he perished. He may also have been executed at the barracks by the Arrow Cross during their killing frenzy in the winter of 1944, or have been killed in the siege bombardment. What is certain is that Ignatz Katz, a talented sportsman and journalist, a loyal Hungarian citizen who wanted nothing more than to survive and be reunited with his beloved wife Ilona and his family, was one of tens of thousands of Budapest inhabitants to be killed in the very last weeks of the war.

*

One day in late November Giorgio Perlasca frantically walked up and down the column of hundreds of frightened Jews being forced onto the train at Józsefváros Station, looking for those under Spanish protection. The deportations had restarted and the station was a scene of utter terror and misery. The SS officers' dogs barked ferociously, straining at their leads, while the gendarmes and Arrow Cross men beat and abused their prisoners. About 300 Jews under Spanish protection had recently disappeared. Some of them, Perlasca was sure, would be at the station. Wallenberg and other neutral diplomats were also there, finding as many Jews as they could with protective papers then taking them aside before the train left. Perlasca had managed to gather a good number of Spanish-protected Jews when he saw two small children together. They looked about eleven years old and were alone, standing in the line of those waiting to get on the train. He walked over to them and told them to run over to the Spanish Legation car, a black vehicle with two Spanish flags in the front, and get in. The chauffeur would close the doors and they would be safe. The two frightened children did as he instructed and the chauffeur slammed the door closed. An enraged German officer appeared demanding that the children be returned. Perlasca informed him that the car was Spanish diplomatic territory and the children were now under Spanish protection. The officer pulled out a gun.

Wallenberg, now standing next to Perlasca, intervened – informing the German that Perlasca was a Spanish diplomat and the car was Spanish territory. 'You're disturbing my work', the Nazi officer snapped. 'You call this work?' replied Perlasca, his voice dripping with sarcasm. The German became even angrier. Everyone began shouting: Perlasca, Wallenberg, the Germans and other neutral diplomats. Then an SS colonel approached, with a narrow face and long, thin nose. He asked what was happening and the situation was explained to him. He looked at the children then back at the neutral diplomats. 'Let it be', he said to the Nazi officer. 'Their time will come.' Once the SS colonel had left Perlasca asked Wallenberg who the colonel was. 'Eichmann', he replied.[4]

On the last day of November Perlasca was woken at 6.00 am and informed that Angel Sans Briz, the Spanish minister, had left Budapest. He left Perlasca a note saying the Spanish Embassy in Vienna could obtain a visa for him for Switzerland. Perlasca had no intention of fleeing to Switzerland or anywhere else. By now around 3,000 people were under Spanish protection in several houses: one overlooking Szent István Park in the very heart of the International Ghetto, and more in the surrounding streets. The rescue operation was becoming increasingly complicated. Once someone was issued with Spanish papers they had to be moved to a protected house in a Spanish diplomatic vehicle. Then they had to be fed. The residents in the houses had to be secured and managed. Perlasca set up a three-person committee in each protected house to oversee hygiene and discipline. Hundreds of frightened, hungry and traumatised people were living in cramped and uncomfortable conditions. And they did stupid things, like going for a walk. No matter how many times Perlasca explained that they had to stay inside, that it was *extremely* dangerous outside, they wandered off to look for missing family members or food or just to breathe fresh air. Every day Perlasca drove around the International Ghetto in the Spanish diplomatic car, flying the flag, checking his protective houses, showing the Arrow Cross, the Germans – and the protected Jews – that Spain was still there, looking after them.

Sans Briz's unexpected departure was a dangerous development. Perlasca went straight to the Spanish-protected house on Károly Légrády Road in the International Ghetto. His instincts were correct. The building was now occupied by the police and the Jews inside were appearing with suitcases. They told Perlasca that they were to be deported. He locked the door and spoke to the senior officer. For once it was the regular police carrying out the round-up rather than the Arrow Cross. Perlasca was indignant and explained that he was surprised at what was happening as the building was under Spanish protection. The Spanish flag was flying. The emblem of Spain was on the wall. This was not acceptable and had to stop immediately. The policeman in charge backed down.

Soon after Perlasca met nearby with officials from the Interior and Foreign Ministries and others. They informed him that as Sans Briz had fled, Hungary no longer had relations with Spain and the Jews were no longer protected. Perlasca was again indignant. Sans Briz had not fled, he retorted. He had gone to Germany for a meeting. In the meantime, he, Giorgio Perlasca, was fully authorised to represent Spain. None of this was true, but the Hungarians were not to know that. It was vital, Perlasca knew, to exude complete confidence. Any semblance of doubt or willingness to negotiate would lead to catastrophe. Hungary was now ruled by a murderous authoritarian regime, the harshest ever in its history. He could not back down for a second. All previous agreements about the protected Jews and Spanish houses must be respected, Perlasca declared. While the discussions continued Perlasca saw a group of other Jews passing by who had been in another Spanish-protected house. They were under armed escort. He then demanded that this group be freed and returned to Spanish protection. It worked.

Crucially, Sans Briz had left a pad with his signature at the embassy. Perlasca changed his first name from Giorgio to Jorge and appointed himself Spanish chargé d'affaires. Like all the neutral envoys Perlasca understood that the safe passes, flags and Spanish signs gave a measure of protection but no guarantees. The whole operation had no real basis in international law. It was all a giant bluff, a deadly game of wartime poker. The stakes were tens of thousands of Jewish lives. Hansi Brand and Rezső Kasztner had set the model in their negotiations with Eichmann: analysing, evaluating, continually probing for vulnerabilities or any information that could be turned to their advantage. Cultivating allies, no matter how cynical or self-interested, at the highest levels of the Arrow Cross regime was crucial. Perlasca had contacts in the Foreign Ministry, the Interior Ministry, the police and the Arrow Cross party itself. Some did large favours, others small. In some ways Perlasca had an advantage over Raoul Wallenberg and Carl Lutz. Sweden and Switzerland were richer and more powerful countries than Spain, but the Arrow Cross was particularly keen to have recognition from Franco's regime, seeing it as a fellow Fascist government. Perlasca used this to develop a connection with Gábor Kemény, the Arrow Cross foreign minister. After the 15 October coup many Hungarian diplomats and embassies remained Horthy loyalists – especially in neutral countries, including Spain. Kemény believed that the path to the much sought after Spanish diplomatic recognition for the Arrow Cross regime lay not through Madrid, but this hybrid Italian–Spaniard-turned-diplomat in Budapest. There was no chance of Spain ever recognising the Arrow Cross regime, but Perlasca made sure to make encouraging noises all through the winter of 1944.[5]

Aranka Klein pushed her fifteen-year-old son, István, out of the packed carriage as hard as she could. It was early December and the trains to the concentration camps were still leaving from Józsefváros Station. The Arrow Cross militiamen and the SS were screaming orders at the terrified Jews when suddenly one of the Nazi officers shouted that nobody under sixteen should get on board. It may have been a rare moment of humanity, or perhaps a concern that such children would be no use as workers. Aranka did not wait to find out. István almost flew in the other direction. His mother pushed a blanket into his hand and he managed to say goodbye. The wagons were sealed and the train left. He never saw her again. From Józsefváros Station, István was taken to an Arrow Cross internment camp at Teleki Square, in District VII, just outside the main ghetto. The drunken, sadistic guards delighted in taunting the young boy, asking why he was still alive and not yet dead, before delivering another beating. Somehow István managed to survive. After eight days István was taken to the main ghetto at 5 Klauzál Square. Conditions there were dreadful, but at least the beatings stopped – and these were very familiar streets.

   István had grown up on Klauzál Square and at nearby 29 Wesselényi Street. His family was born Jewish but had converted to Catholicism in 1939, believing, like many middle-class assimilated, patriotic Hungarian Jews, that changing faiths would provide some protection. István's father, Emil Fenyő, was in the textile business and imported fine cloth from England. Aranka, who had kept her maiden name, was a homemaker. István was a clever boy and the priests at his Catholic school had sent him to a Christian boarding school in Pécs, southern Hungary. István had barely escaped being rounded up after the Nazis invaded. He had travelled back to Budapest on the train with one of the teachers for protection, who told the gendarmes that he and the boy were together. That was enough – István's papers were not checked.

Once he arrived back in Budapest István went home to 29 Wesselényi Street. The building was already allocated as a Yellow Star house, so the Fenyős did not have to move in the first exodus across the city that June. István's uncle and his family moved to the flat. His adored elder brother Pál's room was empty. Pál, ten years older than István, had been killed on labour service in 1942 by Hungarian soldiers. They had hanged him then used his body for target practice. As the summer of 1944 turned into autumn István and his relatives, like most Budapest Jews, were guardedly hopeful. Until 16 October, the day after the Arrow Cross coup, when István and his parents were taken to the synagogue on Rumbach Sebestyén Street. Hundreds of people were crammed into the space with no food. After eight o'clock in the evening it was forbidden to use the toilets, so the floor was soon awash with urine and excrement. There was no heating and the building soon stank. Every now and again a death rattle sounded as somebody took poison and died. After three days István and his parents were finally released. His father Emil managed to obtain Swiss safe passes and they moved to a protected house on Tátra Street, in the International Ghetto. But on 2 December the Arrow Cross appeared, tore up the safe passes and sent the Fenyős to Teleki Square. There István had been separated from his father and taken to Józsefváros Station with his mother.

That evening of 10 December, as István tried to settle in the bomb shelter at the Klauzál Square house, was also the start of the festival of Channukah, the Jewish Festival of Lights. Channukah commemorates the miracle of the oil and the rededication of the Temple in the second century BC. The festival lasts eight days. Candles are lit in a *menorah*, a special candelabra, and it is customary to eat fried food, often including potato pancakes called *latkes*. There were not many miracles in Budapest that winter of 1944, except perhaps for István. The next morning he left Klauzál Square and went back to his childhood home at 29 Wesselényi Street. His father, Emil, was there. He embraced his son as hard as he ever had, tearful but grateful. Emil had believed that both István and his wife were lost. Soon afterwards 5 Klauzál Square was flattened by a bomb. Many of the residents were killed.

A mile or so away, at 29 Vadász Street in District V, Mihály Salamon and his wife, Margit-Mirjam, were celebrating a makeshift Channukah. Salamon, a veteran Zionist leader, was manager of the complex known as the Glass House. The Swiss Embassy, on nearby Szabadság Square, had opened an emigration department in the building in July, thus placing it under diplomatic protection. Since then the Glass House, which had once been the headquarters of a glass manufacturer, had evolved into the city's largest Jewish resistance base. Salamon had managed to make a makeshift *menorah* from nutshells filled with oil and wicks, while Margit-Mirjam had somehow produced makeshift *latkes*. That too was a minor miracle because there had been no potatoes in the house for months. They were very cold, not especially fresh and the dough was covered with a film of grease. But they were the best he had ever tasted.

The Glass House was home to a highly organised and well-run community of around 3,000 Jews, many of them young Zionist activists. The complex was a mini-kibbutz transplanted to the heart of downtown Budapest, a hive of highly organised, motivated activity. The Glass House was built around a courtyard, where a large kitchen served three meals a day, run by a team of cooks assisted by others with preparing, serving and washing up. Sometimes there was coffee or even *langos*, a Hungarian treat of fried dough, but made with potato flour. There was an infirmary where doctors could treat minor ailments as best as they could with extremely limited resources, although the seriously ill were sent to one of the Jewish hospitals. The different Zionist organisations each had their own space. Bnei Akiva, the religious Zionists, were in the attic on the north side. Hanoar Hatzioni, a liberal-minded movement, was in the western attic. The 'Han-Hac' attic also housed the laundry, a large trough where clothes were washed by hand. Habonim Dror, the Socialists, were in a cellar. Members of Hashomer Hatzair, a more left-wing group, also gathered together. The elderly and larger families with children lived in what was called the 'Orthodox cellar'. The young activists ran educational programmes and taught Hebrew. The Orthodox Jews studied the Torah, the five books of Moses, and the Talmud, the rabbinical commentary. The technical department was responsible for the dozens of buildings in the International Ghetto that were under Swiss protection. A continual stream of engineers, mechanics and locksmiths left the Glass House to deal with problems in the protected houses, travelling in Swiss Embassy vehicles.

The Zionists also ran an escape line, modelled on the lines of Joel Brand's 'Tiyul' department. Working with smugglers, they moved people from safe house to safe house in Budapest, into the provinces and across the border into Arad, Romania. Between May and August 1944 as many as 15,000 people were smuggled across the border to Romania, an extraordinary achievement. Each transit was a complicated operation. The fleeing Jews were told how to behave on the train – where travellers were frequently checked – how to meet the smuggler in the border town who would get them across the frontier and how to know when they had reached Romanian territory.[6] After Romania changed sides in August 1944 the frontier was sealed and became much harder to cross. Miklós Krausz, the head of the Palestine Office, and Artúr Weisz, the owner of the Glass House, were strongly opposed to this clandestine activity, believing that it endangered their delicate negotiations with the Arrow Cross and the Germans. They banned several of the young Zionist leaders from entering the building. But they did not care and came in anyway. Some of the activists even stole blank protective papers from the Palestine Office in the Swiss Legation.

The Glass House was comparatively safe. But conditions were cramped and uncomfortable. There was no heating most of the time. The residents slept on bunkbeds or on the floor. Sometimes they slept on their sides, several huddled together at once, although that at least generated some warmth. They were bedevilled by lice and diarrhoea. There was only one toilet, until a pit was dug in the courtyard, where ten people could relieve themselves at once. There was no electricity. In the evenings the cellars were lit by lamps or candles. But they were alive – and liberation would soon be at hand. Many of those in the Glass House were young. Even in such extreme conditions, or perhaps especially so, romance flourished. The passageways between the two sides of the complex were a popular meeting place for romantic assignations. Some young couples who met in the Glass House later married.[7]

The Glass House on Vadász Street was placed under Swiss diplomatic protection and became a centre of Jewish resistance. Crowds of Jewish people queued outside each morning, desperate to receive assistance.

The Galántays finally moved out of their flat on Akácfa Street on 10 December. Ervin took one last look around Klauzál Square before they left. A huge unexploded Russian shell had landed in the middle. He noticed that a large crowd was heading to the market hall. Inside thousands of people were queuing. His description of the scene as Jewish Council officials registered ghetto residents for their ration cards is a rare and finely detailed snapshot of the Ghetto bureaucracy:

> In the middle of the hall, seated behind a table, there are three men. Two of them with beards and black hats seem to be rabbis. In the centre presides a huge bald man in a fur-trimmed coat. He is flanked by two guards with yellow armbands, identifying them as the ghetto police ... Several women are loudly complaining until led away. In the back of the hall white kerchiefed clerks are distributing tins of kosher food and macesz [*matzah*], wafer-like dry pancakes. These are rationed items but there are also sweet wine, beans and bags full of dried fish for sale.

Ervin's parents were offered several large and luxurious flats on Andrássy Avenue, complete with furniture and fittings – now empty after their Jewish owners had been relocated. His mother refused to accept any of them and eventually the family moved to her parents' flat in Óbuda.[8]

By now the Vannay Battalion was at full strength and incorporated into the Hungarian Army. Ervin trained at the Újlaki brickworks in Óbuda. The site had needed a thorough clean after being used as a makeshift concentration camp for the start of the death marches. It was now a comfortable barracks with hot showers and a sauna. Ervin finally got the combat training he longed for. He learnt how to fire a machine gun and use the anti-tank *Panzerfaust*, a single-shot weapon, and translated the instructions from German into Hungarian. The battalion was well fed – at one lunch Ervin had mutton stew and *lecsó*, a vegetable ragout of peppers, tomatoes and potatoes. Meanwhile, at the headquarters at the Toldy Ferenc School on the street of the same name in Buda, Uncle Roth was hard at work. As well as forged documents, he also made a printed instruction leaflet with silhouettes of German and Soviet armoured vehicles. It was vital to be able to recognise them, especially at night, and not fire at the wrong side. He also made dog-tags for the battalion. Ervin received his stamped: 'Galántay Ervin Budapest 1930 October 14'.

31

Days of Hunger and Terror

> Let us behave modestly and quietly in the apartments and the buildings. The instructions of the authorities must be accepted obediently.
>
> Jewish Council instruction to inhabitants of the main ghetto.[1]

David Gur was not thinking about Channukah on 11 December. He checked the time once more, anxiety twisting inside him. It was now late afternoon sliding into evening, and time to make a decision. Feri had still not arrived. Feri was the cut-out, the only person who knew where the workshop was. He arrived each morning with the instructions for the documents to be produced, then returned in the afternoon to collect the finished papers. The protocol was clear: the workshop now had to be packed up and they needed to flee. The workshop had been on the move all through the summer. Each time anything suspicious happened, or a neighbour appeared to be interested in who was coming or going, they packed up and left. For a while the workshop had been based at 52 Damjanich Street, next to the children's home where Judit Ornstein had lived. Then it moved to a bookshop on Baross Street, in the lower edge of District VIII, to Nádor Street in District V, and now back to Baross Street. The location seemed ideal: a Communist contact had found them a place in the headquarters of the far-right Csaba student movement. Gur and his comrades did not go out, but they were hiding in plain sight, in a place with lots of young people coming and going and highly unlikely to be raided.

They waited a little longer then quickly packed up the papers, stamps and equipment. Six suitcases were needed to hold everything. Gur's workshop was now capable of producing any document used in Hungary. As well as fake Hungarian and German government documents and neutral countries' safe passes, it also produced fake papers for Arrow Cross specialised units and death squads. These allowed the Zionist resistance fighters to pose as Hungarian Nazis on their sabotage and attack missions. In November the Zionist youth decided on radical action: to produce a Swiss safe pass for every Jew still alive. Some argued that flooding the city with so many fake safe passes would endanger those with genuine documents. Artúr Weisz and Miklós Krausz were vehemently opposed, believing it endangered the whole safe pass and neutral protection operation. It may be that Lutz himself turned a blind eye to the operation. He certainly did not stop it. In any case the decision was taken: everyone had a right to survival and must be given the opportunity to survive.

Printing 120,000 safe passes was a massive operation, the largest yet. The operation demanded complicated logistics of production, distribution and transportation. The group obtained 45 kg of paper from the same printing house that Lutz used. Just like the genuine documents, the safe passes were made out in German and Hungarian, with the red-and-white emblem of the Swiss Embassy at the top, the words 'Department of Emigration' underneath and the address of 29 Vadász Street. They were all numbered between 1 and 7,000, as only 7,000 genuine passes had been issued. The names were left blank and filled in by hand or typewriter. They were soon distributed all over the city. Some were smuggled into the forced-labour camps, others handed out in children's homes.

The young Zionists produced forged Arrow Cross documents, including 'execution orders'. They then dressed up in Arrow Cross uniforms, including armbands and side arms, and went out on patrol, looking for the Arrow Cross gangs who were rounding up Jews. Posing as an 'execution squad' they then demanded that the Jews be handed over and led them off – soon after, once they were far enough away, they told the startled Jews to run. Posing as an Arrow Cross militiaman was not easy – they had to adjust their language, speak a rough street slang and even hurl abuse at their fellow Jews. They had to steel themselves as their fellow Jews cried and begged, believing they were being led to their deaths. The other danger was of being recognised. On one such mission one of the young Jewish men in Arrow Cross uniform was recognised by someone from his hometown, who started yelling he was a Jew. A hostile crowd soon gathered demanding that he be taken to the police station. At that moment two more Arrow Cross militiamen appeared, drew their guns and jabbed the two fake Arrow Cross men in the back and marched them off down a side street. Once out of sight of the mob, they embraced. The new Arrow Cross gunmen were actually members of Dror, one of the Zionist youth movements, come to rescue their comrades.

Word was spreading among both Allied POWs and the Hungarian resistance about the increasingly effective and professional forgery operation. Gur supplied Swiss birth certificates to a Dutch officer in touch with escaped Allied POWs. The Zionists began to cooperate with the small workers' opposition. As the Glass House became more and more crowded, they opened an annex on neighbouring Wekerle Sándor Street. They exchanged fake documents for accommodation with anti-Nazi workers in factories in District XIV on the edge of the city. They worked with renegade Arrow Cross militiamen who wanted to cooperate with the Jews and with student opposition groups. Famous writers were also supplied with fake papers, including Tibor Déry and Iván Boldizsár, who before the war had attended Caja Odescalchi's salons at the Andrássy Palace and rhapsodised about her beauty. Others received identity papers from the workshop through cut-outs, including the Communist leader László Rajk.

Gur left on a tricycle with the suitcases packed into its luggage area. He then made an extremely risky and dangerous journey far across the city to a safe house in Kőbánya, in the southeast of the city, not far from the advancing Russians, where three young female activists were living. Gur made it to the flat without being seen or arrested and left the suitcases there. But it was going to be very hard to find a new site, he knew.[2]

In December Robi Lichtenstein and his sister, Zsuzsa, were on the move again. The International Ghetto was becoming ever more dangerous. Almost every night their riverside building echoed to the terrible sounds of gunfire as Arrow Cross militiamen shot Jews into the river. Being a child was no protection. It was an agonising decision to split up the family. But Fülöp and Erzsébet decided Robi and Zsuzsa would be safer away from the International Ghetto. They sent their children to the Jewish orphanage on Vilma Királynő Road, near the City Park. The orphanage was protected by the Swedish Embassy, and had supplies of food. A deal had somehow been done with the Arrow Cross and the Germans, Robi's parents thought, and the children would be safe. Even the Arrow Cross were not depraved enough to attack a children's home, they believed. They were wrong.

For a while life was tolerable at the orphanage. It was divided into separate wings for boys and girls and they lived quite freely. There were food supplies and no need for Robi to make hazardous trips to exchange gold chains for bacon. The orphanage was seen as a place of sanctuary – by the time Robi and Zsuzsa got there, so many children had arrived that the managers opened an annex in the neighbouring Munkácsi Mihály Street. But Arrow Cross militiamen frequently harassed the site, looking for young Jewish men who had evaded labour service, threatening the staff and the children. The children and the managers had no means of protecting themselves. Robi's sixth sense told him to find a hiding place. He spent some time exploring the building. Clambering around the cellar, he found a tight passageway to a bombed-out area that was virtually inaccessible, especially for an adult. That was perfect, he thought. The most determined Arrow Cross militiaman would not be able to push his way through that.

One day later in the month several Jewish teenagers who were members of KISKA (Kisegítő Karhatalmi Alakulat), an auxiliary militia, came to the orphanage. Although KISKA had been established under Arrow Cross rule and included former party members, some of its detachments joined the resistance, attacked the Arrow Cross and rescued Jews. Other anti-Nazis and deserters joined.[3] Colonel Lajos Gidófalvy's detachment, one of the city's largest and most effective KISKA groups, worked with Wallenberg's organisation. Robi knew of the militia, some of whose members were connected to the scouts. So when the KISKA fighters asked if he would like to join them on a hunting mission to attack the Arrow Cross, he readily agreed. The boys said that they would come and find him tomorrow. Robi waited outside the orphanage all day but nobody showed up. After the war Robi found out that they had all been caught by the Arrow Cross and shot. After not being sent to his relatives in Abony and escaping from the Újpest sports arena, that was the third in Robi's series of narrow escapes. The fourth was about to happen very soon.

On 24 December the Arrow Cross surrounded both orphanage buildings, shooting in the air and screaming orders. Robi immediately went to get Zsuzsa. The courtyard was full of terrified children running in every direction. He quickly found his sister and pulled her with him, away from the crowd. The two children clambered into Robi's hiding place and sat in the dark, completely silent for several hours, listening to the cries of fear, screaming and shooting as the other children were rounded up and taken away. Eventually the shooting stopped and the orphanage was silent. Accounts differ as to the fate of the children. Some were killed, others may have eventually been rescued by the Red Cross. KISKA fighters engaged the Arrow Cross and ordered them to take the children to the Jewish Council at Síp Street, according to one account. But instead they were taken to an apartment building on Szív Street, and the next day marched down to the Danube. An air raid began and some ran away but many were shot into the river.[4]

Robi and Zsuzsa stayed in the cellar overnight. They set off at dawn the next day, walking through the city, praying that they did not encounter any Arrow Cross patrols. On the Ferdinánd Bridge not far from Nyugati Station, near their original family home, now bombed, they met an armed boy a couple of years older than Robi in a KISKA uniform. Some of the KISKA fighters were in the resistance, but there was no guarantee he was not an Arrow Cross sympathiser. Zsuzsa was frightened of him. At just eight years old her experience of men with guns was terrifying – and she and Robi were now in danger. What were two young children doing, wandering around the city alone at dawn? He could easily shoot them on a whim. The sound of artillery from the south of the city boomed around the streets. Robi kept his cool, chatting with the KISKA fighter. After a while they parted and Robi and Zsuzsa returned to their parents. There were tears of relief, hugs and kisses. Conditions in the International Ghetto were even worse than when they left. There was barely any food, but Robi, his sister and his parents were alive. One day Robi saw a young girl lying on the ground in the entrance of the building while doctors tried in vain to revive her. He would see many more dead bodies over the next few weeks, but the sight of the dying girl would never leave him.

Katalin Karády went into hiding after the Arrow Cross coup. Her public profile, her public sympathy for Jews – especially her own Jewish colleagues – her connections to the resistance and her lover Colonel István Ujszászy all put her high on the most-wanted list. She moved from flat to flat, always staying one step ahead of those pursuing her. It was much harder for Karády to go underground than most Hungarians. She was instantly recognisable – and there were plenty of people who would be glad to denounce her. Her public face also kept her in danger – she was unable to use most air-raid shelters or cellars for fear of being seen.

According to one account, Karády found refuge with friends at their flat on Galamb Street, downtown in District V, near the Erzsébet Bridge – until one day, when two Arrow Cross men pushed their way in. They would all be going for a walk, they sneered, and Karády would soon be very comfortable in the Danube. She tried to distract them with a bottle of brandy, which they quickly downed. Like all Arrow Cross militiamen they prefaced their name with 'brother'. One, called Brother Csiszár, then demanded money. Karády handed over 1,000 *pengős* and offered them another bottle of brandy. The other Arrow Cross man was happy to accept and get drunk. But Brother Csiszár ordered him up. The three of them walked down to the river. Another Arrow Cross patrol walked by with a bound captive. The air-raid sirens started howling. Brother Csiszár followed the other group, ordering the second Arrow Cross man to guard Karády. This was her chance. She tried to persuade him to let her go, saying she only did good things for people. The Arrow Cross man said that was the problem. She had not selected the people for whom she did good things. By now he was quite drunk. He invited Karády back to his room at the nearby Hotel Hungaria on the Corso. She agreed to go. The room was full of empty bottles of alcohol. He asked her to pull off his boots, then fell back on the bed, dead-drunk. Karády left, taking the back staircase, and quickly made her way back to Galamb Street.[5]

After a while she returned home to her villa in Buda, but carried on her work helping Jews. One day in the winter of 1944 a group of freezing, crying and terrified Jewish children were standing on the riverbank, surrounded by Arrow Cross gunmen. Their fate seemed clear. One, János Gömöri, was five years old. He and the others had been marched from their home in the ghetto on Wesselényi Street. Then a large black car suddenly appeared and a 'very pretty lady' got out, he recalled decades later. The lady approached the gunmen and offered them an exchange: gold and jewellery for the children. The Arrow Cross men looked at what was on offer, then nodded. Katalin Karády quickly ushered the children into her car and took them home. There she did everything she could to look after them, feeding them, playing the piano and singing for them. They all survived and after the liberation Karády helped the children find any surviving relatives. Gömöri's father had been killed in Auschwitz but his mother had survived. She and János were reunited. As for István Ujszászy, the love of Karády's life, by now he was in hiding at the Swedish Embassy. They would both survive the war, but would never make a life together.[6]

Robi and his family did not stay much longer in the International Ghetto. In late December, a few days after he and Zsuzsa returned from the orphanage, the Arrow Cross raided their building, screaming at everyone to assemble in the courtyard. Some presented their safe passes. By now these were almost worthless. The militiamen tore them to shreds, screaming abuse and insults. Some of those in the courtyard prepared for death, believing that it was now their turn to be marched to the nearby riverbank. Instead they were all lined up, walked through city and taken to the main ghetto in District VII, the city's traditional Jewish quarter.

It took about an hour for Robi, all his family and the other Jews to walk through the city centre to the entrance of the ghetto, with the Arrow Cross abusing and beating them along the way. Passers-by stared without much sympathy, as though the Jews were an irritant, or an alien species that was nothing to do with their lives. Some laughed, while others shouted abuse and even spat at them. Eventually Robi and his family arrived at Klauzál Square. The Arrow Cross began firing in the air and shouting to make the new arrivals even more afraid as they screamed at the Jews to hand over their valuables. Fülöp slipped a small box with the remains of the family jewellery into Robi's hand. The young boy knew what to do and somehow managed to hide it by a bush nearby.

The ghetto, which covered just 0.3 square kilometres, had been established at the end of November. It was a tight maze of narrow streets of nineteenth-century apartment buildings. The area was surrounded by a high wooden fence, with four gates, including one by the Great Synagogue at the bottom of Wesselényi Street, very near to the Astoria Hotel. Király Street, the main thoroughfare of the Jewish quarter, lay just outside the boundaries. Some of the apartments were spacious, others small and cramped. All were soon extremely crowded. Armed Arrow Cross militiamen and regular police guarded the entrances. Some of the buildings inside the ghetto were already Yellow Star houses, but any Christian tenants, such as the Galántay family, had to leave. Not everyone shared the Galántays' anger at being forced from their home, or their scruples about their new accommodation. Some were quite happy to move into a former Jewish-owned apartment elsewhere in the city. By late December, the Red Cross children's homes were closed down and by Christmas most of the 6,000 children had been relocated to the main ghetto.

Life in the Budapest ghetto was different to that in the Warsaw ghetto. In both capitals tens of thousands of Jews were jammed into cramped, extremely unsanitary conditions with poor hygiene and medical provision. By January 1945 around 70,000 Jews lived in the Budapest ghetto, with an average density of fourteen people per room. But while in Warsaw trains left regularly for the death camps, by the end of 1944 nobody was going anywhere from Budapest. The city was surrounded by the Soviets. The death marches had stopped, the gas chambers at Auschwitz had been blown up. All the Jews had to do was wait and survive the war and the Arrow Cross raids. The narrow streets echoed to the boom of artillery, the rattle of machine-gun fire and the whoosh of Katyusha rockets. But being Jewish was no protection against Soviet munitions. Buildings were frequently hit by mortars and shellfire.

The Jewish Council, which was in charge of the ghetto, developed a well organised system of administration, overseeing food, medical services and as much security as could be provided. It was divided into ten areas, and each local leader oversaw the meagre food supplies, electricity and water, and the fire service if buildings were in flames after being hit by shells or bombs. Each building had its own superintendent, who was the liaison point with the Council. The inhabitants were asked to keep the apartments clean, report any contagious diseases, behave modestly, follow regulations and not make unreasonable demands, especially about food. The ghetto also had its own small police force to keep order – especially necessary after the Jewish inmates of Budapest's prisons were released and transferred into the ghetto. Yet even as the Russians were at the gates of the city, the Arrow Cross still launched raids. Often drunk, they would burst through the gates, massacre the inhabitants of a building, steal their possessions then stagger off. A detachment of a hundred policemen and fifteen comparatively orderly Arrow Cross militiamen was then posted inside the ghetto to keep order and see off any raiders. This worked to an extent – but the policemen and Arrow Cross men had to be fed, further using up meagre food stocks.

These were days of hunger. Communal kitchens were set up, including at the Stern Restaurant on Rumbach Sebestyén Street. The daily ration was 150 grams of bread, 40 grams of flour, 10 grams of oil and 30 grams of vegetables, mostly peas. This was around 800 calories – about half of that provided to prisoners. Few of the ghetto-dwellers actually received that. It was more common to go without food for days. Many starved to death. The price of bread sky-rocketed. The official price was 1.5 *pengős*, the black-market price outside the ghetto was 10 *pengős*, and inside it was 500 *pengős*. There was no fuel – instead the wood was stripped from bombed-out buildings and burnt. Water came from disused wells which were reopened and the well which supplied the ritual bath at the Orthodox synagogue on Kazinczy Street. Flour was sometimes provided by the Red Cross – the only international organisation to open an office inside the ghetto. Ottó Komoly, Hansi Brand and others set up a committee to purchase food from outside suppliers. The sight of food supplies, sometimes including luxuries such as cheese and eggs, entering the ghetto enraged the local Arrow Cross leaders, who frequently prevented the goods from entering.

Despite the Jewish Council's appeals for order and cleanliness, the hygiene and sanitation situation was catastrophic. There was no means of removing rubbish, which piled up in heaps on every street. The scenes at the ghetto's makeshift hospitals – which were just outside its walls – were medieval. Patients lay across the floors while surgeons performed emergency operations on kitchen tables covered with bedsheets, often without anaesthetics. There was no electricity after Christmas Day, so the doctors worked by candle- or torchlight. There was a thriving market in poison and numerous Jews, especially among the middle-class and assimilated, committed suicide. Sometimes Jews were brought in from the river, barely alive after being shot into the Danube by the Arrow Cross. Before Christmas coffins holding around 100 dead bodies a day were taken to the ghetto gate and passed on to Christian drivers, who buried them in a municipal cemetery. By early

January, as the fighting intensified, the dead could no longer be taken away. Instead they were stacked up in the open: at Klauzál Square, in the courtyard of the baths at the Kazinczy Street and at the Great Synagogue, which became a giant open-air grave. An eyewitness account describes the kind of scene usually found at the concentration camps.

In narrow Kazinczy Street enfeebled men, drooping their heads, were pushing a wheelbarrow. On the rattling contraption naked human bodies as yellow as wax were jolted along and a stiff arm with black patches was dangling and knocking against the spokes of the wheel. In the courtyard of the Kazinczy baths behind the weather-beaten façade bodies were piled up, frozen stiff like pieces of wood.

Nearby on Klauzál Square people were hacking lumps of meat off a decapitated dead horse. Its head lay a few yards away, while its yellow-and-blue intestines, 'jelly-like and with a cold sheen', burst out of its body.[7]

The Lichtensteins moved into one room on Akácfa Street, which they shared with Artúr Schwarz and his wife. Fülöp had managed to save a bag of tobacco, which he traded for bread. Even inside the ghetto Robi retained his sense of adventure. One day he climbed over a wall to find some wood to burn for heating. He came face to face with an Arrow Cross militiaman, who pointed his rifle at him. Stealing wood could be a capital crime. Fülöp appeared and acted quickly. It was important not to plead with the Arrow Cross. Pleading only fuelled their sadism, but they appreciated violence. Fülöp slapped Robi hard around the face and yelled at him, calling him a bad boy, saying he had told him not to go there, and started to drag him back. The Arrow Cross man lowered his rifle, gestured for them to get out of there. It was the last of Robi's brushes with death.

32

Siege and Slaughter

In the early morning of 30 December a police officer on duty
stopped five Jewish-looking men, running and soaked to the
skin, who were so confused they were unable to say who they
were or how they had fallen into the Danube.

Hungarian army report.[1]

As the Lichtensteins huddled in their cramped, freezing room in
the ghetto, the Russians steadily advanced towards the city centre.
On 26 December Budapest was finally surrounded by Soviet and
Romanian forces. The outer suburbs were falling rapidly to the
Soviets and the city was cut off. The siege proper began. Marshal
Rodion Malinovsky, commander of the 2nd Ukrainian Front and
Marshal Fyodor Tolbukhin, commander of the 3rd Ukrainian Front,
were attacking from the north and south simultaneously. Shells
and mortars slammed non-stop into the inner city, tracer bullets
arcing through the sky. The streets were lined with corpses and
stank of smoke and dead bodies. Malinovsky and Tolbukhin were
battle-hardened veterans. Malinovsky had served in the Red Army
during the Russian Civil War and fought at some of the bloodiest
engagements of the Second World War, including Stalingrad and
Kursk, before slicing through Ukraine, capturing Transylvania and
advancing into southern and eastern Hungary. He had negotiated
with Horthy's envoys in Szeged, southern Hungary, in one of the
regent's numerous abortive attempts to change sides. Tolbukhin's
troops had recaptured Crimea and southern Ukraine, and liberated
Bulgaria and Yugoslavia.

Some among the Hungarians and Germans, including several senior Hungarian clergy, had wanted to declare Budapest an open city – like Rome or Prague. Eastern and southern Hungary had already been captured. The city itself had powerful symbolic value – especially for Stalin – but little strategic worth. It made more sense for the Germans to withdraw and focus the Axis forces on defending Vienna. Few Hungarians, apart from Arrow Cross fanatics, wanted to see Budapest in flames and reduced to rubble in the coming battle. Hitler had signed the city's death warrant on November 23. He ordered that Budapest must be defended street by street, block by block and building by building. Ferenc Szálasi and the Arrow Cross government agreed – then fled westwards a few days later. On December 1 Hitler issued order No. 11, confirming his order of November 23 and declaring Budapest a *Festung* (Fortress city).

It was easier to defend urban territory than capture it, but the defenders were outgunned and outnumbered. There were around 41,000 Germans and 38,000 Hungarians. But not all of these were experienced soldiers or even combat-ready. Few of the Arrow Cross militiamen, so ready to shoot unarmed Jews into the Danube, were prepared to go into battle against enemy soldiers. The Soviets had around 180,000 battle-hardened troops, many of whom had fought their way through Ukraine, Romania and the Hungarian countryside. They had seen their comrades die, uncovered the evidence of the camps and atrocities on the eastern front and hungered for vengeance.

Hungary was to be in the Soviet sphere of influence. The deals with the West that Stalin had concluded at Yalta and other wartime conferences were now about to bear fruit. There was already a Soviet-backed provisional government operating in Debrecen, eastern Hungary. Béla Miklos, the Horthy loyalist general who had defected to the Russians after 15 October, was the prime minister. There were four opposition parties in the government – the Independent Smallholders, the Social Democrats, the National Peasant Party and the Communists, where the real power lay. For Stalin it was imperative that Budapest was captured as soon as possible, but his orders that the Hungarian capital be swiftly captured had the opposite effect. In his memoir Malinovsky recalled a conversation with Stalin on the evening of 28 October. Stalin ordered Malinovsky to capture the city 'in the shortest possible time' and 'by any means necessary'. Malinovsky asked for five days before commencing the attack, to give reinforcements time to arrive. After that, he promised to deliver a 'severe, absolutely unpredictable blow' and take the Hungarian capital in two to three days. Stalin refused and ordered him to attack immediately. Malinovsky replied that to advance before the reinforcements arrived meant that the Russian forces would be stuck in lengthy battles on the outskirts of the city. Stalin dismissed his concerns. He replied, 'I categorically order you to advance on Budapest tomorrow' and ended the conversation. Malinovsky dutifully ordered his forces to advance the next morning, but his prediction proved correct. Stalin's haste cost the lives of thousands of Russian soldiers and doubtless lengthened the war. As Malinovsky noted, 'Of course the advance dragged on slowly, and the German-Fascist leadership had had enough time to put up a dogged resistance. That was the sole reason for the long fighting in Budapest'.[2]

But by late December the Soviets and Romanian forces had reached a critical mass and were slicing through the German and Hungarian lines like a scythe through a cornfield. The defenders often fought hard, and sometimes even recaptured territory for a few days. But they stood little chance against an army which deployed wave after wave of attackers. Budakalász and Bekásmegyer, just north of Budapest, fell on 26 December. In southern Buda Soviet troops fought their way into Budafok, Albertfalva and Kelenföld, where a decade earlier the Prince of Wales's train had pulled in from Vienna. The next day Soviet forces captured Csillaghegy and Rómaifürdő on the Danube in northern Buda as well as Orbánhegy. Budaörs in the south quickly fell, while in the north the Germans evacuated Dunakeszi and fell back to Rákospalota and Újpest, from where the last Jews to be deported had been rounded up. It was clear to all but the most fanatical Nazi or Arrow Cross militiaman that the city's surrender was inevitable.

The defending forces were riven with tension, rivalry and multiple command lines. The schism between the Germans and Hungarians was deep-rooted. Throughout the war, from the earliest, disastrous Hungarian attack on the Soviet Union in 1941, the Germans had treated the Hungarians with disdain, as lackeys who should be grateful to be allied with the Third Reich. The Nazi high command took strategic decisions that affected the Hungarians without consulting them, deployed poorly armed and under-equipped Hungarian forces where they chose and failed to deliver promised supplies of weapons and ammunition. All this cost many Hungarian lives and continued during the battle for Budapest. German commanders issued orders that purely served their interest without consulting the Hungarians or taking into consideration their needs and military ability. The Germans and Hungarian high commands issued their own military reports, in which they criticised each other. The Germans blew up buildings and destroyed parts of the city as they wished. All the bridges across the Danube, proud symbols of Budapest's sophistication and modernity, were mined and wired. The resistance frequently cut the wires and disabled the fuses. But when the Germans retreated from Pest to Buda in mid-January, they blew up the last bridges, causing fury among the Hungarians whose capital was now cut in two.

The Nazis plundered vast amounts of goods, food and other property. Even László Endre despaired at the extent of the looting. The alliance between the Arrow Cross and the SS was a marriage of convenience, he learned to his dismay. The Germans were pillaging farms, factories, almost anything useful they could move. As the Russians advanced from the east, foodstuff and livestock were supposed to be directed to Budapest, but only a fraction arrived, he wrote in January. Instead, they were sent to the Reich.[3] The German high command itself was divided. The officer in overall charge of the city's defence was SS Obergruppenführer Karl Pfeffer-Wildenbruch. A veteran of the First World War, he had joined the SS in 1939, where he commanded the SS Police. But he had little combat experience and even less understanding of very-close-quarter urban warfare. Pfeffer-Wildenbruch had become commander almost by accident. He was essentially a policeman and had been sent to Budapest in autumn 1944 to ensure that the Arrow Cross took power. Nor was he very courageous – he conducted the defence of the city from his bunker and did not visit the frontline or the fighting troops. His example was followed by others. As one officer observed, 'Pfeffer-Wildenbruch is ... not a leader of men. In any case it is a novelty for a commanding general not to leave the tunnel for six weeks. This also spread to the officers of his staff, who only visit their troops as a formality after the award of the Knight's Cross.'[4]

Although Malinovsky and Tolbukhin had fought at Stalingrad, they had not commanded operations within the city itself. They lacked experience of high-intensity urban warfare. For a while the Soviet forces, like the Germans, were hampered by lack of coordination as different corps received orders from separate command centres. On 11 January Malinovsky brought all the attacking forces under the command of Lieutenant General Ivan Afonyin. Afonyin was experienced in urban warfare, having served inside the cauldron of Stalingrad, at Kursk and at the liberation of Kiev. Pest would fall within a few days.

A few blocks from the Lichtensteins, István Fenyő was still living with his father, Emil, in their family home at 29 Wesselényi Street in the heart of the ghetto. At least a dozen people were crammed into the flat, surviving in atrocious conditions. There was no running water, no heating and barely any food. At first they received bread from the communal authorities but then supplies stopped in mid-December. Sometimes there were beans or peas, but István and the others were constantly ravaged by hunger. The building shook and rattled from the constant explosions and air raids but István and Emil could not go to the shelter. Like many in the ghetto they were ravaged by a disease called the 'Ukrainian sickness' – a kind of dysentery that produced constant yellow diarrhoea. In a strange way the illness was a kind of blessing. Those who were sick had to stay in their apartments. When the Arrow Cross raided, they usually targeted the cellars but did not bother going upstairs and sweeping through each floor.

For István, half-starved, frightened, filthy and desperately missing his mother, a new nightmare was about to unfold. Dozens of people were dying every day from starvation, sickness, suicide and the freezing cold. Some simply gave up. Hundreds of bodies were stacked up on Klauzál Square and Kazinczy Street, near the Orthodox synagogue. Many were frozen, but they were still a health hazard. The Germans ordered that the bodies be buried and instructed the Jewish Council to organise it. All able-bodied men – such as there were in the ghetto – were ordered to assist. István did his part. It was a horrendous task. Apart from the psychological trauma of seeing so many dead people, many of the dead bodies had begun to decompose. Worst of all, István and the others had no gloves. They had to place the corpses into wheelbarrows with their bare hands. They then wheeled the bodies to the courtyard of the Great Synagogue on Dohány Street. A train of wheelbarrows trekked back and forth, piled high with corpses, heads and blackened limbs hanging from the edges, seeping fluids. A large pit was dug in the Great Synagogue courtyard. István and others unloaded the dead bodies and placed them into a mass grave. That was at least a kind of dignity.[5]

Ten days after fleeing the base on Baross Street, despite his every effort, David Gur could not find a new site to set up the workshop. The Russians were advancing, Budapest was under non-stop bombardment and the Arrow Cross were rampaging through the streets. The city was collapsing into chaos. After days of inaction and no new documents being produced, the Zionists' new allies began to turn on them. Where were the papers that they had promised? Why weren't they being produced? Who were these people – these 'Zionists' – anyway? Some even accused Gur's group of being saboteurs, threatening them with retribution after the war. Gur was working with Miki Langer and Andrej Fabry, two of the group's most talented draughtsmen and forgers. Both were in their early twenties and refugees from Slovakia.

Langer proposed that they set up the workshop in the building department of the Budapest municipality on the Erzsébet Boulevard. He knew the building supervisor and trusted him. They would set up in a back room. It would be safe. Gur and Fabry reluctantly agreed. They moved in on 21 December and began to unpack and set up the workshop. The Arrow Cross raided the building the same day. As they stormed down the corridors Gur and the others frantically searched for their weapons. They had left them in their jackets, which were outside in the hall. There were more guns in the suitcases but they did not find them in time. All three were arrested and tied up. Their money, watches and valuables were taken.

The Arrow Cross also swept through the building, checking every resident's papers. One of them called the police to complain that drunk Arrow Cross men were causing a nuisance. Gur and the others tried to bribe the Arrow Cross men with 10,000 *pengős* to let them go. It might have worked. But the police, too frightened to enter the building after the complaint, called the Arrow Cross headquarters. An Arrow Cross security squad, fanatics and sadists, turned up and took over the whole affair. They took the three prisoners to the Arrow Cross headquarters, where they opened up the suitcases. Their eyes opened wide when they saw what they had found: Arrow Cross documents, military permits, a Swiss passport and much more. This was clearly a huge catch. Gur, Langer and Fabry were beaten but for a short while were left alone. They managed to shred and eat their identity documents. This was vital, as they included their addresses.

The Arrow Cross militiamen returned and ordered them to unpack and sort the material. Gur and the others surreptitiously destroyed as much as they could. Several of the Arrow Cross were extremely young, still in their mid-teens. They larked about, trying out the stamps on the forms. Then the serious violence began. The young Arrow Cross were the worst, eager to show their zeal, hitting the prisoners as hard as they could. Gur, Fabry and Langer were stripped to their underpants and beaten continuously from midnight till dawn. They were beaten with fists, clubs and chairs.

This was not any kind of interrogation seeking information – it was pure, untrammelled violence and savagery. At seven o'clock in the morning high-up Arrow Cross officials arrived to see the three captives. They were dressed, brought out to the corridor and seated separately. Fabry was severely concussed and could not stand. Miki Langer was in the worst shape, covered with bleeding wounds, blue circles around his eyes. At eleven o'clock he collapsed. Gur and Fabry tried to help with mouth-to-mouth respiration. It was to no avail. Soon after, he died. The Arrow Cross men appeared, kicked him, stripped his clothes and took his body away.

That afternoon Gur and Fabry were taken to the military prison on Margit Boulevard. The suitcases were the cause of their catastrophe, but also helped to keep them alive. Without the intriguing evidence they would doubtless have been quickly shot. The two prisoners were clearly part of a much wider network, which had to be investigated. By now, 22 December, the Russians were just a few hundred yards from the prison. Shells flew overhead and continually exploded nearby. But the round-ups continued. Several Zionist comrades, including members of Dror, were also held at the prison. Fabry was first to be summoned for interrogation. But he was still suffering from severe concussion and could not even stand up. Gur was next. He was led in. A chair with an electric-shock machine stood in the centre of the room. It was Gur's bad luck that his interrogator was one of the most notorious torturers, a Lieutenant Balassa, who was also well informed about the Zionists. Balassa asked Gur which Zionist movement he was from. Gur replied, Hashomer Hatzair. Balassa smiled, and replied that he already had people from Dror and Maccabi Hatzair, so he was happy to welcome someone from Hashomer Hatzair.

Gur was forced into the chair. The clips were attached to his skin and the switch thrown. The pain was unlike anything he had ever experienced, an agony tearing through him. His entire body shook and twitched. He lost control of himself. The torturers were enjoying themselves. Sometimes they switched the current on quickly, one burst after another. Sometimes more slowly. Then they interrogated Gur again. None of them knew that outside the prison Gur's comrades were about to mount a rescue operation. A Polish man had appeared several times at the Glass House annex on Werkele Sándor Street, saying that he could get prisoners released. On 21 December, the day of the arrest, he appeared again. The price was 300 gold Napoleons for Gur, Fabry and Langer, and 20 more for each extra captive that was freed. This was an incredible sum, especially at this stage in the war, but somehow they found the money. Gur's comrades then drew up a fake official execution order with a list of names. The Pole was to present this at the prison, extract their comrades and hand them over. The Pole agreed to the terms.

Giorgio Perlasca planned to spend the evening of 24 December having dinner at the Spanish Legation villa in Buda. He left in the late afternoon but when he drew near he was stopped by Hungarian soldiers. They said it was not possible to go ahead as the Russians were just a few hundred yards away. Perlasca explained that he was a Spanish diplomat and he needed to get to the villa. The soldiers said he could pass through for fifteen minutes. At the villa Perlasca was warmly welcomed – sixty people had now taken refuge there. They even had a giant Christmas tree, festooned with presents for him. He stayed for a while, but did not take his presents, fearing that would send the wrong message, that he was leaving for good.

Perlasca later had supper at a downtown hotel with a high-ranking Arrow Cross minister. Perlasca assumed that he wanted Spanish passports in exchange for the security of the protected houses. Years later he said that he would have done the deal, if that was necessary. But the Arrow Cross official did not ask for anything. In fact, he left suddenly. On his way home Perlasca was stopped by an Arrow Cross patrol. He showed them his diplomatic identity papers. The militiamen said they were no longer valid. At that moment Perlasca saw a regular army patrol on the other side of the street. He called them over and they told the Arrow Cross militiamen to respect Perlasca's status and to leave. They did. The next morning, Christmas Day, brought terrible news. Perlasca tried to get in touch with the Legation villa as there were still two cars there. The villa had been hit in the fighting and burned to the ground.[6]

Károly Odescalchi decided to risk a visit home for Christmas. He called his wife, Culi, and asked her to arrange everything and to try and make sure that their son Pál was also there. Károly had been in hiding since 15 October, moving from place to place to avoid arrest. The Arrow Cross had immediately targeted Ganz, which was known for the high number of Jewish directors. They gave the managing director a long list of employees whom they wanted to be sacked. Károly, well known for his anti-Nazi views, was number one. The managing director had warned Károly and he immediately packed a bag and moved out of the city. Another director, denounced by a pro-Nazi, had been taken to the riverbank and shot into the Danube. Károly was living in a small inn at the top of Sváb Hill, not far from the Majestic Hotel where Eichmann had his headquarters. Only Károly's wife and trusted secretary knew where he was. The hill was an excellent vantage point and he could watch the shifting frontlines. Meanwhile, Károly had laid in three months' worth of food at the family home on Piroska Street, and distributed the family's valuables to different hiding places around and outside the city.

Even in the midst of the inferno some of the city's infrastructure, including public transport, kept functioning. Across the city Hungarian soldiers jumped on and off the trams, making their way to their dugouts and positions. Károly took the cog-wheel railway from his hiding place down Sváb Hill. At the bottom a crowd of Hungarian soldiers waited to travel upwards, towards the frontline. Károly then took the tram home. The cook had somehow managed to prepare a hearty Christmas dinner. Károly was very happy to see that Pál was also there. He often had little news of his son. Pál had joined the Hungarian resistance movement and could be away for days at a time, in great danger, without communicating.

Pál worked with two army officers, Guidó Görgey and Jenő Thassy, in a group based in a hospital. Both had long been part of the anti-Nazi resistance. Görgey was related to Vince Görgey, the

Arrow Cross man who had provided the Wallenberg operation with protective Gendarmes in exchange for plundering its food supplies. Guidó Görgey was hiding a young Jewish girl, moving her between his family's country house and a convent in Budapest. The Budapest hospital director used to 'forget' his official stamp and leave it unattended, so the resistance group could make fake medical papers, to bring their friends and comrades inside. In his memoir Görgey gives a detailed account of an action the group carried out, in which Pál Odescalchi played a leading role.[7] Pál managed to obtain some explosives and carried out surveillance on a villa on Gellért Hill that senior German officers used as a base. One evening Guidó and the others drove to the villa, with a piece of newspaper obscuring his number plate. Guidó waited nearby with his engine running. Pál and the others planted the explosives, then walked back to the car. Three loud explosions soon sounded. Pál returned the next day, nonchalantly strolling past the house, to see the wreckage all over the road, being searched by German soldiers. Pál also made contact with the small military resistance, who invited his group to link up and work together. Pál said that he needed to consult his comrades. The next time he made contact, he telephoned before as a precaution. A Hungarian Gestapo agent answered. Pál learned later that the officers had been arrested and were shot.

On Christmas Day David Gur and the other Jewish inmates of the prison were separated. The Christians were taken away. The Jewish prisoners expected to be walked to the nearby riverbank and machine-gunned into the Danube. But they were not executed and their jailers opened negotiations. Gur and the others offered them huge sums of money to let them go. The jailers wanted guarantees, promises of protection, testimonies that they had protected the Jewish prisoners. Gur agreed to everything, promised the jailers whatever they wanted.

Two days later, the remaining Jewish prisoners, including Gur, were called out and ordered to stand in rows on the prison parade ground. A military officer in uniform appeared with several soldiers and began to read a list of prisoners' names who were to step forward. Clearly, these unfortunates were about to be taken away and executed. But the names were not accurate. Many were not in the prison. Gur then heard a name that he knew very well indeed: Tibor Rapos Farkas. That was his underground name – only known to his comrades. Gur identified himself as that Tibor Rapos Farkas. Sixteen more comrades also stepped forward. The officer and the soldiers escorted them towards the exit. The prison guards shrugged – the Jews were being taken away to be shot. It was no longer their business.

Outside the prison gate a Swiss diplomatic car was parked. It was a sign. The Glass House operatives had access to such a vehicle. The officer and the soldiers walked the prisoners along the riverbank to the Chain Bridge and crossed over into Pest. Gur understood what was happening but it was important that the pretence was kept up in case they ran into an Arrow Cross or German patrol. But eventually there was no more need. Once they had crossed the river Gur immediately led the group to the Swiss-protected building on Wekerle Sándor Street. There his comrades were waiting for them at the entrance. The Pole was paid and left with his 'soldiers'. Gur and his comrades kissed and embraced. Their joy and relief was tempered with terrible grief when Gur broke the news of Miki Langer's murder. The whole operation was repeated the next day, rescuing the members of Dror and several Communists. In total, 117 people were saved in a brave and audacious operation.

The Budapest Zionists' document workshop was one of the most successful long-term resistance operations of the Second World War. For months in the heart of a Nazi-occupied city – one later ruled by murderous street gangs – a group of courageous, determined activists produced tens of thousands of documents, including 120,000 safe passes from neutral countries, birth and marriage certificates, identity cards, military exemption papers, certificates of American, Polish and Yugoslav citizenship, residence permits, sugar ration cards, Gestapo and Arrow Cross papers and more. The papers saved thousands of lives. When Andrej Fabry arrived in Budapest in 1942 he asked Samu Stern to help absorb the Jewish refugees from Slovakia and Poland. Stern refused, saying, 'I will allow no intruders to endanger the relative safety of Hungarian Jews.' Had the Jewish Council shown similar courage and steadfastness in the spring and summer of 1944, the history of the Hungarian Holocaust may have been very different.

33

Shells Rain Down

The poor child was literally torn to pieces and it was lucky that she did not regain consciousness any more.

Edina Zichy Pallavicini, diary entry for 26 December 1944.

Up in the Castle Edina Zichy Pallavicini was doing her best to make whatever Christmas she could. She had gone shopping a couple of days earlier, but there was nothing on sale, apart from books, dried mushrooms, ersatz coffee and lemon juice. No sweets, cakes or biscuits were available anywhere. But she managed to find enough trinkets at home to prepare a tombola and a small Christmas tree. Edina's sister-in-law, Ceta Sardagna, and her children were staying with the Zichys. The children were very excited, also preparing small gifts for everyone. It was a cosy evening on 24 December and on Christmas Day Edina attended mass. Guns sounded in the distance but the war was everywhere. There were constant air raids and bombing, devastating the once-picturesque streets and alleys of the Castle District. The streets were covered with rubble, fragments of bricks and shards of glass. The worst were the mines, which silently floated down on parachutes then exploded with devastating effect. Coming out of church, Edina met two friends who were now unable to return to their villa in Hűvösvölgy, a distant suburb of Buda. The Russians were already there and they could not cross the frontline. They too came to stay.

Many of the houses in the Castle District dated back to the Ottoman era and had plenty of space underground, often in a maze of tunnels. The Zichy home had several cellars on different levels, including a wine cellar and other alcoves that would later be used as hiding places. Part of the underground network was turned into a bunker, with mattresses and bedding, where some of the servants were already sleeping. Edina began to prepare the food supplies. Quite a lot had arrived from the countryside and the house already had its own stocks. Edina and the cook took down a goose-liver pie, a game pie, marmalade, jam, ham and bacon. Everything would have to be rationed and parcelled out as almost two-dozen people needed to be fed. But compared to the conditions in the ghetto, these were supplies of unimaginable luxury.

After Christmas the bombardment intensified. Castle Hill was a small world, inhabited by many aristocratic families who knew and were related to each other. Even as the Russians advanced, they still paid social calls. On 26 December Lili Széchenyi arrived. Edina told her she was not sure if she was completely sane, to walk around in the bombardment. Then the house shook from several loud explosions followed by a thunderous crash. It had taken a direct hit, the first of many to come and also the deadliest. Two servants emerged, wrote Edina, carrying a bloody mess – one of the Sardagna children, who had been ripped apart by shrapnel. 'I could just see the bluish-black face of the poor child, the eyeballs glaring white, unconscious but groaning and breathing stentoriously. I knew at once that she was dying.' Soon after Szampa, one of the servants, gently closed her eyes. Once the first shell had hit the house the young girl had run to the bathroom to find her mother. Just as she passed the window, a mine exploded outside. 'All this was so sudden and horrible that I could scarcely realise what had really happened.'

Edina reproached herself for the girl's death. She was the air-raid warden for three houses and should have ordered everybody into the cellars once the shells started landing. 'Alas we had to go through this awful lesson to learn how to behave during a siege.' Beyond the grief and misery at the death of the young girl was the problem of the funeral. No coffins were available and there were no officials to help. The church graveyards had already been captured by the Russians. The best on offer was a potential place in a mass grave in a few days. And the child had to be washed and dressed. Mercedes, one of the servants, started the grim task, but was very clumsy. Nobody wanted to help, so Edina forced herself:

> I saw how dreadfully inefficient she was. I could hand her the clothes that we had selected for her last toilet but I could not get myself to touch the poor child. The face was now very quiet and nearly smiling – that horrible look was gone – but the rest was one bleeding mass – with gaping wounds all over. I was frightfully ashamed of myself – but I was no good at all at this last act of Christian charity I ought to have fulfilled. I always tried to look in another direction and felt like a coward.

The girl – unnamed in Edina's diary – was buried in the garden on 28 December. Somehow Edina found a priest to officiate. Two days later she was talking in the kitchen about food with another child and the staff when a loud crash sounded. The tree in front of the kitchen collapsed, the house windows broke and 'an immense cloud of dust and smoke blackens the air'. Edina grabbed the young girl and rushed to the back of the kitchen, cowering with the cook and laundress. One explosion followed another as they sank on their knees and prayed. After ten minutes the 'infernal din' suddenly stopped. Edina rushed out to see what had happened to the house and the others. The courtyard was full with debris – shattered bricks, tiles, broken glass and wooden beams from the roof. Everyone was alive but half the dining room had been destroyed. It was a simultaneous attack of aerial bombing and artillery. From then on everyone slept in the cellars.

For Captain John Coates Christmas meant a narrow escape and liberation, of sorts. Coates and Lieutenant Gordon had planned to break out of the Zugliget POW camp on 16 November. But that evening the two SOE officers were taken by the Germans to the SD headquarters. This was very bad news. Coates believed that 'the game was up'. The initial interrogation was quite civilised. Coates was not beaten or tortured. But the SD officer told Coates that he would be sent to Vienna – where the Gestapo would know what to do with him. In the meantime Coates was taken to the prison on Gyorskocsi Street. Held on the fifth floor, which was controlled by the Germans, Coates was placed into a freezing cell. He spent three weeks there, each day expecting to be tortured or sent to Vienna. There was no way to escape from the place but he resolved to make a run for it as soon as he was outside the building.

Coates was neither beaten up nor sent to Vienna. By this stage of the war transporting a POW would demand considerable resources. Instead, on the morning of 7 December, Coates was told to clear his cell. All three SOE officers were taken back to the Zugliget camp. Their fortunes had turned again, this time in their favour. Zugliget was certainly a better place to be than Gyorskocsi Street prison or the SD headquarters. But like many Hungarian institutions it was half-packed up by the time Coates returned. The camp rumour mill said that like the Arrow Cross government, the camp was moving westwards, away from the advancing Russians. Coates ordered Lieutenant Thomas, the third officer in their group, to get himself to a hospital and escape from there. He was in the most danger as he had been captured in civilian clothes, so might be shot as a spy.

A few days later Coates and Gordon finally escaped. They went to a safe house on Krusper Street, on the very outskirts of Budapest. Karola Koschwitz, a courageous Hungarian woman living there, was working for SOE and already hiding two Jewish women in her bathroom. Coates stayed for five days then moved on. Koschwitz showed extraordinary courage. Two rooms of her apartment were taken over by the Germans. The flat was searched three times by the Arrow Cross and Hungarian police but the hiding places remained undiscovered.[1] By Christmas Day Coates had relocated to a villa in southern Budapest. The sound of battle was very close. Around seven o'clock in the evening of 26 December a Russian patrol consisting of an officer and eight men came to the house where he was staying and demanded to be let in. Coates greeted them in Russian. They were extremely suspicious, especially when he explained that he was English. His British ID card was barely legible and his forged Hungarian papers made him look even more suspicious. A drunken officer arrived and started to bark questions in pidgin-German. 'The situation', noted Coates, 'began to look rather black'.

Eventually Coates was taken to a field headquarters. There he was treated decently and the Russians were friendly. Two days later Coates was taken to another Russian officer, who agreed to contact Allied headquarters in Bari and confirm Coates's identity. Eventually he was allowed to leave. He arrived in Bucharest on 12 January and reported to the British Military Mission. Operation Dibbler was over. Coates had not succeeded in organising Partisan attacks or sabotage. But he had gathered an enormous amount of useful, high-grade intelligence about conditions in Hungary and the German and Hungarian military and intelligence operations.[2] And Coates was lucky. Not all Allied POWs who fell into Russian hands in Budapest at the end of the war fared as well. Reginald Barratt, the British officer who was in contact with Colonel Howie in Budapest, was captured by the Russians in Slovakia, imprisoned and eventually shot. Lieutenant Gerrit van der Waals, the courageous Dutch officer who introduced Howie to Lolle Smit, the Dutch businessman and Allied agent, was arrested by the Soviets. Van der Waals had been active in the resistance but that proved no protection. He was taken to Moscow and died there in prison.

As the Russians moved forward and the bombardment intensified the Arrow Cross attacks became more and more frequent. The Jewish hospital on Bethlen Square was raided. A group of men were taken away and shot into the Danube. On New Year's Eve dozens of Arrow Cross gunmen attacked the Glass House complex. Three people were killed and twenty wounded as the militiamen stormed inside. The Arrow Cross were wide-eyed at what they found. They had thought they were plundering a Swiss warehouse. Instead they had discovered thousands of Jews in hiding. This was a prize far beyond what they had been expecting. They immediately ordered 800 people into the street to be 'relocated', although everyone knew what that meant.

Miklós Krausz, the head of the Palestine Office, who worked out of the Swiss Legation, quickly went into action. Over the previous few weeks he and some other Jewish leaders had developed a relationship with Pál Szalai, the Arrow Cross's liaison with the Budapest police. Szalai had left the party in 1942, but rejoined in the autumn of 1944. He soon became a surprisingly helpful ally of the Jewish community. Szalai even banned the removal of property left behind by Jews when they were relocated, without an official warrant. Szalai was friends with Károly Szabó, a key member of the Wallenberg operation. He also helped the Swedish rescue mission, doubtless with an eye on the end of the war and the looming arrival of the Russians. Krausz quickly contacted Szalai, who moved swiftly. Several police and military vehicles soon arrived at the Glass House – a notable but rare example of the Hungarian authorities protecting their Jewish citizens against the Szálasi regime. The Arrow Cross men dispersed, but returned the next day to invite Artúr Weisz, the building owner, for 'negotiations'. Weisz, having little choice, accepted the offer. Sándor Hunwald, known as Simha, and one of the most daring activists went to look for him. Hunwald had fake papers identifying him as an employee of the Swiss Embassy, but he was caught carrying 500 forged safe-conduct passes. He was executed soon after in the basement of the Interior Ministry. Weisz never returned.

Another group of Arrow Cross invaded the Dunapalota Hotel on New Year's Eve, looking for Ottó Komoly, who was still living there. Komoly had decided not to go into hiding or move into the main ghetto, which, despite its horrific conditions, offered a modicum of protection. His status as a war veteran and his connections had so far kept him safe and would continue do so, he believed. And somehow the hotel kept functioning, even during the siege. The menu, such as it was, was often limited to rice and peas, but even that was still served with the Dunapalota's trademark style and elegance, from tureens by white-shirted waiters. The hotel was known as a place of refuge. Imre Biederman, a member of Pál Odescalchi's resistance cell, recalled how one evening in the winter of 1944 a naked young woman, drenched, crying and shaking from cold and terror, ran into the dining room. The others rushed to help and wrapped her in their coats, while the waiters led her upstairs to a room. The next day she told how she had been marched to the Margit Bridge by the Danube, near the International Ghetto, by the Arrow Cross. Once at the riverbank the terrified Jews had been ordered to strip off before being shot into the water. She had jumped in before the gunmen opened fire and somehow managed to avoid being shot. She had then swam downriver in the freezing waters, before climbing out by the nearby Chain Bridge. She was given new clothes and hidden in the hotel.[3] But while the staff could hide someone and provide shelter, they were powerless against an Arrow Cross raiding party. Komoly was taken away and murdered.

As 1944 turned into 1945 the neutral powers' safe passes offered less and less protection. Tibor Marcel was crossing Liszt Ferenc Square on New Year's Day with his daughter to take her to a Swiss-protected house when he was stopped by a deaf and dumb Arrow Cross man. He signalled for Marcel to show him his papers, then took them both to one of the Arrow Cross headquarters on Andrássy Way. Marcel and his daughter were robbed of all their valuables, jewellery and papers. The two were separated. The horror began. Marcel was taken for interrogation. The Arrow Cross men began with a slapping competition. He was hit seventy times on the left side of his face. After that the Arrow Cross forced the prisoners to hit each other. If the blows were not hard enough the Arrow Cross joined in with truncheons, breaking the men's bones until they collapsed. This lasted till eight o'clock in the evening, with new groups of prisoners being brought in every thirty to forty minutes. Occasionally the Arrow Cross guards told a prisoner to take off his shirt, then sliced strips of skin from his back with razor blades.

The prisoners were forced to kneel facing the wall until three o'clock in the morning. They were then tied together in two with a rope, and taken down into the street, barefoot in their shirts and underwear. Marcel had no news of his daughter. The men were marched down in a group from Andrássy Way to the Chain

Bridge, shivering from the cold, beatings and terror. They were told to sit down at the riverside quay. Everyone knew what was coming next. The shooting started. Marcel jumped into the river, taking the other man with him. The rope came off. Others also jumped into the Danube and the bullets were whizzing all around him in the water. Marcel swam downriver towards the floating dock on Petőfi Square and climbed out. From there he watched the prisoners being executed. Somehow, barefoot in a sopping shirt, he made it through the city to the Glass House, where he was tended to and his testimony was collected.[4]

There were around 4,000 Arrow Cross militiamen in Budapest at this time. Accounts such as Tibor Marcel's of torture and murder raise several questions. How did such a small number of gunmen terrorise a city of 1 million people? Many of the Arrow Cross were still teenagers, feral psychopaths living out their most violent, sadistic fantasies of torture and murder. Party members were ordered to kill and torture to prove their loyalty, which they did with enthusiasm. But they were far outnumbered and outgunned by the army. Many regular soldiers loathed the Arrow Cross, seeing them, rightly, as undisciplined thugs and murderers. Most Arrow Cross gunmen had little, if any military expertise. It would have been comparatively easy to bring them under control and disarm, imprison or shoot them. Not all the killers were men; women also took part in the massacres. After the war 10 per cent of those Hungarians prosecuted for war crimes were women.[5] Mária Mádi asked in her diary, where were the police while these atrocities unfolded? Or even the gendarmes and the army? These were sharp questions, which still resonate today. There were individuals among all three forces who intervened to save Jews and scattered resistance operations. But the leaderships of the police, the Gendarmes and the army, like Admiral Horthy during the deportations of the countryside Jews, simply stood aside. As the Hungarian historian Krisztián Ungváry notes, nowhere else in Nazi-occupied Europe were Jews killed in public in such large numbers over such a long period of time. Nor was there any meaningful attempt by the non-Jewish resistance movement, such as it was, to stop the massacres.

'This could not have happened without a deep and far-reaching moral crisis among the population', writes Ungváry. Such a crisis was perhaps best embodied by Pál Hódosy, the national police commissioner, who said, 'The problem is not that Jews are being murdered. The only trouble is the method. The bodies must be made to disappear, not put out on the streets.'[6]

The Arrow Cross leadership was furious that the neutral countries refused to extend diplomatic recognition to Szálasi's government. The neutral diplomats' fanciful promises that everything was in hand were no longer believed. By January 1945 Budapest had descended into a new level of barbarity. Imre Nidosi, a former manager of the Gellért baths, appointed himself commander of all Arrow Cross forces. Nidosi was a psychopathic mass murderer. Each night the Jews were marched to the riverside and each morning the half-frozen Danube was slick with blood, the ice holding the twisted bodies of the victims, grimacing in their death agonies. Death could come at any time. One of Wallenberg's employees was shot with his family on the Chain Bridge and their bodies thrown into the river.

Wallenberg moved some of his team to a new base at the headquarters of the Hazai Bank at 6 Harmincad Street, in the heart of downtown, by the historic Gerbeaud Café. Aware that he too was now in danger – Eichmann had threatened to shoot him – Wallenberg was continually on the move, spending more and more time moving between safe houses and the bank. But the bank building was safe. It was a solid construction with thick walls and a deep basement vault, where dozens of bank employees and protected Jews took shelter. The corridor to the vault was crooked. A large mirror was placed on the wall, giving a view into the distance, so the Jews could hide if the place was raided. During the siege the building was hit twenty times, and caught fire three times. Nobody inside was injured. But outside was ever more dangerous as the Russian shells and mortars rained down on the city centre. On 2 January a shell exploded near Wallenberg's car. Tivadar Jobbágy, his driver, was hit by shrapnel and died.[7]

34

Fresh Depths of Savagery

In the holy name of Christ, fire!

Order to shoot Jewish prisoners given by Father András Kun,
Catholic priest and Arrow Cross death squad leader.

It was midnight on a freezing winter evening in early January 1945
in the basement torture chamber of the Arrow Cross headquarters
at 60 Andrássy Way. Father András Kun looked at his captives
with sadistic pleasure. Ernő Ligeti, his wife and young son, Károly,
had all been brutally interrogated and tortured. Now the three of
them had been stripped naked and tied together. Shaking with
terror and grief, they awaited their deaths. Even by the depraved
standards of the Arrow Cross this would be a particularly cruel
murder, plumbing new depths of trauma and degradation. But
such psychopathic savagery was Kun's speciality. The Ligetis
had been living in a Swiss-protected house in the International
Ghetto on Pozsonyi Way. Kun had personally ordered them to be
brought in. Ernő Ligeti enraged him. An eminent Jewish writer
from Transylvania, Ligeti had moved to Budapest in 1940. He
worked for *Magyar Nemzet*, a conservative daily newspaper, but
was a socially progressive democrat. Ligeti's prolific, lyrical output
was full of warm, affectionate portraits of Transylvanian society
between the war. And now he was going to die. The gunmen took
aim. The order was issued and they opened fire. Ernő and his wife
were killed instantly. Four bullets hit their son Károly. Incredibly,
he survived the shooting and managed to live through the last days
of the war.[1]

Kun revelled in his quasi-religious role as he led his killers. A former monk, he wore a cassock, a priest's collar and a crucifix and always carried a pistol. His sadism often had a sexual edge. He liked to strip female prisoners naked and leer at them. One former prisoner of Kun's, who survived a severe beating in his headquarters, watched a young woman prisoner being suffocated with her own bloody sanitary towel and a man whose penis was nailed to a table before he was killed.[2] Many Jews would soon die at the hands of Kun's gunmen. His murderous squad would target the most vulnerable Jews, the sick and the elderly, as they slaughtered hundreds in three carefully organised massacres. Hungary now had its own Einsatzgruppen, who followed the same modus operandi as the SS on the eastern front. Kun's gang began on 12 January at the Jewish hospital on Maros Street in Buda, which operated under the protection of the International Red Cross. The streets around the hospital were blocked off and the gunmen stormed in. Anyone who could not walk was immediately shot in their bed. Those who were mobile were ordered to take the bodies into the courtyard and dig a mass grave. Once this task was completed they were shot into the grave themselves. Ninety-two doctors, patients and nurses were killed. Just as on the eastern front, one victim, a nurse named Joli, survived by pretending to be dead and then crept out of the mass grave hours later.[3]

Two days after that, Kun's militiamen invaded another Jewish hospital on Városmajor Street, near the local Arrow Cross headquarters. By now the Soviets were just two or three hundred yards away. The street echoed to the boom of artillery, the rattle of machine-gun fire and the crash of exploding shells. Emil Börszöményi-Nagy, a Christian man who lived nearby, was at home waiting nervously for the Russians to arrive. His apartment overlooked the courtyard of the hospital. He suddenly heard a different sound to the usual cacophony of war. This was much nearer. Börszöményi-Nagy looked out of his window, from where he could see into the courtyard of the Jewish hospital. He staggered back in horror at the sight. Several nurses were standing in a row in the courtyard, shaking with terror as the Arrow Cross militiamen screamed at them. The gunmen took aim and opened fire. The nurses collapsed, crying in their death agonies as their white uniforms flooded crimson with blood. The sight of the killing was unbearable, but Börszöményi-Nagy had no means of stopping the shooting. The building was surrounded by Arrow Cross militiamen armed with sub-machine guns. 'We sat, sunk into ourselves and listened to the repeated gunshots and death screams for another hour', he later testified.

Börszöményi-Nagy was a judge and his detailed testimony provides a haunting eyewitness account of the massacre. The gunmen had arrived around 11.00 am. One group of militiamen ordered all patients who could walk to get out of bed and get dressed. They were sent in small groups into the hospital courtyard, ordered to turn around and were then shot in their back or the back of their head. The courtyard was soon filled with bodies, piled one on top of another, some still groaning in their death agonies. Another group went through the wards, one by one, shooting everybody they saw, including the elderly and children in their beds. The bodies of two little boys were found hugging their mother, who had also been shot. The hospital director lay in the courtyard under two dead bodies, moaning for a long time before he died. About 150 people were killed in two hours. The next day the bodies were covered with a red carpet. Petrol was poured over it and the corpses before they were set on fire, together with the building, which burned for two days.[4]

Such savagery was not confined to Jewish prisoners. On 2 January 1944 the Arrow Cross arrested fourteen members of the Communist resistance, known as the Red Brigade. They were taken to the Royal Palace and savagely tortured. A young woman called Éva Braun was raped with a piece of wood. A fellow prisoner later recalled, 'I could hear terrible screaming and panting from the next room ... After my interrogation I was led through that room where I saw Éva Braun lying on the floor half-naked and weeping.' Most of the prisoners, including Braun, were executed soon after, many shot on the Palace terrace by the Gendarmes.[5]

After the war, mass graves across the city were opened so relatives could identify the victims. The remains of those murdered in the Arrow Cross Maros Street massacre were exhumed in April 1945.

Ervin Galántay gave a nostalgic look over the top of the ghetto wall as he dashed up Kiralyi Street in the heart of the Jewish quarter. He could just see the upper floors of 62 Akácfá Street, the former family home. By now, 6 January, he was a battle-hardened soldier and had seen plenty of action. He was very lucky to be alive – he was a runner for the Vannay Battalion, traversing the city with orders and documents on extremely perilous missions. At this time it was often still possible to make telephone calls across the city. Hungarian scouts and reconnaissance units sometime rang up residents in areas that had been captured by the Soviets to gather intelligence about the Russian forces. Friends and relatives often called each other when the Russians arrived, saying 'Ivan is here'. But open telephone lines were not secure enough to transmit military orders and intelligence reports.

Repeatedly under fire in several engagements, Ervin dodged bullets, shellfire and even fragments of an exploding tyre when he took refuge behind a car. He had been wounded in the stomach, but miraculously his leather belt stopped another shell fragment. One day Ervin had managed to make it to his parents' flat. There he had read the story of the battle of Thermopylae, when a few hundred Spartans had, according to legend, beaten back a Persian army many times their number, to his entranced little brother, Tibor. The Greek legend seemed especially apposite. The Russian assault was relentless as it advanced street by street, house by house and room by room. Each time they were beaten back, they just advanced again; Marshall Malinovsky and his commanders hurled waves of men and machines into the maelstrom, while bombs and shells rained down. At the start of the month the Russians had tried to capture Margit Island, in the middle of the Danube. The Hungarians and Germans beat them back and the river was soon full of corpses. Another attack soon followed. The Russians just kept coming. Sooner or later, the island and all of Budapest would fall. With the city surrounded the defenders were running out of food, medicine and ammunition. In a daring feat of airmanship, the Germans managed to land half-a-dozen gliders on the Vérmező , an open space near Déli Station. Vérmező, an eighteenth-century execution site, meant 'Field of blood' in Hungarian and so it proved. The Soviets immediately launched a precisely targeted mortar barrage, setting several aeroplanes ablaze.

Ervin's mission that day was to deliver a set of reports to a captain of a unit stationed near Keleti Station, right across the other side of the city from the battalion's base in Buda. He passed by the Liszt Ferenc Academy of Music, where he and his family had enjoyed so many concerts in happier times. To his amazement – and pleasure – he heard the sounds of stringed instruments, flutes and a piano playing. He stopped inside for a moment to find it full of Arrow Cross militiamen, who had taken over the building. The Russians were just two kilometres away now. One Arrow Cross man was threatening to blow the place up rather than surrender. Ervin protested that it was a beautiful part of the city's heritage. The Arrow Cross man replied, 'Then what should I blow up, the ghetto?'

Ervin, thinking of his family, said that not all buildings there were owned by Jews. By now thoroughly angry, the Arrow Cross man demanded Ervin's documents. Who was he anyway, and why was he wandering around the city? The documents did not pass muster. There was one way to tell. He ordered Ervin to drop his trousers. For Jewish boys this was usually a death sentence and they were shot on the spot. But Ervin had not been circumcised. He was allowed to leave. He visited his grandmother in a nearby hospital, where he was very well fed with veal schnitzel, noodles and preserved plums. He even received a second portion of schnitzel to take home. Ervin eventually found the officer he was looking for, at Vigadó Square, just behind the Corso and the grand hotels, and delivered his reports.

Back at the Vannay Battalion's base, he had another delivery to make: to Katille and Lilla, the precocious young teenage daughters of Ilona, a senior nurse. Ervin and the girls enjoyed a not-so-innocent flirtation, involving lots of hugs, cuddles and petting. He had drawn erotic sketches of the girls in his diary, which they found, to their amusement. The girls proposed that they pose properly and take off their tops. Ervin agreed and had another idea. He divided the schnitzel into small pieces and pretended to be a Catholic priest as he placed each piece on their tongues, as though he was delivering communion. Ervin took his time with the drawing, directing the giggling sisters through pose after pose, but made sure to leave before Ilona returned. Ervin had two worries: that he would be killed and that he would die a virgin. Sex was a mystery. He looked at a medical book which had illustrations of the inside of a woman's body. But all he could think about was the body of the woman he had found on Margit Boulevard at Christmas time, lying in a pool of her own blood, her fur coat open and her underwear exposed.

At the Zichy Palace on Werbőczy Street – or what was left of it – January 1945 was getting off to a hideous start. The bombings and the air raids were intensifying and the food supplies were running low. There was not enough water for everyone to keep clean. The hall took a direct hit overnight and all the windows were blown out. Wardrobes had been placed in front of the empty space to stop shrapnel coming into the house, but they had been blown over by the blast. One of the residents, a lady called Stepsi, was being looked after by a nurse in one of the rooms. It was clear that she had to be relocated to the bunker. This was extremely complicated and inconvenient as Stepsi was bed-bound, and so took up much valuable space. Edina asked her nurse to bring down as little as possible. Instead the nurse fetched a stream of trunks, parcels, bags and blankets, while screaming 'my poor invalid countess must have everything she is used to'. Eventually Edina managed to persuade the nurse to place some of the goods in the lower cellar. Her reward was a stream of abuse. 'I never in my life heard expressions such as she used. It made me shiver all over. She must be a genuine witch … what is most astonishing is Stepsi is thoroughly attached to this most vulgar woman', wrote Edina.

Edina was a highly intelligent, courageous and capable person. But she had never experienced anything like this. There was the fear and terror of the bombardments, the deep distress at the destruction of her family home and her possessions, the trauma of the dead child, now buried in the garden, and the responsibility of keeping almost two-dozen people safe and fed. She was being tested to the very limits. At times Edina tried to work out a means of saving the most valuable furniture and paintings. But the bombs fell randomly across the whole complex and courtyard. On 2 January she went upstairs to gather by hand whatever valuables she could find. But the stress and anxiety meant that whatever she picked up, she dropped. 'I think I have a sort of nervous breakdown.'

On 10 January, when the bombardment stopped for a while, she ventured upstairs to her bed and sitting room. The contents had been hurled all over the floor: not from a bomb but the Arrow Cross raiding parties that were now scouring the Castle, looking for men to press-gang, and food and valuables to loot. For a short while she ventured outside – but not too far because if the bombing resumed she did not want to be stuck in a bunker with unknown people. The Castle District, once a maze of pretty, pastel-coloured houses, narrow streets and airy courtyards, was a scene of complete devastation. 'The houses are ruins to a great part and there are lots of dead horses everywhere', she wrote. The news from the Szikla Hospital on Castle Hill, where Ilona Horthy had once worked as a nurse, was also grim. It was overflowing with wounded soldiers and victims of the bombing raids, and the air was very bad. The Jewish doctors working there had been arrested by the Arrow Cross, known in Hungarian as the Nyilas. 'These Nyilas people are of a criminal stupidity. It does not matter that so many wounded suffer unnecessarily – the principal thing according to them is that every Jew be under lock and key.'

Across the river in Pest, the Jews in the ghetto feared the same fate, or worse. On 8 January Arrow Cross gunmen launched the largest raid of the war on a protected house. Number 1 Jókai Street was not in the ghetto, but it was a Swedish-protected building where around 260 people lived, including many working for Wallenberg's operation. Everyone was ordered out and marched to the Arrow Cross headquarters on Városház Street in the city centre. There they were held for hours, beaten and robbed and stripped of their shoes. The women and children were separated and ordered out into the freezing night to walk barefoot, down towards the river. They believed that they were about to be shot into the river and prepared for death. In fact they were taken to the gate of the ghetto and allowed to walk in. But dozens of others, including their menfolk, were murdered at the riverbank. That night Wallenberg actually visited Nidosi, the Arrow Cross commander, in the shelter at Városház Street. Wallenberg had no idea that his employees and protected Jews were being held there and tortured. The scene that greeted them was demonic. Nidosi's girlfriend was lying on a sofa eating biscuits, while he and other Arrow Cross leaders were sitting a table on which a skull was ringed by burning candles.[6]

In another raid on a house on Wesselényi Street, one of the ghetto's main thoroughfares, Arrow Cross militiamen shot forty-three people in a single building. In response Pál Szalai, the Arrow

Cross liaison with the police, an ally of the Jewish leadership, came to the rescue. Szalai deployed a hundred Hungarian policemen inside the ghetto, together with a special Arrow Cross unit that was ordered to guard the gates and keep the inhabitants safe. The Russians were so near now, and liberation was at hand. But the freezing, dark, narrow streets swirled with rumours and questions. Surely the Arrow Cross and the SS would destroy the ghetto before the Red Army arrived? A massacre was doubtless planned, or the ghetto would be flattened by the Luftwaffe, or both. Accounts differ as to what happened next.

In his post-war testimony Pál Szalai recounted that one afternoon in mid-January, as the Soviet forces were rapidly advancing to the centre of the city and were almost at the gates of the ghetto, a police officer ran into his office in the shelter at the City Hall with alarming news: 500 German soldiers had gathered and 200 policemen were mobilising at the Hotel Royal for an operation later that day to seal off the ghetto and kill everyone inside. Szalai immediately asked Gábor Vajna, the Arrow Cross interior minister, to stop the planned massacre. He refused.

Szalai then went to see General Gerhard Schmidhuber, the German officer in command of the defence of Pest, who was also in the City Hall shelter. Szalai informed him that he was representing Raoul Wallenberg and he had a message from the Swedish diplomat: if the planned massacre was not stopped Schmidhuber would be held accountable and tried as a war criminal. This was partly true – Szalai had no means of contacting Wallenberg, but the two men had agreed that he could invoke his name if necessary. And Wallenberg was hardly likely to object. Schmidhuber agreed. He summoned Gábor Vajna, the German officer in charge, the local Arrow Cross leader and the police commissioner and ordered them to stop the planned operation.[7]

After the war Giorgio Perlasca also claimed some credit for saving the ghetto by confronting Gábor Vajna in his office in the City Hall shelter. According to Perlasca, Vajna admitted that, yes, he wanted to 'solve' the Jewish question by killing everyone. Perlasca tried several arguments saying how much the

Hungarians would suffer if the massacre went ahead. The Soviets were at the gates and the Western Allies would brutally bomb the city. Nothing was working. Perlasca then had a brainwave: if the massacre was not stopped, he said, the Spanish government would intern all 3,000 Hungarians in Spain and seize their goods. Madrid would also ask the Brazilian and Paraguayan governments to do the same with the Hungarians in their countries. There were in fact only around a hundred Hungarians in Spain and Perlasca had no authority to make any such threat. But Vajna had no idea how many Hungarians lived in Spain and after months of bluffing a few more lies made no difference. Vajna said he was shocked that a 'friendly government' would issue such a threat. He offered to save the Jews under Spanish protection. Perlasca stood his ground: all the Jews, in both the main ghetto and the International Ghetto, needed to be safe. Eventually, Vajna agreed.[8] Whichever account is correct – and both may be accurate – the planned attack was stopped. The remaining Jews of Budapest were saved.

At the Zichy Palace the eight horses were starving to death, howling all night and gnawing at their stables. On 13 January Edina told the stable-master that he had to deal with the situation. It was 'too cruel and too dangerous to have starving animals there'. If they escaped they would be frantic with hunger and uncontrollable. That evening they heard Russian for the first time – music sounded through a megaphone, then a Russian voice reciting a list of towns and villages – presumably those that had been captured.

The house still had food supplies – not luxurious, to be sure, but enough to ensure that everyone was fed with at least one meal a day, often soups such as minestrone or *gulyás*. Those sheltering there had little idea how fortunate they were. For most of the city, and especially inside the ghetto, the idea of hot soup was an extraordinary luxury. Yet still Edina's charges complained. Eventually she snapped, and said that she had not turned the house into an open-air dwelling on purpose to inconvenience them. The situation was beyond her control, so please stop criticising everything and try to make the best of it. They listened. Her friend Marie-Louise was a great help, always remaining calm, putting on a smile and ensuring plenty of small talk to keep people calm. 'A thoroughly well-bred lady amounts to much in such times', noted Edina gratefully.

35

Pest Liberated, Buda Fights On

'You don't need that any more.'

Russian soldier as he cut off István Fenyő's Yellow Star,
17 January 1945.

István Fenyő watched with wonder as the soldier strode down Wesselényi Street towards him, his face set and determined, bayonet in hand. Weakened with dysentery, barely able to stand, surrounded by corpses, the fifteen-year-old boy felt no fear, only a strange kind of joy and relief. The officer raised his blade to István – and carefully cut away the threads holding the Yellow Star to his tattered, filthy clothing. István stared at the Red Army insignia on the soldier's uniform, barely able to understand that the day he, his father, all the Jews of the ghetto, had waited for for so long had arrived. It was the morning of 17 January 1945. The Germans and the Arrow Cross were gone, fleeing for their lives. The Russians had smashed through the gates. The ghetto was liberated. István and his father had survived.

The Russian soldier threw István's Yellow Star on to the ground. Emil, István's father, asked him where they could go now. 'Anywhere you want, you are free now', replied the Russian.[1] In later years, when Hungary was a Communist dictatorship, István had some troubles with the Russians. But this moment he would never forget. His heart ached though for his mother. For months after the end of the war, he and Emil, the last two of what had once been a happy family of four, hoped against hope that somehow Aranka would return from the camps. But she had died in Ravensbrück.

More Jews ventured out, almost unbelieving at what they saw and heard: soldiers wearing the grey uniforms of the Red Army with the Red Star on their caps, speaking Russian. Some, weakened by hunger and disease, crawled out of the cellars and simply lay on the street in front of the Soviet soldiers. Others sobbed, prayed or just watched, now too numb to feel much at all. As word spread, the trickle turned into a flood and the ghetto-dwellers poured out, clambering down the stairs of the bombed-out apartment buildings, emerging blinking from the crowded tenements. The streets were soon full of Soviet soldiers, rushing here and there, shouting orders, setting up telephone lines, as they took control of the area.

Robi Lichtenstein was standing in the doorway of the apartment building on Akácfa Street as he watched the Russians walk in. He too felt no fear but a great joy and relief. Most families had lost one or two members, especially among their menfolk. Miraculously, Robi, his little sister and both his parents had survived. But there was still no news of his grandmother Katalin. They thought she was somewhere in the ghetto but had not managed to find her. Out of the blue, a familiar voice sounded, shouting, 'Robi, Robi'. For a moment he could not believe what he saw. It was a former schoolmate, now in Russian Army uniform. He smiled, walked over and gave Robi the most vital gift of all in those days: a loaf of black bread. The family went back to Váci Way. Their original home had been destroyed in the air raid, but Fülöp found a flat in another building. Robi's grandmother, Katalin, also survived and a few days later appeared at the flat. She was skin and bone. But she was alive.

Across the river in Buda, where the Arrow Cross and the Germans were still holding out, the Jews were not celebrating. Not far from the burned-out Városmajor Hospital, the residents of the Jewish nursing home on Alma Street were living in fear. They had already survived two attempts to kill them in November. In the first they had been protected by the Budapest police chief and soon after that by Friedrich Born of the Red Cross. On 19 January German soldiers appeared and took away most of their food – just as they had done at the Városmajor Hospital before the massacre. The frail, elderly residents were terrified. Dead Jews would not need to eat.

One of the Christian workers at the home, Ferenc Jóska, went to the commander of the nearby Hungarian military hospital and asked him for protection. He declined, claiming he had no means. Jóska went back to the home and advised the residents to flee. But most were over seventy, the area was now under continual shellfire and where would they go? Only four took his advice. The others awaited their fate. Father Kun's death squad arrived that evening. They separated the men and women and made them walk down to the nearby park. Those who could not walk were carried. The elderly Jews were lined up and shot, falling quickly into the snow. Some were only wounded and begged the Arrow Cross men to finish them off. They threw hand-grenades into the tangle of dead and wounded but only one exploded. The clothes of the dead and wounded caught fire. The flames, the cold and their wounds then killed them. It was a miserable death, when liberation was just days away.[2]

There were no Jews remaining in those parts of western Hungary still under the control of the Arrow Cross. Instead, they turned their fury onto the local Roma, carrying out a series of massacres as the Russians advanced. Some time in late January or early February 1945 Roma families from the city of Székesfehérvár, forty-five miles from Budapest, were rounded up and taken to Várpalota, further west. (Székesfehérvár had fallen to the Russians but was recaptured on 23 January.) The local Roma were rounded up as well and both groups were forced into a barn, making a total of 113 men, women and children. The next morning the Arrow Cross, together with the local gendarmes, picked out the men and took them to the edge of the town. There they forced the men to dig a pit. All the men, apart from five, were lined up on the edge then shot into the pit. The five survivors were marched to the centre of Várpalota and made to stand facing the wall of the local castle. The gendarmes formed a firing squad and shot the men in the back. One man was still alive after the fusillade – a gendarme delivered the coup de grace to his head.

The gendarmes and Arrow Cross then force-marched the Roma women and children to the pit where their brothers, husbands and fathers had been murdered and ordered them to line up by the mass grave.[3] A witness account records what happened next:

Women were sent there to the edge, their baby in their hand, the smaller children next to them, clutching their dress. It was horrible to see how they were shot one by one. And as the Arrow Cross men were shooting them, they were falling into the hole; a small child did not die so they went there and shot him.

There were two survivors: Angéla Lakatos and Margit Raffael, a fourteen-year-old girl. Angéla was four months pregnant. She was shot eight times, and wounded in her hand, leg, side and other places. Like the survivors of the Einsatzgruppen mass executions on the eastern front, Angéla played dead when the gunmen checked if anyone was still alive. Once they had left, she pushed each of the bodies nearby to see if there were other survivors. Her hand landed on Margit, who pushed back. Angela asked who she was, and then if she could help her, as she was not able to stand up alone. Margit had survived by jumping into the pit when the executioners opened fire. Somehow she avoided being shot, and only received a minor wound from a ricochet. She set off on foot to the nearby town of Veszprém in her blood-drenched dress, arriving two days later.[4]

As the Soviets advanced through the City Park and the nearby zoo, Raoul Wallenberg was staying on nearby Benczúr Street, once a wide tree-lined avenue of splendid villas and art-nouveau apartment buildings. He was naïvely looking forward to the Russians' arrival, planning to explain everything about his work and his future plans for the Jews of Budapest. The Russians finally swept through the German lines and arrived at Wallenberg's base around lunchtime on 13 January. He explained, through an interpreter, that the building hosted the Red Cross and the Swedish Legation. Some hours later Major Demchenko, a Soviet officer, appeared. Wallenberg said that he was a Swedish diplomat and wanted to contact Marshall Malinovsky, the Soviet commander. Demchenko posted two guards outside the building and came back in the evening. The next day Wallenberg and his driver Vilmos Langfelder set off with Major Demchenko. Accounts differ as to what happened next, but Ingrid Carlberg, author of the most authoritative biography of Wallenberg, records that Wallenberg and Langfelder eventually arrived at the headquarters of the 151st Infantry Division, five miles east of the City Park. Their car was confiscated and Wallenberg protested strongly. He was then interrogated – a series of polite, apparently friendly conversations.

Wallenberg had made a catastrophic error in making himself available to the Russians. They had lost tens of thousands of men as they fought their way through Budapest, street by street, building by building, room by room. Budapest was still an active front – across the river the fighting still raged. The Russians were extremely suspicious of foreign and neutral diplomats. The Wallenberg name – and Enskilda Bank's dealing with the Nazis – were well known in Moscow. The War Refugee Board, which had sent Wallenberg to Budapest, the Russians believed, with some justification, was a front for American intelligence-gathering. A Swedish diplomat who had been negotiating with the Nazis and the Arrow Cross, who had access to foreign currency and who claimed to be rescuing Jews set off multiple alarms. Moscow was informed. The outcome was never in doubt.

On 17 January, as the Russians fought their way into the main ghetto, Wallenberg and Langfelder returned to Benczúr Street. But this time they were accompanied by Soviet officers, including Major Demchenko, on a motorcycle with a sidecar. Wallenberg was given time to gather his possessions and say goodbye to his colleagues. From there Wallenberg and Langfelder went to the Swedish office on Tátra Street in the International Ghetto, which had just been liberated. Wallenberg explained that he was going to Debrecen to make contact with high-ranking Soviet officers – and quietly reminded them that there were valuables in the safe at the base on Harmincad Street. He would be back in a week or so, he thought. Unknown to Wallenberg, that same day a telegram had arrived from Moscow to the commander of the 2nd Ukrainian Front: Wallenberg should be arrested and sent to Moscow. Neither Wallenberg nor Langfelder ever returned.

Raoul Wallenberg was not the only courageous anti-Nazi to be arrested by the Russians and incarcerated. After Pest was liberated, Pál Odescalchi and his comrades Guidó Görgey and Jenő Thassy emerged from their cellar in downtown Pest and went to liaise with the Communists at Tisza Kálmán Square, not far from Keleti Station. The palatial former headquarters of the Volksbund, the German pro-Nazi organisation, was now the Communist Party headquarters. János Kádár, the Communist leader who would later rule Hungary for more than thirty-two years, thanked the three young men for their work fighting the Germans. He offered them party membership with special low numbers, which would have been valuable currency in the years to come. All three declined. They were later arrested by a Russian military patrol who locked them in a cellar with a crowd of other unfortunates. After a while the Russian soldier demanded three people to volunteer for work. Pál and his comrades quickly moved forward but someone else stood in front of him at the last moment and took his place. Guidó and Jenő went out with the Russians and eventually escaped.

Pál though was marched to Gödöllő, just outside Budapest, where Admiral Horthy had had his summer palace. Pál languished there for weeks. Károly had no idea of his son's fate. Conditions at the makeshift camp were appalling. Many thousands of prisoners, from teenage boys to elderly men, were held there or passed through, most deprived of shelter and forced to sleep outside. There was nothing to eat and no medical attention. Every morning dozens of corpses were collected and buried. Word came through that Pál was held at Gödöllő and was sick with dysentery. Károly tried everything he could think of to rescue or help his son. Gödöllő was on the other side of the river, but it was impossible to cross the Danube. All the bridges were blown and their remains lay in the water. Great blocks of ice had formed against the wreckage. Corpses bobbed in the freezing waters. In places the waters were frozen solid, but anyone trying to cross would be shot by the Russians.

Eventually Károly managed to secure Pál's release papers. He sent a detective to the camp to bring him out, but the Russians threatened to shoot him. There was no word of Pál for months. Károly feared the worst. One day in July 1945 he came home to find an emaciated, sickly looking man standing in the corner of the room. At first he did not recognise him, then realised it was his son. The Russians had released him as an invalid. Pál slowly recovered.

In Castle Hill, two Hungarian soldiers appeared at the Zichy Palace in mid-January, bringing news that the Soviet troops had already captured the area around Astoria. The fall of Buda was inevitable. Other news was sadder. The cook had died at the Szikla Hospital. She, her husband and daughter had left the bunker and been caught in the bombardment. 'If they had stayed on in our bunker nothing would have happened to them. One cannot escape one's destiny', wrote Edina. The house was hit again and the courtyard was now so full of rubble that it was hard to move across it. To add to everything, the stable-master had still not dealt with the horses, which were howling ever louder and stamping even more frantically from hunger.

At night the sky burned red with fire. The air was thick with ashes and the acrid stink of cordite. The sky was sometimes full of coloured parachutes. The Germans were dropping supplies to the garrison on Castle Hill, who were now surrounded. Red for ammunition, yellow for food and white for medicine. Inside the bunker, it was increasingly hard to sleep, wrote Edina, such was the cacophony, not just from the war but the noises of her fellow inhabitants. 'Lying there among all those snores, sighs, puffings and chewings is too awful for words ... Sometimes the concert is so loud that I nearly get a fit of laughter.' Mrs Bartl, an elderly family friend living with them, was barely eating and getting weaker and weaker. A German ambulance had crashed into the house's entrance and was now blocking the courtyard.

A few days later the horse problem was finally solved. The Zichy Palace took multiple hits, blowing off the door of the bunker and destroying a whole wing, which came down on the stables. The horses were killed. Edina despaired of trying to preserve any of the family's possessions. 'There is no way of saving anything, no combination is worthwhile to think about – we are just helpless toys in the hands of destiny and have to bear whatever is meant for us.' The Russians were very near now. Two days later even more problems arose. There was a large unexploded bomb by the German ambulance and a dead German soldier had been found in one of the rooms. Fearful of the consequences if she did not inform the authorities, Edina sent notes to the municipality about the bomb and the German headquarters about the dead soldiers. The Germans arrived on the last day of the month. In fact there were two dead soldiers, whom they placed in the crashed ambulance by the entrance and tagged with their names. Edina despaired that they had not taken the bodies away – the dead soldiers and the dead horses were a serious health hazard. 'This is now even worse than before, when they were in the room. Nobody can come and go without passing them.'

Across Budapest the streets were littered with dead horses. Crowds gathered around the animals, hacking off pieces of meat, was a common sight. One of the Hungarian soldiers who had moved into the house shot a starving horse and brought back a leg. Mrs Bartle's nurse was very pleased, if not excited by this, and promised to make *gulyas* soup from it. Edina felt sick at the sight of the horseflesh. 'The whole proceeding is most disgusting and the smell of the raw meat horrid.' The nurse was enjoying herself so much that she did not answer Mrs Bartle, who was calling her, to Edina's exasperation. 'At last I have to order her severely to go and attend to her patient and leave her amateur butchery.'

Pest had fallen but across the river in Buda the battle was still raging. The Russians fought their way forward street by street, building by building, sometimes room by room. The terrified, half-starved inhabitants huddled in freezing, stinking shelters. Bombs and shells exploded all around them reducing whole streets to piles of smoking rubble. The remnants of once-grand apartment buildings stood like rows of jagged, broken teeth. At night the city was lit up by the flash of artillery and the arc of tracer bullets. It was clear that the defenders' situation was hopeless and Budapest would soon surrender, but not before many more lives were lost. Soon after midnight on Saturday, 20 January Ervin Galántay received a tin of liver-paste, crackers, brandy and a champagne cork in a baby-sock from a red-haired woman who ran the Golden Pheasant pub. The battalion was going into action at 5.00 am and these were their rations. The cork in a sock was to be used if someone was wounded to stop them screaming. Their nose was to be squeezed, the cork inserted into their mouth and brandy poured over the sock.

Ervin was paired with a soldier called Talpas. Their first stop was a nearby bunker. It was a revolting place, with a nauseating stink of filth, unwashed bodies and decay. Some of the soldiers were wounded and moaning in agony. Others were suffering from the Ukrainian disease, as was Talpas. After two hours Ervin and Talpas were sent to wait in a dugout. The Hungarian frontline was only fifty metres from the railway yard at Déli Station, which was held by the Russians. Somehow Ervin and Talpas fell asleep. Talpas defecated in his trousers, the stink filling the dugout. The attack started on time at 5.00 am. The Hungarian Zrínyi mobile assault guns advanced and the German half-tracks opened fire. The air was full of the cacophony of war: the rattle of machine-gun fire, the boom of cannons, the cries of the wounded and dying. Orange tracer bullets cut through the night air, towards the Soviets massed in the railway yard.

A whistle sounded and Ervin shook Talpas, trying to wake him. He stayed asleep. Ervin advanced without him, hurling grenades as Hungarian and German soldiers were shot and blown to pieces all around him. He watched a soldier in front of him fall, holes 'opening up on the back of his white smock' as they formed 'a red lake'. Out of the carnage a Russian soldier appeared and took aim at Ervin. A grenade landed by the Russian and he fell. Pain shot through Ervin's neck. He touched it with his white glove, which turned red. Ervin stumbled back to the Hungarian lines, surrounded by dead and dying soldiers. A German soldier staggered up to him and collapsed while vomiting blood. He shuddered and died. Ervin made it back to the dugout where, incredibly, Talpas was still asleep. Ervin finally woke Talpas told him to get him back to the first-aid station. He passed out. Soviet corpses were piled up by the Hungarian trenches. The line was held but at high cost: sixty-eight of the battalion were killed or missing in action – more than 10 per cent.

Some time after, Ervin woke up in the first-aid station. He had been shot in the neck. Somehow the bullet passed through without cutting a major artery or vein. Talpas had taken him back. A wounded man was then brought in, with his foot blown off. He looked familiar. It was Talpas – he had gone outside for a smoke when a mortar landed. But there was no hope for him. An army doctor gave Ervin a certificate that he was wounded in combat and could go home. He was sent back in an ambulance, but when a bomb landed nearby it crashed. Ervin continued on foot and visited a gendarme he knew called Csuka. They shared some pálinka, which turned out to be a serious mistake.

Soon after Ervin was arrested by a Hungarian military policeman, who could smell the alcohol on his breath. Ervin was taken to some kind of holding facility, a grim place that echoed to the sound of gunfire. A Hungarian officer and an SS officer questioned him. Ervin looked frantically for his papers – but he had left them with Csuka, the gendarme. Wounded in the neck and stomach, his mouth dried out by the strong alcohol, he could barely speak. The young boy was shoved into a dimly lit, stinking room crowded with hostile men. Several were led out, one by one. None returned. In the courtyard the crack of rifle fire sounded, followed by pistol shots. The men were deserters and were being executed.

After midnight Ervin started banging on the door, screaming that he was a Vannay runner and had been wounded. Miraculously, Csuka the gendarme appeared with his papers. He admitted that he gave Ervin the pálinka. Ervin was released but Csuka was told to start saying his prayers for drinking on duty. Even then the longest day did not end. Weakened by his wounds and loss of blood, Ervin got lost on the way home. He somehow found his way to the street leading to his grandmother's housing estate in Óbuda. As he walked down the road a barrage of shells landed nearby, destroying several houses, covering him in dust and rubble. Somehow he survived and eventually made it to the shelter of the building where his parents were staying. A familiar stink wafted up: cheap tobacco, foul breath, nappies, urine, excrement and unwashed bodies. His mother, overjoyed, cried out his name. But not everyone was happy to see Ervin. The warden forbade him to sleep in the shelter, as he was in uniform and the Russians were now just 400 metres away. Ervin stayed in the apartment, where his mother and great-aunt looked after him.

A few days later he managed to cross town and visit his paternal grandfather who lived in Buda. Richárd, a patrician gentleman who had once served as an imperial councilor, was known as 'His Excellency'. He greeted Ervin dressed in a mink-trimmed house coat and a Turkish-style cap. His flat was still elegant, but mattresses were pushed against the broken windows. Richárd offered Ervin sherry or a cigar, then invited him to help himself from his collection of antique watches. He had to trade valuables to get some thin soup from the house warden. Once a stout, confident man, he was now thin with trembling hands. The flat's kitchen was empty – Richárd previously had his meals delivered from a restaurant, now long closed. Ervin realised he was starving. He searched in his pocket and found some crackers, which Richárd gratefully accepted.

By 4 February Ervin Galántay was used to death. He had seen his comrades dying in front of him, blood spouting over him like a fountain, snow-covered corpses splayed in their death agonies, dead Russian soldiers stacked up like lumber. But the scene in front of him in the Vannay Battalion's position in an apartment on Retek Street was something completely out of his experience. Lieutenant Horváth was smacking a wounded Hungarian soldier called Tamás and screaming abuse at him, calling him a 'fucking idiot', while

Ildi, a nurse in a blood-stained white uniform, tried to restrain him. Nearby a dead corporal lay on the floor with his eyes open, blood seeping from his chest. Then Horváth saw Ervin, together with Viki, another nurse who had accompanied him, walk into the room. The madness left him and he collapsed into a chair.

The two nurses advanced on the wounded man and started attending to his wound. A single bullet had passed through Tamás, somehow missing his major organs. An hour earlier the Soviets had fired a barrage of flares which lit up the streets. Tamás looked out of the window to see a red-haired woman, naked but for a pair of boots, being chased across the road. The woman was well known to the Hungarian soldiers – she was the publican from the Red Pheasant who a few days earlier had handed out their rations and emergency brandy. Tamás excitedly called over the corporal. As soon as they stood in the window a Soviet sniper opened fire. The corporal was killed immediately. Tamás was shot through the chest but survived.

He was definitely out of action. But Tamás's machine gun needed to be manned, with someone else feeding through the ammunition belt. The gun was positioned in the corner of the room. Ervin was to fire the gun, while Viki fed the bullets. Viki was twenty-one, tall and slender, dressed in trousers, felt boots and a helmet, carrying a pistol. They huddled together to keep warm. For a moment Ervin thought of Ilona and her flirtatious daughters, Katilla and Lilla. One freezing evening the three of them had huddled in bed together, the girls' hands roaming over him under the cover – until Ilona burst in, furiously shouting, slapping Ervin and sending the girls out of his room. They had all left the battalion base at the start of the month. Katilla and Lilla had both said they would be willing to 'go all the way' with him, but he too was a virgin and was nervous that he would not know what to do. The girls left a note for him – a drawing of two linked hearts with a dedication, 'We love you Ervinke, stay out of harm's way, lots of kisses.'

Viki and Ildi had been working as maids in the house of a judge elsewhere in Buda when the Russians arrived. Both had been violently gang-raped, held down while a succession of soldiers forced themselves onto the girls, one after another. Viki had been violated so brutally that she had suffered internal injuries. Doctors had told her that she would never be able to have children. Infected with a sexually transmitted disease, Viki suffered from a foul-smelling white discharge. No treatment was available. The two young women had been freed by Vannay fighters who had mounted a long-distance commando raid through the sewers into Soviet-controlled territory, raided the villa and brought them back to the battalion headquarters. There Ilona, the mother of Ervin's girlfriends, had given them accelerated combat nurse training. The only thing Viki now cared about was killing Russians, as many as possible.

For a moment Viki and Ervin huddled together and prayed, then a red flare lit up the street. The first Soviet tank advanced, smashing through the barricade. A shell hit and it exploded, the turret flying in the air. A second tank moved slowly behind it. Four Russian soldiers rode the vehicle, holding on to handles behind the turret. Ervin opened fire with the machine gun. The Russian soldiers' white smocks turned red and they slid off the vehicle. The tank kept going and suddenly the machine gun was out of bullets. Viki yelled at Ervin to fire, fire and kill the Russians.

Ervin frantically changed the ammunition belt. A loud explosion thundered through the building, likely a heavy mortar hitting the roof. A second explosion boomed through the room and the ceiling collapsed. Stunned by the blast, Ervin choked on the thick dust. He looked at Viki. Blood oozed from her ears, mouth and eyes. He shook her but she did not move. She was unconscious – although she was alive. He grabbed Viki's pistol and ran downstairs. The street was thick with acrid smoke, bullets flying in every direction. Ervin rolled into the gutter as another T-34 rumbled by. Just as he stood up a shell exploded nearby. The Hungarian gunners were firing at the Soviet tanks. The blast-wave lifted him up, hurled his helmet into the air and Ervin down onto the pavement.

He passed out. When he woke up he saw that his trousers had been blown off. Ervin stood by a burning Soviet tank, in his white underwear, surrounded by dead Russian soldiers, with Viki's pistol in his hand. Hungarian soldiers, believing him to be a Russian, opened fire. Dodging their bullets, Ervin peeked into the T-34 – the crew were blackened corpses and he emptied his pistol into their charred bodies. There was nothing more for him to do. Dizzy and weak, he tried several doors before an old lady let him into an apartment building on Logodi Street, where he collapsed.

At Werbőczy Street the war ground on. Pest had fallen but Buda was still holding out – but at a high cost for its surviving inhabitants. The food supplies began to run lower and lower. The Arrow Cross were raiding continually now, looking for food, valuables and men's clothes, so they could change into civilian suits and shirts when the Russians arrived. On the evening of 7 February Mrs Bartle was getting weaker and weaker. She suddenly announced in a strong voice, 'The Buda Castle is Hungarian – Germans get out.' Then she died. It was a moment of great sadness – she had been a family friend for more than fifty years, even if she was spoiled and fussy.

Edina and the others knelt around her bed and prayed. Mrs Bartle's remains were carried out and laid out in the hall. The ground was frozen solid and there were no coffins, so she was placed in a bomb crater. It took several days to bury her, in the brief intervals between the shelling. The Russians were very near now and the bombardment was intense. The next day the Arrow Cross returned, strutting and arrogant. Edina showed them some of the food supplies in the bunker, but managed to keep them away from the entrance to the lower cellar, where more was stored. The footman Misi also helped by distracting them. Had the Arrow Cross militiamen seen that Edina was concealing food, she would likely have been shot. Eventually the regular Hungarian Army turned up and arrested the Arrow Cross men.

Rumours swirled that the Germans and Russians were negotiating. Edina feared that the Germans would not surrender and the Russians would starve them out. 'The whole situation is very precarious and disgusting', she wrote. She feared that there would be the kind of intense street-fighting that had taken place across the city. Such an urban battle would add a whole new level of terror and destruction. 'How often did I lie awake at night thinking of the horrors of a street fight, when they will fight from house to house, occupy the cellars and throw us all out, as it happened to some of those who lived in a district which surrendered first', she wrote. On Sunday, 11 February the servant Mercedes managed to attend a mass and make her way safely back to the house. The outside was a scene of horror and utter ruination, she reported. 'Dead horses lying among the ruins, wounded soldiers carried by their comrades to the underground hospital, before the Ministry of Finance large puddles of blood – everywhere wrecks of motorcars, tanks, lorries.'

That night Edina did not sleep at all. She and the others hid in the bunker, listening to the sound of non-stop shooting outside, vehicles coming and going and voices as people tramped around upstairs in the house. What was going on? In the morning they found out: the rooms were filled with cast-off uniforms, weapons, helmets and military blankets. Fleeing soldiers had used the house

Arrow Cross militiamen parading in Budapest with German soldiers. The Hungarian Nazis instituted a reign of terror, arresting Jewish people at will, savagely torturing them and shooting them into the Danube.

as a dumping ground before changing into civilian clothes. Globus the stable-master appeared. The Russians were already at Number 7, where the SS commander had been living, he told Edina. This was good news, she knew – it meant the Germans had evacuated, so they would at least be spared the street-fighting, about which she had worried intensely. Soon after the Russians were at her house. They were friendly enough to the Hungarians, but as they roamed through the shattered streets, they killed any Germans they found. 'Is this now really the end of the siege? Should these awful weeks of darkness, dirt and anxiety be really past?' Edina wrote.

For Edina and her charges, it was the end and the war was over. But in other parts of Buda the fighting was still raging. Ervin Galántay had spent six days in the shelter on Logodi Street, sharing a room with a heavily pregnant young woman called Ágnes and using a bucket for a toilet, when a doctor arrived on 11 February. He changed the bandage on Ervin's neck and took out some stitches from his stomach wound. Ervin asked if the doctors could get a message to the Vannay Battalion headquarters on nearby Toldy Street. The doctor shook his head. It was almost impossible to move around the city now. The fighting was intense, room by room. Even the building next door had changed hands several times. There was no water and snow was being melted to make tea or soup. The doctor explained to Ervin what to do when the Russians arrived. He must say 'Vengerszky', Hungarian, and not 'Nemetzky', German.

Finally that day, Ágnes went into labour. Ervin turned away, facing the wall, as the other women rushed in to help, and he fell asleep. By the time he woke up the following morning, the baby had been born – a pretty girl with blue eyes and auburn hair. But she was crying from hunger. Ágnes, half-starved, could not produce milk. A priest arrived to baptise the baby. He rushed through the ceremony – all the Hungarian soldiers had left to fight at nearby Széna Square. The Russians were expected very soon.

Ervin was lucky to be wounded and recuperating. His comrades believed he was dead and he had been listed as killed in action. Had Ervin been combat ready he would doubtless have volunteered for the Vannay Battalion's last mission. Its fighters were deployed in the break-out, the Germans and Hungarians' attempt to smash their way through the Russian siege lines and regroup in German-controlled territory outside Budapest. In fact the best option would have been to surrender the city to the Russians. The defenders were encircled, outnumbered and outgunned. Pest had been captured. Both sides knew that it was inevitable that all of Budapest would soon fall. The Russians had indicated that they were open to negotiations. But SS Obergruppenführer Karl Pfeffer-Wildenbruch, the German officer in charge of the defence of the city, refused. Hitler had declared Budapest a *Festung*, a fortress city, and so it would remain – at a terrible cost both for its inhabitants and Budapest itself. Pfeffer-Wildenbruch had 23,900 troops under his command, of whom 9,600 were wounded. The Hungarians mustered around 20,000 with around 2,000 wounded. Some of those fighting in German uniforms were known as HiWis, or volunteers. The HiWis were Ukrainians, Balts or other Soviet nationalities who had changed sides. They, and the SS troops, felt they had no choice but to try and fight their way out. They knew the Russians would shoot them on sight if they surrendered.

The break-out began at 8.00pm on the evening of 11 February. The plan was for the Germans and Hungarians to descend from the Castle area, which overlooked the city, down to Széll Kálmán and Széna squares, two large open areas at the bottom of the hill, then smash their way through the Russian lines and head into open country. An advance guard of Russian-speaking Vannay fighters and others, posing as Soviet soldiers, were deployed in late afternoon to clear the Russian forward positions. At first the attack went well. Morale was high, some of the Germans and Hungarians believing that they would almost saunter across the lines. Schmidhuber, the German commander who had helped prevent the destruction of the Budapest ghetto, said 'We won't let them trap us. The day after tomorrow we will be sitting together over a drink.' Crowds of civilians prepared to join the soldiers, including many women and elderly, sometimes pushing prams with young children. They believed they would somehow be protected and would it make through the Russian lines. This would prove a catatastropic mistake.

The Soviets were long expecting some kind of break-out from the Castle and were waiting. There was only one feasible way out of the city. As Ungváry notes, the direction of the break-out could be guessed by 'using common-sense'. The push forward soon turned into a massacre. The Soviets watched the first wave of soldiers come through, fired their flares, then opened up with machine-guns, mortar and artillery fire. Széll Kálmán and Széna squares quickly turned into a charnel house, the icy roads and pavements slick with blood, covered with moaning wounded and twisted corpses. Three Soviet tanks rumbled into view and opened fire on the crowd which rushed inside any nearby building. The tanks were destroyed, the crowd rushed forward again but then more Russian tanks appeared and opened fire again. The freezing winter air was thick with the acrid stink of cordite and the metallic tang of blood. Across the squares the wounded begged to be finished off. 'Doesn't anyone have a heart,' pleaded one. 'Here's my pistol by my side. Please shoot me because I can't. Both my arms are gone.' Numerous German officers, especially those in SS uniforms, shot themselves. 'It was a cruel night,' recorded one Soviet account. 'The thunder of guns and the whistle of shells mingled with the frightened yells of the escapees and the death rattle of the wounded, as muzzle flashes lit up groups of people dementedly running to and fro in the deep darkness.'[5]

The break-out was one of the Germans' worst military defeats of the war. Some 17,000 German and Hungarian soldiers were killed, most in the first six hours, along with an unknown number of civilians. More than 22,000 soldiers were captured. Hundreds of bodies were piled up and burnt or buried in mass graves. A few thousand did make it through to the Buda Hills, but most were later taken prisoner. Just 700 or so German and Hungarian soldiers finally made it across the Russian lines into German-controlled territory, including a handful of Vannay Battalion fighters. Several hundred soldiers found refuge in the city. Pfeffer-Wildenbruch and a group of officers escaped through an underground culvert.

Much of of the historic Castle District was levelled in intense street-fighting, air-raids and artillery bombardments.

They surrendered to the Russians the next morning, demanding guarantees they would not be shot and would be received by at least a Major. General Iván Hindy, the Hungarian turncoat who had played a pivotal role ensuring that the Arrow Cross and SS took power in October 1944, was also captured. László Vannay was killed in the fighting, as was General Schmidhuber. The nurses Viki and Ildi, Ilona and her two engaging daughters, Katille and Lilla, all disappeared, presumed killed in the fighting.

The Russians arrived at Logodi street, where Ervin and Agnes were sheltering, on the morning of 13 February. Two young soldiers kicked the door open, demanding to know if Ervin and Ágnes were 'Nemetszky'. 'Magyar, Vengerszky', said Ervin. The soldiers gave Ervin and Ágnes bars of chocolate then stormed off. Soon after more Russians arrived, these less friendly. Bullets smashed into the door of the shelter and three soldiers stormed in, stinking of alcohol. One pulled the blanket off Ágnes and another turned Ervin bodily to the wall while they raped Ágnes, even though she had just given birth. Paula néni, Auntie Paula, was dragged out of the shelter and taken upstairs by the soldiers.

Ágnes screamed for help, but none came. One of the soldiers sat on Ervin, then turned the boy on his back, pouring brandy down his throat, snarling '*Na zdarovye*', 'Cheers', as the drink splashed everywhere.

Soon after the Russians left. Ágnes moaned and sobbed while the baby fell silent. When Ervin woke the next day Ágnes was gone and the baby was dead. The priest appeared with Auntie Paula and wrapped the dead baby in newspaper, before placing it in a suitcase. Auntie Paula had been raped three times and Ágnes had been taken to hospital. That day, 14 February, Ervin made his way home for good. It was still a dangerous journey – the fighting was over but the Russians were rounding up Hungarian men, Christians and Jews, for *málenkij robot*, 'a little work'. Sometimes that meant clearing rubble and corpses for a few hours. But for thousands it meant a one-way ticket to the Gulag.

Ervin avoided the main roads, and kept to the side streets, where there were fewer Soviet patrols. Eventually he made it to Óbuda and the housing estate where his parents were staying. The street was deserted apart from stray dogs. He knocked on the door to a joyous reunion. There were tears, hugs and indescribable relief. All of his immediate family there had survived: his father, mother, great-aunt and two brothers, Eugene and Tibor. Grandfather Richárd, though, had starved to death. Margit even managed to make a homecoming dinner of pancakes with apricot jam. They never tasted so good. After breakfast his little brother, Tibor, sat in his lap, while their father, Jenő, played a Bach violin sonata. 'Did you bring me a gun?' Tibor asked innocently.

Afterword

When I moved to Budapest in 1991 to work as a foreign correspondent, I quickly noticed two things. The first was the city's physical scars. Buildings, especially downtown, were still pitted with bullet holes and gouged by shrapnel. Sometimes the bullet holes were grouped around the corner of a particular window. It was easy to imagine a soldier shooting from his eyrie before the fusillade of shots in return. Easy too, to imagine the click of a German officer or Soviet commissar's heels as they strode down still-haunted streets. The second thing I noticed was how few elderly men there were. It was less than fifty years after the end of the war, so a man aged, say, thirty in 1945, would only be in his mid-seventies. Elderly women were everywhere, but where were their husbands and brothers? Often in one of several places, I later learned: turned to ashes in Auschwitz, buried in a military cemetery in Ukraine or vanished into the Danube.

Budapest and its inhabitants emerged from the war shattered and traumatised. Some of the city, especially the once-glamorous Corso, looked more like Stalingrad than the centre-piece of a cosmopolitan European capital. The Dunapalota Hotel and its neighbours were a charred wreck of shattered walls, piles of rubble and broken glass. None were rebuilt. All seven bridges had been blown up and lay in pieces in the river. About eighty per cent of the city was damaged, a quarter severely damaged and only one in four buildings remained intact. Much of the historic Castle District, the scene of heavy fighting, was almost levelled. Around 80,000 Soviet troops lost their lives. About 39,000 German and Hungarian soldiers were killed and another 40,000 captured during the siege.

About as many civilians were killed including thousands of Jews who were shot into the Danube.

For weeks after the end of the war, the frozen river brought forth a harvest of bloated, bloodied bodies as it slowly thawed out. As in Berlin and other cities, Soviet troops systematically looted and stole valuables, especially jewellery and watches. Tens of thousands of women and girls were raped, often with extreme violence, leaving terrible legacies of internal damage, infertility and disease. Youth or age was no protection. Alaine Polcz, a young woman in Csákvár, west of Budapest, was repeatedly gang-raped. The first time she tried to fight back but banged her head and lost consciousness. She woke up with a Russian on top of her, hearing a voice calling for 'Mummy, Mummy,' before she realised it was her own. Eventually the Russians left, leaving her half-naked and bleeding profusely. Some time later another group of soldiers arrived. They laid the women on the ground. Polcz, who later became a renowned psychologist, recorded in her memoir what happened next:

Eight to ten Russians on their haunches surround me, first one lies on me, then another. They specified the time allotted to each of them. They looked at a wristwatch; they lit a match from time to time and one of them had a cigarette lighter; they kept track of the time. They hurried each other. One asked, 'Dobre rabota?' (Nice work?). I didn't move. I thought I would die from it.

Some of the victims were so violently raped that their spines snapped. Polcz's back was not broken but was badly injured. Her skin tore and turned into a bleeding sore, where her bloodied clothes became stuck.[1]

Of the pre-war population of around 250,000 Jews, including Christian converts, around 100,000 survived in the main and International ghettos. Around another 20,000 survived hiding with false papers. Several tens of thousands eventually returned from the camps and forced labour. (There are no exact figures.) In 1945 the Budapest Jewish community was the largest single group of survivors in Nazi-occupied Europe, although a large number emigrated to the west or Palestine. Survivors often returned home to a cold welcome from their neigbours, who had emptied their home of their possessions and taken over their homes. Tens of thousands of Budapest's inhabitants were deported to the Soviet Union. Many died in captivity or did not return home until the 1950s. Hungary's ethnic German minority paid a high price for its widespread collaboration with the Nazis. More than 200,000 were expelled to Germany and Austria.

Numerous war criminals and Nazi collaborators faced swift, if selective and often rough justice, under the People's Tribunals, which operated between February 1945 and April 1950. The first trial on the Pest side, of two former guards in a penal army squadron who had participated in the murder of 124 Jewish labour servicemen, took place as early as 3 February 1945 while fighting was still raging in Buda. Both guards were immediately found guilty and hanged from lampposts the next day in public at Oktogon – nine days before Budapest finally surrendered. Such gruesome spectacles aimed to satisfy the public's desire for vengeance – onlookers called on the hangman to make sure they died slowly. Overall, around 59,000 people were tried of whom just under 27,000 were convicted. Most were imprisoned. Of 477 death sentences, 189 were carried out, including, remarkably, those of three prime ministers and a head of state (see pp.425–34). In the fevered atmosphere after the war, the Hungarian authorities even gathered evidence to indict the leaders of the Jewish Council and the Vaada for collaborating with the enemy, although no charges were brought.

Eighty years on, the profound trauma of the Holocaust and the passive role of the Jewish Council still stirs powerful emotions and unresolved questions. Survivors asked why more of their fellow Jews had not fought back. Ernest Stein was a twenty-one-year-old student in 1944, living near the Great Synagogue on Dohány Street. He refused to wear a Yellow Star and surreptitiously took photographs of Jewish men being arrested. Stein met with the Jewish Council and gave them the photographs – they refused to circulate the images, for fear of causing a panic. After the Arrow

Cross coup Stein escaped from labour service. He joined the Jewish resistance and lived illegally, moving between safe-houses and abandoned buildings. Like Róbert Lichtenstein, Stein refused to do as he was told. Those who disobeyed had a higher chance of survival.

Stein wondered in his memoir why so few followed his example. It would have been easy, he wrote, for the labour servicemen to overpower their camp guards. 'Some of the labour camps had thousands of these men and only a handful of guards ... And yet none of the prisoners seized the guns of the guards to try to attack them and escape. Why were we not successful at doing that? How was it all possible?'. Resistance ran in the family. Stein's sister Ibolya obtained false papers for eighteen people and sheltered them. Stein was ready to fight with his fists and any weapon he could find. Confronted by two young Arrow Cross militiamen, he slammed their heads together, knocked them out and stole their uniforms. When the Arrow Cross planned a raid on the Glass House, Stein and his comrades, dressed in stolen Arrow Cross uniforms, arrived first. As soon as the actual Arrow Cross men arrived Stein and the others attacked them. He choked one to death with his bare hands while his comrades killed all the others and then disposed of their bodies. 'If we had all removed the Star of David, if we had disarmed those few guards controlling us in the [labour service] camps, maybe we could have interrupted this outrageous genocide, this extermination of the Jews,' he later wrote. But Stein and his group, like David Gur and his comrades, were in the minority.

Matyas Rákosi and other exiled Communist leaders returned from Moscow. They steadily and diligently planned their takeover. In the first elections, in November 1945, the Smallholders, a conservative agrarian party, won an absolute majority. But the crucial Ministry of the Interior, which controlled the police and security services, was handed to the Communists. By August 1949, through a well-honed mix of intimidation and brutality, backed by the Soviets, Rákosi had turned Hungary into a 'People's Republic' – a fully-fledged Marxist dictatorship and loyal ally of the Soviet Union. Numerous lower-level Arrow Cross functionaries were allowed to join the Communist party. The old Arrow Cross headquarters at 60, Andrássy Way, with its basement cellars and torture chambers, was handed to the new secret police – with some of the same staff that had served the Arrow Cross. It was not until May 1990, as the Soviet bloc collapsed across Eastern Europe, that Hungary held a genuinely free election. The country's first post-Communist democratic prime was József Antall Jr., whose father József had worked with Caja Odescalchi and Britain to organise the wartime Polish rescue operation. The last Soviet troops left Hungary in June 1991 and the country is now a member of the European Union and NATO.

Hungary, like every nation that was occupied by the Nazis, is still coming to terms with its wartime history and its participation in the Holocaust. There is still a notable current of nostalgia for the Horthy era and a reluctance among some to face the country's role in the deportation of the countryside Jews. Yet at the same time, government officials now speak openly of Hungary's catastrophic failure to protect its Jewish citizens in 1944 and its terrible human cost. Each year on 16 April the country observes a day of remembrance for its Holocaust victims. Budapest boasts an excellent Holocaust Memorial Centre in a former synagogue (hdke.hu/en), and numerous memorials including a row of metal shoes along the Danube embankment near Parliament, marking the place where the Arrow Cross shot their victims into the river. Many key wartime sites are still standing but have nothing to indicate their historical importance. The Majestic Hotel on Minerva Street in the Buda Hills, where Adolf Eichmann once negotiated with Joel and Hansi Brand, is once again an apartment building, and Eichmann's former office a residence. Hannah Arendt, reporting from Eichmann's trial in Jerusalem in 1961, described him as embodying the 'banality of evil', a faceless bureaucrat following orders. Arendt's characterisation is wrong because it removes his agency. As this book shows, Eichmann was a fanatical anti-Semite, who seized every opportunity to deport and murder as many Jews as he could.

Perhaps the real banality of evil lies in the building's unremarkable features: the tree-lined walkway to the entrance, along which

Eichmann walked; the plain staircase inside that led to his office; the corridors down which bloodied victims staggered and the steps to the basement storage area that was once a torture chamber. Inside the cellar the site's original metal sign rests against the wall. It was repainted after the war and the building given a different name. But that layer has faded in places and the faint outline of the word 'Majestic' is still partly visible. Eichmann's former residence at 13b Apostol Street now houses several businesses, including a Pilates studio. Nothing outside indicates that he once lived there. The Andrássy Palace, Caja Odescalchi's home that was the centre of the Polish resistance, is now a somewhat run-down apartment house – although here at least a plaque by the rear entrance does commemorate its wartime importance.

The ongoing dialogue about Hungary's wartime history is perhaps best embodied at Szabadság Square, near the former US Legation where Carl Lutz ran his rescue operation – now the site of the US embassy. In 2014, a bust of Miklós Horthy was installed at the entrance of the Hungarian Reform Church, looking onto the square. That same year Hungarian authorities erected a new memorial to the victims of the Nazi occupation. Intended to unite Jewish and non-Jewish survivors and the descendants of victims, it had the opposite effect. The memorial features a statue of the Archangel Gabriel holding the orb and cross of Hungarian kings, while a menacing eagle swoops down onto him. Gabriel represents an innocent Hungary, the eagle the bloodthirsty Germans. The memorial, widely seen as an attempt to whitewash history, triggered anger among Hungary's Jewish community and their allies. In response they constructed one of Europe's most poignant and moving Holocaust commemorations. The People's Memorial, as it is known, has gathered family stories, copies of documents, photographs of victims, testimonies and personal possessions – all carefully displayed in front of the statues.

Nowadays, such a construct in a Western capital would likely not last long before being destroyed or daubed in red paint. Ironically, Hungary, the graveyard of so many Jews, has become one of the safest places in Europe to be Jewish. Klauzál Square, the epicentre of the wartime ghetto, where frozen bodies were stacked like logs and Róbert Lichtenstein hid his family's remaining valuables behind a bush as Arrow Cross gunmen screamed at him, is now the centre of the Buli-negyed, the city's party quarter. Old stereotypes still endure, but Hungary has proved immune to the explosion of anti-Semitism across Europe that followed 7 October 2023. In 2024, on Holocaust Memorial Day, Kaddish, the Jewish prayer for the dead, was recited in Parliament where more than eighty years earlier three sets of anti-Jewish legislation had been passed. Budapest's Jews were once forced to wear yellow stars but now freely wear Stars of David. Amid the ghosts of the city's last days, the People's Memorial remains unguarded and untouched, the fading family stories and photographs gently rippling in the breeze.

The People's Memorial on Szabadság Square in downtown Budapest includes moving family testimonies from relatives of those killed in the Holocaust.

Acknowledgements

The Last Days of Budapest reaches back to late autumn 1990 when I first arrived in the city to write a travel article for *Elle* magazine. A pale mist hovered over the Danube as I walked across the Chain Bridge. A chill wind gusted, threaded with the faint smell of lignite. The grand war-ravaged apartment buildings of Pest shone in the sunshine. I was instantly captivated. The following summer I set up shop as a foreign correspondent. I ended up staying for more than twenty-five years, covering Hungary, Central Europe and the Balkans for several national newspapers including the *Independent*, *The Times* and the *Economist*. My family has no Hungarian roots but I think by now I have become a part-Magyar, at least by osmosis.

My thanks go first of all to Budapest and its inhabitants, a city that has given me so much more than a career. It was listening to the stories of my in-laws, Róbert and Zsuzsa Ligeti, at the Sunday lunch table that first gave me the idea for this book. I am grateful to them for sharing and allowing me to publish such personal accounts of their lives. *The Last Days of Budapest* was originally conceived as a book about the later years of wartime Budapest. Neil Belton at Head of Zeus and Clive Priddle, formerly of PublicAffairs in New York, showed great faith and patience in allowing me to expand its scope to cover the whole of the wartime period. Neil and Clive's guidance, insight – and patience as the project grew – have been invaluable. Huge thanks to everyone at Head of Zeus, especially Karina Maduro, Amy Wong and Kate Wands, to Dan Shutt for his copy editing, Neil Burkey for his proofreading and to Anthony and Nicholas Cheetham for their support over the years. My highest compliments go to Matt Bray and Pete Garceau, the cover designers of the British and American editions, both of which are works of art. It has been a pleasure to work with Lara Heimart and the team at PublicAffairs who have been sterling advocates for this book. Special thanks go to my agents Georgina Capel and Simon Shaps for their unwavering support and enthusiasm and to Rachel Conway, Irene Baldoni and Polly Halladay.

Much of *The Last Days of Budapest* is based on Hungarian-language material and contemporaneous accounts. Krisztina Fenyő has been a steadfast and invaluable colleague, researching in archives and online, translating and fact-checking everything from espionage memoirs and accounts of wartime nightlife to the price of groceries and the horrors of the Arrow Cross era – while sharing her own in-depth knowledge and nuanced perspective. Some thirty years ago I was privileged to meet and interview her late father, Professor István Fenyő, who took us on a moving and unforgettable walk through the backstreets of District VII in the former main ghetto where he and his parents were incarcerated. The richness and complexity of stories recounted in this book reflect Krisztina's diligent work. Mark Odescalchi generously shared his knowledge of his grandmother Caja and their family history, extracts from his grandfather Károly's unpublished memoir and Edina Zichy Pallavicini's unpublished diary of Budapest under Nazi rule. György Antall helped open doors to learn about his grandfather's sterling efforts to save Polish and Jewish refugees in the early years of the war. I am grateful to Judit Ornstein's relatives in the United States, especially Sharone Ornstein, for supplying me with an English-language edition of Judit's wartime diaries and to George Deak for allowing me to reproduce extracts of his sensitive translation. Thomas Komoly and Anna Porter generously shared their knowledge of and insight into the activities of the wartime Budapest Vaada, especially Ottó Komoly and Rezső Kasztner. Arcanum.hu, an excellent digital archive of Hungarian newspapers and magazines, was an invaluable resource. I am especially grateful to Gábor Lengyel for his historical insight and his diligent text-editing of Hungarian spellings. Any mistakes are mine.

Professor Michael Miller and Maria Gabler of Central

European University provided much-appreciated assistance with obtaining access to several Hungarian archives. Thanks to the staff of all the archives who ably assisted our research: in Britain the UK National Archives, the Imperial War Museum, the Wiener Holocaust Library and the Churchill Archives Centre; in Hungary the Hungarian National Archives and the Institute of Political History and Trade Unions; in Israel the Central Zionist Archives, Yad Vashem World Holocaust Remembrance and Moreshet (the Mordechai Anielewicz International Centre for Holocaust Documentation, Research and Education), and in the United States the US National Archives and Yale University Archives. Thanks also to the always helpful staff at the British Library in London where I spent many productive hours. Edward Serotta, the founding director of centropa.org, a digital archive of twentieth-century Jewish life in Central and Eastern Europe, deserves a special mention. Readers wishing to explore the lives of many others who lived through the events described in this book will find numerous moving accounts there.

A work of history such as this naturally draws on the insight and expertise of other specialists and experts. Several historians and writers kindly shared their knowledge of and writing about this period, including Duncan Bare, Judy Batalion, Professor Béla Bodó, Bryan Cartledge, Claerwen Howie and Professor Zoltan Peterecz. Many other friends and colleagues helped along the way with knowledge, insight, documentary material and contacts. They include: Yuval Alpan, Ottó Bihari, Gloria von Berg, Gergely Börszöményi-Nagy, the late Hansi Brand, Natasha Cooper, the late László Devecseri, Eleonora Dragi, David Gur, Andrew Finkel, the late Gábor Forgacs, Ruth Ellen Gruber, George Gömöri, Dina Kraft, Zoltan Ligeti, Sam Loewenberg, István Miklauzič, László Petrovics-Ofner, Judit Rajk, István Rajkai, Charles Rosenbaum, Luciana and Franco Perlasca, István Rajkai, Panni Roman, Joan Stein Schimke, Frank Shatz, the late Ernest Stein, Andrew Shiels, András Török, Zsuzsanna Toronyi, Shaun Walker and Anne Zwack. Oleg Beyda located and translated several Russian accounts of the siege, including extracts from the memoirs of

Marshal Rodion Malinovsky. A special shout-out goes to Roger Boyes, Adrian Brown and Peter Green for their friendship and encouragement over the years – and especially to Justin Leighton, a sterling ally on so many journeys to and from Budapest and its surrounds. Thanks also to Rabbi Tamás Verő, Linda Verő Ban and everyone at Frankel Leo synagogue in Budapest for their warm welcome and so much more.

Lengthy periods of sitting and thinking can make writing a lonely and potentially unhealthy occupation. Many of the stories recounted here, especially after spring and October 1944, make for dark reading. When I needed company or exercise, or both, I found unfailing camaraderie and encouragement at the Dynamic Self Defence Academy in north London. My grateful thanks to everyone there, especially Gideon Hajioff, Shaun McGinley and Ali Safari, the kings of Krav Maga and Muy Thai, who chased away any writer's blues. A special mention, as always, for Tony Lang and the staff of Budapest's marvellous Bestsellers bookshop. If you are in the city and plan to buy this book, or any books, please give Bestsellers your custom. My thanks most of all go to my wife Katalin and children Daniel and Hannah for their love and support for a husband and father who was all too frequently absorbed in wartime Budapest. Nagyon szeretlek titeket. Finally, every book deserves a sound-track, or at least a key song. Miles Davis, John Coltrane, Dexter Gordon, Harold Budd, Brian Eno and others all brought background inspiration. This book's musical muse is jazz pianist Hank Jones. His version of the 1940 classic *How High the Moon* will, for a few minutes at least, transport you to a vanished world.

Notes

Readers wishing to see some of the lost architectural beauties of pre-war Budapest, including the original Erzsébet Bridge and the Dunapalota Hotel can visit 'Budapest's Lost Glories' by Amos Chapple at: www.rferl.org/a/budapest-lost-glories-then-now-slider-gallery/32732512.html

The surviving dramatis personae and their fate

József Antall, the Interior Ministry official who helped save thousands of Polish and Jewish refugees, served in Hungary's first post-war government. After the Communist takeover in 1948 he withdrew from public life. Antall was honoured as a Righteous Among the Nations by Yad Vashem, the World Holocaust Remembrance Centre in Jerusalem. He died in 1974.

László Baky, the Hungarian official in charge of the deportations, was convicted of war crimes and hanged with his colleague László Endre in March 1946. Footage of their execution can be seen at: collections.ushmm.org/search/catalog/irn1000595

Endre Bajcsy-Zsilinszky, the anti-Nazi politician and resistance leader, was arrested by the Arrow Cross in November 1944 and executed the following month.

László Bárdossy, the Hungarian prime minister who steered Hungary into war with the Soviet Union, was convicted of war crimes and executed by firing squad in Budapest in January 1946.

Kurt Becher, the SS officer and Himmler's envoy who negotiated with Rezső Kasztner, the Weiss family and other Jewish leaders, was appointed Special Reich Commissioner for the concentration camps in January 1945. Becher and Kasztner travelled to Germany and may have helped save the lives of prisoners at Bergen-Belsen and other places. Becher was arrested by the Allies and imprisoned at Nuremberg. Becher was not prosecuted – mainly because of supportive testimony provided by Kasztner. He later became one of the richest businessmen in West Germany. Becher testified for the prosecution in the Eichmann trial from Germany, as he feared arrest if he travelled to Israel. He died in 1995.

István Bethlen, prime minister between 1921 and 1931, was arrested by the Soviets and taken to Moscow where he died in prison in October 1946.

Joel Brand remained in Palestine after he was released by the British. Hansi Brand moved to Palestine after the war with their two sons. The family lived on a kibbutz before moving to Tel Aviv where they spent the rest of their lives. Joel died in 1964, Hansi in 2000.

Basil Davidson, who ran the SOE operation in Budapest, was parachuted into Yugoslavia in 1943. He fought with Tito's Partisans until summer 1944 and was then deployed in Italy. Davidson was awarded the Military Cross. He returned to journalism and became an expert on Africa. He died in 2010.

Adolf Eichmann was one of many high-ranking Nazi war criminals to disappear after the war with the help of the Catholic church's 'Rat-lines'. He moved to Buenos Aires with his family and worked in a Mercedes factory. Eichmann was kidnapped by the Mossad in 1960, put on trial in Jerusalem the following year and executed in 1962.

László Ferenczy, the Gendarmerie liaison officer with the Germans, was convicted of war crimes and executed in May 1946.

István Fenyő and his father Emil remained in Budapest after the war. István later became a distinguished historian and professor of nineteenth-century Hungarian literature and an acclaimed literary editor. He published twenty-six books and mentored several notable poets and writers. He died in 2017.

Ervin Galántay, the teenage soldier in the Vannay Brigade, left Hungary in 1948. He became a renowned international architect and also lectured on urban warfare to military audiences. He moved to Switzerland, where he died in 2011. His younger brother Tibor was killed during the 1956 uprising.

Wilhelm Götz, the Abwehr and SD agent in Budapest and Istanbul, was interned by the British at the end of the war, interrogated at length and eventually released to the Turkish authorities in October 1945. In July 1949 British intelligence tried to locate Götz but no trace of him could be found.

Andor Grosz, the 'smuggler-king' of wartime Budapest and quadruple agent, stayed in Israel until in the mid-1950s when he moved to Germany. There he lived modestly until he died in the early 1970s.

Ilona Edelsheim Gyulai remained interned at Schloss Hirschberg in Germany with her father-in-law Miklós Horthy until the arrival of American troops in May 1945. After the war she moved to Portugal with her family, then married a British army officer and diplomat. She often returned to Budapest in her last years and died in Lewes, Sussex, in 2013.

David Gur remained in Hungary, organising Jewish emigration to Palestine, until 1949 when he moved to Israel. He had a successful career as an engineer, married and had three daughters and ten grandchildren. At the time of writing he lived in Ramat Gan, Israel.

Péter Hain, Admiral Horthy's security chief who later became chief of the Hungarian Gestapo, was arrested and tried for war crimes. After feigning lunacy, he was executed in July 1946.

Miklós Horthy and his family initially remained in Germany after the war, surviving on charity and assistance organised by John Montgomery Flournoy and Herbert Pell, the former American ministers in Hungary. Horthy testified in in the war crimes trial of Edmund Veesenmayer at Nuremberg. But despite his role in the Hungarian Holocaust, and the massacres at Kamenets-Podolsk and Novi Sad, Horthy was neither charged with war crimes nor returned to Hungary – where he would have been put on trial. In 1948 Horthy, his wife and son Miklós Jr. went into exile in Portugal, where he died in 1957. In 1993 he was reburied in his home town of Kenderes, where tens of thousands attended the ceremony.

Miklós Horthy Jr. was sent to Dachau, and eventually liberated by US troops in May 1945. He moved to Portugal with his family and remained in exile until he died in 1993.

Wilhelm Höttl, the regional SD chief, surrendered to American forces. After serving as a prosecution witness in the Nuremberg trials, like many senior Nazis, he escaped justice and was recruited by the US Counter-Intelligence Corps to work against the Soviets. He later opened a school and was honoured for his work in education. Höttl died in 1999.

Charles Telfer Howie, the South African army officer who negotiated with Miklós Horthy, returned to Cape Town and worked at the family firm until he retired. Appointed an Order of the British Empire (Military Division) and decorated by South Africa and Poland, he died in 1993.

Béla Imrédy, prime minister between 1938 and 1939 who oversaw anti-Jewish legislation and served as minister of the economy during the Nazi occupation, was tried for war crimes and executed in February 1946.

Andor Jaross, the minister of the interior during the Nazi occupation, was tried for war crimes and executed in April 1946.

Miklós Kállay, prime minister until March 1944, was eventually captured by the Nazis. Sent first to Dachau and then Mauthausen, he was liberated by US troops in May 1945. Kallay left Hungary and eventually settled in the United States. He died in New York in 1967.

Katalin Karády, Hungary's best-known actress, left Hungary in 1951, moved first to São Paulo in Brazil, then settled in New York where she opened a hat shop. She never returned to Hungary but is buried in Budapest. Karády was honoured by Yad Vashem as a Righteous Among the Nations. She died in New York in 1990.

Katinka Károlyi (Andrássy) and her husband Mihály returned to Budapest after the war. Sent to Paris as ambassador, Mihály protested the Communist show trials and again went into exile with his wife. Mihály died in 1955. Katinka died in Antibes, France, in 1985.

Rezső Kasztner moved to Israel and became a spokesman for the Ministry of Trade and Industry. As well giving testimony in favour of Kurt Becher, he intervened on behalf of SS officers Dieter Wisliceny and Hermann Krumey. In 1953 Malchiel Grünwald, a Hungarian Holocaust survivor, published a pamphlet accusing Kasztner of collaborating with the Nazis. Kasztner sued for libel but the judge accepted most of Grünwald's arguments. In March 1957 Kasztner was shot by three former members of the Stern Group and died of his injuries. The Supreme Court overturned most of the judgement of the lower court in January 1958. The Kasztner Affair, as it is known, still haunts Israel and Hungarian Jewry to this day.

Ferenc Keresztes-Fischer, the wartime interior minister, was arrested after the Arrow Cross coup and sent to Mauthausen. Liberated by American troops, he died in Austria in 1948.

Arthur Koestler moved to Palestine, the Soviet Union and Paris where he wrote Communist propaganda. He reported on the Spanish Civil War and eventually settled in London where he became an acclaimed author and prominent anti-Communist. Koestler committed suicide in London, together with his wife Cynthia, in 1983.

Emil Kovarcz, the death squad leader during the White Terror and minister in the Arrow Cross government, was tried for war crimes and hanged in Budapest in May 1946.

András Kun, the Roman Catholic monk and death squad leader during the Arrow Cross terror, was tried for mass murder and hanged in Budapest in September 1945.

Béla Kun, the leader of the short-lived Hungarian Soviet Republic in 1919, fled to Vienna. After several failed attempts to organise Communist uprisings in Germany and Austria he moved to the Soviet Union. Kun was executed during Stalin's purges in 1938.

Géza Lakatos, prime minister from late August 1944 until the Arrow Cross coup, was not imprisoned but had his assets and pension confiscated by the Communist authorities. He later worked as a book illustrator and emigrated to Australia in 1965. He died two years later.

Róbert Lichtenstein, my late father-in-law, remained in Budapest with his family. He worked as a history teacher and child psychologist. During the 1980s, in the last years of the Communist system, he wrote and published a best-selling series of childrens' books. He died in November 2024.

Carl Lutz, the Swiss diplomat who saved tens of thousands of Budapest Jews, returned to Switzerland with his wife Gertrude to a hostile reception. The Swiss authorities, angry about his unauthorised rescue activities, launched an enquiry and criticised him for overstepping his powers. Lutz sank into depression and struggled with financial difficulties. He continued as a diplomat, serving in minor posts, until he retired in 1961. Lutz died in 1975. Twenty years later he was finally honoured by Switzerland. A small memorial commemorates him on Szabadság Square, by the US embassy, while a section of the Danube quayside has been named in Lutz's honour. Carl and Gertrud were recognised by Yad Vashem as a Righteous Among the Nations.

Dr Mária Mádi, the doctor and diarist, emigrated to the United States, where she worked as a psychiatrist. Her friend Irene and her nephew Alfred, whom she sheltered, survived. Mádi, who died in 1970, was honoured by Yad Vashem as a Righteous Among the Nations.

John Flournoy Montgomery, US minister to Hungary, did not receive another posting. After the war he became one of Admiral Horthy's staunchest supporters and helped arrange his release from Nuremberg where he had faced being charged with war crimes. Montgomery, and later his daughter Jean, organised regular payments to the Horthys in exile, some of which were provided by wealthy Hungarian Jewish families. Montgomery died in 1954.

Owen O'Malley, British Minister to Hungary, returned to London in 1941 and was appointed Minister to the Polish government-in-exile. In May 1943 he submitted a detailed report on the Katyn massacre of more than 20,000 Polish prisoners by the Soviet secret police to the British government, a truth then politically inconvenient. Hopeful of being sent to Madrid after the war, O'Malley was sent to Lisbon instead, a downgrading. He retired and moved to Ireland in 1947. He died in 1974.

Ernő Munkácsi, the secretary of the Jewish Council and author of How It Happened, remained in Hungary. He died in 1950.

Károly Odescalchi remained as deputy managing director of Ganz until he was sacked in 1947. Tipped off by a Russian general, he narrowly escaped being assassinated by the Communist secret police and escaped to Austria with a single suitcase. He moved to Britain and became a successful and prosperous businessman. The Andrássy Palace that had housed the Polish resistance organisations was seized by the authorities in 1948. The second, neighbouring Andrássy Palace was destroyed during the war. The French Institute now stands on the site. Károly Odescalchi died in 1989.

Pál Odescalchi moved to Britain in 1947 where he studied at Bristol University. He had a successful career as an industrial psychologist before retiring to France where he supported several charities working in Hungary and Transylvania. He died in April 2014.

Pál Ornstein, brother of Judit, escaped from forced labour and joined the Zionist underground in Budapest. He and his father Lajos survived the war. Pál married his childhood sweetheart Anna in 1946 and they moved to the United States. Pál became a renowned professor of psychology and psychiatry and died in 2017. Lajos moved to Israel after the war and changed his name to Abraham Eliezer. His diary of his experiences on a death march is a unique record of the last months of the Holocaust. See: youtube. com/watch?v=ETogAMY8LVo

Yoel Palgi, who parachuted into Yugoslavia and crossed into Hungary, was imprisoned and sent to Germany with his fellow parachutist Peretz Goldstein. Palgi managed to escape and returned to Budapest where he worked with the Zionist underground. Goldstein was taken to Oranienburg to work as a forced labourer and was probably killed in an Allied air-raid. Palgi survived the war and emigrated to Israel where he helped found El-Al, the national airline. He died in 1978.

György Pálóczi-Horváth, the Hungarian journalist and SOE operative, returned to Budapest in 1947. He was imprisoned for five years and frequently tortured. He fled Hungary in 1956 and moved to London, where he worked as a journalist and writer. Pálóczi-Horváth died in 1973.

Herbert Clairborne Pell, American Minister to Hungary from 1941-1942, served as the United States representative on the United Nations War Crimes Commission. He died in 1961.

Giorgio Perlasca, the Italian-Spanish diplomat who saved thousands of Jews, returned to Italy in summer 1945. He wrote a long memorandum about his rescue work, but otherwise did not speak about his time in wartime Budapest. Even his family were unaware of his achievements. Finally in 1987, after decades of searching, a group of Hungarian Jews tracked him down and his story gained widespread publicity. Perlasca was honoured by Hungary, Italy and Yad Vashem which appointed him a Righteous Among the Nations. He died in 1992.

Pál Prónay, the militia leader during the White Terror, set up a death squad after the Arrow Cross coup and resumed his killing. He was captured by the Soviets in early 1945 and died in the Gulag in the late 1940s.

Krystyna Skarbek continued working for SOE in the Middle East. In July 1944 she was parachuted into France where she worked with the resistance with her customary flair and courage. Appointed an Order of the British Empire after the war, but lacking proper financial support from the authorities, she eventually became a cabin steward on an ocean liner. In 1952 she was stabbed to death in her lodgings in London by a fellow steward who had become obsessed with her.

Otto Skorzeny, the SS officer who planned the October 1944 Arrow Cross coup, escaped from American custody and moved to Spain, then Egypt where he worked as a government adviser. Several authors claim that Skorzeny was later recruited by Mossad, the Israeli intelligence service. Skorzeny died in 1975.

Samu Stern, the president of the Jewish Council, remained in Budapest. Traumatised by his role in the Jewish Council, he died in 1946.

Samuel Springmann, who ran the Vaada's courier network, and his wife Ilona finally arrived in Palestine in July 1944. They settled in Tel Aviv. Springmann died in 1988.

Ferenc Szombathelyi, chief of the wartime General Staff, and a leading figure in the secret negotiations with the Western allies, was tried in Budapest after the war and sentenced to ten years in prison. Extradited to Yugoslavia, he was found guilty of war crimes for the Novi Sad massacre and executed in November 1946.

Ferenc Szálasi, the Arrow Cross leader, was executed in Budapest in March 1946.

Erzsébet Szapáry, who worked with Caja Odescalchi and József Antall on the Polish rescue operation, emigrated to Switzerland after the war where she died in 1980. Szapáry was honoured by Yad Vashem as a Righteous Among the Nations.

Sándor Szent-Iványi, the head of the Unitarian Church who sheltered Howie and worked with the resistance, left Hungary and moved to the United States with his family. He worked for Radio Free Europe until 1978 and died in 1983.

Döme Sztójay, prime minister during the deportation of Hungarian Jewry, was tried for war crimes and executed in March 1946.

Satvet Lütfi Tozan returned to Istanbul and resumed his career as a businessman, unofficial diplomat and broker. Appointed an Order of the British Empire, he died in 1975.

István Ujszászy, the wartime intelligence chief, was arrested by the Soviets in early 1945 and taken to Moscow. He returned to Budapest in late 1948 where he was interrogated at length about the structure and activities of Hungary's wartime intelligence agencies. Ujszászy disappeared soon after. The details of his eventual fate still remain unknown but he was probably executed soon after his interrogation was completed.

Edmund Veesenmayer, Reich plenipotentiary in Hungary and a key architect of the Holocaust in Croatia and Hungary, was convicted of war crimes at Nuremberg and sentenced to twenty years in prison. He was released in 1951, one of numerous senior Nazis and Holocaust perpetrators to be set free by John McCloy, the US High Commissioner in Germany. Veesenmayer died in 1977.

László Veress, the Hungarian diplomat who negotiated with the Allies in 1943, married his girlfriend Laura-Louise. They moved to London after the war, where he worked for the BBC Hungarian service. Veress died in 1980.

Raoul Wallenberg, the Swedish diplomat who saved tens of thousands of Budapest Jews, and his driver Vilmos Langfelder, were sent to eastern Hungary, then on to Moscow and the Lubyanka prison. Eighty years on, the precise details of their fate still remain unknown. In 1957 the Soviet authorities admitted that Wallenberg had been imprisoned but claimed he had died of natural causes in 1947. Many believe that he and Langfelder were shot, probably in the late 1940s. Mystery also surrounds the failure of both the Swedish authorities and Wallenberg's powerful family – in particular Jacob and Marcus Wallenberg, who ran Sweden's most important bank – to actively intervene on his behalf. Raoul's mother, Maj, and his step-father Fredrik von Dardel spent the rest of their lives searching for him or details of his fate. Both committed suicide in 1979.

Dieter Wisliceny, the SS officer who worked closely with Adolf Eichmann, was a witness at the Nuremberg trials. He was extradited to Czechoslovakia, tried for war crimes and executed in February 1948.

Edina Zichy Pallavicini left Hungary after the war and moved to Spain, where several of her children lived. The Zichy Palace was seized by the Communist authorities and is now a private dwelling. She died in 1964.

Archives Cited

CIARR – CIA Reading Room (www.cia.gov/readingroom/home)
CZA – Central Zionist Archive, Jerusalem
IWM – Imperial War Museum, London
MNL – Magyar Nemzeti Léveltár (Hungarian National Archives), Budapest
PSL – Politikatörténeti és Szakszervezeti Levéltár (Institute of Political History and Trade Unions), Budapest
UKNA – UK National Archives, London
USHMM – United States Holocaust Memorial Museum, Washington DC
USNA – United States National Archives, College Park, Maryland
WHL – Wiener Holocaust Library, London
YV – Yad Vashem, Jerusalem

Bibliography

Books

1944 Glass House Memorial Room, Carl Lutz Foundation (Budapest, undated).

Adam, István Pál, *Budapest Building Managers and the Holocaust in Hungary* (London, 2016).

Anger, Per, *With Raoul Wallenberg in Budapest* (New York, 1981).

Antall, József (eds. Károly Kapronczay, Szilárd Biernaczky), *Menkültek Menedéke: Emlékek és Iratok* (Shelter for Refugees: Memoirs and Writings) (Budapest, 1997).

Arnothy, Christine (trans. Antonia White and Catherine Castledine), *I am fifteen and I do not want to die* (London, 2009).

Aronson, Shlomo, *Hitler, the Allies and the Jews* (Cambridge, 2004).

Atkinson, Linda, *In Kindling Flame* (New York, 1992).

Bailey, Roderick, *Forgotten Voices of the Secret War: An Inside History of Special Operations During the Second World War* (London, 2009).

Barber, Annabel, *Budapest Blue Guide* (Taunton, 2018).

Barker, Elizabeth, *British Policy in South–East Europe in the Second World War* (London, 1976).

Bársony, János and Daróczi, Ágnes (eds), *Pharrajimos: The Fate of the Roma during the Holocaust* (New York, 2007).

Batalion, Judy, *The Light of Days: Women Fighters of the Jewish Resistance* (London, 2021).

Bauer, Yehuda, *Jews for Sale: Nazi-Jewish Negotiations, 1933-1945* (New Haven, London, 2009).

Benshalom, Rafi, *We Struggled For Life: The Hungarian Zionist Youth Resistance During the Nazi Era* (Tel Aviv, 2001).

Ben-Tov, Arieh, *Facing the Holocaust in Budapest: The International*

Committee of the Red Cross and the Jews in Hungary, 1943–1945 (Geneva, 1988).

Bernath, Gábor (ed.), *Porrajmos: Recollections of Roma Holocaust Survivors* (Budapest, 2000).

Birnbaum, Marianna D. (trans. Marianna D. Birnbaum and Judith Flesch Rose), *1944: A Year Without Goodbyes* (Budapest, 2015).

British Embassy, *Harmincad utca 6: A Twentieth Century Story of Budapest* (Budapest, 2000).

Boldizsár Iván, *Keser-Édes* (Bitter-sweet) (Budapest, 1987).

Braham, Randolph, *The Politics of Genocide: The Holocaust in Hungary Vols. I and II* (New York, 1980).

Brand, Daniel, *Trapped by Evil and Deceit: The Story of Hansi and Joel Brand* (Brookline, MA 2020).

Breitman, Richard, Goda, Norman J.W., Naftali, Timothy and Wolfe, Robert, *US Intelligence and the Nazis* (New York, 2005).

Brewster, Ralph, *Wrong Passport*, Blue Danube (Budapest, 2022).

Bridge, Ann, *A Place to Stand* (London, 1953).

Bridge, Ann, *The Tightening String* (London, 1962).

Bridges, Tyler, *The Flight: A Father's War, A Son's Search* (Baton Rouge LA, 2021).

Bonhardt, Attila, 'The Role of Colonel Ferenc Koszorús in the Prevention of the Deportation of the Jews of Budapest', in Géza Jeszenszky (ed.), *July 1944: Deportation of the Jews of Budapest Foiled* (Saint Helena CA, 2017).

Carlberg, Ingrid, *Raoul Wallenberg: The Heroic Life of the Man Who Saved Thousands of Hungarian Jews from the Holocaust* (London, 2015).

Cartledge, Bryan, *The Will to Survive: A History of Hungary* (London, 2011).

Cesarani, David, *Eichmann: His Life and Crimes* (London, 2005).

Cockburn, Claud, *In Time of Trouble: An Autobiography* (London, 1956).

Cohen, Asher (trans. Carl Alpert), *The Halutz Resistance in Hungary 1942–1944* (New York, 1986).

Cole, Tim, *Holocaust City: The Making of a Jewish Ghetto* (New York, London 2003).

Cookridge, E.H., *Inside SOE: The Story of Special Operations in Western Europe* (London, 1966).

Davidson, Basil, *Special Operations Europe: Scenes from the Anti-Nazi War* (London, 1980).

Dawidowicz, Lucy S., *The War Against the Jews 1933-1945* (London, 1979).

Deák István, *Europe on Trial: The Story of Collaboration, Resistance and Retribution During World War II* (New York and London, 2015).

Debreczeni, József (trans. Paul Olchváry), *Cold Crematorium: Reporting from the Land of Auschwitz* (London, 2024).

Denes, Magda, *Castles Burning: A Child's Life in War* (London, 1997).

Dévényi Sándorné [Anna] (eds. Heléna Huhák, András Szécsényi and Erika Szivós) *Kismama Sárga Csillaggal: Egy Fiatalasszony Naplója A Német Megszállástól 1945 Júliusaig* (New Mother with a Yellow Star: A Young Lady's Diary from the Nazi Occupation to July 1945) (Budapest, 2015).

Eber, George F., *Pinball Games* (2010).

Eby, Cecil D, *Hungary at War: Civilians and Soldiers in World War II* (University Park, PA, 1998).

Edelsheim Gyulai, Ilona, *Honour and Duty: The Memoir of Countess Ilona Edelsheim Gyulai, Widow of Vice-Regent Stephen Horthy of Hungary* (Arundel, 2005).

Elon, Amos *Timetable: The Story of Joel Brand* (London, 1981).

Farago, Ladislas, *The Game of the Foxes: British and German Intelligence Operations and Personalities Which Changed the Course of the Second World War* (London, 1971).

Farago, Ladislas, *Burn After Reading: The Espionage History of World War II* (Annapolis, 1961).

Farkas, Charles, *Vanished by the Danube* (Albany, NY 2013).

Frank, Tibor (ed.), *Discussing Hitler: Advisers of U.S. Diplomacy in Central Europe 1934–1941* (Budapest, 2003).

Felix, Christopher, *A Short Course in the Secret War*, (Lanham, MA, 1992).

Freedland, Jonathan, *The Escape Artist: The Man Who Broke Out of Auschwitz to Warn the World* (London, 2022).

Frey, David, *Jews, Nazis, And The Cinema of Hungary: The Tragedy of Success 1929-1944* (London, New York, 2018).

Foot M.R.D. and Langley JM, *MI9: Escape and Evasion* (London, 2020).

Foot, M.R.D. *SOE: An Outline History of the Special Operations Executive 1940–1946* (London, 1999).

Friling, Tuvia, 'Istanbul 1942–1945: The Kollek-Avriel and Berman-Ofner Networks', in Bankier, David (ed.), *Secret Intelligence and the Holocaust* (New York, 2006).

Fry, Helen, *Women in Intelligence: The Hidden History of Two World Wars* (London, 2023).

Galántay, Ervin Y, *Boy Soldier: Budapest, 1944–1945* (Budapest, 2007).

Gilbert, Martin, *Auschwitz and the Allies: The truth about one of this century's most controversial episodes* (London, 1981).

Gilbert, Martin, *The Holocaust: The Jewish Tragedy* (London, 1989).

Görgey, Guidó, *Két Görgey (Two Görgeys)* (Budapest, 2004).

Grose, Peter, *Gentleman Spy: The Life of Allen Dulles* (London, 1995).

Gur, David (ed. Eli Netzer, trans. Pamela Segev and Avri Fischer) *Brothers for Resistance and Rescue: The Underground Zionist Youth Movement in Hungary during World War II* (Jerusalem, New York, 2007).

Hagen, Louis, *The Secret War for Europe: A Dossier of Espionage* (London, 1968).

Haslam, Jonathan and Urbach, Karina (eds.) *Secret Intelligence in the European States System 1918-1989* (Stanford, 2014).

Hingyi Lászlo, *Budapest Ostroma (The Siege of Budapest) 1944-1945* Vols. 1 and 2 (Budapest, 2019).

Hirschi, Agnes and Schallié (eds.), *Under Swiss Protection: Jewish Eyewitness Accounts from Wartime Budapest* (Stuttgart, 2017).

Horthy, Miklós, *Admiral Nicholas Horthy: Memoirs*, Annotated by Andrew L. Simon (Safety Harbour, 2000).

Horthy, Miklós, *Titkos Iratai (Secret writings)* (Budapest, 1963).

Howie, Claerwen, *Agent by Accident* (Cape Town, 1997).

Höttl, Wilhelm, *The Secret Front: The Story of Nazi Political Espionage* (New York, 1954).

Juhász, Eszter, *Ostromnapló: Budapest 1944-45* (Budapest, 2018).

Kántás, Balazs, *A Brief and Fragmented History of Radical Right-Wing Paramilitary Formations in Hungary in the 1920s* (Delhi, 2021).

Jangfeldt, Bengt (trans. Harry D. Watson and Bengt Jangfeldt) *The*

Hero of Budapest: The Triumph and Tragedy of Raoul Wallenberg (London, 2014).

Jeffrey, Keith, *MI6: The History of the Secret Intelligence Service* (London, 2010).

Kádár, Gábor and Vági Zoltan, *Self-Financing Genocide: The Gold Train, the Becher Case and the Wealth of Hungarian Jews* (Budapest, New York, 2004).

Kahn, David, *Hitler's Spies: German Military Intelligence in World War II* (New York, 1978).

Kapronczay, Károly, *Refugees in Hungary* (Toronto, Buffalo, 1999).

Károly, Kristóf, *A Halálos Tavasztól A Gestapo Fogságaig* (From Deadly Spring to Gestapo Prison) (Budapest, 1987).

Károlyi, Michael, *Faith without Illusion: Memoirs of Michael Károlyi* (trans. Catherine Károlyi) (London, 1956).

Károlyi, Catherine, *A Life Together: The Memoirs of Catherine Károlyi* (London, 1966).

Kershaw, Alex *The Envoy: The Epic Rescue of the Last Jews of Europe in the Desperate Closing Months of World War II* (New York, 2010).

Kertész Imre (trans. Tim Wilkinson) *Fateless* (London, 2004).

Koch, Stephen, *Stalin, Willi Münzenberg and the Seduction of the Intellectuals* (London, 1996).

Koestler, Arthur, *Arrow in the Blue* (London, 1954).

Koestler, Arthur, *The Invisible Writing: Autobiography 1931-53* (London, 1954).

Korb, Alexander and Ümit Üngor, Ugur (eds.), *Mass Violence in Modern History* (Abingdon, 2019).

Komoly, Thomas, *Orphans of the Holocaust: Ottó Komoly's Diary, Budapest 1944* (London, 2024).

Kurimay, Anita, *Queer Budapest 1873-1961* (Chicago, 2020).

Merkin, Yakov, *Crosscurrents: Navigating the Turbulent Politics of the Right During the Horthy Era in Hungary, 1920-1944* (New York, 2017).

Lambert, Gilles, *Operation Hazalah: How Young Zionists Rescued Thousands of Hungarian Jews in the Nazi Occupation* (New York, 1974).

Landwehr, Richard, *Budapest: The Stalingrad of the Waffen-SS* (Bennington, VT 2012).

Langlet, Valdemar (trans. Graham Long) *Reign of Terror: The Budapest Memoirs of Valdemar Langlet 1944-1945* (New York, 2013).

LeBor, Adam, *Hitler's Secret Bankers: How Switzerland Profited from Nazi Genocide* (London, 2020, updated edition).

LeBor, Adam, *Tower of Basel: The Shadowy History of the Bank That Rules the World* (New York 2013).

Leigh Fermor, Patrick, *Between the Woods and the Water* (London, 2013).

Lendvai, Paul, *The Hungarians: A Thousand Years of Victory in Defeat* (London, 2021).

Lester, Elenore, *Wallenberg: The Man in the Iron Web* (Englewood Cliffs, NJ 1982).

Litchfield, David R.L., *Hitler's Valkyrie: The Uncensored Biography of Unity Mitford* (Cheltenham, 2015).

Lipstadt, Deborah E., *The Eichmann Trial* (New York, 2011).

Löb, Ladislau, *Dealing With Satan: Rezső Kasztner's Daring Rescue Mission* (London, 2008).

Lukacs, John, *Budapest 1900: A Historical Portrait of a City and its Culture* (London, 1993).

Macartney, C.A., *Hungary: A Short History* (Edinburgh, 1962).

Macartney, C.A., *October 15th: A History of Modern Hungary, 1929-1945* Vols. I and II (Edinburgh, 1957).

Marton, Kati, *Wallenberg: Missing Hero* (New York, 1995).

Masson, Madeleine, *Christine: SOE Agent & Churchill's Favourite Spy* (London, 2005).

Masters, Anthony, *The Summer That Bled: The Biography of Hannah Senesh* (London, 1972).

Montgomery, John Flournoy, *Hungary: The Unwilling Satellite* (London, 2017).

Mihályi, Balázs *Siege of Budapest 1944-45: The Brutal Battle for the Pearl of the Danube* (Oxford, 2022).

Miller, Michael L., and Szapor, Judith (ed.), *Quotas: 'The Jewish Question' and Higher Education in Central Europe 1880-1945*, New York 2024.

Miller, Russell, *Behind the Lines: The Oral History of Special Operations in World War II* (London, 2002).

Mirga-Kruszelnicka, Anna and Dunajeva, Jekatyerina (eds.) *Rethinking*

Roma Resistance Throughout History: Recounting Stories of Strength and Bravery (Budapest, 2020).

Mueller, Michael (trans. Geoffrey Brooks), *Canaris: The Life and Death of Hitler's Spymaster* (London, 2007).

Mulley, Clare, *The Spy Who Loved: The Secrets and Loves of Christine Granville, Britain's First Special Agent of World War II* (London, 2012).

Munkácsi, Ernő, ed. Nina Munk, *How It Happened: Documenting the Tragedy of Hungarian Jewry*, (Montreal, 2018).

Nagy, Zsolt, *Great Expectations and Interwar Realities: Hungarian Cultural Diplomacy 1918-1941* (Budapest, New York, 2017).

Newby, Eric (ed.), *A Book of Travellers' Tales* (London, 1985).

Ogden, Alan, *Through Hitler's Back Door: SOE Operations in Hungary, Slovakia, Romania and Hungary 1939-1945* (Barnsley, 2010).

O'Connor, Bernard, *Blowing up the Danube: British Intrigues in the Balkans during the Second World War* (North Carolina, 2022).

O'Malley, Owen, *The Phantom Caravan* (London, 1954).

O'Sullivan, Michael, *Patrick Leigh Fermor: Noble Encounters between Budapest and Transylvania* (Budapest, 2018).

Ornstein, Paul with Epstein, Helen, *Looking Back: Memoir of a Psychoanalyst* (Lexington, MA 2015)

Ozsváth, Zsuzsanna *When the Danube Ran Red* (Syracuse, NY 2017).

Palgi, Yoel, *Into the Inferno: The Memoir of a Jewish Paratrooper Behind Nazi Lines* (New York, 2002).

Pálóczi-Horváth, George, *The Undefeated* (London, 1993).

Pálóczy-Horvath, G., [sic] *In Darkest Hungary* (London, 1944).

Peterecz, Zoltán, *Royall Tyler and Hungary: An American in Europe and the Crisis Years 1918-1933*, (Saint Helena, CA, 2022).

Petersen. Neal H. (ed.), *From Hitler's Doorstep: The Wartime Intelligence Reports of Allen Dulles 1942–1945* (University Park, PA, 1996).

Polcz, Alaine (trans. Albert Tezla), *One Woman in the War: Hungary 1944-1945* (Budapest, New York, 2002).

Porter, Monica, *Deadly Carousel: A Singer's Story of the Second World War* (London, 1990).

Porter, Anna, *Kasztner's Train: The True Story of Rezső Kasztner, Unknown Hero of the Holocaust* (Toronto, 2007).

Prohászka, László, *The Danube Promenade – Our Budapest series* (Budapest, 1998).

Pusztaszeri, Laszlo, *Karády és Újszászy: Párhuzamos életrajz történelmi háttérrel* (Karády and Ujszaszy: Parallel Biography With Historical Background). (Budapest, 2008).

Révész Peretz (trans. Isabella Arad) *Standing Up to Evil: A Zionist's Underground Rescue Activities in Hungary* (Jerusalem, 2019).

Rona, Jutka (trans. Tibór Bérczes, Sára Zorándy) *Magyar Cigányok Túlélok vallanak, Hungarian Gypsies Survivors' Stories* (Budapest, 2011).

Rubin, Barry, *Istanbul Intrigues: A True-Life Casablanca* (1989, New York).

Ruina, Edith, *How They Lived To Tell 1939-1945* (Green Bay, WI 2005).

Sakmyster, Thomas, *Hungary's Admiral on Horseback: Miklós Horthy 1918-1944* (New York, 1994).

Schandl, Catherine Eva, *The London Budapest-Game* (London, 2007).

Seaman, Mark (ed.) *Special Operations Executive: A new instrument of war* (London and New York, 2006).

Sebestyen, Victor, *Budapest between East and West* (London, 2022).

Senesh, Hannah, *Hannah Senesh: Her Life and Diary, The Complete First Edition* (Nashville, TN 2013).

Shatz, Frank, *Reports from a Distant Place,* (Columbus, OH 2012).

Schellenberg, Walter (trans. Louis Hagen) *The Labyrinth: Memoirs of Walter Schellenberg, Hitler's Chief of Counterintelligence* (New York, 2000).

Shiels, Duncan, *The Rajk Brothers*, Paris, 2006.

Shukman, Harold (ed.) *Stalin's Generals* (New York, 1993).

Skorzeny, Otto, *Skorzeny's Special Missions: The Memoirs of Hitler's Most Daring Commando* (Barnsley, 2011).

Smith, Bradley F., *The Shadow Warriors: OSS and the Origins of the CIA* (London, 1983).

Smith, Stuart, *Otto Skorzeny: The Devil's Disciple* (Oxford, 2018).

Soros, Tivadar, *Maskerado: Dancing Around Death in Nazi Hungary* (Edinburgh, 2000).

Stafford, David, *Britain and European Resistance 1940-1945: A Survey of the Special Operations Executive with Documents* (Toronto, Buffalo, NY, 1983).

Stone, Norman, *Hungary: A Short History* (London, 2019).

Surányi J. András, *A pesti Broadway: Személyes bejárás történelmi kitérőkkel* (Pesti Broadway: a personal tour with historical detours) (Budapest, 2009).

Szálasi Ferenc (ed. László Karsai), *Naplói* (Diaries) 1942-1946 (Budapest, 2016).

Szebeny Klára, *103 el nem küldött levél Buda ostromáról* (103 unsent letters about the siege of Buda) (Budapest, 2015).

Szegedy-Maszák Marianne, *I Kiss Your Hands Many Times: Hearts, Souls and Wars in Hungary* (New York 2013).

Szent-Miklosy, Istvan, *With The Hungarian Independence Movement 1943-1947: An Eyewitness Account* (New York, 1988).

Szép, Ernő (trans. John Bátki), *The Smell of Humans: A Memoir of the Holocaust in Hungary* (Budapest, 1994).

Szita, Szabolcs, (trans. Sean Lambert), *Trading in Lives? Operations of the Jewish Relief and Rescue Committee in Budapest, 1944-1945* (Budapest, New York 2003).

Szita, Szabolcs, *A Gestapo Magyarországon* (*The Gestapo in Hungary*) (Budapest, 2002.)

Temkin, Gabriel, *My Just War: The Memoir of a Jewish Red Army Soldier in World War II* (Novato, CA 1998).

Tickell, Jerrard, *Miss May: The Story of an Englishwoman* (London, 1958).

Török, András (trans. Peter Doherty and Ágnes Enyedi), *Budapest: A Critical Guide* (Budapest, 2014).

Tschuy Theo, *Dangerous Diplomacy: The Story of Carl Lutz, Rescuer of 62,000 Hungarian Jews* (Grand Rapids, MI, 2000)

Tucker-Jones, *The Battle for Budapest 1944-1945: Rare Photographs from Wartime Archives* (Barnsley, 2016).

Ungváry, Krisztián (trans. Ladislaus Löb), *Battle for Budapest: 100 Days in World War II* (London, 2011).

Vági Zoltán, Csősz Lászlo and Kádár Gábor (trans. Zsofia Zvolenszky) *The Holocaust in Hungary: Evolution of a Genocide* (Lanham, MA 2013).

Veress, Laura-Louise, *Clear the Line: Hungary's Struggle to Leave the Axis during the Second World War* (Chapel Hill, NC, 1995).

Vrba, Rudolf and Bestic Alan, *I Escaped from Auschwitz: The Shocking True Story of the World War II Hero Who Escaped the Nazis and Helped Save Over 200,000 Jews* (New York 2020).

Wallenberg, Raoul, *Letters and Dispatches 1924-1944* (New York, 1995).

Weissberg, Alex, *Desperate Mission: Joel Brand's Story as Told by Alex Weissberg* (New York, 1958).

Wetzler, Alfred (trans. Ewald Osers), *Escape from Hell: The True Story of the Auschwitz Protocol* (Oxford, New York, 2007).

Wilkinson, Peter, *Foreign Fields: The Story of an SOE Operative* (London, New York, 2002).

Wilson, Francesca M., *In the Margins of Chaos: Recollections of Relief Work in and between Three Wars* (London, 1944).

Ullein-Reviczky, Antall (trans. Lovice Mária Ullein-Reviczky) *German War, Russian Peace: The Hungarian Tragedy* (Reno, NV 2014).

Zsolt, Béla (trans. Ladislaus Löb), *Nine Suitcases* (London, 2005).

Zweig, Ronald, *The Gold Train: The Destruction of the Jews and the Second World War's Most Terrible Robbery* (London, 2002).

Academic papers, journal articles and theses

Alström, Göran and Carlson, Benny, 'What Did Iver Olsen Tell Harry White: Sweden at the End of World War II from the "Olsen Angle"', *Lund Papers in Economic History*, No. 98, 2005.

Bare, Duncan, 'Hungarian Affairs of the US-Office of Strategic Services in the Mediterranean Theatre of Operations from June 1944 until September 1945', Master Thesis, University of Graz, 2015.

Bare, Duncan, 'A Hungarian Show with American Assistance': The OSS "Sparrow" Mission to Detach Hungary from the Axis in March 1944', Bachelor Thesis, University of Graz, 2013.

Barna, Ildiko, 'Post-Holocaust Transitional Justice in Hungary: Approaches, Disputes and Debates', East European Holocaust Studies, published online September 5 2023.

Bartha, Ákos, 'Terrorists and Freedom Fighters: Arrow Cross Party Militias, "Ragged Guard" and "KISKA" Auxiliary Forces in Hungary (1938–1945)', *Studia historica Brunensia*, Vol. 69, No. 2, 2022.

Becker, Andras, 'British Strategy in Hungary in 1944 and the

Hungarian Jewish Commandos of the Special Operations Executive', *Hungarian Studies Review*, September 2017.

Bittera, Éva, 'Andrássy Klara, Egy (a)typikus arisztocrata' ('Klara Andrassy, An (A)typical Aristocrat'), *Folio Historica*, 35, 2020.

Bodó, Bela, 'Paramilitary Violence in Hungary After the First World War', *East European Quarterly*, XXXVIII, No. 2 June 2004.

Bodó, Béla, 'Hungarian Aristocracy and the White Terror', *Journal of Contemporary History*, Vol. 45, No. 4, October 2010.

Borhi, László, 'The Allies, Secret Peace Talks, and the German Invasion of Hungary, 1943-1944', *Hungarian Studies Review*, Vol. 46-47, October 2020.

CIA, 'The Tangled Web – Allied Deception Operations in Hungary', *Studies in Intelligence*, Anonymous, Approved for Release July 29 2014.

Cohen, Asher, 'He-Halutz Underground in Hungary: March – August 1944', *Yad Vashem Studies* Vol. 14 1981.

Deák, István, 'Budapest and the Hungarian Revolutions of 1918–1919', *The Slavonic and East European Review*, Vol. 46, No. 106, 1968.

Dobos Dóra, 'Az angol-magyar titkos diplomacia, a Special Operations Executive (Különleges Hadműveletek Bizottsága) angol titkosszolgálati szerv szerepe a magyar kiugrasi kísérletben' (The role of Anglo-Hungarian diplomacy and the SOE English secret service in Hungary's attempt to leave [the Axis]), *Válóság*, September 2016.

Dobos Dóra, 'Fekete rádiózás a Közel-Keleten 1941-1942 között' (Black Radio in Central-East [Europe] between 1941-1942) *Nemzembiztonsági Szemle*, 2018/2.

Dragoni, Eleonora, 'Maria Madi's Budapest Diaries: A Testimony of War and Courage', Master thesis, University of Leiden, 2019.

Eden, Robert J. P., 'An Autobiography', Imperial War Museum.

'Final Report of the International Commission on the Holocaust in Romania', 11 November 2004.

Erez, Zvi, 'The Jews of Budapest and the Plans of Admiral Horthy August-October 1944', *Yad Vashem Studies*, Vol. 16, 1984.

Frey, David S., 'Mata Hari or the Body of the Nation: Interpretations of Katalin Karády', *Hungarian Studies Review*, Vol. 41, No. 1–2, 2014.

Fürj, Orsolya, 'A brit diplomáciai jelenlét Magyarországon 1924 és 1941 között: A British Legation szervezete és működése' ('The British diplomatic presence in Hungary between 1924 and 1941: The organisation and operation of the British Legation') PhD thesis, Debrecen University 2017.

Hajdu, Tibor, 'A Magyar ellenállás legitimista hercegnője: Odescalchi Károlyné' (A Hungarian opposition legitimist princess: Mrs Károly Odescalchi), *A történet-tudomány szolgálatában. Tanulmányok a 70 éves Gecsényi Lászlo tiszteletére*, ed. Baráth Magdolna – Molnár Antal. Budapest-Győr 2012.

Kovacs, Mária, 'The Case of the Teleki Statue: New Debates on the History of the Numerus Clausus in Hungary', *Jewish Studies at the Central European University, IV, Yearbook 2004–2005*.

Jeszenszky, Géza, 'Overcoming the Baneful Legacy of Trianon', *Hungarian Review*, Vol. 11, No. 4, 2020.

Leimbach, Diane, 'Failure to Free an Enemy: How the Dynamics of WWII Prevented the Success of OSS Operations in Hungary', *Report: West Point Undergraduate Historical Review*, Vol. 2 Iss. 1, Article 8.

MacKay, Craig Graham, 'A Friend Indeed: The Secret Service of Lolle Smit', August 2010. Available at: https://www.raoulwallenberg.net/wp-content/files_mf/1288788709Lolle-Smit.pdf

MacKay, Craig Graham, 'An American Perspective on Lolle Smit', December 2015.

Meszerics Tamas, 'Undermine or Bring Them Over: SOE and OSS Plans for Hungary in 1943', *Journal of Contemporary History*, Vol. 43, No. 2, 2008.

Ornstein, Judit, copy of original Hungarian language diary, received from Moreshet, the Mordechai Anielewicz International Centre for Holocaust Documentation, Research and Education, Givat Haviva, Israel. English language translation by George Deak.

Peterecz, Zoltán, 'Sparrow Mission: A US Intelligence Failure during World War II', *Intelligence and National Security*, Vol. 27, No. 2.

Peterecz, Zoltán, 'A Certain Amount of Tactful Undermining: Herbert C. Pell and Hungary in 1941', *Hungarian Quarterly*, Vol. 202–203, 2011.

Pető, Andrea, 'Gendered Exclusions and Inclusions in Hungary's

Right-Radical Arrow Cross Party (1939–1945): A Case Study of Three Party Members', *Hungarian Studies Review*, Vol. 41, No. 1–2, 2014.

Pelle, János, 'A holokauszt utolsó felvonasa a Józsefvárosban' (The Holocaust's last act in Jozseftown) *Válóság*, September 2016.

Pelle, János, 'Zsidók es arisztokraták a negyvenes években' (Jews and aristocrats in the 1940s) *Válóság*, November 2013.

Somogyi Allison, 'The Bitter End: Life and Survival in the Holocaust Diaries of Young Jewish Women In Budapest Under the Arrow Cross Regime, October 1944 – February 1945'. Dissertation for partial fulfilment of Doctor of Philosophy, Chapel Hill, 2019.

Szekér, Nora, 'Domokos Szent-Iványi and his Book', Parts I and II, *Hungarian Review*, 9 November 2013 and 8 January 2014.

Szelke, László, 'Katonák, kémek, kalandorok: Az SOE és a 2. vkf. osztály a második vilaghaboruban (1940-1942)' ('Soldiers, Spies, Adventurers: the SOE and department 2. vkf during the second world war'), *Honvédségi Szemle* (*Hungarian Defence Review*), November 2018.

Szelke, László, 'Secrets, Legends, Destinies: The History of the Gresham Palace and Its Anglo-Saxon Connections', doctoral thesis, Piliscsaba, 2012.

Stenge, Csaba B., 'Olimpiai éremszerszők tragediája a Donnal: Petschauer Attila és Székely Andras, mint zsidó munkaszolgálatosok a Magyar 2. Hadseregnel' ('The Tragedy of Olympic Medallists at the River Don: Attila Petschauer and Andras Székely as Jewish Labour Servicemen with the Hungarian Second Army'), *Seregszemle, The Journal of the Hungarian Forces Joint Command*, Vol. 14, No. 1, January–February 2016.

Szita, Szabolcs, 'Ujszászy István tabornok palyafutasa' ('General István Ujszászy's Field Run'), *Múltunk*, Vol. 2, 2006.

Tóth Vásárhelyi, Éva, 'Gróf Andrássy Klára, A Szociális Legitimista' ('Countess Andrássy Klára, the Social Legitimist'), *Múltunk*, Vol. 2, 2008.

Vago, Bela, 'The Intelligence Aspects of the Brand Mission', *Yad Vashem Studies*, Vol. 10, 1974.

Vago, Bela, 'Budapest Jewry in the Summer of 1944: Ottó Komoly's Diaries', *Yad Vashem Studies* Vol. 8, 1970.

Vasvári, Louise O., 'The Yellow Star and Everyday Life under Exceptional Circumstances: Diaries of 1944-1945 Budapest', *Hungarian Cultural Studies*, Vol. 9 2016.

Vrba, Rudolf and Wetzler, Alfred, '*The Auschwitz Protocol: The Vrba Wetzler Report*', April 1944.

Print media and website articles

Adam, Christopher, 'The Genocidal Priest: The Last Interview with András Kun', *Hungarian Free Press*, 11 March 2019.

Andrássy Klára Odescalchiné 'Asszonyszemmel végig az égő Spanyolországon' ('A Woman's Eye through Burning Spain'), *Újság*, 6, 13 March 1938.

Bányai, Viktória, Frojimovics, Kinga and Gombocz, Eszter, 'Gyerekmentés Budapesten 1944-45' (Child Rescue in Budapest 1944-45), *Szombat*, 29 January 2021

Bard, Mitchell, 'The Vatican and the Holocaust: Pope Pius XII and the Holocaust', jewishvirtuallibrary.org, undated.

Brown, Cyril, 'Charles Crowned Amid Great Pomp', *The New York Times*, 2 January 1917.

Bodó, Péter, 'The last coronation – Charles IV became a Hungarian king 105 years ago', pestbuda.hu, 30 December 2021.

Bruce Teicholz obituary, *The New York Times*, 10 September 1993.

Council of Europe, '*Project Education of Roma Children in Europe, Austria and Hungary 1850–1938*' (undated).

Cserépfalvi, Katalin, 'Cserépfalvi Imre és Társai Bűnügy Története 1942' ('The Story of Imre Cserépfalvi and His Partners' Criminal Case'), Lili Groszmann blog, liligro.hu, 2 September 2023.

Csaba Nagy, Attila, 'Az arisztokrácia és az úri középosztály megszólításai a Magyar Királyságban' ('Modes of Address of the Aristocracy and Middle Classes in the Kingdom of Hungary'), regnumportal.hu, 5 May 2010.

Deák, István, 'Could the Hungarian Jews Have Survived?', *New York Review of Books*, 4 February 1982.

'Eichmann Tells His Own Damning Story', *Life*, 12 November 1960.

'Europa Plan', jewishvirtuallibrary.org (undated)

Finkel, Andrew, 'House of Great Illusions', *Cornucopia*, Vol. 11, 1996.

Fiziker, Róbert, 'Pest Mmegér Egy Eestet – Edward of Windsor Látogatasai Fővárosunkban' ('Pest is worth an evening – Edward of Windsor's visits to our capital'), mnl.gov.hu, 26 September 2022.

Howard, E., 'World War II: Siege of Budapest', historynet.com, 6 December 2006.

István, Gabor Benedek, 'A csodarabbi ismeretlen megmentője' ('The Unknown Saviour of the Miracle Rabbi'), *Népszabadság*, 21 June 1997.

Ivanovic S, and Marin R., 'Kémek Világa Budapesten: Hírszerzők Harca a II. Világháborúban' ('The World of Spies in Budapest: The Agents' Fight in the Second World War') *Magyar Szó* (*Hungarian Word*), Novi Sad, Yugoslavia, November – December 1969.

Kraft, Dina, 'Anne Frank of Budapest': Newly Discovered Diary Chronicles Jewish Girl's Life in Nazi-Occupied Hungary', *Haaretz*, May 1 2019.

Lambert, Sean, 'The Horthy Era' (1920-1944), the orangefiles.hu (undated).

Jewish Telegraphic Agency, 'Reveal Disruption Caused by Ouster of Jews from Hungary's Economy', *Daily News Bulletin*, 24 July 1944.

LeBor, Adam, 'Painful Memories', *Budapest Week*, 24 November 1994.

Łubczyk, Grzegorz, 'The Story of Henry Slawik', translated by Andrew Rajcher, sprawiedliwi.org, September 2019.

Petschauer, Attila, 'Akik együtt vacsoraztak vele' ('Who Dined Together with Him'), *Színházi Élet*, February 1935.

Pilecki Institute, articles on Edith Weiss, Erzsébet and Antal Szapáry https://instytutpileckiego.pl/

Prince Paul Odescalchi, obituary, *The Telegraph*, 30 June 2014.

'Vannay, Ford's Protege, Guilty of Attack on Hungarian Jewish Statesman', Jewish Telegraphic Agency, 27 June 1927.

Waldner, Nicole, 'Gloomy Sunday: Macabre Stories Have Surrounded Rezső Seress's 1930s Lament', *Financial Times*, 14 August 2023.

Yad Vashem, 'The Story of Munkács, A Jewish Community in the Carpathian Mountains'.

Zemplényi, Lily, 'Remembering the Aster Revolution Laying the Foundation of the Hungarian Republic', *Hungarian Conservative*, 31 October 2022.

Websites

arcanum.hu
ceeol.com (Central and Eastern European Online Library)
centropa.org
collections.milev.hu (Hungarian Jewish Museum and archives)
discovery.nationalarchives.gov.uk/
ehri-project.eu (European Holocaust Research Infrastructure)
www.facebook.com/groups/budapestregikepeken
historynet.com
hungarianconservative.com
hungarianfreepress.com
jewishvirtuallibrary.org
jta.org (Jewish Telegraphic Agency)
liligro.hu
library.hungaricana.hu/en
machtereti1944.org (Zionist resistance memorial)
mnl.gov.hu
nytimes.com
pestbuda.hu
instytutpileckiego.pl
raoul-wallenberg.eu
raoulwallenberg.net
regnumportal.hu
sprawiedliwi.org
the orangefiles.hu
telegraph.co.uk
tortenelemportal.hu
ushmm.org
vrbawetzler.eu
wienerholocaustlibrary.org

Private accounts and diaries

Selected extracts from the memoir of Károly (Carlo) Odescalchi.
Zichy Pallavicini, Edina, *Diary from March 17 1944 to November 12 1945*.
Stein, Ernest and Stein Schimke, Joan, *One Man Army: The Wartime*

Experiences of Ernest Stein, Budapest, Hungary 1944. New York, June 2012.
Memories of the Sternberg Family, Collected by Moshe Nahum Sternberg, ed. Miriam Ben David, Jerusalem, 2017.

Selected documentaries

Budapest Ostroma (The Siege of Budapest/City of Terror)
(2020, available with English sub-titles on YouTube)
A Gyilkosok Emlékműve (Monument to the Murderers)
(2021, available with English sub-titles on YouTube)
Killing Kasztner: the Jew Who Dealt with Nazis (2009, available on Prime Video)
The Last Days (1998, available on Netflix)

Endnotes

1 The End of Empire

1. Cyril Brown, 'Charles Crowned Amid Great Pomp', *The New York Times*, 2 January 1917.
2. Footage of the coronation can be viewed on YouTube, www.youtube. com/watch?v=afnnfaDxi14. See also the detailed account by Péter Bodó at pestbuda.hu/en/cikk/20211230_the_last_coronation_charles_iv_became_a_hungarian_king_105_years_ago, 30 December 2021.
3. John Flournoy Montgomery, *Hungary: The Unwilling Satellite*, Arcole Publishing, 2017, p. 22.
4. John Lukacs, *Budapest 1900*, London, 1993, pp. 71–73.
5. Lily Zemplényi, 'Remembering the Aster Revolution Laying the Foundation of the Hungarian Republic', *Hungarian Conservative* hungarianconservative.com/articles/culture_society/remembering-the-aster-revolution-laying-the-foundation-of-the-first-hungarian-republic/, 31 October 2022.
6. Arthur Koestler, *Arrow in the Blue*, London, 1954, p. 43.
7. Lenin's *Collected Works*, 4th English Edition, Volume 29, Moscow, 1972, pp. 242–243.
8. István Deák, 'Budapest and the Hungarian Revolutions of 1918–1919', *The Slavonic and East European Review*, Vol. 46, No. 106, 1968, p. 139.
9. Original Hungarian source: 'Kilencven éve vonult be Horthy Budapestre' ('Horthy Arrived in Budapest Ninety Years Ago'), https://tortenelemportal.hu/2009/11/horthy-bevonulasa-budapestre/. Translated by Sean Lambert, 'The Horthy Era (1920–1944)', The Orange Files, https://theorangefiles.hu/the-horthy-era-1920-1944-long/#.

10. Lukacs, *Budapest 1900*, pp. 21, 22.
11. Michael L. Miller and Judith Szapor (ed.) *Quotas: The Jewish Question and Higher Education in Central Europe 1880–1945*, New York 2024, includes a detailed discussion of the numerus clausus law.
12. Bryan Cartledge, *The Will to Survive: A History of Hungary*, London, 2011, p. 354.

2 A Nation Traumatised

1. Claud Cockburn, *In Time of Trouble: An Autobiography*, London, 1956, p. 48.
2. Cockburn, *In Time of Trouble*, p. 48.
3. Béla Bodó, 'Hungarian Aristocracy and the White Terror', *Journal of Contemporary History*, Vol. 45, No. 4, October 2010.
4. Alexander Korb and Ugur Ümit Üngor (ed), Mass Violence in Modern History: Béla Bodó, 'The White Terror: Antisemitic and Political Violence in Hungary 1919-1921', Abingdon, 2019, pp. xiv-xvi.
5. Balázs Kántás, *A Brief and Fragmented History of Radical Right-Wing Paramilitary Formations in Hungary in the 1920s*, Delhi, 2021, pp. 30–31.
6. Bela Bodó, 'Paramilitary Violence in Hungary After the First World War', *East European Quarterly*, XXXVIII, No. 2 June 2004, p. 145.
7. Bodó, 'Paramilitary Violence', pp. 134-135.
8. Bodó, 'Hungarian Aristocracy and the White Terror', p. 720.
9. Prince Paul Odescalchi, obituary, *The Telegraph*, 30 June 2014. https://www.telegraph.co.uk/news/obituaries/10936111/Prince-Paul-Odescalchi-obituary.html
10. Géza Jeszenszky, 'Overcoming the Baneful Legacy of Trianon', *Hungarian Review*, Vol. XI, No. 4, 2020, pp. xx–xy.
11. György Pálóczi-Horvath, *The Undefeated*, London, 1993, pp. 24–25.
12. Attila Csaba Nagy, 'Az Arisztokrácia És Az Uri Középosztály Megszólításai A Magyar Királysagban' ('Modes of Address of the Aristocracy and Middle Classes in the Kingdom of Hungary') regnumportal.hu
13. Cartledge, *The Will to Survive*, p. 335.
14. Éva Bittera, 'Andrassy Klara, Egy (A)typikus Arisztokrata' ('Klara

Andrassy, An (A)typical Aristocrat'), *Folio Historica*, 35, 2020.

15. Lukacs, *Budapest 1900*, p. 23.

16. Francesca M. Wilson, *In the Margins of Chaos: Recollections of Relief Work in and between Three Wars*, London, 1944, pp. 263–264.

17. Lukacs, *Budapest 1900*, p. 82.

18. Michael O'Sullivan, *Patrick Leigh Fermor: Noble Encounters between Budapest and Transylvania*, Budapest, 2018, p. 75.

19. Miklós Horthy, *Admiral Nicholas Horthy: Memoirs*, Annotated by Andrew L. Simon, Florida, p. 161.

3 The Most Seductive City

1. Quoted in Éva Tóth Vásárhelyi, 'Gróf Andrássy Klára, a szociális legitimista' ('Countess Klára Andrássy, the Social Legitimist'), *Múltunk*, Vol. 2, 2008, pp. 105–121.

2. Patrick Leigh Fermor, *Between the Woods and the Water*, London, 2013, p. 29.

3. Victor Sebestyen, *Budapest between East and West*, Weidenfeld & Nicholson, 2022 includes a lively and informative discussion about the revival and modernisation of the Hungarian language.

4. Leigh Fermor, *Between the Woods and the Water*, p. 24.

5. Sir Cecil Beaton, *A Night Out in Budapest, 1936*. Included in *A Book of Travellers' Tales*, assembled by Eric Newby, London, 1985.

6. A detailed account of the royal visit and Edward's subsequent journeys to Hungary, compiled by Róbert Fiziker from Hungarian government archives, is available at: mnl.gov.hu/mnl/ol/hirek/pest_meger_egy_estet_edward_of_windsor_latogatasai_fovarosunkban

7. Attila Petschauer, 'Akik együtt vacsoráztak vele' ('Who Dined Together with Him'), *Színházi Élet*, February 1935.

8. Andrássy Klára Odescalchiné, 'Asszonyszemmel végig az égő Spanyolországon' ('A Woman's Eye through Burning Spain'), *Újság*, 6 March 1938.

9. Tóth Vásárhelyi, 'Countess Andrássy Klára, the Social Legitimist', p. 119, quoting the continuation of Caja's account of her time in Spain, *Újság*, 13 March 1938.

10. Catherine Kiralyi, *A Life Together: The Memoirs of Catherine Károlyi*, London, 1966, p. 302.
11. Wilson, *In the Margins of Chaos*, p. 264.
12. Pálóczi-Horváth, *The Undefeated*, p. 53.
13. Pálóczi-Horváth, *The Undefeated*, pp. 55–56.
14. Nicole Waldner, 'Gloomy Sunday: Macabre Stories Have Surrounded Rezső Seress's 1930s Lament', *Financial Times*, 14 August 2023.
15. Cartledge, *The Will to Survive*, p. 355.
16. Cartledge, *The Will to Survive*, p. 346.

4 Diplomatic Dances

1. Montgomery, *Hungary, The Unwilling Satellite*, p.41.
2. Tibor Frank (ed.), *Discussing Hitler: Advisers of U.S. Diplomacy in Central Europe 1934–1941*, Budapest, 2003, p. 40.
3. Frank, *Discussing Hitler*, p. 20.
4. Frank, *Discussing Hitler*, p. 26.
5. Owen O'Malley, *The Phantom Caravan*, London, 1954, p. 204.
6. Randolph Braham, *The Politics of Genocide: The Holocaust in Hungary, Volume One*, New York, 1980, pp. 123–125.
7. Braham, *The Politics of Genocide*, pp. 126–127.
8. János Bársony and Ágnes Daróczi (eds), *Pharrajimos: The Fate of the Roma during the Holocaust*, New York, 2007.
9. Council of Europe, *Project Education of Roma Children in Europe, Austria and Hungary 1850–1938*, rm.coe.int/austria-and-hungary-1850-1938-factsheets-on-romani-history/16808b1a93.
10. Cartledge, *The Will to Survive*, p. 363. Translated by John Batko and quoted in Csigany, L., in 'The Oxford History of Hungarian Literature', Oxford University Press, 1984, p. 358.
11. Braham, *The Politics of Genocide*, p. 147.
12. Alexander Szanto testimony, original German held at the Wiener Holocaust Library, 1656/3/9/578. English translation available at European Holocaust Research Infrastructure early-testimony.ehri-project.eu/document/EHRI-ET-WL16560578

5 Brothers in Sword and Glass

1. Wilhelm Höttl, *The Secret Front: The Story of Nazi Political Espionage*, New York, 1954, pp. 203–204.
2. Laura-Louise Veress, *Clear the Line: Hungary's Struggle to Leave the Axis during the Second World War*, Chapel Hill, NC, 1995, pp. 5–7.
3. C.A. Macartney, *October 15th: A History of Modern Hungary, 1929–1945*, pp. 456–7.
4. Cartledge, *The Will to Survive*, p. 377.
5. Károly Kapronczay, *Refugees in Hungary*, Toronto, 1999, p. 105.
6. Wilson, *In the Margins of Chaos*, p. 264.
7. Kapronczay, *Refugees in Hungary*, p. 47.
8. Kapronczay, *Refugees in Hungary*, p. 65.
9. Wilson, *In the Margins of Chaos*, pp. 248–249.
10. Quoted in Tibor Hajdu, '*A Magyar ellenállás legitimista hercegnője: Odescalchi Károlyné*' ('A Hungarian opposition legitimist princess: Mrs Károly Odescalchi'). In: *A történet-tudomány szolgálatában. Tanulmányok a 70 éves Gecsényi László tiszteletére. Ed: Baráth Magdolna – Molnár Antal*. Budapest-Győr, 2012. pp. 431–9.

6 A Sackful of Trouble

1. UKNA HS 4/93 Section D report, anonymous author, 22 August 1940.
2. UKNA HS 9/612, 7 December 1939, 433 advised D/H.
3. UKNA HS 9/612, Statement made on 23 February 1941 by 'X'.
4. Clare Mulley, *The Spy Who Loved: The Secrets and Loves of Christine Granville, Britain's First Special Agent of World War II*, London, 2012, pp. 39–40.
5. Madeleine Masson, *Christine: SOE Agent & Churchill's Favourite Spy*, London, 2005, p. 44.
6. UKNA FO 371/2446, O'Malley, 26 February 1940.
7. Keith Jeffrey, *MI6: The History of the Secret Intelligence Service*, London, 2010, pp. 411–412.
8. UKNA HS 4/93, Section D report, anonymous author, 22 August 1940.

9. László Szelke, 'Secrets, Legends, Destinies: The History of the Gresham Palace and Its Anglo-Saxon Connections', doctoral thesis, Piliscsaba, 2012.

10. Szelke, 'Secrets, Legends, Destinies'. Szelke quotes Ujszászy's interrogation after the war by the Communist secret police.

11. UKNA FO 371/2446, Summary of work undertaken by Mr. Davidson in Budapest, undated.

12. Tamás Meszerics, 'Undermine or Bring Them Over: SOE and OSS Plans for Hungary in 1943', *Journal of Contemporary History*, Vol. 43, No. 2, 2008, pp. 195–216.

13. UKNA HS 7/162, SOE Hungarian Section History, Major G.I. Klauber, p. 4.

7 A Surfeit of Spies

1. Ilona Edelsheim Gyulai, *Honour and Duty: The Memoir of Countess Ilona Edelsheim Gyulai, Widow of Vice-Regent Stephen Horthy of Hungary*, Arundel, 2005, pp. 26–27.

2. UKNA FO 371/24430, Somers-Cocks to Kirkpatrick, sent 9 February 1940.

3. Lászlo Pusztaszeri, *Karády és Ujszászy: Párhuzamos életrajz történelmi háttérrel*, (Karády and Ujszászy: Parallel Biography With Historical Background), Budapest, 2008.

4. UKNA KV 2/387, Willi Götz, interrogation report.

5. The author is grateful to a relative of Ignatz's, who kindly provided access to his correspondence home in 1940 and 1944. Translation by Krisztina Fenyő.

6. UKNA HS 9/830/3, recommendation for an MBE, which he received in 1946.

7. UKNA HS 9/612, Statement made on 23 February 1941 by 'X'.

8. Basil Davidson, *Special Operations Europe: Scenes from the Anti-Nazi War*, London, 1980, pp. 58–59.

9. UKNA FO 371/24426, Sir Alexander Cadogan to O'Malley, 9 October 1940.

10. UKNA FO 371/24426, O'Malley to Sir Alexander Cadogan, 11

October 1940. Davidson in his memoirs writes that O'Malley threatened to denounce him in early 1941. However, the correspondence about the incident is dated September and October 1940, so the author has placed the incident then.

11. UKNA KV 2/387, Willi Götz, interrogation report.
12. UKNA FO 954/11C/611, Budapest Telegram 104, Military Attache to Director of Military Intelligence, 17 February 1941.
13. UKNA HS 9/612, Statement made on 23 February 1941 by 'X'.

8 The Die is Cast

1. Hajdu Tibor, Litván György (eds.), *Károlyi Mihály levelezése IV, 1930-1944*, Budapest, 2014, page 444. See also: PSL 704.f 215. ő.e
2. Ibid.
3. Höttl, *The Secret Front*, New York, 1954, p. 192.
4. UKNA FO 1093/246. On the London and Budapest radio transmitters and SIS decision-making, see UKNA FO 1093/301.
5. Mária Kovacs, 'The Case of the Teleki Statue: New Debates on the History of the Numerus Clausus in Hungary', *Jewish Studies at the Central European University, IV, Yearbook 2004–2005*, Budapest, 2005, pp. 191–208.
6. UKNA FO 371/26602, O'Malley telegram to Foreign Office, 3 April 1941.
7. Pálóczi-Horváth, *The Undefeated*, p. 83.
8. UKNA FO 371/3463, O'Malley to London, 4 April 1941.
9. UKNA FO 371/3463, O'Malley to London, 16 April 1941.
10. UKNA FO 371/3463, London to O'Malley, 16 April 1941.
11. Pálóczi-Horváth, *The Undefeated*, p. 93.
12. UKNA FO 371/3463, O'Malley to London, 24 November 1941.
13. Quoted in Kapronczay, *Refugees in Hungary*, p. 241.
14. UKNA HS 7/162, SOE Hungarian Section History, p. 6.
15. UKNA HS 4/133, Basil Davidson notes on sources and SOE collaborators, undated.
16. Email to author from Mark Odescalchi (grandson of Caja), 9 January 2023.

17. Károlyi, *Faith without Illlusion*, p.298.
18. Károly Odescalchi, unpublished family memoir,   extracts kindly provided by Mark Odescalchi.

9 City of Spies

1. Quoted in Zoltán Peterecz, 'A Certain Amount of Tactful Undermining: Herbert C. Pell and Hungary in 1941', *Hungarian Quarterly*, Vol. 202–203, pp. 124–127.
2. László Szelke, 'Katonák, kémek, kalandorok' ('Soldiers, Spies, Adventurers'), *Honvédségi Szemle* (*Hungarian Defence Review*), November 2018.
3. UKNA KV 2/412, Wilhelm Höttl.
4. David Kahn, *Hitler's Spies: German Military Intelligence in World War II*, New York, 1978, pp. 312–316.
5. UKNA KV 2/1496_2, Interrogation of KLATT or KAUDER by Mr. Johnson, 27 January 1947, p. 17.
6. Michael Muller, *Canaris: The Life and Death of Hitler's Spymaster*, London, 2007, pp. 213–214.
7. UKNA KV 2/1496_1, p. 37.
8. Höttl, *The Secret Front*, p. 9.
9. Quoted in Peterecz, 'A Certain Amount of Tactful Undermining', p. 127.
10. Quoted in Peterecz, 'A Certain Amount of Tactful Undermining', p. 131.

10 Hungary Goes to War

1. Edelsheim, *Honour and Duty*, p. 71.
2. Cartledge, *The Will to Survive*, pp. 385–386.
3. Braham, *The Politics of Genocide*, pp. 198–199.
4. Final Report of the International Commission on the Holocaust in Romania, 11 November 2004, pp. 15–22.
5. WHL P.III.c No. 583

6. Braham, *The Politics of Genocide*, pp. 200–207.
7. USHMM, Hansi Brand interview transcript: collections.ushmm. org/film_findingaids/RG-60.5002_01_trl_en.pdf.
8. Ladislas Farago, *The Game of the Foxes: British and German Intelligence Operations and Personalities Which Changed the Course of the Second World War*, London, 1971, pp. 416–423.
9. Farago, *The Game of the Foxes*, p. 421.
10. The author has drawn on Peterecz's account of Pell's departure.
11. Farago, *The Game of the Foxes*, p. 422.
12. Edelsheim, *Honour and Duty*, p. 76.

11 A Time of Dying

1. Edelsheim, *Honour and Duty*, p. 83.
2. UKNA HS 4/131, D/H18 [Basil Davidson] to London and Cairo, 17 December 1941.
3. Braham, *The Politics of Genocide*, pp. 207–212.
4. Edelsheim, *Honour and Duty*, p. 90.
5. UKNA HS 5/825 AH/6 to SOE London, 24 February 1943.
6. Andrew Finkel, 'House of Great Illusions', *Cornucopia*, Vol. 11, 1996.
7. UKNA HS 5/825 DH13 to London, 16 March 1942.
8. Katalin Cserépfalvi, 'Cserépfalvi Imre és Társai Bűnügy Története 1942 ('The Story of Imre Cserépfalvi and His Partners' Criminal Case'), Lili Groszmann blog, liligro.hu/2023/09/02/cserepfalvi-imre-es-tarsai-bunugy-tortenete-1942/.
9. The author has drawn on a lengthy detailed series of articles about Satvet Lütfi Tozan published in *Magyar Szó* (*Hungarian Word*), the Hungarian-language newspaper published in northern Yugoslavia, from November to December 1969. The articles, by S. Ivanovic and R. Marin, were based on interviews with Tozan, archival documents and court papers and published under the headline 'Kémek Világa Budapesten: Hírszerzők Harca a II. Világháborúban' ('The World of Spies in Budapest: The Agents' Fight in the Second World War'). Translations by Krisztina Fenyő.
10. Jerrard Tickell, *Miss May*, London, 2017. See also: UKNA KV 2/3324

Mary Miske-Gerstenberger; HO 382/18 Miske-Gerstenberger, Baroness Mary, SOE operative.

11. UKNA HS 5/825, Arrests in Hungary, DH/18 from Istanbul to Cairo and London, 15 May 1942.

12. Szelke, 'Soldiers, Spies, Adventurers', p. 195.

12 A New Spring's Hope Dies

1. Edelsheim, *Honour and Duty*, p. 499.
2. Edelsheim, *Honour and Duty*, p. 104.
3. Edelsheim, *Honour and Duty*, p. 105.
4. Edelsheim, *Honour and Duty*, p. 499.
5. Edelsheim, *Honour and Duty*, p. 107.
6. FO 371/3099, quoted in Stockholm to London, 21 August 1942.
7. Veress, *Clear the Line*, p. 60.
8. Anthony Masters, *The Summer That Bled: The Biography of Hannah Senesh*, London, 1972, p. 137.
9. Cartledge, *The Will to Survive*, pp. 384–385.
10. Cartledge, *The Will to Survive*, p. 390.
11. Bársony and Daróczi, *Pharrajimos*, p. 47.
12. Csaba B. Stenge, 'Olimpiai éremszerzők tragédiája a Donnál: Petschauer Attila és Székely András, mint zsidó munkaszolgálatosok a magyar 2. hadseregnél.' ('The Tragedy of Olympic Medallists at the River Don: Attila Petschauer and Andras Székely as Jewish Labour Servicemen with the Hungarian Second Army), *Seregszemle, The Journal of the Hungarian Forces Joint Command*, Vol. 14, No. 1, January–February 2016.

13 A Marriage of Convenience

1. UKNA KV 2/129, Interrogation report of Samuel Springmann, 15 May 1944.
2. UKNA KV 2/129, Interrogation report of Samuel Springmann, 23–29 May 1944.

3. UKNA KV 2/129, Interrogation report of Samuel Springmann, 23–29 May 1944.
4. UKNA KV 2/129, Interrogation report of Samuel Springmann, 15 May 1944.
5. USHMM: Hansi Brand interview.
6. Jewish Virtual Library, 'Europa Plan', www.jewishvirtuallibrary.org/europa-plan.
7. UKNA KV 2/387, Willi Götz. The author has drawn extensively on this file, which contains a wealth of detail about Abwehr and SD operations and personalities in wartime Budapest.

14 An Agreement in Istanbul

1. Author interviews with Róbert Lichtenstein, Budapest 2021-2023.
2. Szelke, 'Soldiers, Spies, Adventurers', pp. 96–97, quoting Hungarian documents.
3. Zoltán Peterecz, 'Sparrow Mission: A US Intelligence Failure during World War II', *Intelligence and National Security*, Vol. 27, No. 2, pp. 241–260. See also Peterecz's work *Royall Tyler and Hungary: An American in Europe and the Crisis Years 1918–1953*, Saint Helena, 2022.
4. Neal H. Petersen (ed.), *From Hitler's Doorstep: The Wartime Intelligence Reports of Allen Dulles 1942–1945*, University Park, PA, 1996, Telegram 1432, 2 March 1943, pp. 45–46.
5. Petersen, *From Hitler's Doorstep*, Telegram 4158, 14 July 1943, p. 82.
6. Horthy, *Admiral Nicholas Horthy*, p. 206.
7. Petersen, *From Hitler's Doorstep*, Telegram 811–820, 2 October 1943, pp. 137–138.
8. Petersen, *From Hitler's Doorstep*, Telegram 1140–1145, 24 November 1943, p. 162.
9. *Magyar Szó* (Tozan series), 24 November 1969, p. 8.
10. Ibid.
11. Szabolcs Szita, 'Ujszászy István tabornok palyafutasa' ('General István Ujszászy's Field Run'), *Múltunk*, Vol. 2, 2006, p. 8. The author has drawn on this thoroughly researched and detailed study.
12. Szita, 'General István Ujszászy's Field Run', p. 16.

13. Pusztaszeri, Karády and Ujszászy, p. 163.
14. Szita, 'General István Ujszászy's Field Run', p. 21.
15. Frey, p. 96.
16. Some details are also corroborated in the interrogation report of Samuel Springmann: UKNA KV2/129, 15 May 1944.
17. Gabor Benedek István, 'The Unknown Saviour of the Miracle Rabbi', *Népszabadság*, 21 June 1997. István draws on the work of Hungarian historian Ágnes Godó. See also Pusztaszeri, Karády and Ujszászy p. 210.
18. USHMM Mária Mádi diaries, File 2, 13 October 1944, available at the United States Holocaust Memorial Museum: collections. ushmm.org/search/catalog/irn50967?rsc=138863&cv=0&x=1039&y= 1323&z=1.6e-4

15 A South African in Budapest

1. UKNA HS 9/753/2, Major G. S. Morton, Personal Impression of 'H', 5 October 1944.
2. Claerwen Howie, *Agent by Accident*, Cape Town, 1997. The author has drawn on this authoritative account of Howie's time in Budapest.
3. UKNA HS 9/753/2, Report on Lieutenant Colonel Howie, 30 September 1944.
4. Howie, *Agent by Accident*, pp. 115–116.
5. UKNA HS 9/753/2, 16 June 1945.
6. CIARR: Report on X-2 Activities in Bucharest, Major Robert Bishop, 25 April 1945, cia.gov/readingroom/docs/BISHOP%2C%20 ROBERT_0101.pdf.
7. C. G. MacKay, 'An American Perspective on Lolle Smit', documentary appendix, undated. See also MacKay, 'A Friend Indeed: The Secret Service of Lolle Smit', August 2010: raoulwallenberg.net/wp-content/ files_mf/1288788709Lolle-Smit.pdf.
8. Alex Weissberg, *Desperate Mission: Joel Brand's Story as Told by Alex Weissberg*, New York, 1958, pp. 44–49. Claerwen Howie notes that Colonel Howie did not recall this event, but 'it might concern Howie': Howie, *Agent by Accident*, p. 212 n. 13, p. 220, n. 36.

9.   FO 371/34451 8353, Brief by Roberts for Moscow talks: Hungary, 22 September 1943.

10. Edelsheim, *Honour and Duty*, p. 153.

11. HS 4/90 Lieutenant Colonel Howie, 30 September 1944.

12. HS 4/90 Lieutenant Colonel Howie, 30 September 1944.

13. Braham, *The Politics of Genocide*, p. 363.

14. UKNA KV 2/129, Interrogation Report of Samuel Springmann, 23–29 May 1944.

15. UKNA KV 2/129, Interrogation Report of Samuel Springmann, 23–29 May 1944.

16. *Magyar Szó*, 26 November 1969, p. 14.

17. Petersen, *From Hitler's Doorstep*, Telegram 1534–1538, 2 January 1944.

18. Petersen, *From Hitler's Doorstep*, Telegram 205–207, 6 January 1944.

19. E Howard, *World War II: Siege of Budapest*, December 6 2006. Available at: w.historynet.com/world-war-ii-siege-of-budapest/

16 Operation Margarethe

1.   Braham, *The Politics of Genocide*, p. 744.

2.   *Hannah Senesh: Her Life and Diary, The Complete First Edition*, Nashville, TN, 2013, p. 43.

3.   *Hannah Senesh: Her Life and Diary*, p. 135.

4.   Masters, *The Summer That Bled*, pp. 143–144.

5.   Imperial War Museum, Robert J. P. Eden, *An Autobiography*, Private Papers of R. J. P Eden.

6.   Veress, *Clear the Line*, pp. 197–198.

7.   Höttl, *The Secret Front*, p. 195.

8.   Höttl, *The Secret Front*, p. 195.

9.   Masters, *The Summer That Bled*, p. 158.

10. Braham, *The Politics of Genocide*, p. 396.

11. Edelsheim, *Honour and Duty*, p. 162.

12. Duncan Bare, 'A Hungarian Show with American Assistance: The OSS "Sparrow" Mission to Detach Hungary from the Axis in March 1944', bachelor's thesis, Graz, 2013.

17 Head of State in Absentia

1. Anita Kurimay, *Queer Budapest 1873-1961*, Chicago, 2020, includes a detailed account of the divorce and accompanying scandal, pp. 124–133.
2. Braham, *The Politics of Genocide*, p. 403.
3. Braham, *The Politics of Genocide*, p. 404.
4. Braham, *The Politics of Genocide*, p. 373.
5. Horthy, *Admiral Nicholas Horthy*, p. 219.
6. Edelsheim, *Honour and Duty*, p. 150.
7. Kapronczay, *Refugees in Hungary*, pp. 141–142.
8. USHMM, Holocaust Encyclopedia, Denmark: encyclopedia. ushmm.org/content/en/article/denmark.
9. Braham, *The Politics of Genocide*, p. 379.
10. Eichmann Tells His Own Damning Story, *Life* magazine, November 28 1960.
11. Braham, *The Politics of Genocide*, p. 419.
12. Braham, *The Politics of Genocide*, pp. 434–435.
13. Braham, *The Politics of Genocide*, pp. 437–438.
14. Braham, *The Politics of Genocide*, pp. 496–497.

18 A Wave of Arrests

1. Kapronczay, *Refugees in Hungary*, p. 121.
2. Kapronczay, *Refugees in Hungary*, pp. 122–123.
3. The author has drawn on Claerwen Howie's detailed account.
4. Edelsheim, *Honour and Duty*, p. 177.
5. Braham, *The Politics of Genocide*, p. 494.
6. 'The Story of Henryk Slawik', Polish Righteous: sprawiedliwi.org. pl/en/stories-of-rescue/story-henryk-slawik.
7. David Frey, 'Mata Hari or the Body of the Nation: Interpretations of Katalin Karády', *Hungarian Studies Review*, Vol. 41, No. 1–2, 2014.
8. Szita, 'General István Ujszászy's Field Run', p. 21.
9. Szita, 'General István Ujszászy's Field Run', pp. 21–23.
10. Szabolcs Szita, *A Gestapo Magyarországon (The Gestapo in Hungary)*,

Budapest, 2002, pp. 142–146. Károly Kristof, *A halálos tavasztól a Gestapo Fogságaig* (*From deadly spring to Gestapo prison*), pp. 7–14.

19 Warnings Ignored

1. English translation of Judit Ornstein's diary by George Deak, used gratefully with permission.
2. Braham, *The Politics of Genocide*, pp. 923–925.
3. Paul Ornstein with Helen Epstein, *Looking Back: Memoir of a Psychoanalyst*, Lexington, KY, 2015, p. 43.
4. Braham, *The Politics of Genocide*, pp. 552–557.
5. Braham, *The Politics of Genocide*, p. 693.
6. Braham, *The Politics of Genocide*, p. 704. Bruce Teicholz, obituary, *The New York Times*, 10 September 1993.
7. Ernő Munkácsi, *How It Happened: Documenting the Tragedy of Hungarian Jewry*, ed. Nina Munk, Montreal, 2018, pp. 92–94.
8. *The Auschwitz Protocol: The Vrba-Wetzler Report*, https://vrbawetzler.eu/img/static/Prilohy/The-Auschwitz-Protocol.pdf.
9. See Braham, *The Politics of Genocide*, pp. 708–731 for a detailed examination of the arrival of the *Auschwitz Protocols* in Budapest and the report's reception.
10. Interview with Lea Furst Komoly, conducted by Yehoshua Ben Ami, Ramat Gan, 26 January 1995. With thanks to Thomas Komoly.
11. David Gur, author interview, Tel Aviv, July 2022.
12. Weissberg, *Desperate Mission*, pp. 122–123.

20 Mission Impossible

1. Weissberg, *Desperate Mission*, chapter 5, 'Money for Blood'. The author has drawn on Weissberg's account.
2. Tuvia Friling, 'Istanbul 1942–1945: The Kollek-Avriel and Berman-Ofner Networks', in David Bankier (ed.), *Secret Intelligence and the Holocaust*, New York, 2006.
3. UKNA FO 371/42711, Interrogation report of Andor Grosz, June 1944.

4. Weissberg, *Desperate Mission*, p. 145.
5. Braham, *The Politics of Genocide*, p. 581.
6. CZA, Alexandra Leitner, *The Tragedy of the Jews in Nagyvárad*, Oradea, undated.
7. Jewish Telegraphic Agency, 'Reveal Disruption Caused by Ouster of Jews from Hungary's Economy', *Daily News Bulletin*, 24 July 1944.
8. Braham, *The Politics of Genocide*, p. 926.
9. USHMM, Barbara Marton Farkas testimony: encyclopedia. ushmm.org/content/en/oral-history/barbara-marton-farkas-describes-deportation-from-hungary-to-auschwitz.
10. Braham, *The Politics of Genocide*, pp. 587–588.
11. Yad Vashem, 'The Story of Munkács, A Jewish Community in the Carpathian Mountains': yadvashem.org/yv/en/exhibitions/communities/munkacs/László_ferenczy.asp.
12. István Deák, 'Could the Hungarian Jews Have Survived?', *New York Review of Books*, 4 February 1982.

21 Exodus

1. Munkácsi, *How It Happened*, pp. 153–155.
2. MNL Endre László Iratok HU-MNL-OL-X 10872-53176 X 10627-1944, István Bertényi to Lászlo Endre, 20 June 1944.
3. Munkácsi, *How It Happened*, p. 736.
4. Munkácsi, *How It Happened*, p. 156.
5. WHL, Alexander Szanto, Jewish Forced Labour in Hungary, P III i, No. 763, January 1958.
6. Edelsheim, *Honour and Duty*, p. 165.
7. HS 4/108, Conversations with Lieutenant Colonel Howie, 2 October 1944.
8. HS 4/108, Conversations with Lieutenant Colonel Howie, 2 October 1944.

22 A Dirty Business

1. Masters, *The Summer That Bled*, pp. 158, 159.
2. Masters, *The Summer That Bled*, part 4, 'Hungary 1944'. The author has drawn on Masters' account.
3. Weissberg, *Desperate Mission*, p. 138.
4. Hansi Brand, author interview, Tel Aviv, March 1998.
5. USHMM, Hansi Brand interview.
6. USHMM, Hansi Brand interview.
7. Pilecki Institute, 'Edith Weiss', https://instytutpileckiego.pl/en/medal/odznaczeni/edith-weiss.
8. Adam LeBor, *Hitler's Secret Bankers: How Switzerland Profited From Nazi Genocide*, London, 2020, pp. 254–256.
9. CIARR, Interrogation of Albert Speer, Seventh Session, 1 June 1945, 10.15 am to 12.30, cia.gov/readingroom/document/05892361.
10. Bauer, pp. 201–209. The author has drawn on Bauer's account.
11. Braham, *The Politics of Genocide*, pp. 952–966.

23 Summer Salvation

1. *Magyar Vilaghirado*, 1059, June 1944, Nemzeti Film Intezet: filmhiradokonline.hu/#home.
2. Munkácsi, *How It Happened*, p. 72, n. 105.
3. Braham, *The Politics of Genocide*, pp. 500–501.
4. MNL, Endre Lászlo Iratok, HU-MNL-OL-X 10872-53176 X 10627-1944 Endre to Sztojay, 22 June 1944 and anonymous poem.
5. Munkácsi, *How It Happened*, p. 189.
6. Braham, *The Politics of Genocide*, p. 753.
7. Mitchell Bard, 'The Vatican and the Holocaust: Pope Pius XII and the Holocaust', Jewish Virtual Library, www.jewishvirtuallibrary.org/pope-pius-xii-and-the-holocaust#N_23_.
8. Munkácsi, *How It Happened*, pp. 208–211.
9. Munkácsi, *How It Happened*, p. 206, n. 53.
10. Edelsheim, *Honour and Duty*, pp. 182–186.
11. Attila Bonhardt, 'The Role of Colonel Ferenc Koszorús in the

Prevention of the Deportation of the Jews of Budapest', in Géza Jeszenszky (ed.), *July 1944: Deportation of the Jews of Budapest Foiled*, Helena History Press, 2017, p. 216. The author has drawn on Bonhardt's detailed account.

12. Munkácsi, *How It Happened*, p. 234.
13. Braham, *The Politics of Genocide*, pp. 772–773.
14. Braham, *The Politics of Genocide*, pp. 792–793.

24 Neutral Rescuers

1. Gloria von Berg (daughter of Tibor), author interview, Budapest, 5 November 2010.
2. Ingrid Carlberg, *Raoul Wallenberg: The Heroic Life of the Man Who Saved Thousands of Hungarian Jews from the Holocaust*, London, 2015, pp. 251–252.
3. Carlberg, *Raoul Wallenberg*, pp. 262–263; Gábor Forgács, author interview, Budapest, June 2010.
4. Göran Alström and Benny Carlson, 'What Did Iver Olsen Tell Harry White: Sweden at the End of World War II from the "Olsen Angle"', *Lund Papers in Economic History*, No. 98, 2005.
5. Yoel Palgi, *Into the Inferno: The Memoir of a Jewish Paratrooper Behind Nazi Lines*, New York, 2002, pp. 100–113.
6. Masters, *The Summer That Bled*, pp. 244–247.
7. Braham, *The Politics of Genocide*, pp. 792–793.
8. Braham, *The Politics of Genocide*, p. 795.
9. Munkácsi, *How It Happened*, p. 256.

25 A Time of Alibis

1. Braham, *The Politics of Genocide*, p. 799.
2. Edelsheim, *Honour and Duty*, p. 197.
3. Thomas Komoly, *Orphans of the Holocaust: Ottó Komoly's Diary, Budapest 1944*, London, 2024, pp. 95–96.
4. Komoly, *Orphans of the Holocaust*, p. 115.

5. Masters, *The Summer That Bled*, p. 260.
6. WHL, Alexander Szanto, Jewish Forced Labour in Hungary, P III i, No. 763, January 1958.

26 A New Year's Promise

1. Kantas, *Brief and Fragmented History of Radical Right-Wing Paramilitary Formations in Hungary in the 1920s*, pp. 35–39.
2. Stuart Smith, *Otto Skorzeny: The Devil's Disciple*, Oxford, 2018, p. 154.
3. USNA RG 226, Entry 191, Box 4, Copy of Wallenberg Report, 29 September 1944.
4. Carlberg, *Raoul Wallenberg*, p. 245.
5. Carlberg, *Raoul Wallenberg*, pp. 272–274.

27 A False October Dawn

1. Edelsheim, *Honour and Duty*, pp. 219–226.
2. Edelsheim, *Honour and Duty*, pp. 228-230.
3. UKNA WO 204/11601, Report on SOE Mission in Hungary, 13 February 1945.

28 The Gates of Hell

1. Braham, *The Politics of Genocide*, pp. 829–838.
2. István Pál Adam, *Budapest Building Managers and the Holocaust in Hungary*, London, 2016, pp. 96–98. The author has drawn on Adam's detailed account.

29 Death March

1. Masters, *The Summer That Bled*, pp. 294–296.
2. Arieh Ben-Tov, *Facing the Holocaust in Budapest: The International*

Committee of the Red Cross and the Jews in Hungary, 1943–1945, Geneva, 1988, pp. 302–303.
3. Bársony and Daróczi, *Pharrajimos,* pp. 160–161.
4. Gábor Forgács, author interview, Budapest, June 2010.
5. Carlberg, *Raoul Wallenberg,* pp. 291–293.
6. Braham, *The Politics of Genocide,* pp. 841–842.
7. Masters, *The Summer That Bled,* pp. 299–302.
8. Braham, *The Politics of Genocide,* pp. 847–848.

30 To the Ghetto

1. Braham, *The Politics of Genocide,* page 852.
2. 'Vannay, Ford's Protege, Guilty of Attack on Hungarian Jewish Statesman', Jewish Telegraphic Agency, 27 June 1927.
3. Ervin v. Galántay, *Boy Soldier: Budapest, 1944–1945,* Budapest, 2007, chapters 1 and 2. The author has drawn on Galántay's detailed account.
4. USHMM, Interview with Giorgio Perlasca, 5 August and 5 September 1990, RG-50.030*0178.
5. USHMM, Perlasca interviews.
6. David Gur, author interview, Tel Aviv, July 2022.
7. 1944 Glass House Memorial Room, Carl Lutz Foundation, Budapest, undated. The author has drawn on this account.
8. Galántay, *Boy Soldier,* chapters 1 and 2.

31 Days of Hunger and Terror

1. Braham, *The Politics of Genocide,* page 857.
2. David Gur, author interview, Tel Aviv, July 2022; Rafi Benshalom, *We Struggled For Life: The Hungarian Zionist Youth Resistance During the Nazi Era,* Tel Aviv, 2001; 'The Zionist Youth Resistance Movement in Hungary 1944', YouTube, user 'Benny Barzilay', www.youtube.com/watch?v=EcrVlMbkRS4.
3. Ákos Bartha, 'Terrorists and Freedom Fighters: Arrow Cross Party Militias, "Ragged Guard" and "KISKA" Auxiliary Forces in

Hungary (1938–1945)', *Studia historica Brunensia*, Vol. 69, No. 2, 2022, pp. 67–89.

4. Viktória Bányai, Kinga Frojimovics and Eszter Gombocz, *Gyerekmentes Budapesten*, (*Child Rescue in Budapest*) Szombat, 29 January 2021.
5. Kristóf Károly, *A halálos tavasztól a Gestapo fogságaig* (*From deadly spring to Gestapo prison*) Budapest, 1987 pp. 56–62. (The book is based on a series of articles first published in Budapest in 1947-1948.) An Arrow Cross man called Gábor Csiszár was tried by the People's Tribunal and executed in October 1945.
6. YV Testimony of János Gömöri at Yad Vashem, 30 September 2003, Katalin Karády file.
7. Krisztián Ungváry, *Battle for Budapest: 100 Days in World War II*, London, 2011, p. 247.

32 Siege and Slaughter

1. Ungváry, *Battle for Budapest*, p. 238.
2. Ia. Malinovskii (ed.) *Budapesht – Vena – Praga: Istoriko-memuarnyi trud* (Budapest – Vienna – Prague: A work of historical memoir), page 81 (Moscow, 1965). Translated by Oleg Beyda.
3. Duncan Shiels, *The Rajk Brothers*, Paris, 2006, page 71.
4. Ungváry, *Battle for Budapest*, p. 67.
5. Krisztina Fenyő, interview with István Fenyő, Budapest, August 2013.
6. USHMM, Perlasca interviews.
7. Guidó Görgey, *Két Görgey* (*Two Görgeys*), Budapest, 2004. The author has drawn on Görgey's account.

33 Shells Rain Down

1. UKNA HS 9/859/7 Karola Koschwitz SOE personnel file.
2. UKNA WO 204/11601 Report on SOE Mission in Hungary (Operation Dibbler) February 1945. See also: IWM Private Papers of Major JG Coates DSO.

3. Görgey, *Two Görgeys*, p. 129.
4. 1944 Glass House Memorial Room, p. 39.
5. Andrea Pető, 'Gendered Exclusions and Inclusions in Hungary's Right-Radical Arrow Cross Party (1939–1945): A Case Study of Three Party Members', *Hungarian Studies Review*, Vol. 41, No. 1–2, 2014.
6. Ungváry, *Battle for Budapest*, p. 239.
7. British Embassy, *Harmincad utca 6: A Twentieth Century Story of Budapest*, Budapest, 2000.

34 Fresh Depths of Savagery

1. Christopher Adam, 'The Genocidal Priest: The Last Interview with András Kun', *Hungarian Free Press*, 11 March 2019.
2. Monica Porter, *Deadly Carousel: A Singer's Story of the Second World War*, London, 1990, p. 137.
3. Braham, *The Politics of Genocide*, p. 872.
4. EHRI, 'Eyewitness Testimony on the Arrow Cross Massacres in Városmajor and Alma Streets', Budapest Municipal Archives, reproduced at EHRI, https://visualisations.ehri-project.eu/items/show/94.
5. Ungváry, *Battle for Budapest*, p. 261.
6. Carlberg, *Raoul Wallenberg*, pp. 360–361.
7. Braham, *The Politics of Genocide*, p. 873.
8. USHMM, Perlasca interviews.

35 Pest Liberated, Buda Fights On

1. Adam LeBor, 'Painful Memories', *Budapest Week*, 24 November 1994.
2. EHRI, 'Eyewitness Testimony on the Arrow Cross Massacres in Városmajor and Alma Streets'.
3. Bársony and Daróczi, *Pharrajimos*, p. 108. The account is based on witness testimony in the post-war trial of Imre Kemenes, one of the perpetrators.

4. Gábor Bernath (ed.), *Porrajmos: Recollections of Roma Holocaust Survivors*, Budapest, 2000, pp. 134–136.
5. Ungváry, *Battle for Budapest*, p. 208. The author has drawn on Ungváry's account.

Afterword

1. Alaine Polcz, *One Woman in the War: Hungary 1944–1945*, pp. 88–90.

Image Credits

Index

About the Author

Credit: Zoltan Tuba

ADAM LEBOR is a veteran former foreign correspondent who lived in Budapest for many years, reporting on Hungary and Central Europe for newspapers including *The Times*, the *Independent* and the *Economist*. He is the author of seven novels and nine non-fiction books including *Hitler's Secret Bankers*, which was shortlisted for the Orwell Prize. He is an editorial trainer for several publications and organisations, and writes for the *Financial Times*, *The Times* and the *Critic*. He divides his time between London and Budapest.

www.adamlebor.com @adamlebor
www.thelastdaysofbudapest.com